By _____

NO LONGER PROPERTY OF
SEATTLE PUBLIC LIBRARY

D0056283

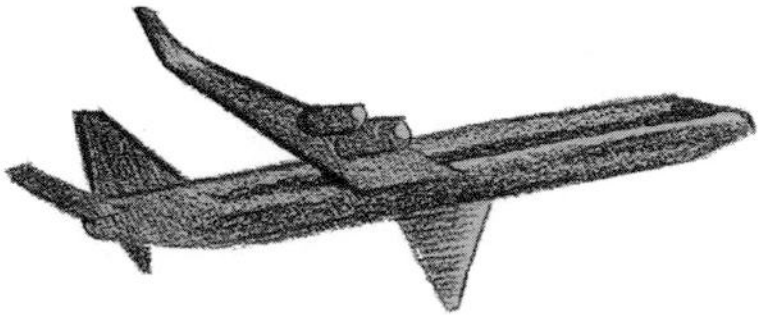

PASSPORT

SOPHIA GLOCK

LB
LITTLE, BROWN AND COMPANY
NEW YORK BOSTON

ABOUT THIS BOOK

THIS BOOK WAS EDITED BY SUSAN RICH AND DESIGNED BY SASHA ILLINGWORTH. THE PRODUCTION WAS SUPERVISED BY KIMBERLY STELLA, AND THE PRODUCTION EDITOR WAS MARISA FINKELSTEIN. THE TEXT WAS SET IN TEXTURE PASSPORT REGULAR. THE DISPLAY TYPE IS HAND-LETTERED WITH CORRESPONDENCE HAND-LETTERED BY JULIA WHITEHOUSE.

Copyright © 2021 by Sophia Glock • Colors by Mike Freiheit • Cover illustration copyright © 2021 by Sophia Glock. Cover design by Sasha Illingworth. • Cover copyright © 2021 by Hachette Book Group, Inc. • Hachette Book Group supports the right to free expression and the value of copyright. The purpose of copyright is to encourage writers and artists to produce the creative works that enrich our culture. The scanning, uploading, and distribution of this book without permission is a theft of the author's intellectual property. If you would like permission to use material from the book (other than for review purposes), please contact permissions@hbgusa.com. Thank you for your support of the author's rights Little, Brown and Company • Hachette Book Group • 1290 Avenue of the Americas, New York, NY 10104 • Visit us at LBYR.com • First Edition: October 2021 • Little, Brown and Company is a division of Hachette Book Group, Inc. • The Little, Brown name and logo are trademarks of Hachette Book Group, Inc. • The publisher is not responsible for websites (or their content) that are not owned by the publisher. Photographs courtesy of Sophia Glock • Library of Congress Cataloging-in-Publication Data • Names: Glock, Sophia, author. • Title: Passport / Sophia Glock. • Description: First edition. | New York: Little, Brown and Company, 2021. | Summary: Teenage Sophia, living with her American family in Central America, discovers that her parents are living double lives, leading her to explore her own boundaries around honesty and deception. • Identifiers: LCCN 2020005069 | ISBN 9780316458986 (hardcover) | ISBN 9780316459006 (paperback) | ISBN 9780316458993 (ebook) | ISBN 9780316458979 (ebook other) • Subjects: LCSH: Graphic novels. | CYAC: Graphic novels. | Secrets—Fiction. | Families—Fiction. | Central America—Fiction. • Classification: LCC PZ7.7.G63 Pas 2021 | DDC 741.5/973—dc23 • LC record available at https://lccn.loc.gov/2020005069 • ISBNs: 978-0-316-45898-6 (hardcover), 978-0-316-45900-6 (trade paperback), 978-0-316-45899-3 (ebook), 978-0-316-49507-3 (ebook), 978-0-316-49506-6 (ebook) • PRINTED IN CHINA • APS • Hardcover: 10 9 8 7 6 5 4 3 2 1 • Paperback: 10 9 8 7 6 5 4 3 2 1

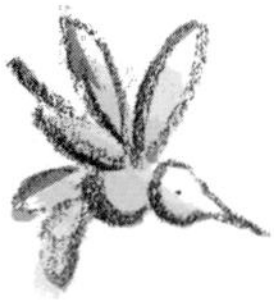

TO TATIANA & MONEIRA

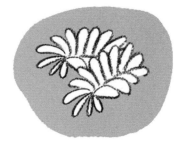

ALL STATEMENTS OF FACT, OPINION, OR ANALYSIS
EXPRESSED ARE THOSE OF THE AUTHOR AND DO
NOT REFLECT THE OFFICIAL POSITIONS OR VIEWS OF
THE U.S. GOVERNMENT. NOTHING IN THE CONTENTS
SHOULD BE CONSTRUED AS ASSERTING OR IMPLYING
U.S. GOVERNMENT AUTHENTICATION OF INFORMATION
OR ENDORSEMENT OF THE AUTHOR'S VIEWS.

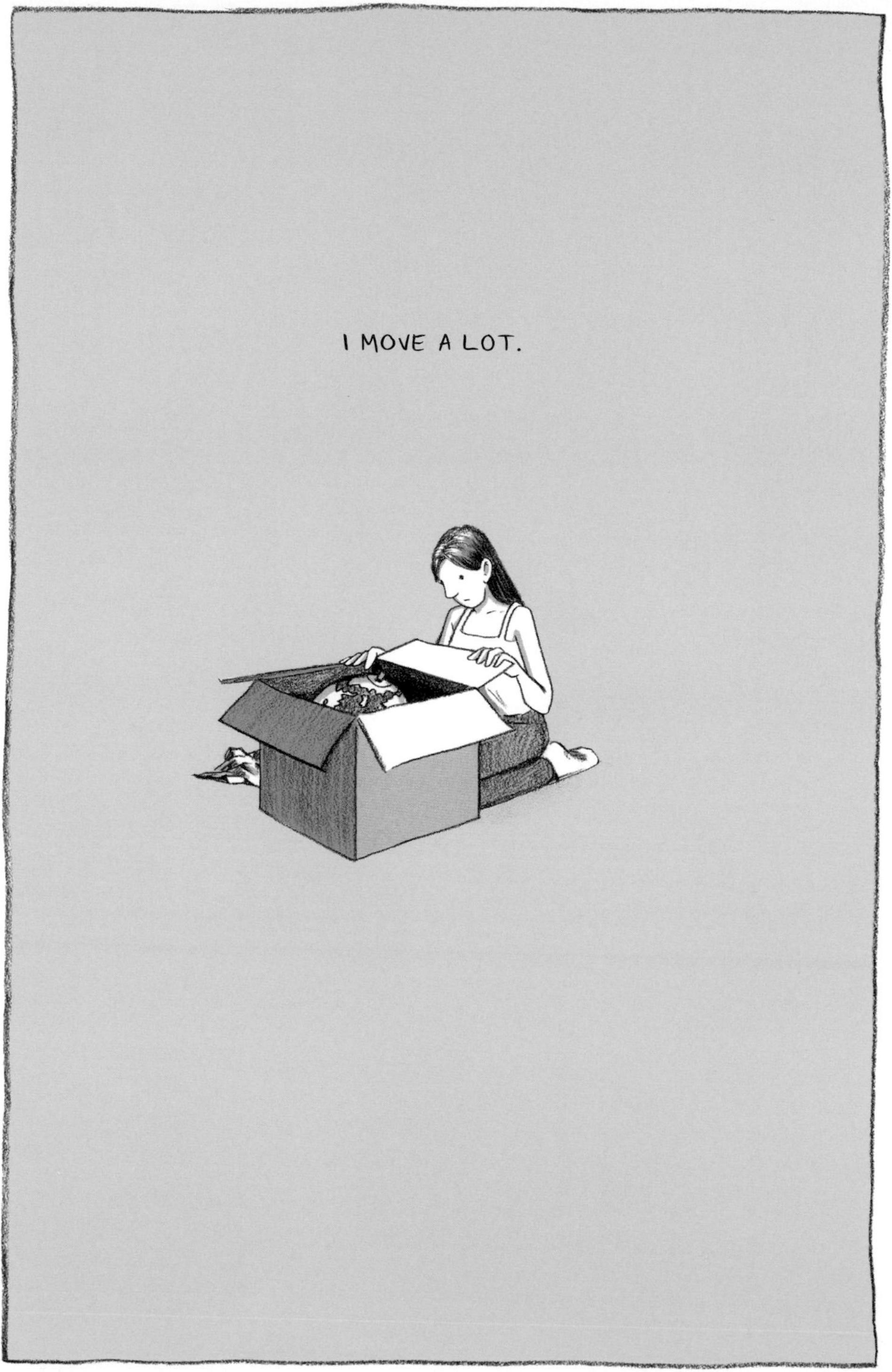
I MOVE A LOT.

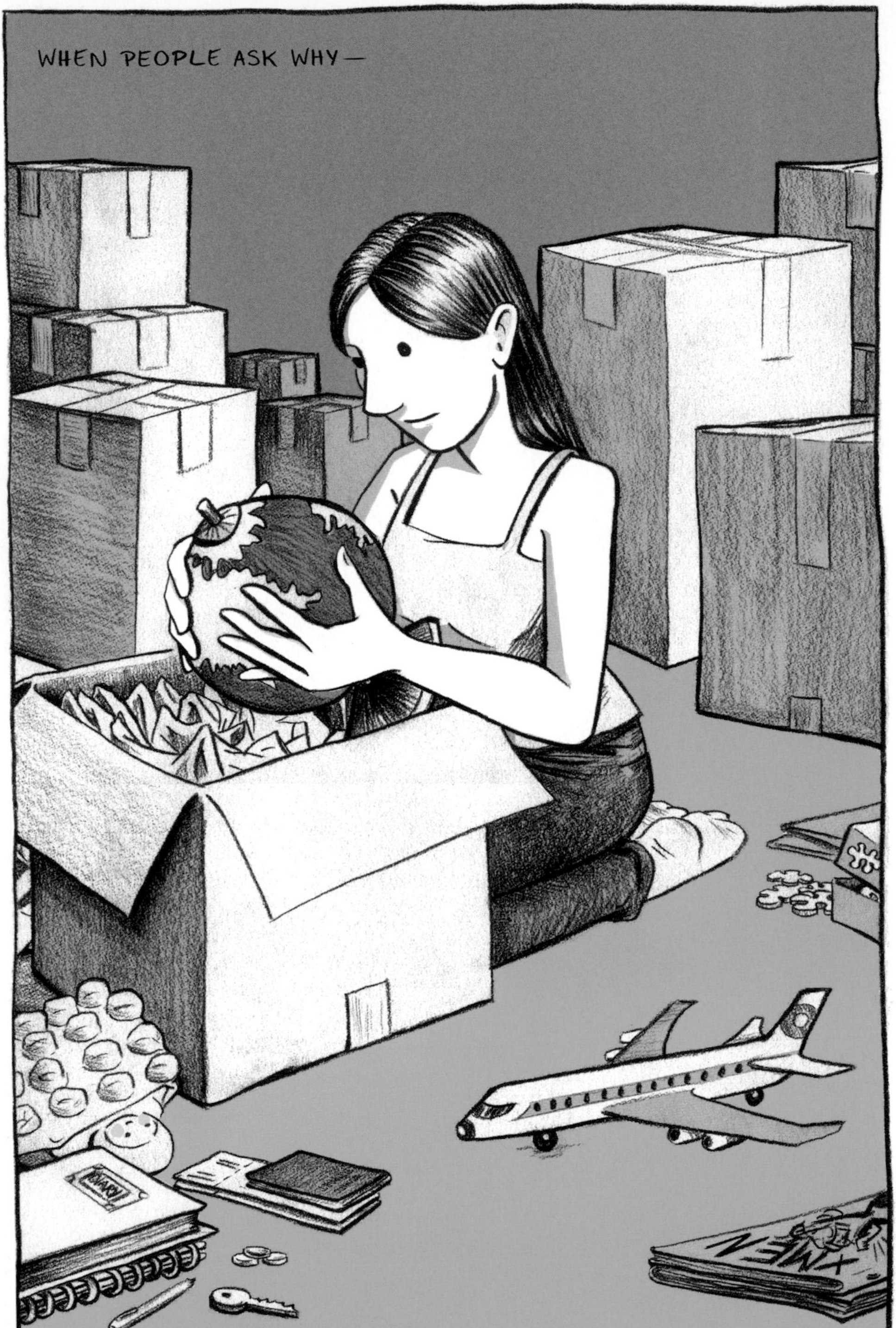
WHEN PEOPLE ASK WHY—

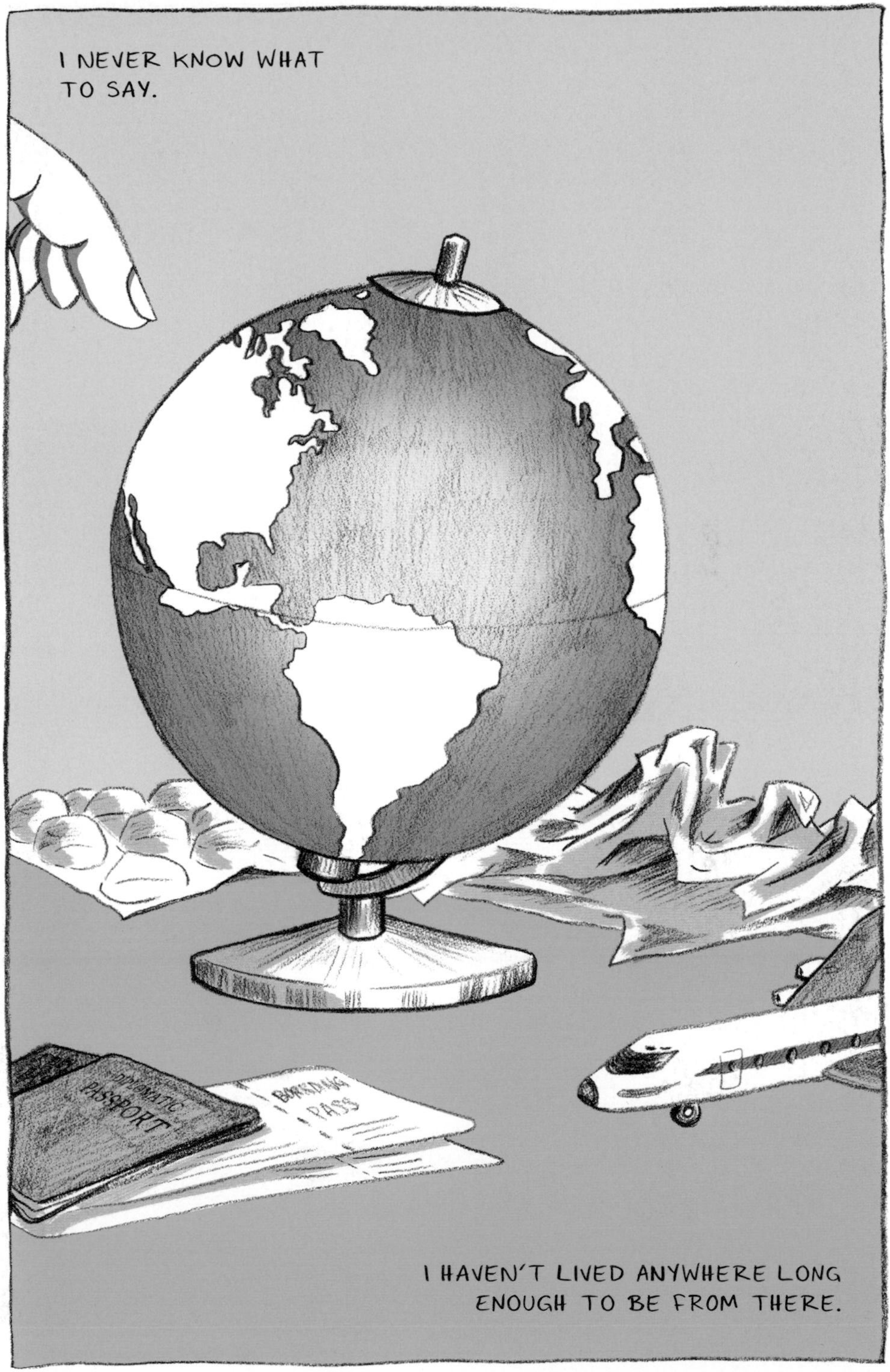
I NEVER KNOW WHAT
TO SAY.
DIPLOMATIC
PASSPORT
BOARDING
PASS
I HAVEN'T LIVED ANYWHERE LONG
ENOUGH TO BE FROM THERE.

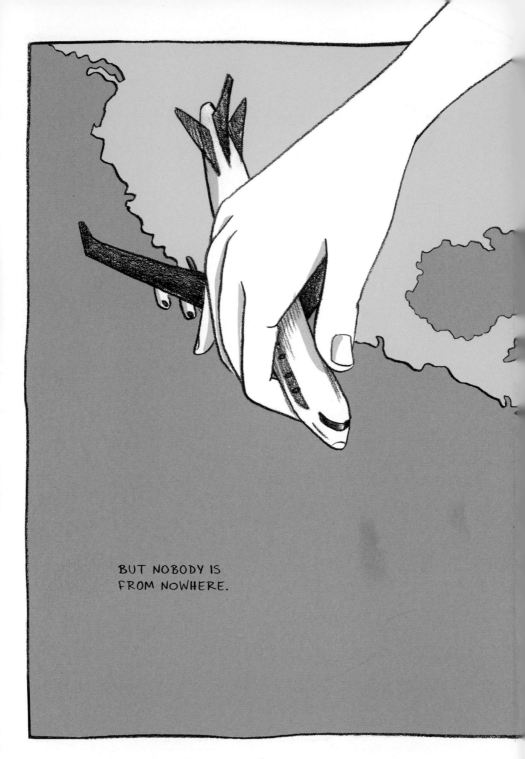

BUT NOBODY IS
FROM NOWHERE.

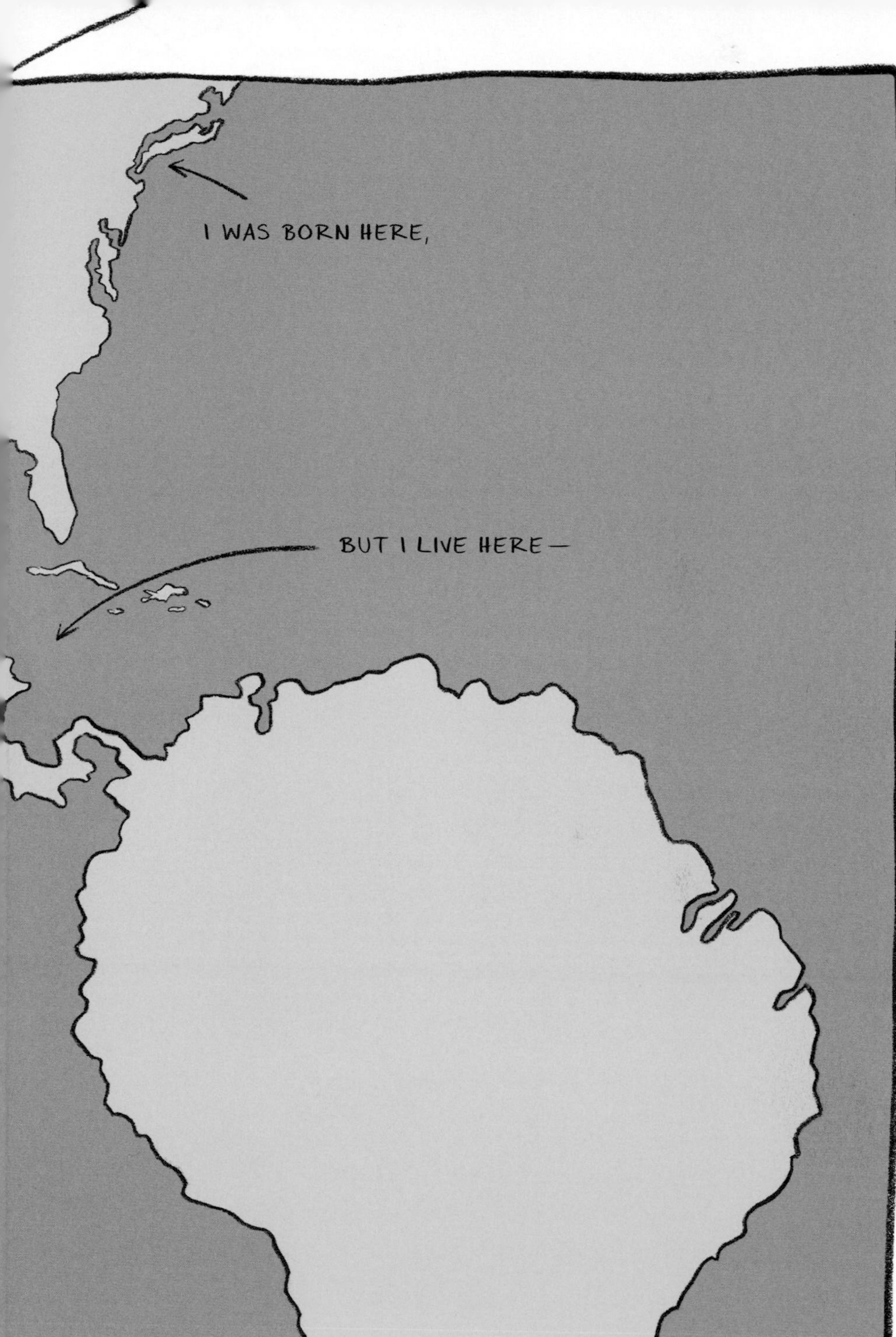
I WAS BORN HERE,
BUT I LIVE HERE—

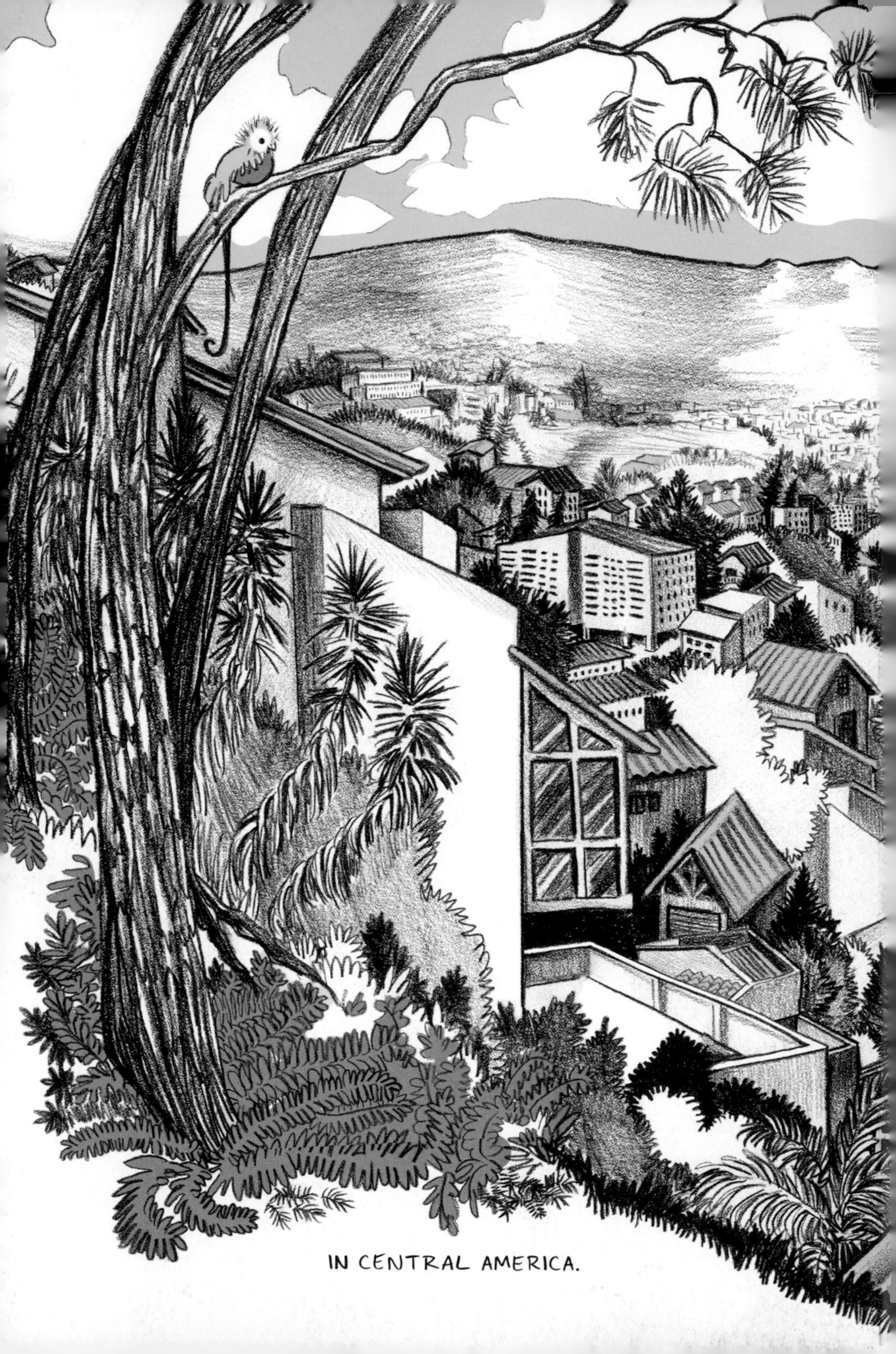
IN CENTRAL AMERICA.

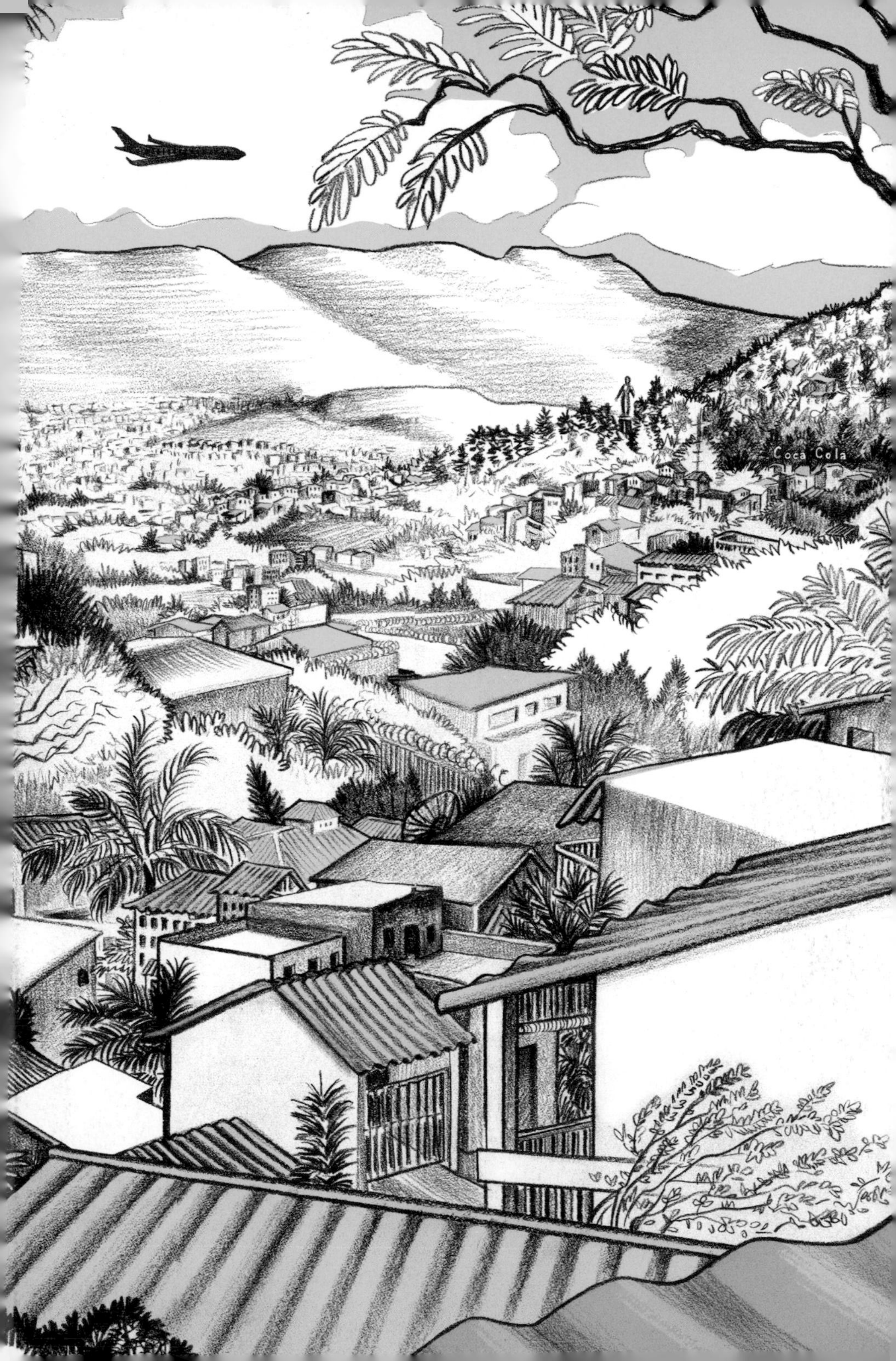
Coca Cola

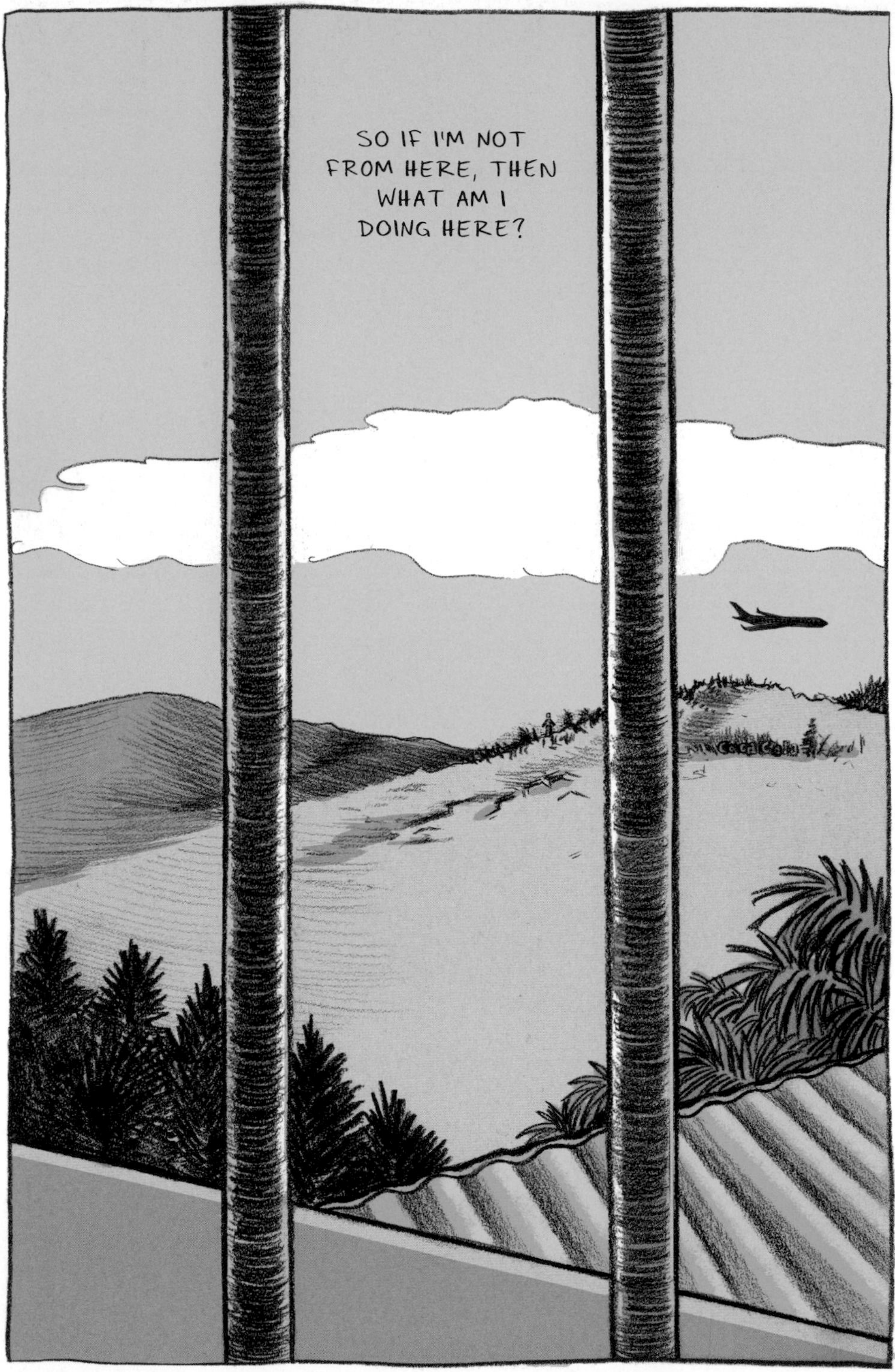
SO IF I'M NOT FROM HERE, THEN WHAT AM I DOING HERE?

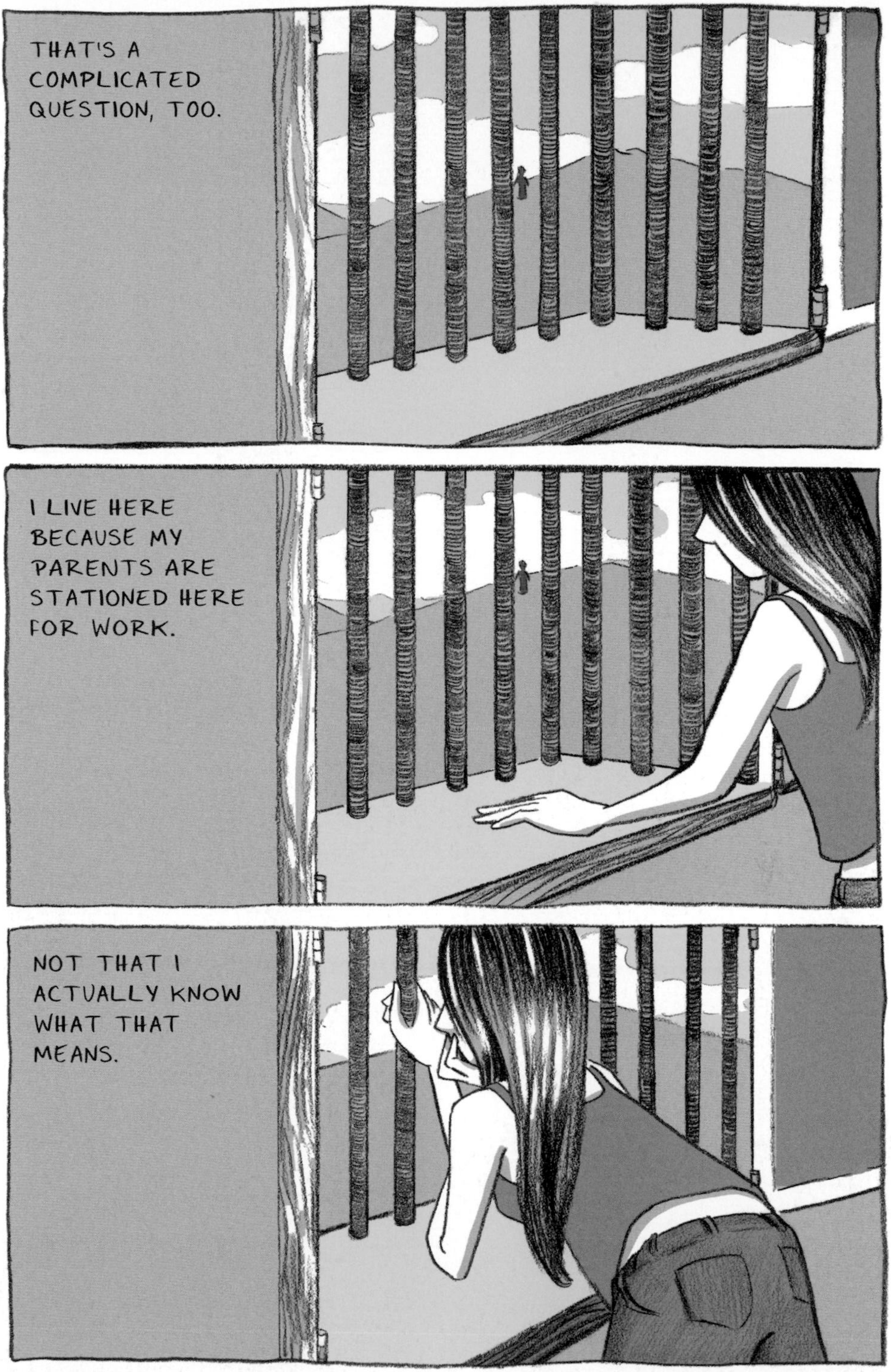
THAT'S A COMPLICATED QUESTION, TOO.
I LIVE HERE BECAUSE MY PARENTS ARE STATIONED HERE FOR WORK.
NOT THAT I ACTUALLY KNOW WHAT THAT MEANS.

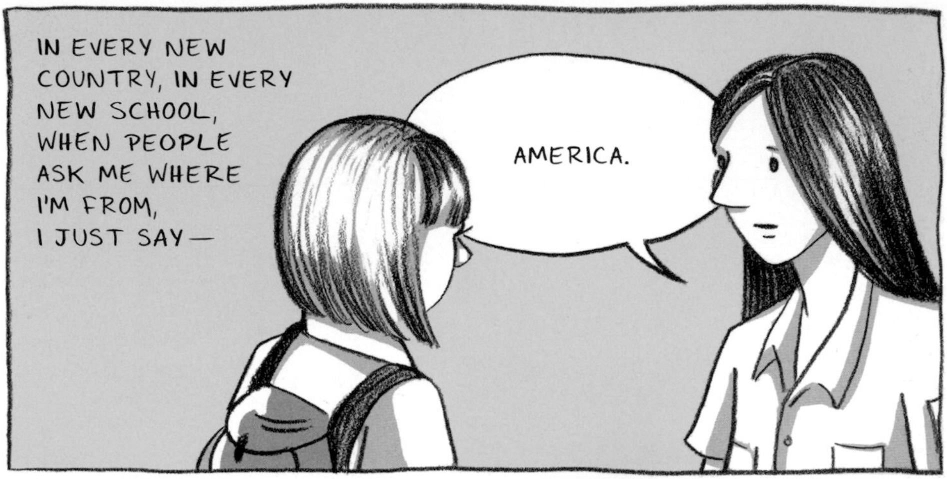
IN EVERY NEW COUNTRY, IN EVERY NEW SCHOOL, WHEN PEOPLE ASK ME WHERE I'M FROM, I JUST SAY—
AMERICA.

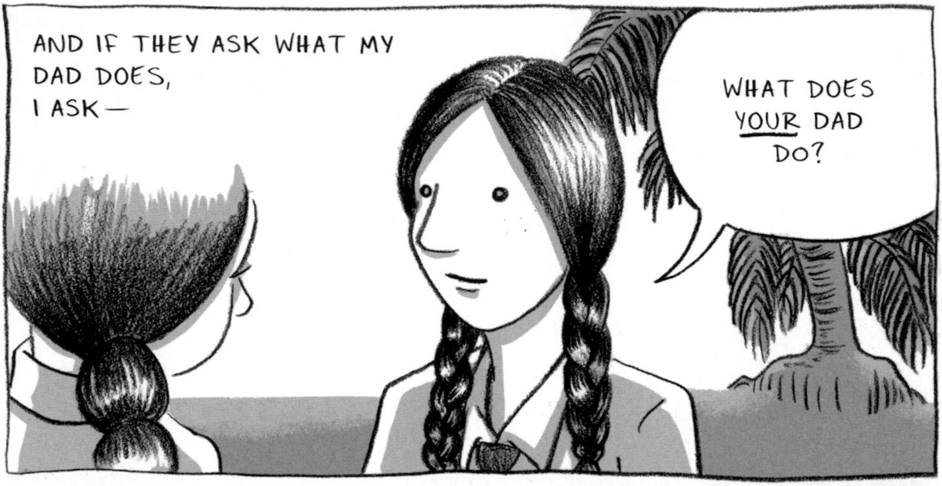
AND IF THEY ASK WHAT MY DAD DOES, I ASK—
WHAT DOES YOUR DAD DO?

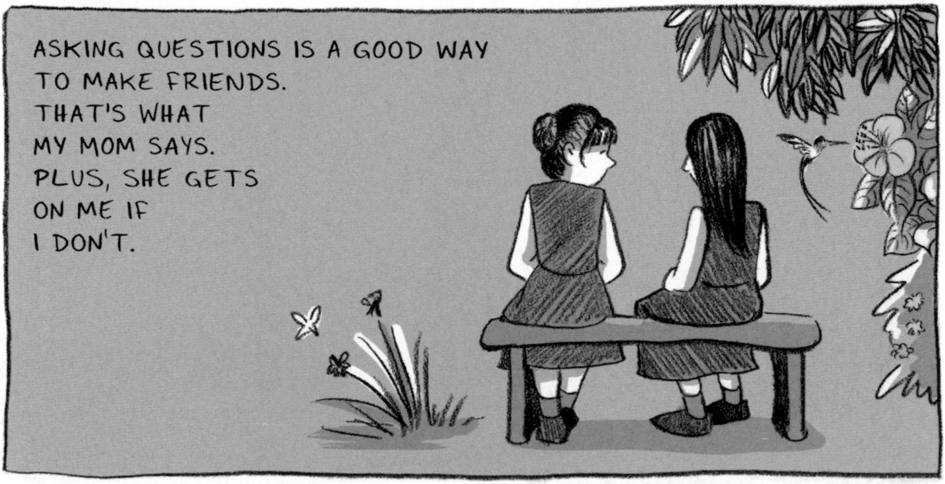
ASKING QUESTIONS IS A GOOD WAY TO MAKE FRIENDS. THAT'S WHAT MY MOM SAYS. PLUS, SHE GETS ON ME IF I DON'T.

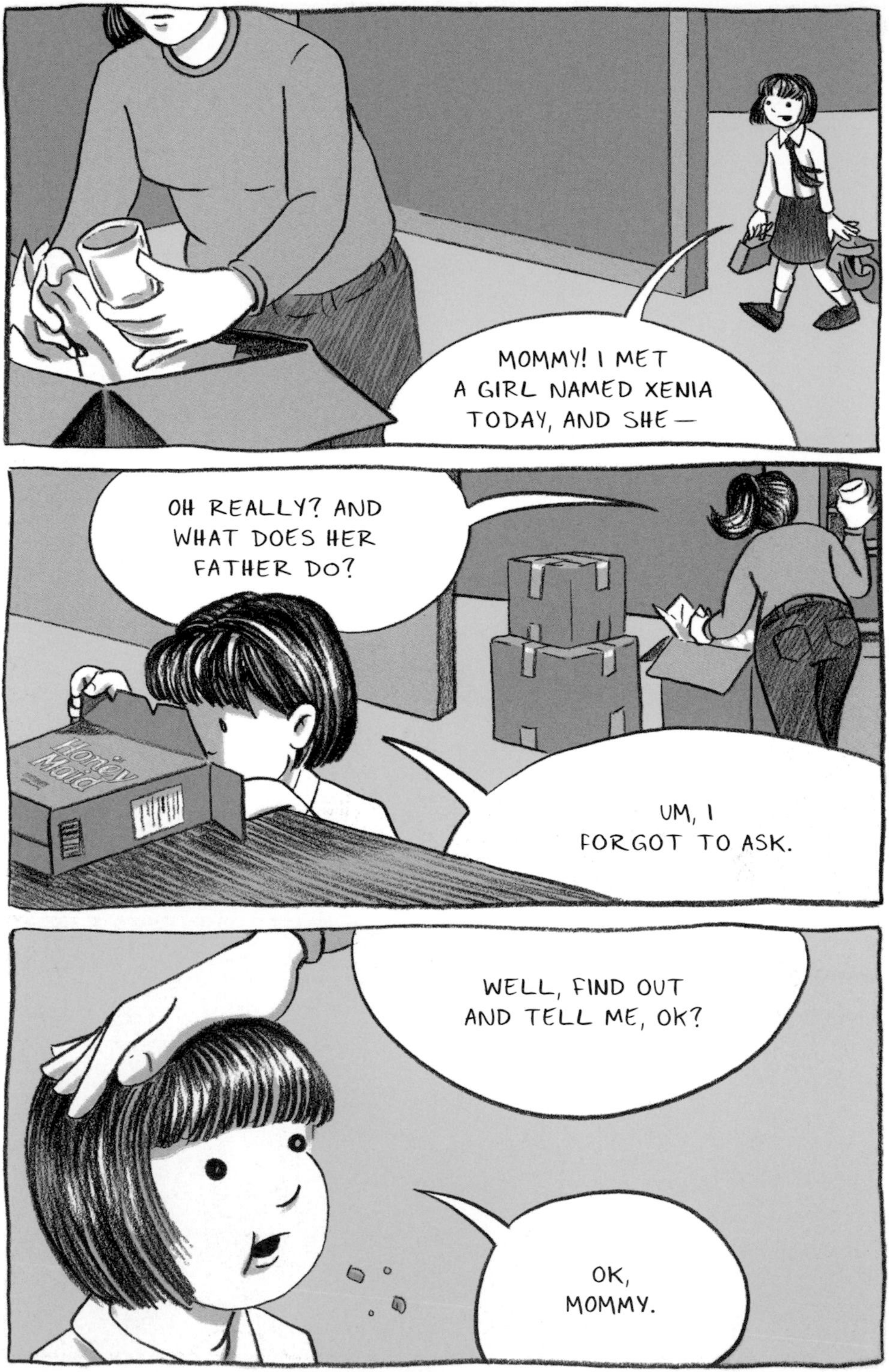
MOMMY! I MET A GIRL NAMED XENIA TODAY, AND SHE—
OH REALLY? AND WHAT DOES HER FATHER DO?
Honey Maid
UM, I FORGOT TO ASK.
WELL, FIND OUT AND TELL ME, OK?
OK, MOMMY.

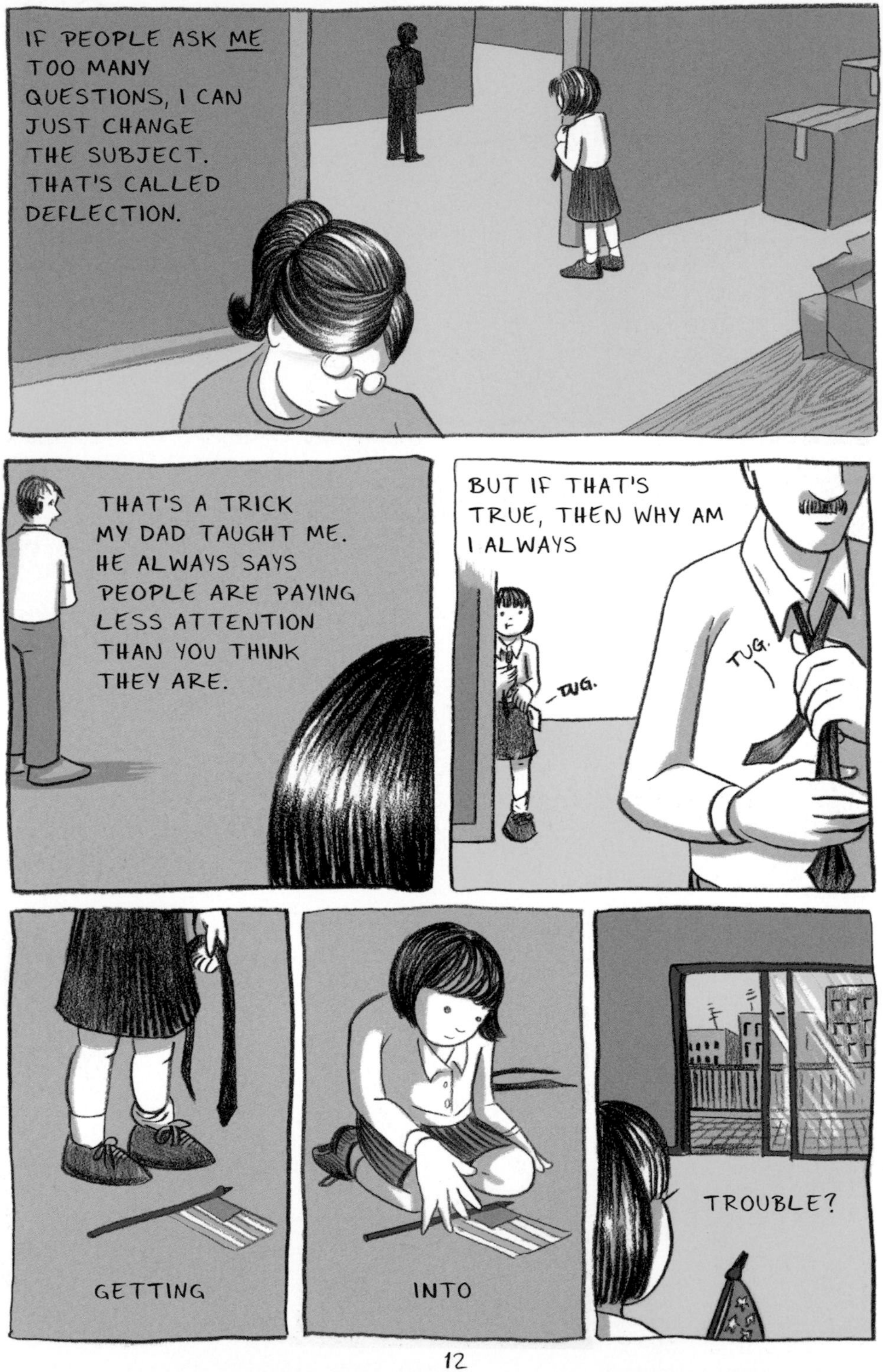
IF PEOPLE ASK ME TOO MANY QUESTIONS, I CAN JUST CHANGE THE SUBJECT. THAT'S CALLED DEFLECTION.
THAT'S A TRICK MY DAD TAUGHT ME. HE ALWAYS SAYS PEOPLE ARE PAYING LESS ATTENTION THAN YOU THINK THEY ARE.
BUT IF THAT'S TRUE, THEN WHY AM I ALWAYS
TUG.
TUG.
GETTING
INTO
TROUBLE?

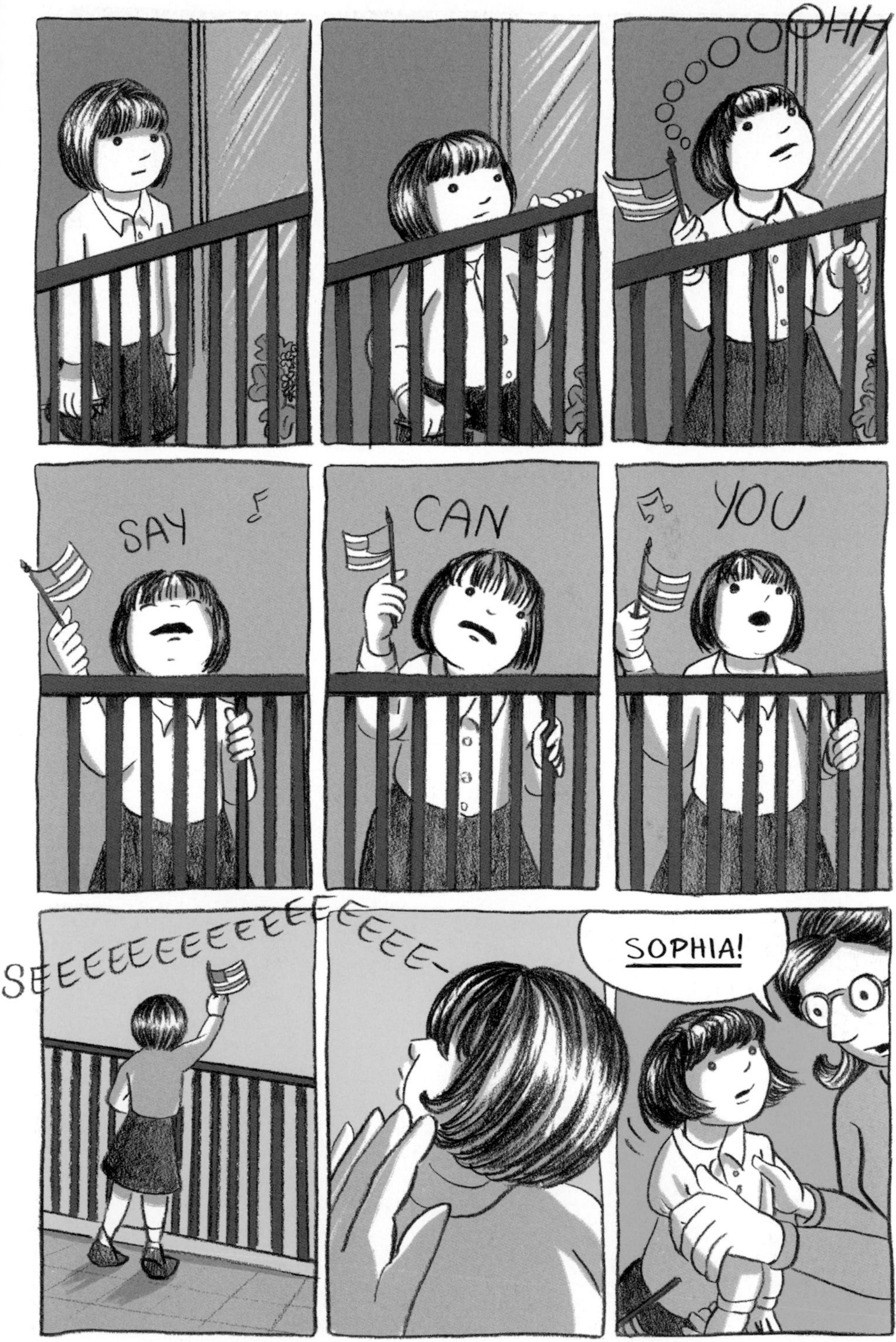
OOOOOOOHH
SAY
CAN
YOU
SEEEEEEEEEEEEEEEEEEEE-
SOPHIA!

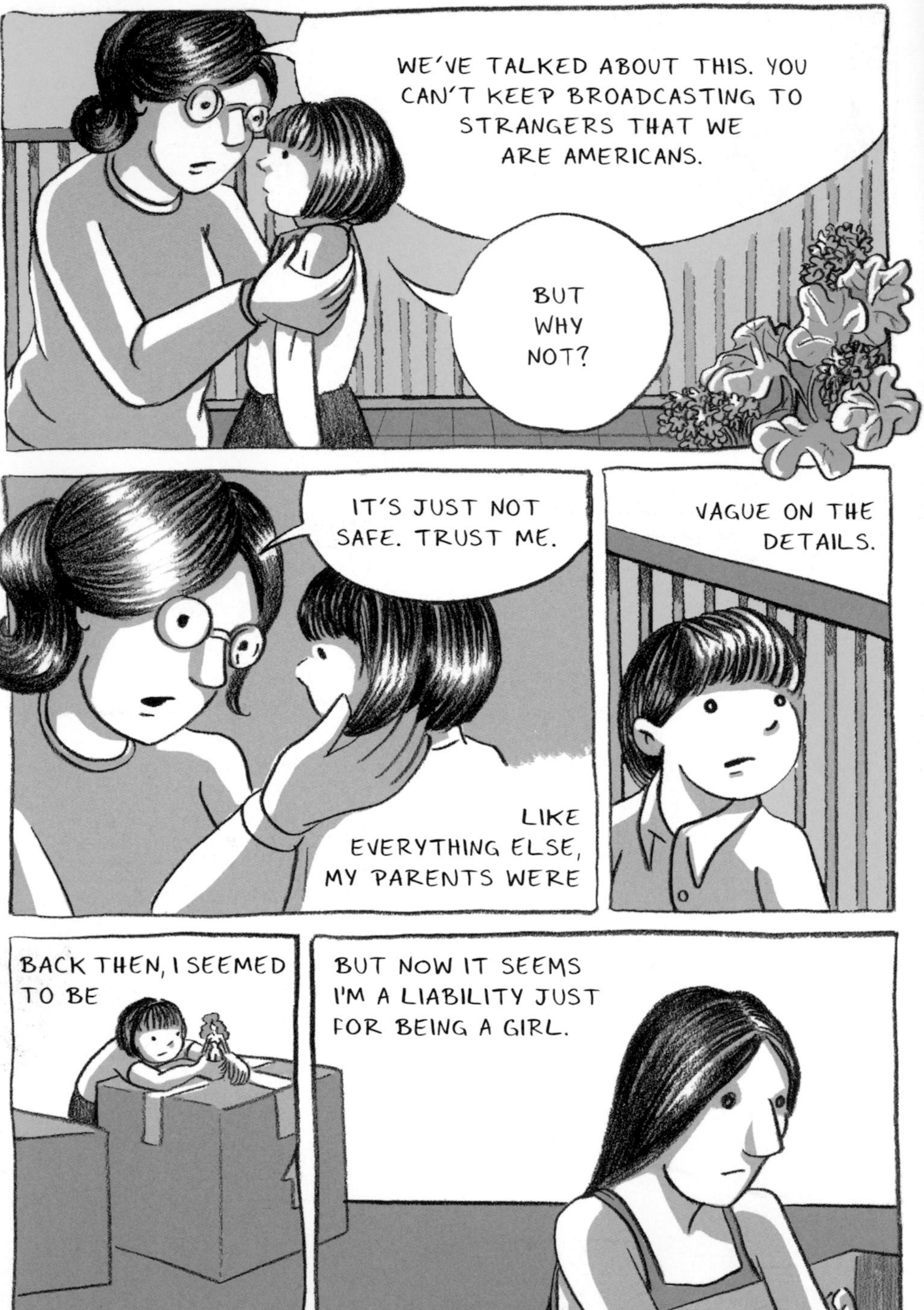
WE'VE TALKED ABOUT THIS. YOU CAN'T KEEP BROADCASTING TO STRANGERS THAT WE ARE AMERICANS.
BUT WHY NOT?
IT'S JUST NOT SAFE. TRUST ME.
LIKE EVERYTHING ELSE, MY PARENTS WERE
VAGUE ON THE DETAILS.
BACK THEN, I SEEMED TO BE
A LIABILITY FOR HAVING A BIG MOUTH—
BUT NOW IT SEEMS I'M A LIABILITY JUST FOR BEING A GIRL.

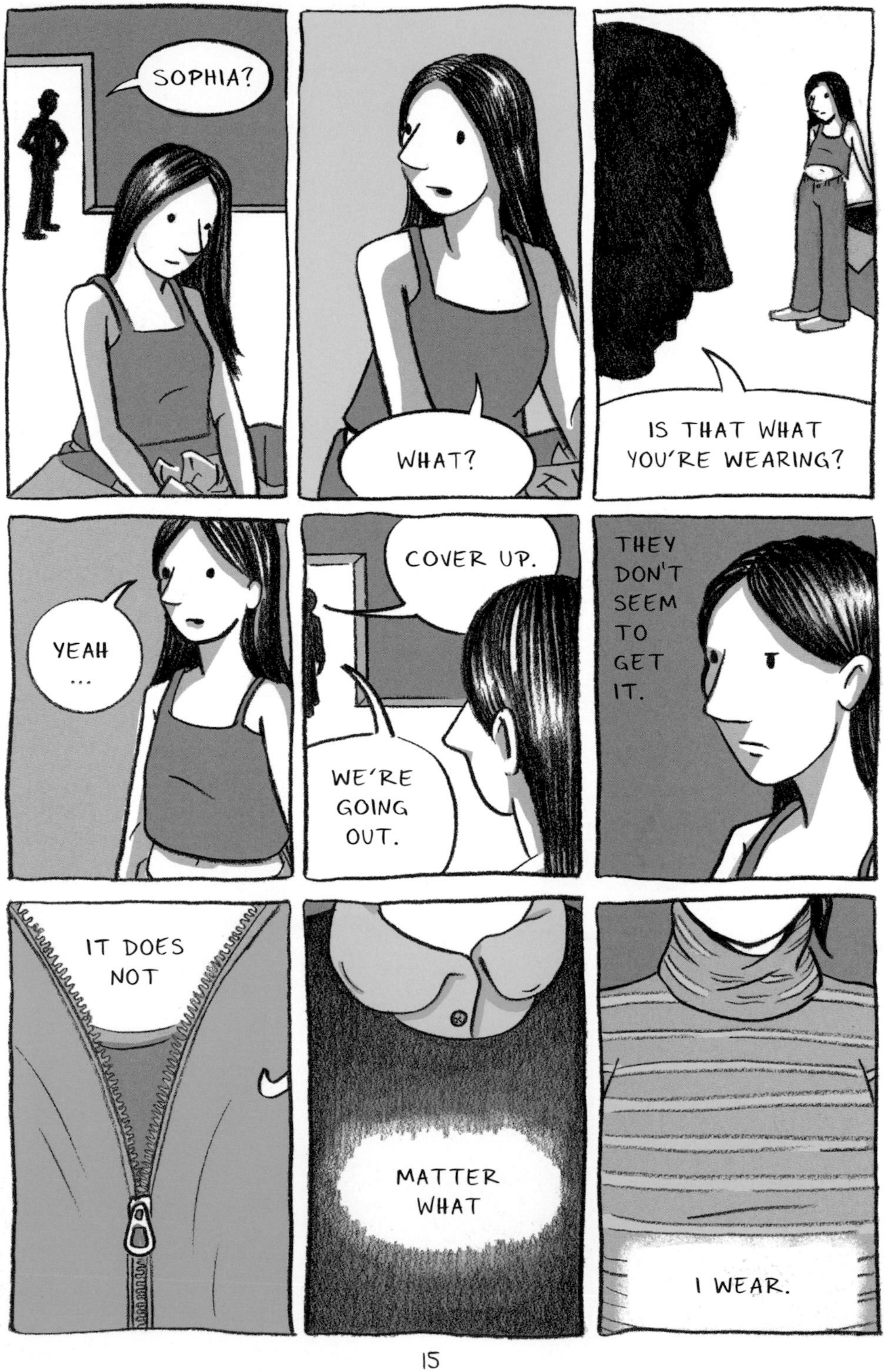
SOPHIA?
WHAT?
IS THAT WHAT YOU'RE WEARING?
YEAH ...
COVER UP.
WE'RE GOING OUT.
THEY DON'T SEEM TO GET IT.
IT DOES NOT
MATTER WHAT
I WEAR.

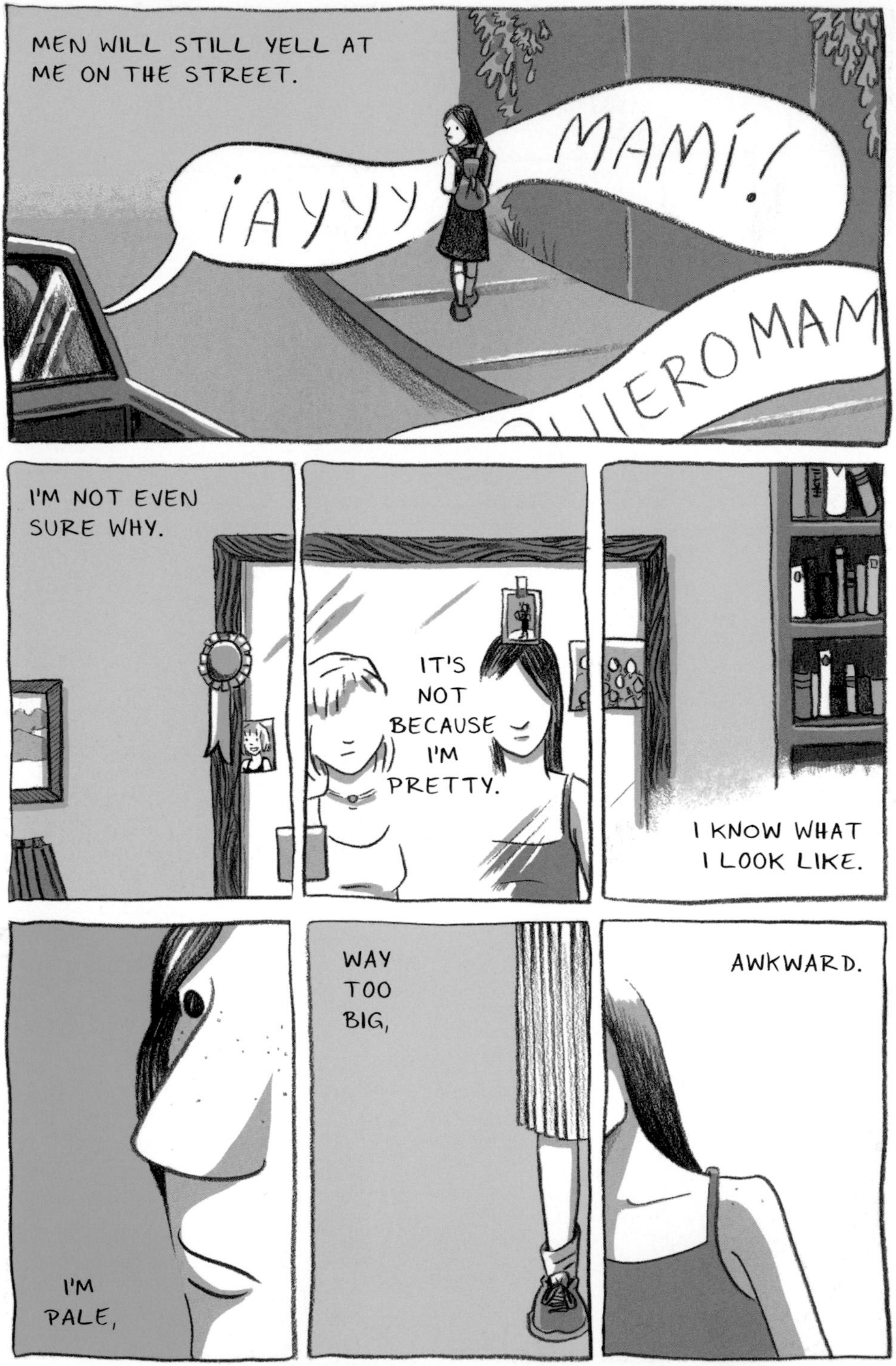
MEN WILL STILL YELL AT ME ON THE STREET.
¡AYYY MAMÍ!
QUIERO MAM
I'M NOT EVEN SURE WHY.
IT'S NOT BECAUSE I'M PRETTY.
I KNOW WHAT I LOOK LIKE.
I'M PALE,
WAY TOO BIG,
AWKWARD.

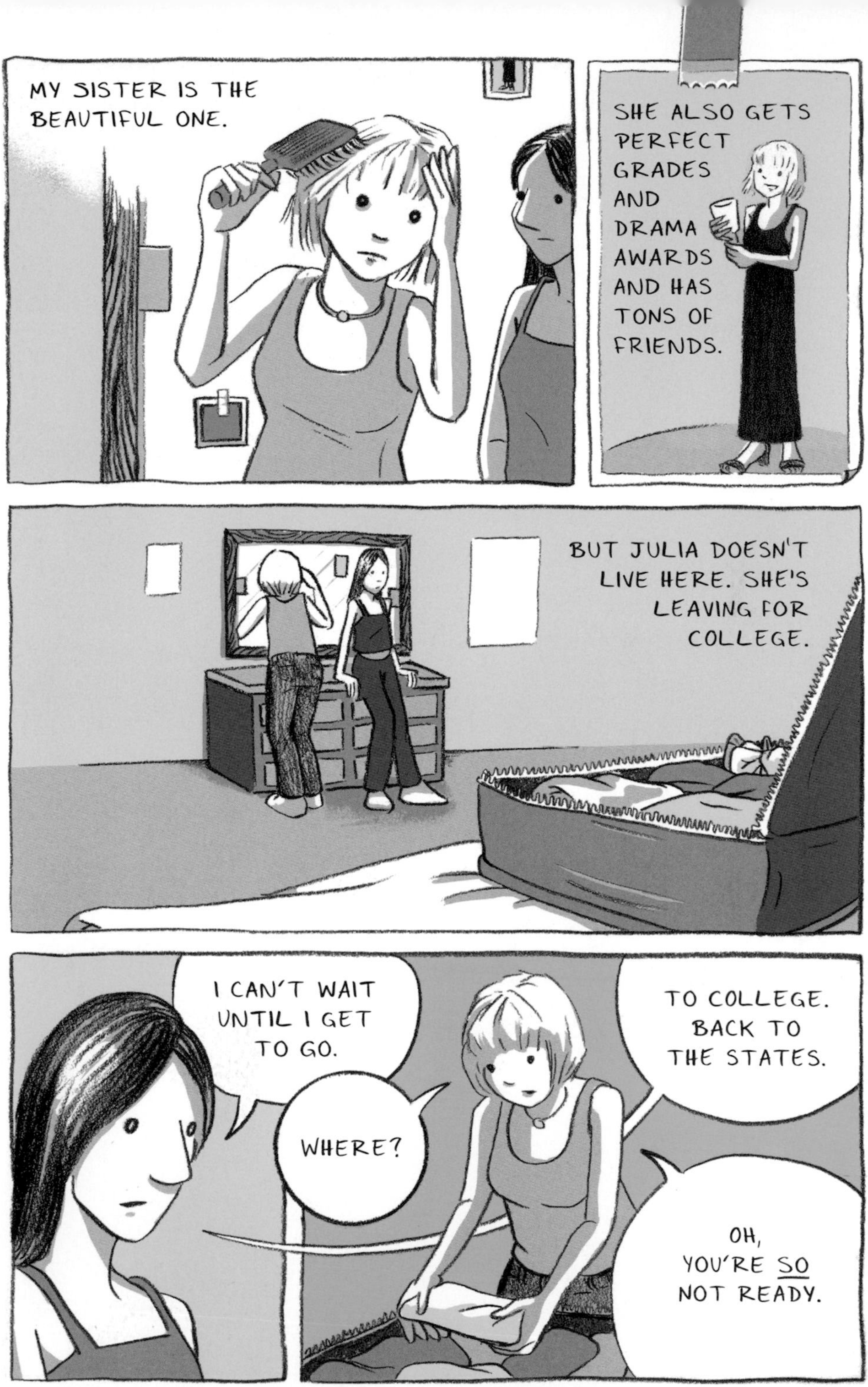
MY SISTER IS THE BEAUTIFUL ONE.
SHE ALSO GETS PERFECT GRADES AND DRAMA AWARDS AND HAS TONS OF FRIENDS.
BUT JULIA DOESN'T LIVE HERE. SHE'S LEAVING FOR COLLEGE.
I CAN'T WAIT UNTIL I GET TO GO.
WHERE?
TO COLLEGE. BACK TO THE STATES.
OH, YOU'RE SO NOT READY.

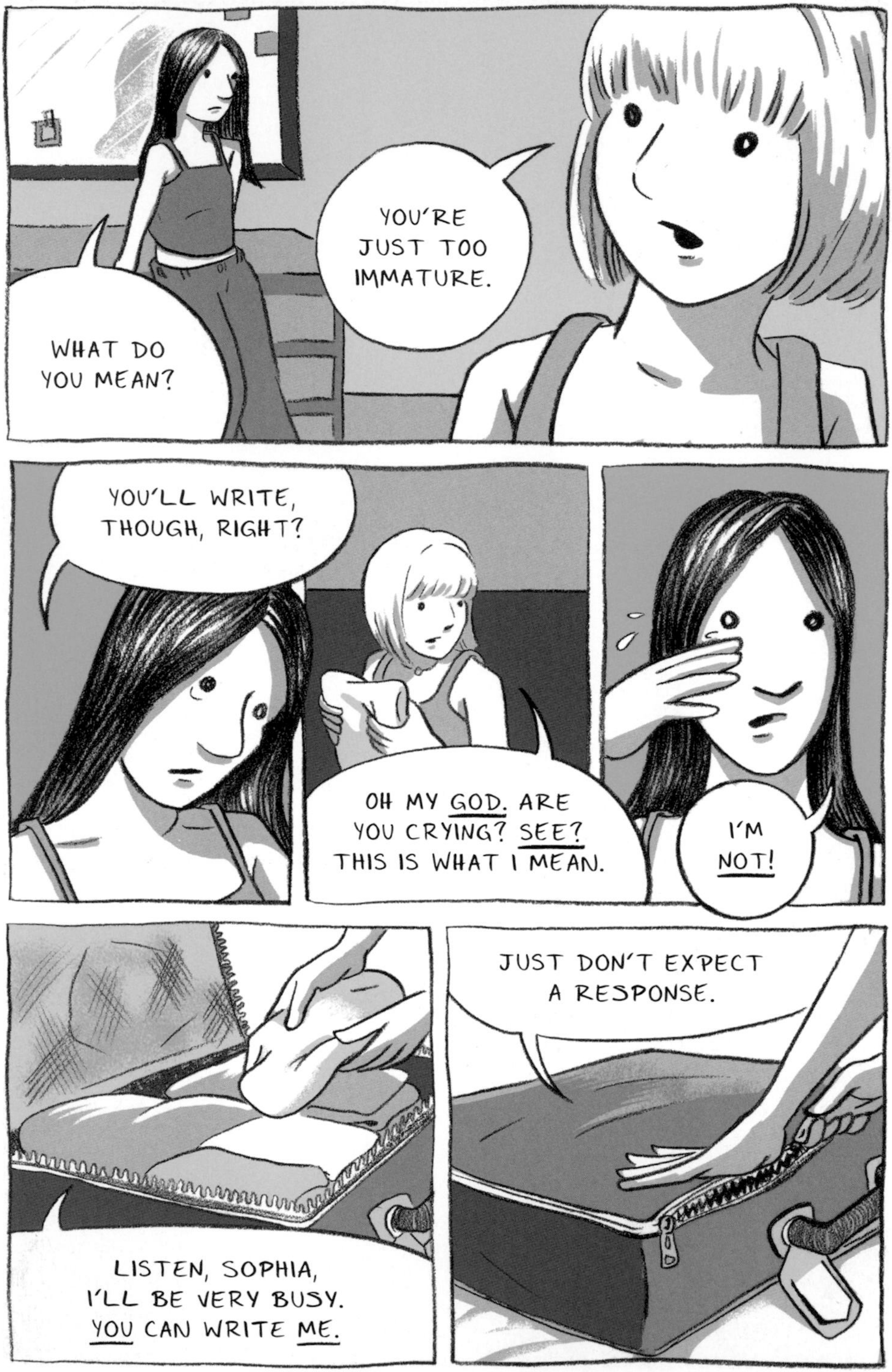
WHAT DO YOU MEAN?
YOU'RE JUST TOO IMMATURE.
YOU'LL WRITE, THOUGH, RIGHT?
OH MY GOD. ARE YOU CRYING? SEE? THIS IS WHAT I MEAN.
I'M NOT!
LISTEN, SOPHIA, I'LL BE VERY BUSY. YOU CAN WRITE ME.
JUST DON'T EXPECT A RESPONSE.

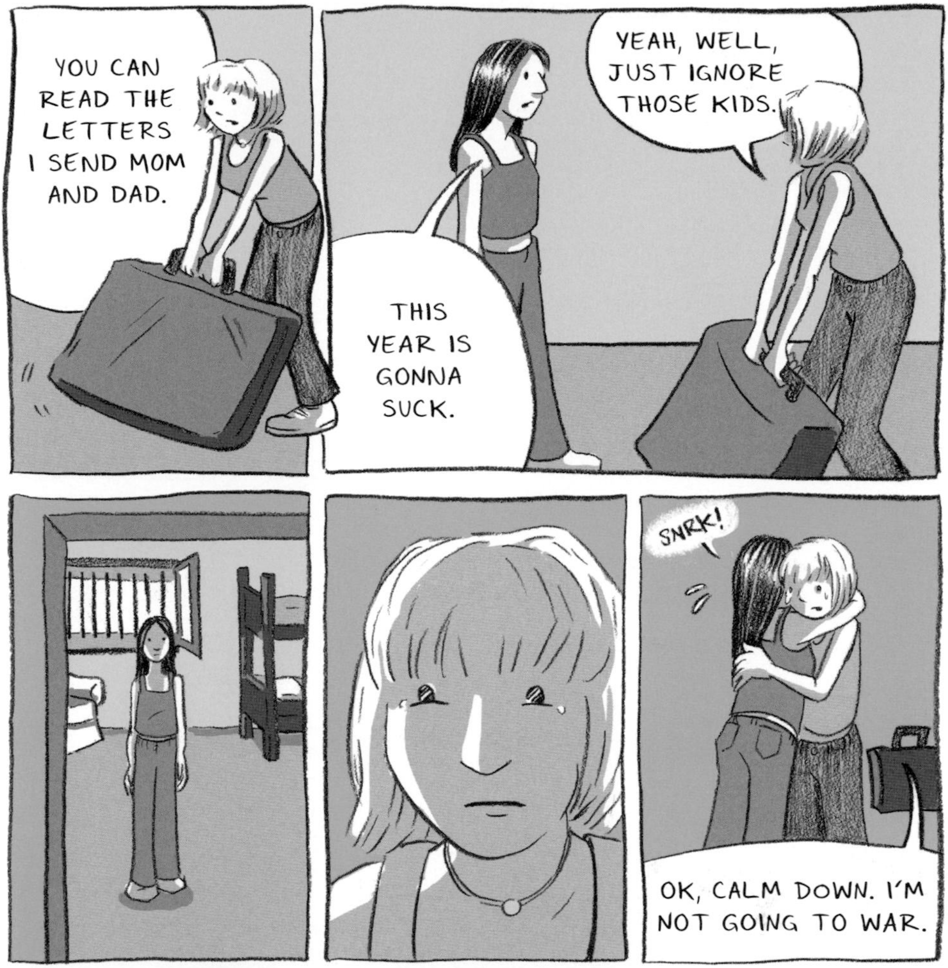
YOU CAN READ THE LETTERS I SEND MOM AND DAD.
THIS YEAR IS GONNA SUCK.
YEAH, WELL, JUST IGNORE THOSE KIDS.
SNRK!
OK, CALM DOWN. I'M NOT GOING TO WAR.

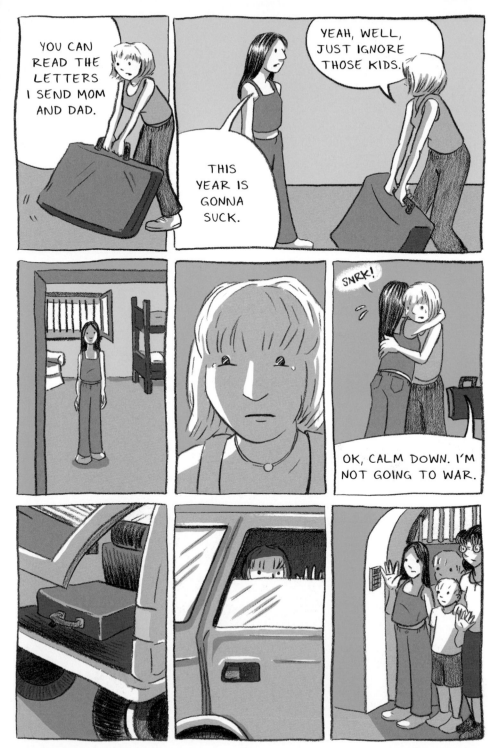

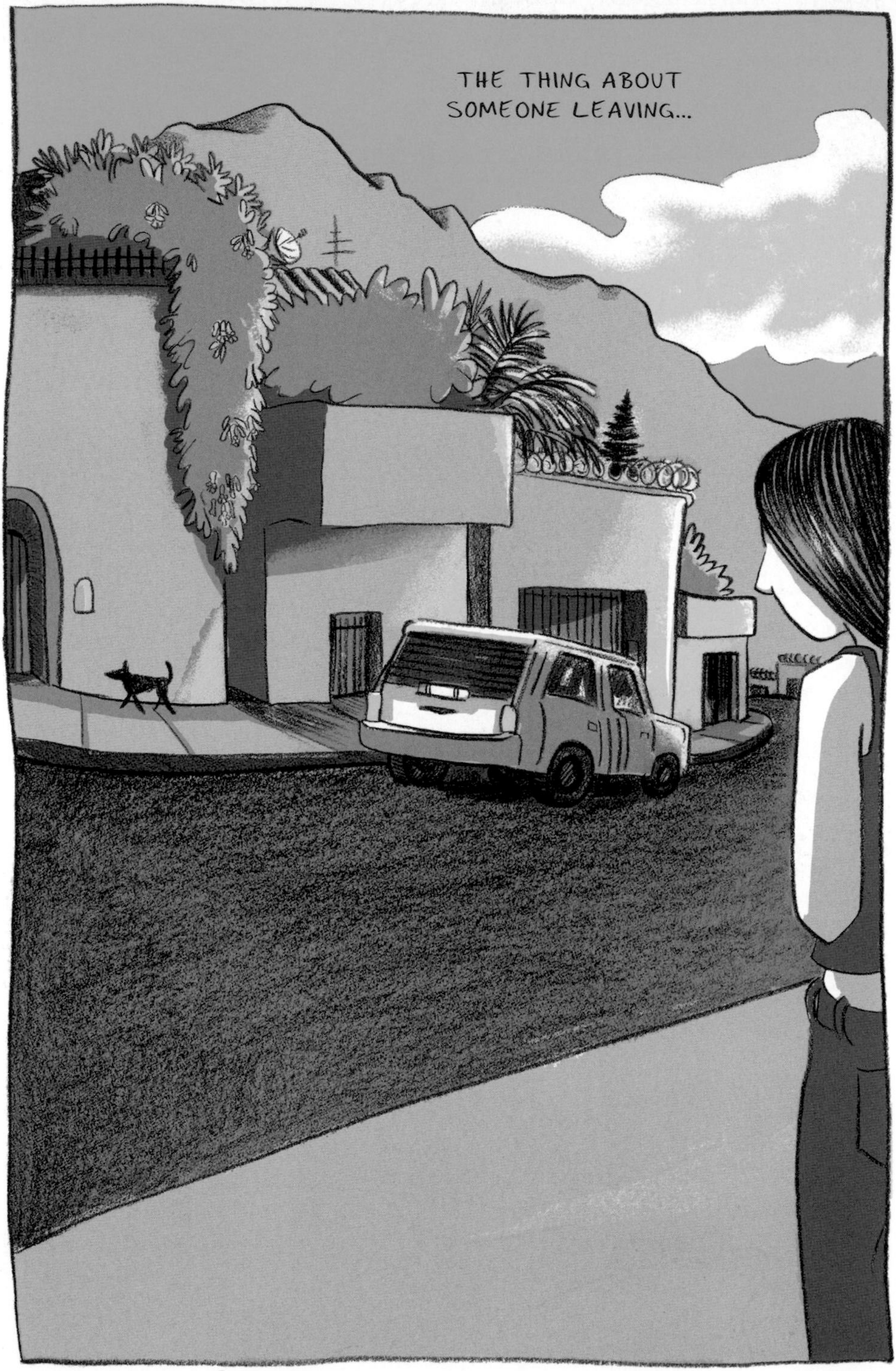
THE THING ABOUT
SOMEONE LEAVING...

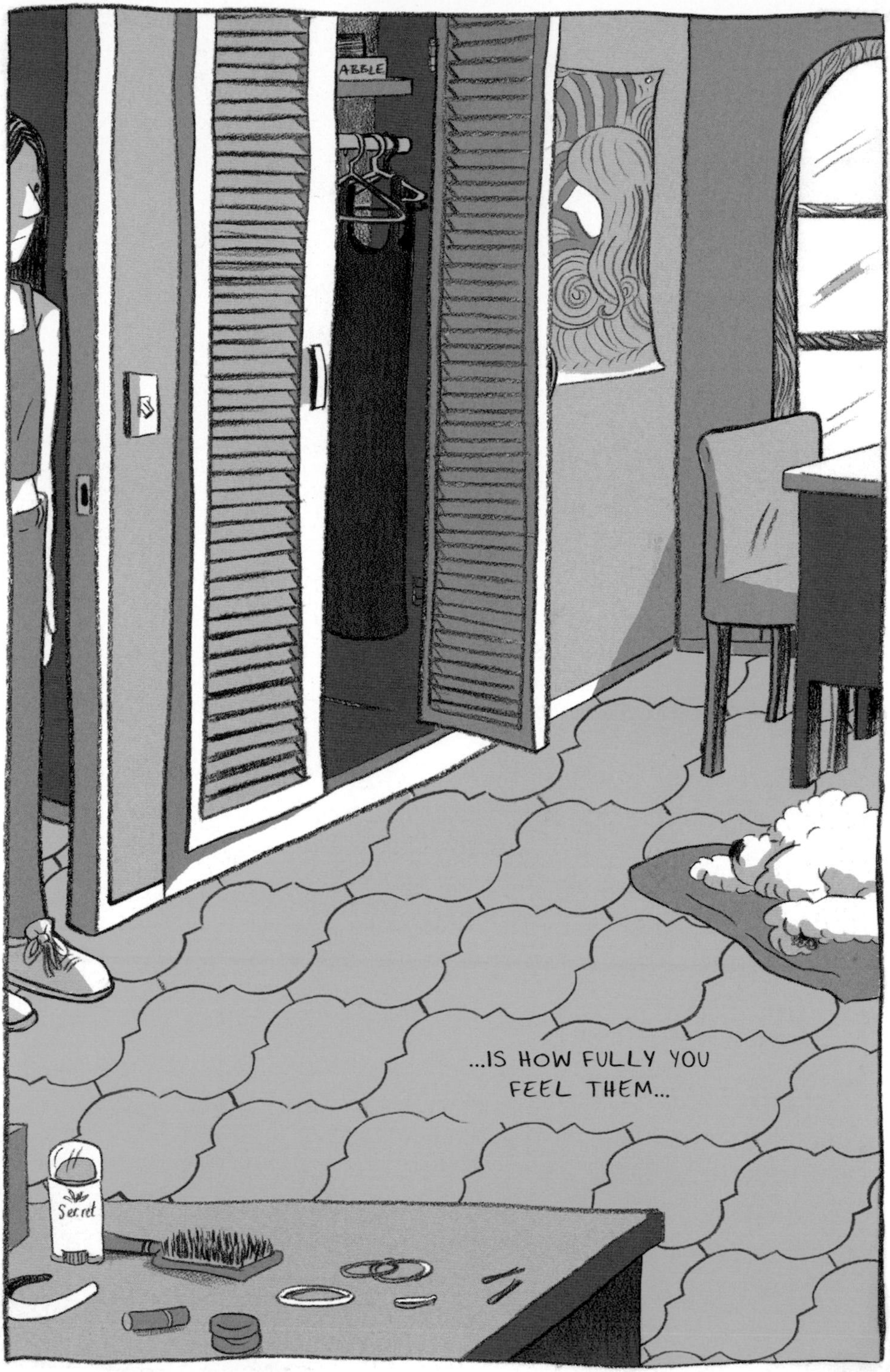
ABBLE
...IS HOW FULLY YOU FEEL THEM...
Secret

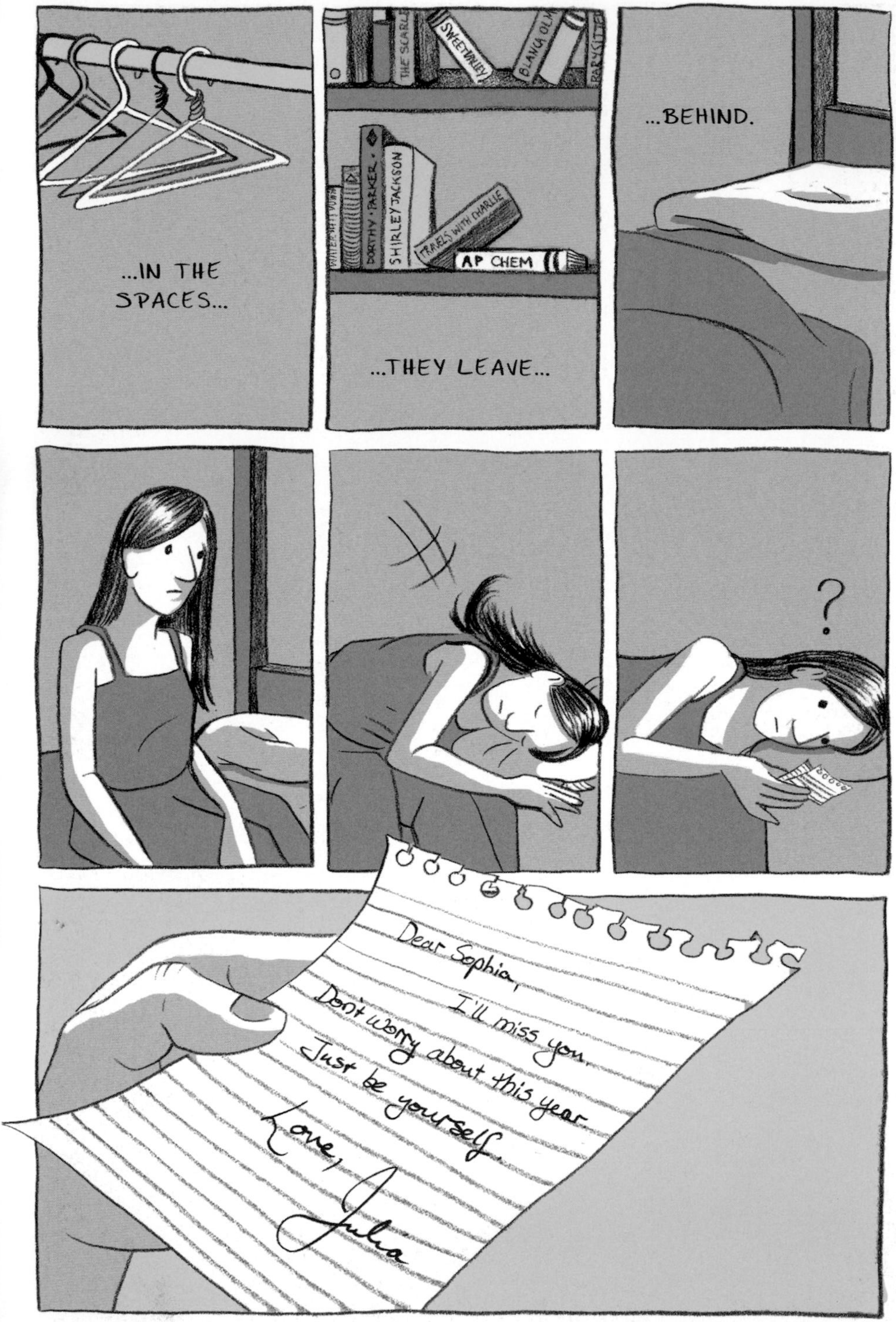
...IN THE SPACES...
SWEET VALLEY
DORTHY · PARKER
SHIRLEY JACKSON
TRAVELS WITH CHARLIE
AP CHEM
...THEY LEAVE...
...BEHIND.
?
Dear Sophia,
I'll miss you.
Don't worry about this year.
Just be yourself.
Love,
Julia

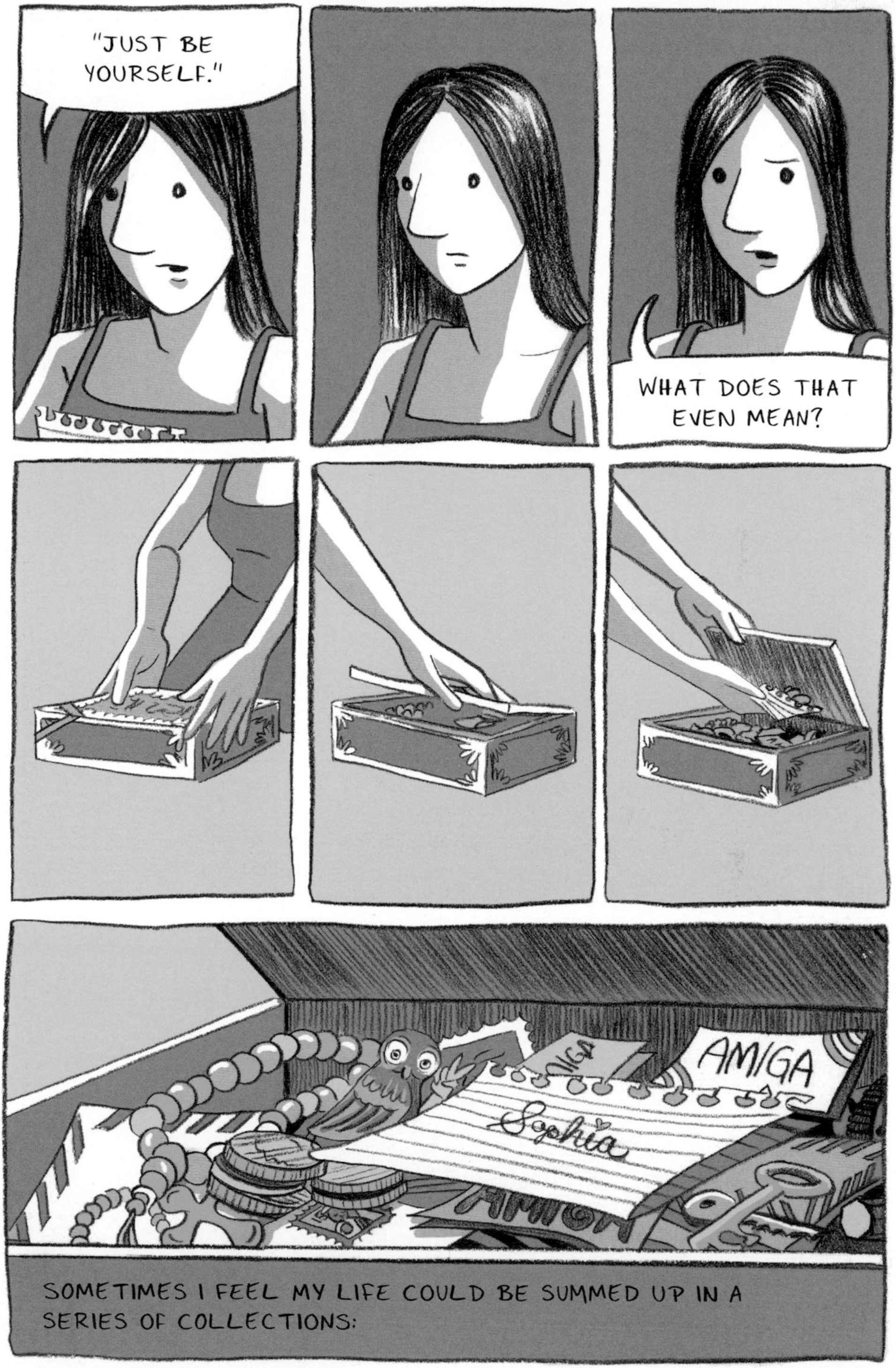
"JUST BE YOURSELF."
WHAT DOES THAT EVEN MEAN?
AMIGA
Sophia
SOMETIMES I FEEL MY LIFE COULD BE SUMMED UP IN A SERIES OF COLLECTIONS:

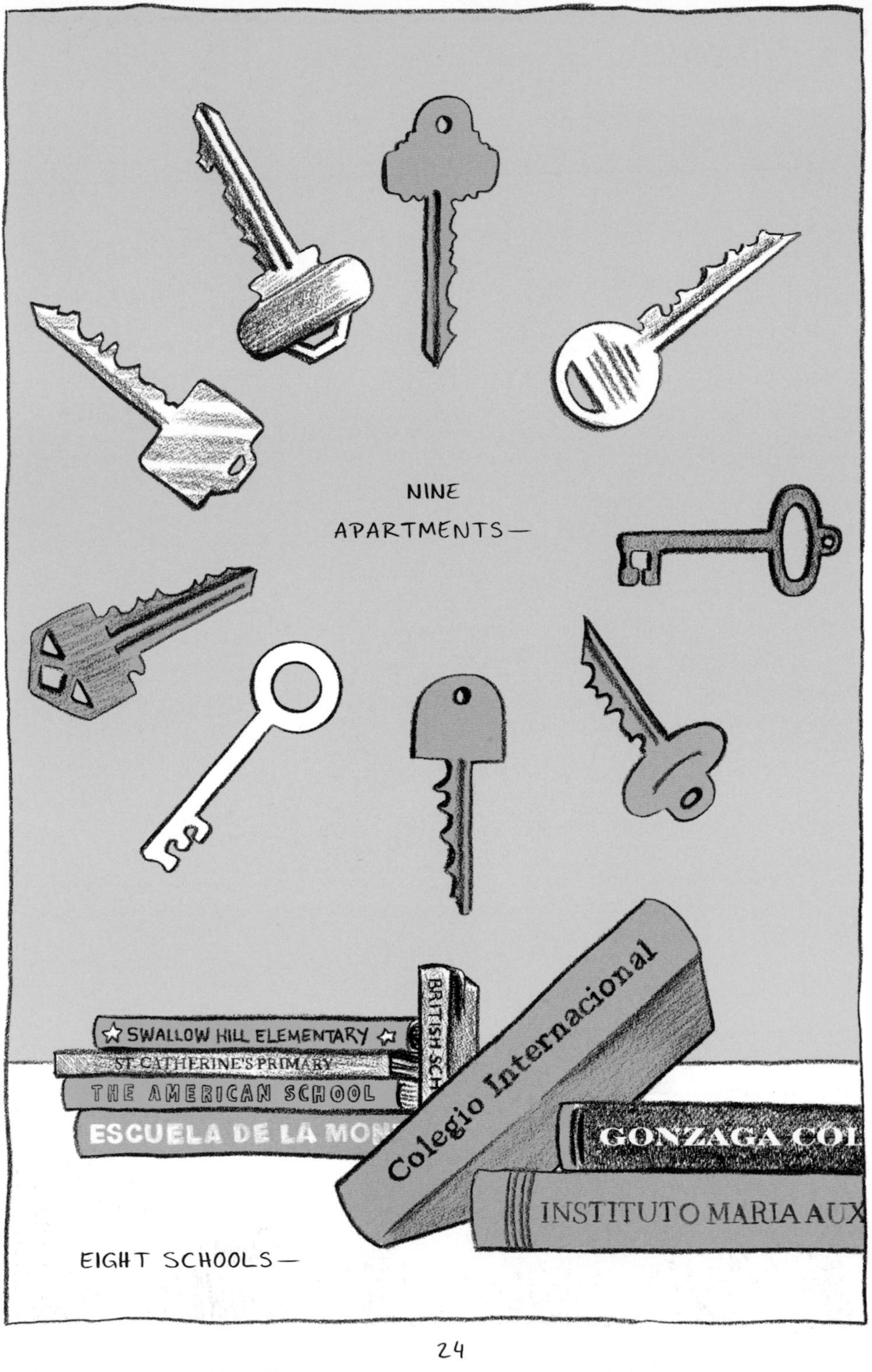

NINE
APARTMENTS—
SWALLOW HILL ELEMENTARY
ST. CATHERINE'S PRIMARY
THE AMERICAN SCHOOL
ESCUELA DE LA MON
BRITISH SCH
Colegio Internacional
GONZAGA COL
INSTITUTO MARIA AUX
EIGHT SCHOOLS—

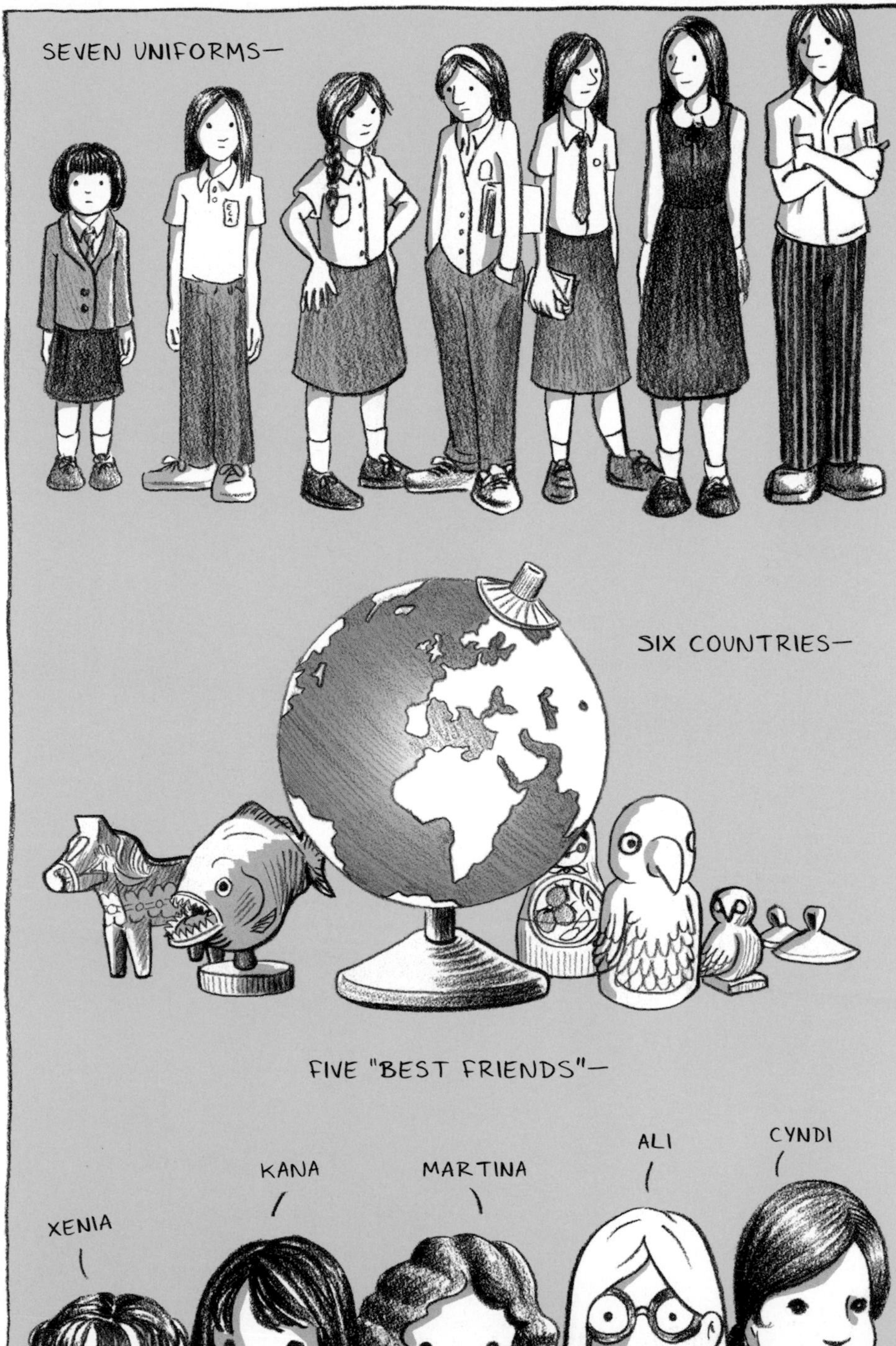
SEVEN UNIFORMS—
SIX COUNTRIES—
FIVE "BEST FRIENDS"—
XENIA
KANA
MARTINA
ALI
CYNDI

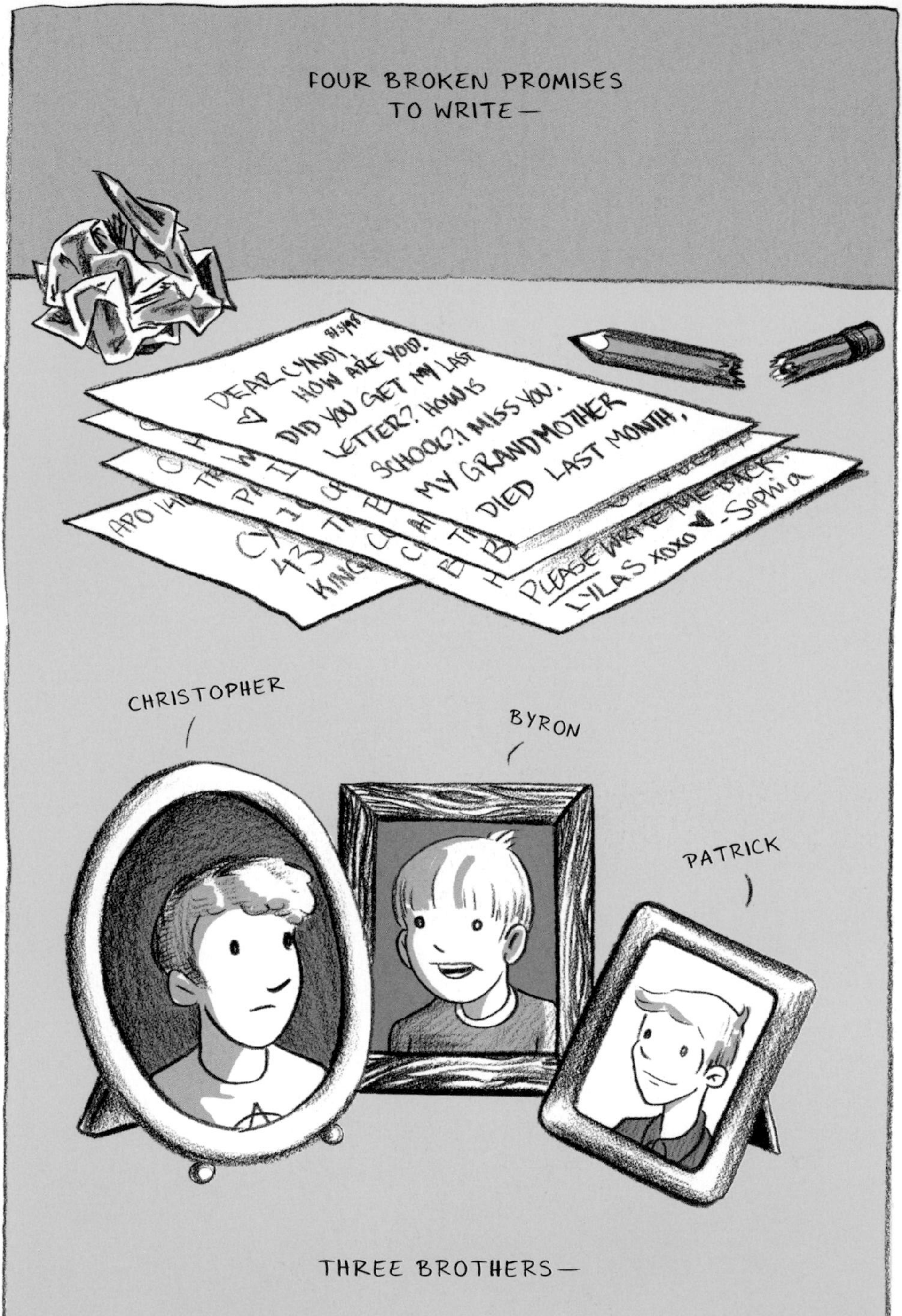
FOUR BROKEN PROMISES
TO WRITE—
DEAR CYNDI,
HOW ARE YOU?
DID YOU GET MY LAST
LETTER? HOW IS
SCHOOL? I MISS YOU.
MY GRANDMOTHER
DIED LAST MONTH.
PLEASE WRITE ME BACK!
LYLAS XOXO ♥ -Sophia
CHRISTOPHER
BYRON
PATRICK
THREE BROTHERS—

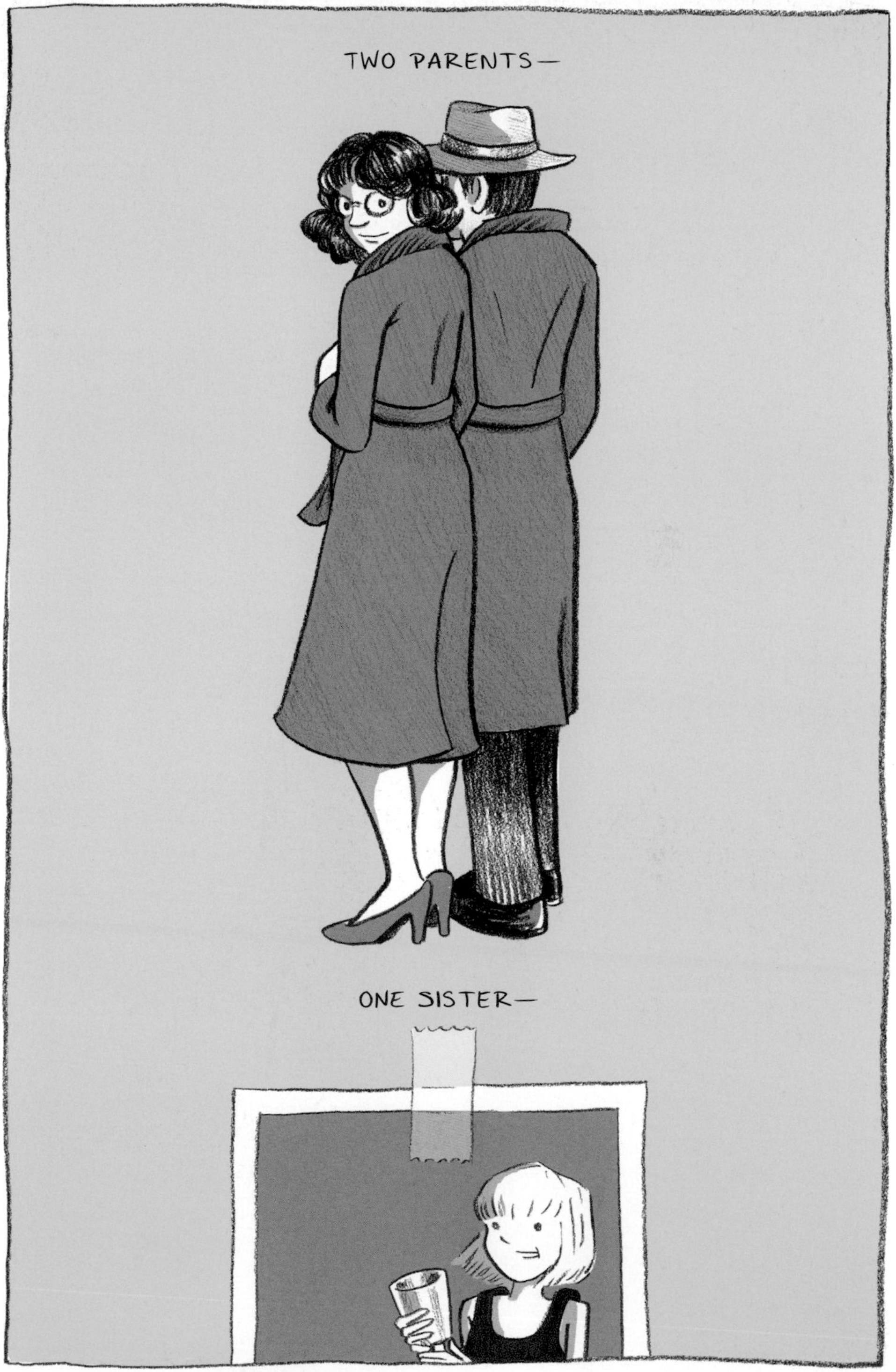
TWO PARENTS—
ONE SISTER—

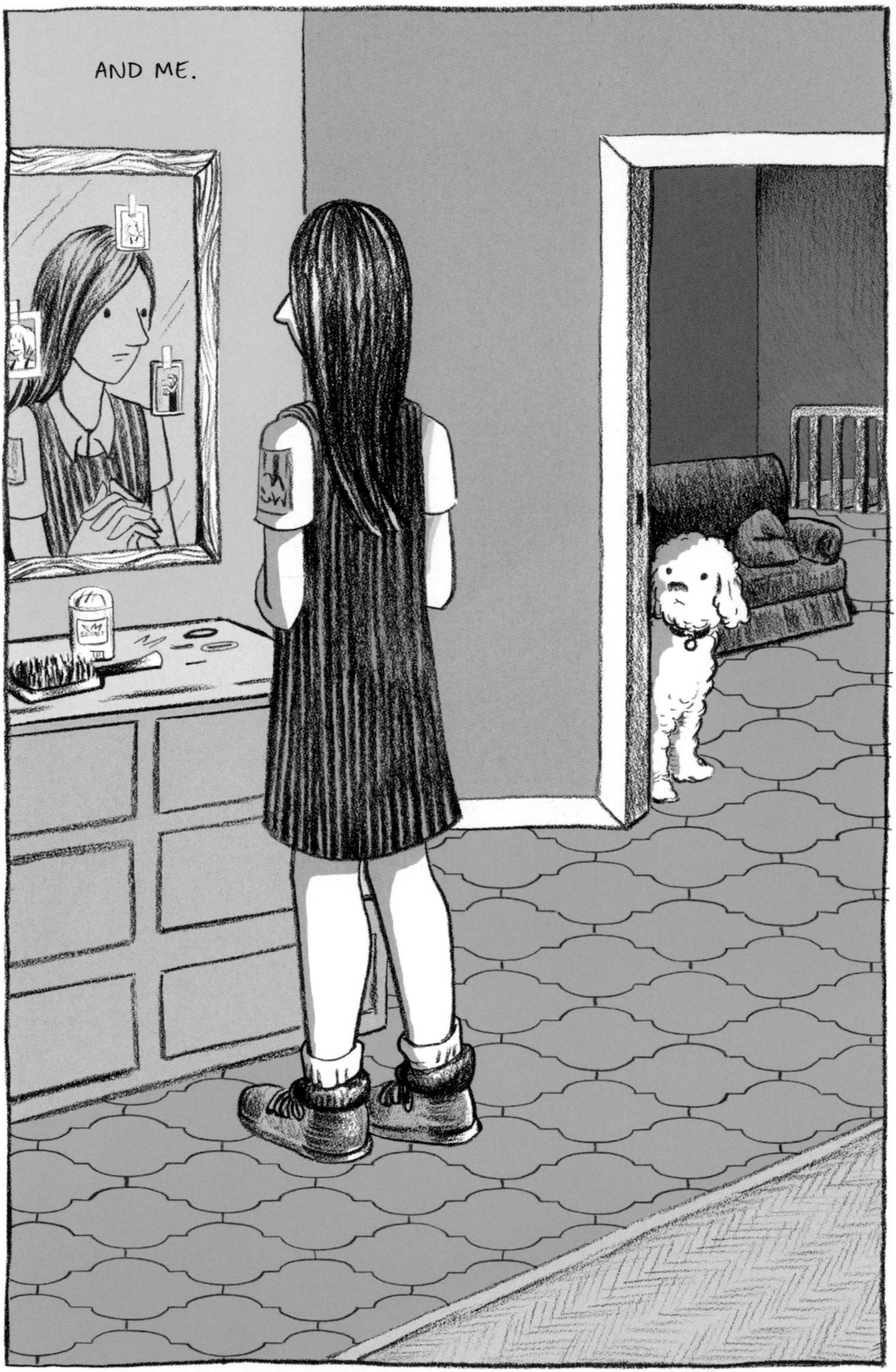
AND ME.

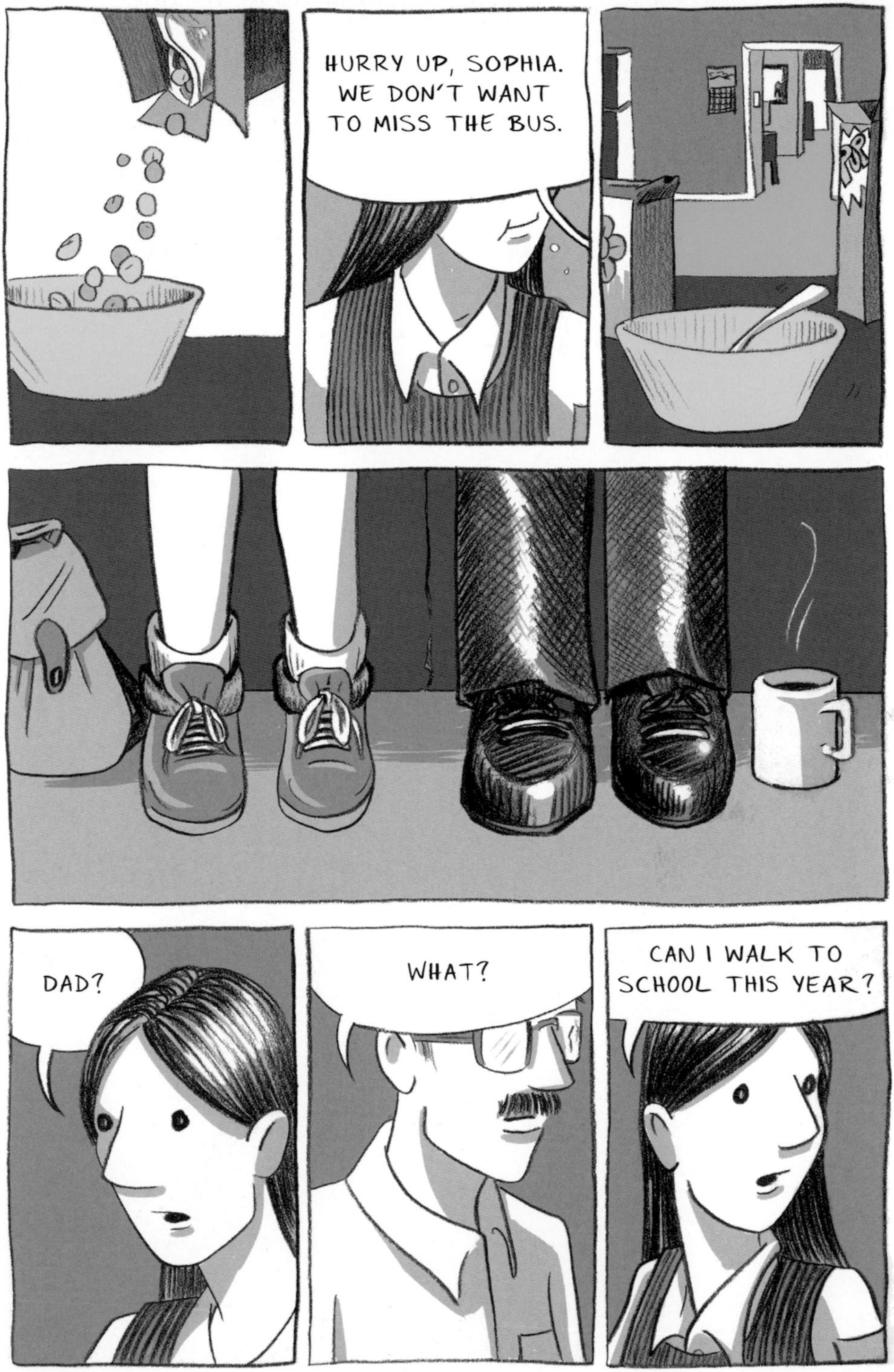
HURRY UP, SOPHIA. WE DON'T WANT TO MISS THE BUS.
POP
DAD?
WHAT?
CAN I WALK TO SCHOOL THIS YEAR?

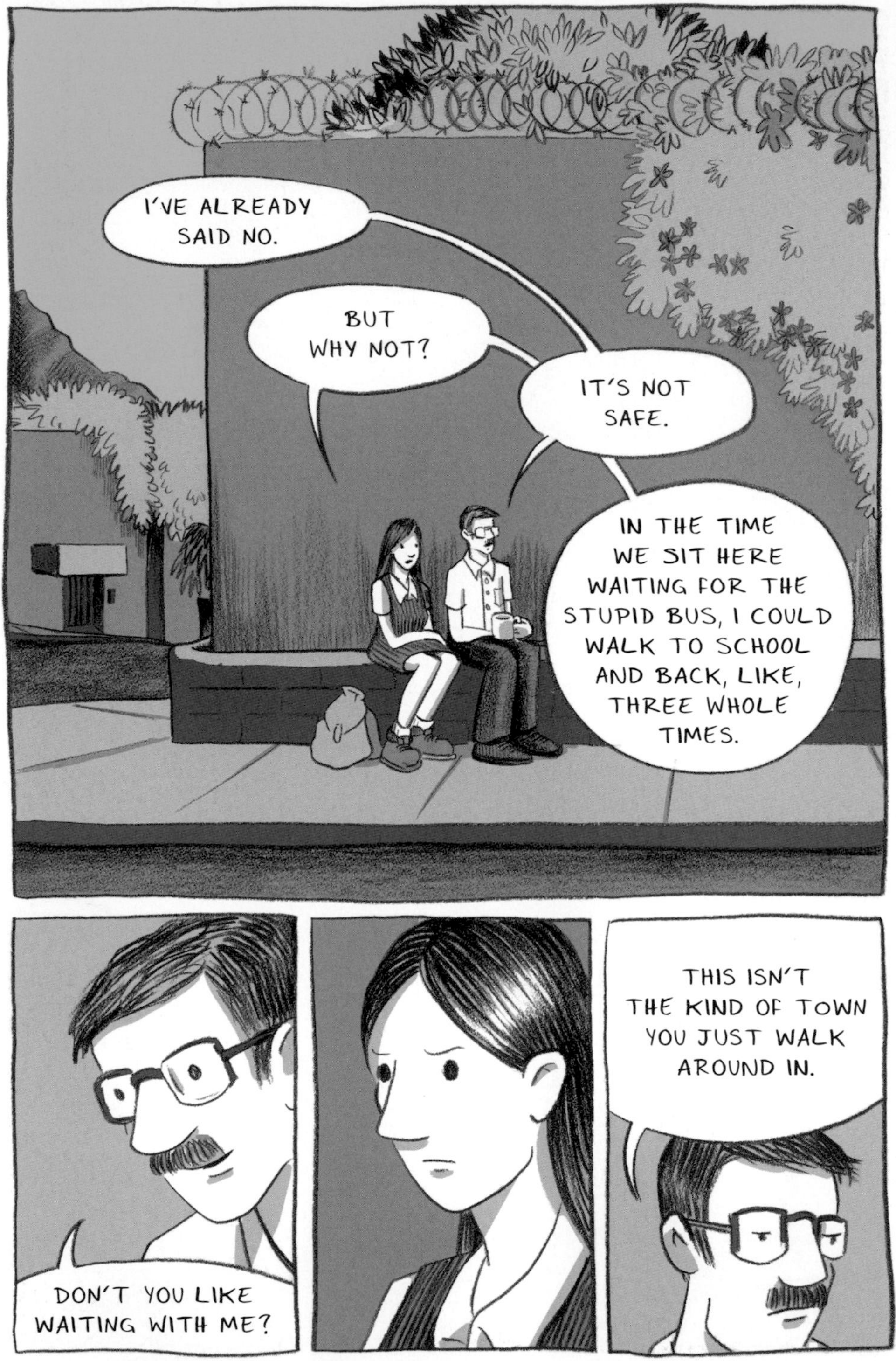
I'VE ALREADY SAID NO.
BUT WHY NOT?
IT'S NOT SAFE.
IN THE TIME WE SIT HERE WAITING FOR THE STUPID BUS, I COULD WALK TO SCHOOL AND BACK, LIKE, THREE WHOLE TIMES.
DON'T YOU LIKE WAITING WITH ME?
THIS ISN'T THE KIND OF TOWN YOU JUST WALK AROUND IN.

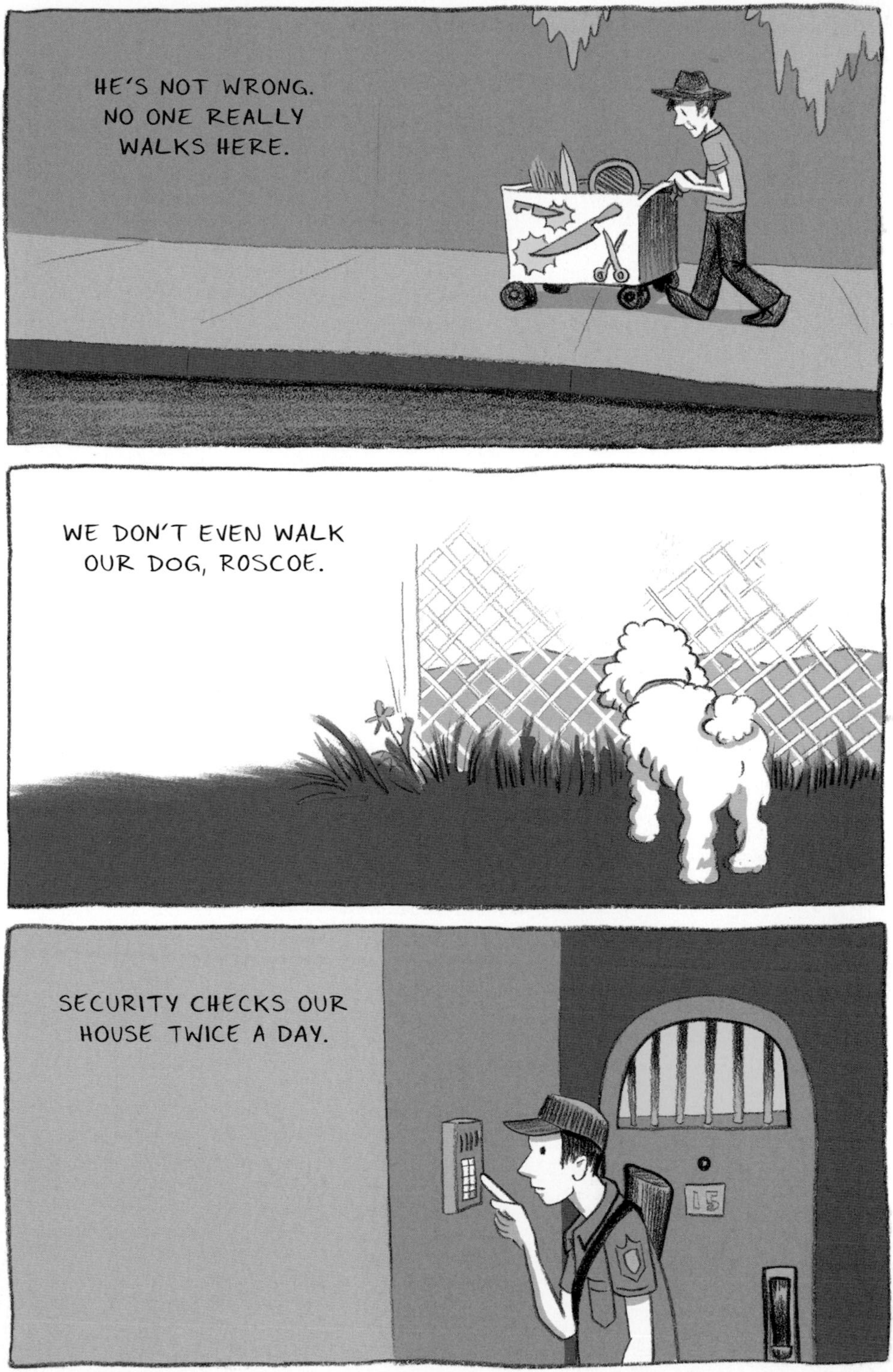
HE'S NOT WRONG. NO ONE REALLY WALKS HERE.
WE DON'T EVEN WALK OUR DOG, ROSCOE.
SECURITY CHECKS OUR HOUSE TWICE A DAY.
15

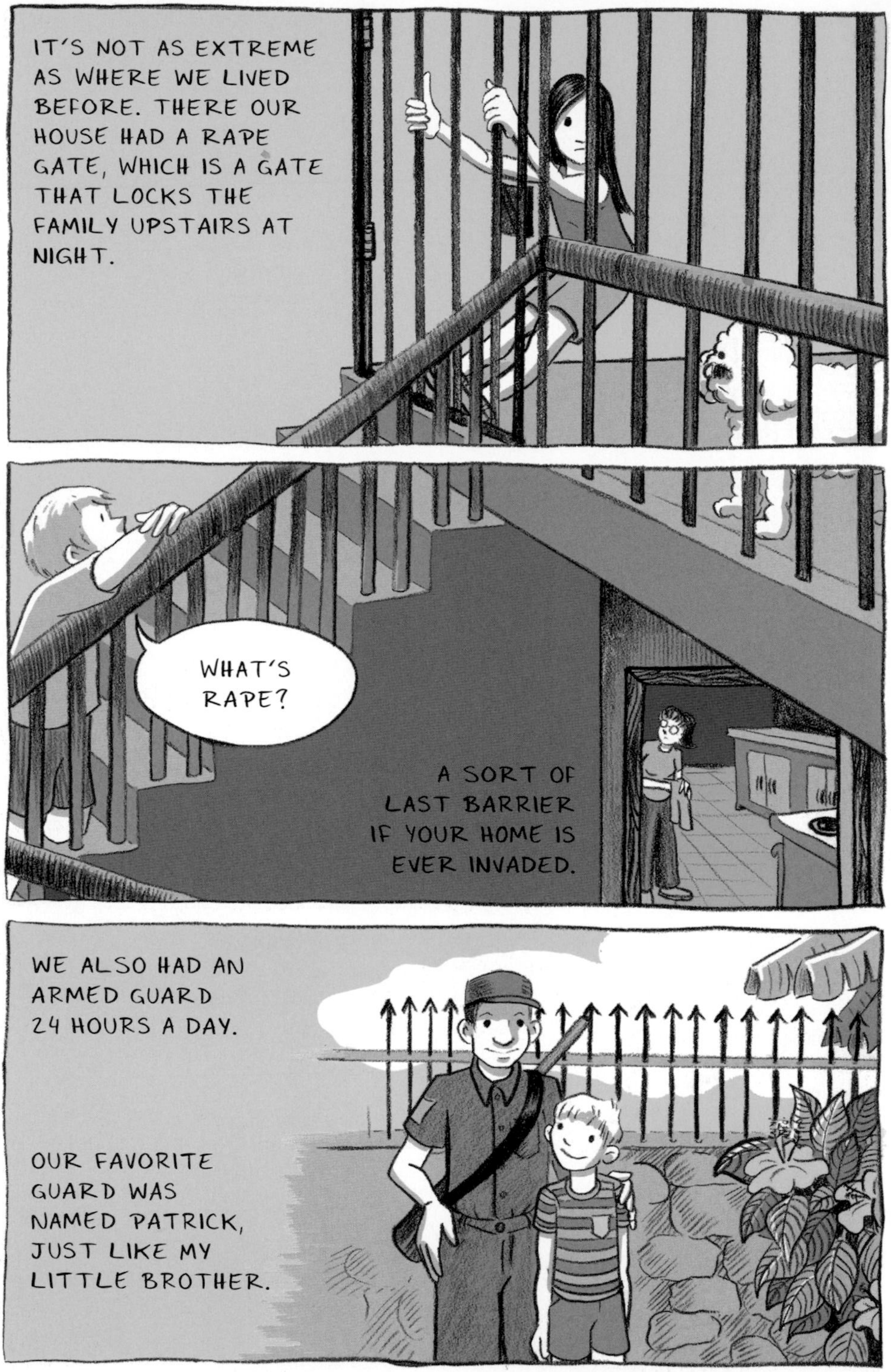
IT'S NOT AS EXTREME AS WHERE WE LIVED BEFORE. THERE OUR HOUSE HAD A RAPE GATE, WHICH IS A GATE THAT LOCKS THE FAMILY UPSTAIRS AT NIGHT.
WHAT'S RAPE?
A SORT OF LAST BARRIER IF YOUR HOME IS EVER INVADED.
WE ALSO HAD AN ARMED GUARD 24 HOURS A DAY.
OUR FAVORITE GUARD WAS NAMED PATRICK, JUST LIKE MY LITTLE BROTHER.

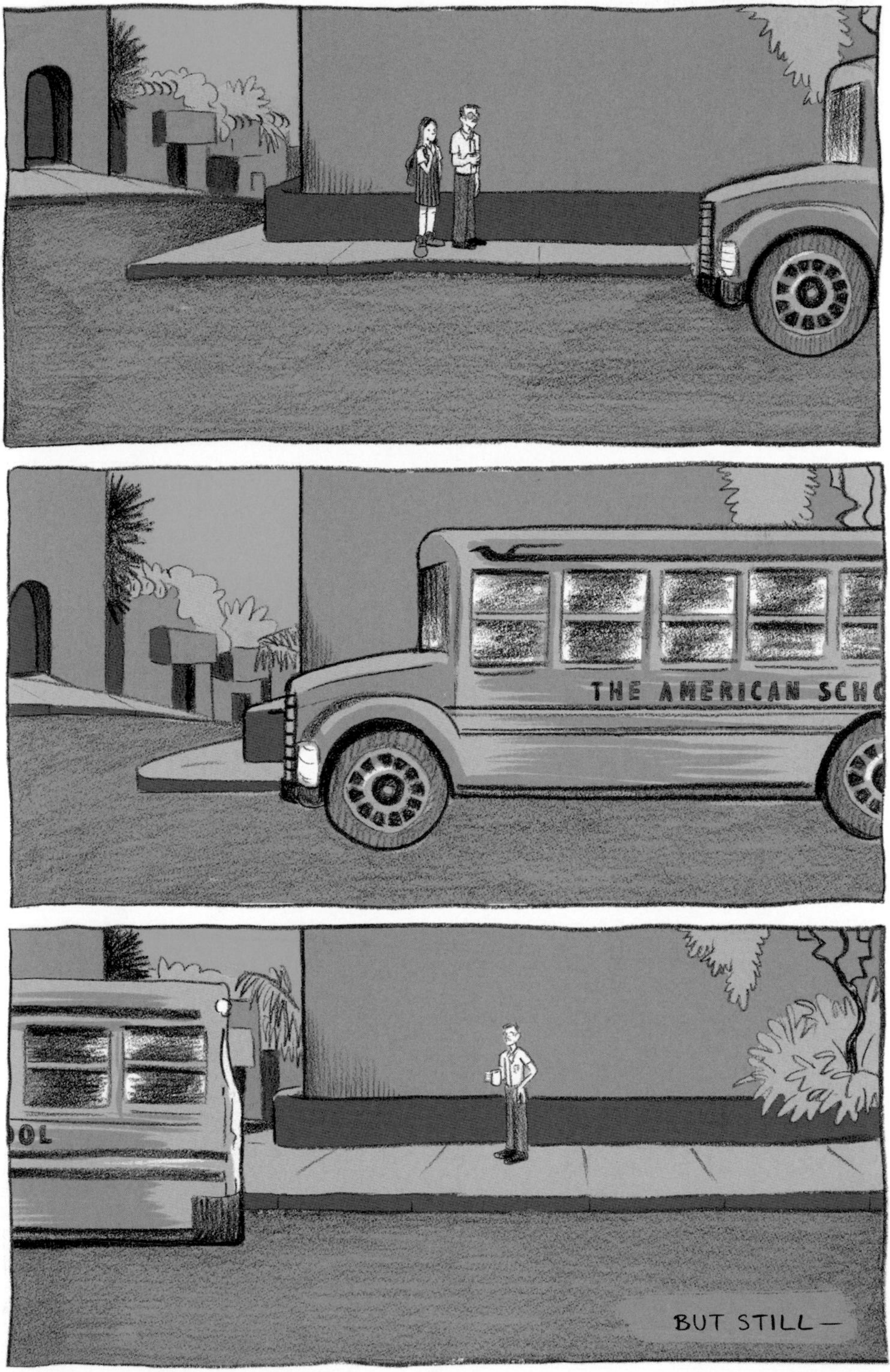
THE AMERICAN SCHO
BUT STILL—

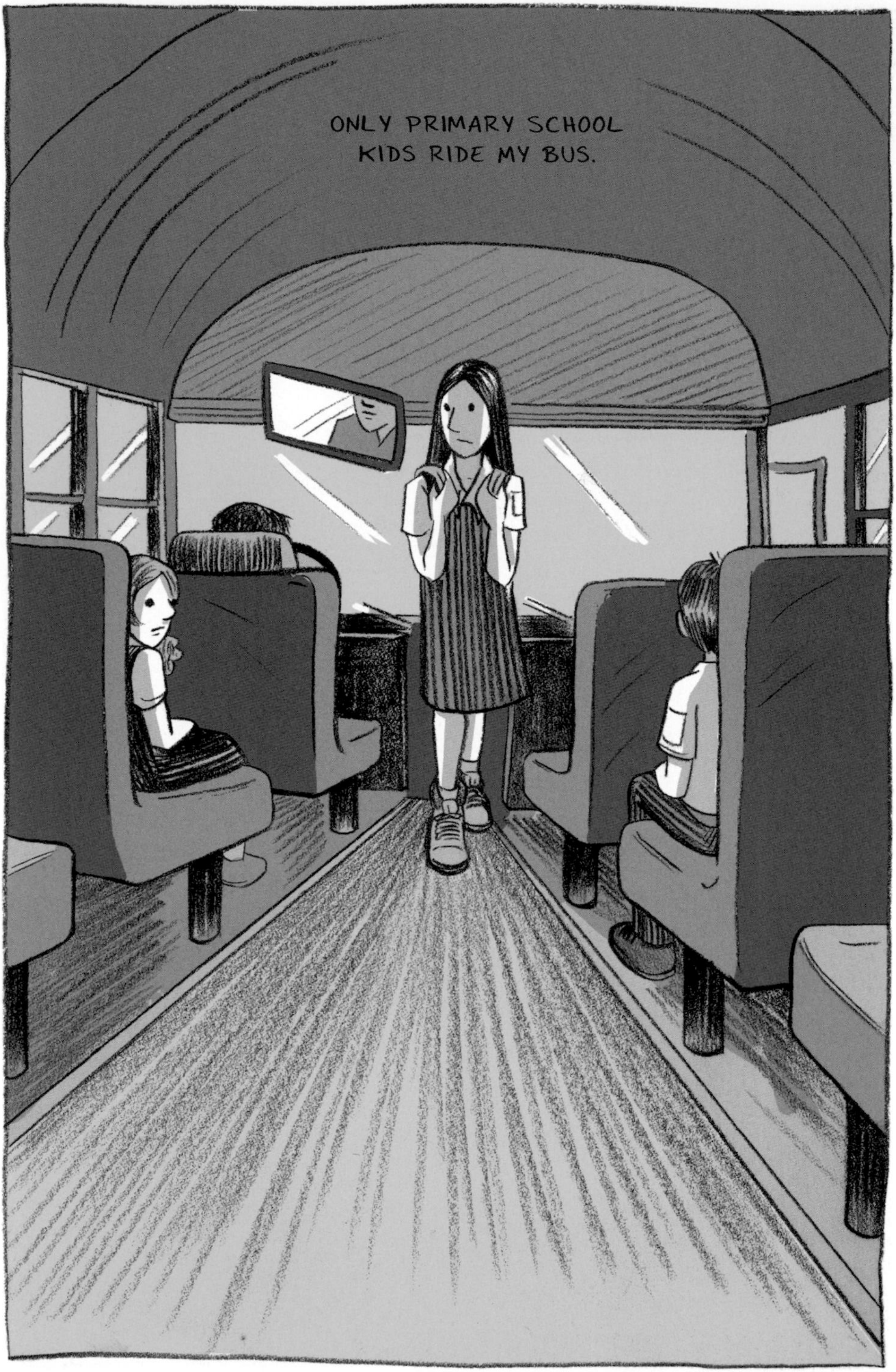
ONLY PRIMARY SCHOOL
KIDS RIDE MY BUS.

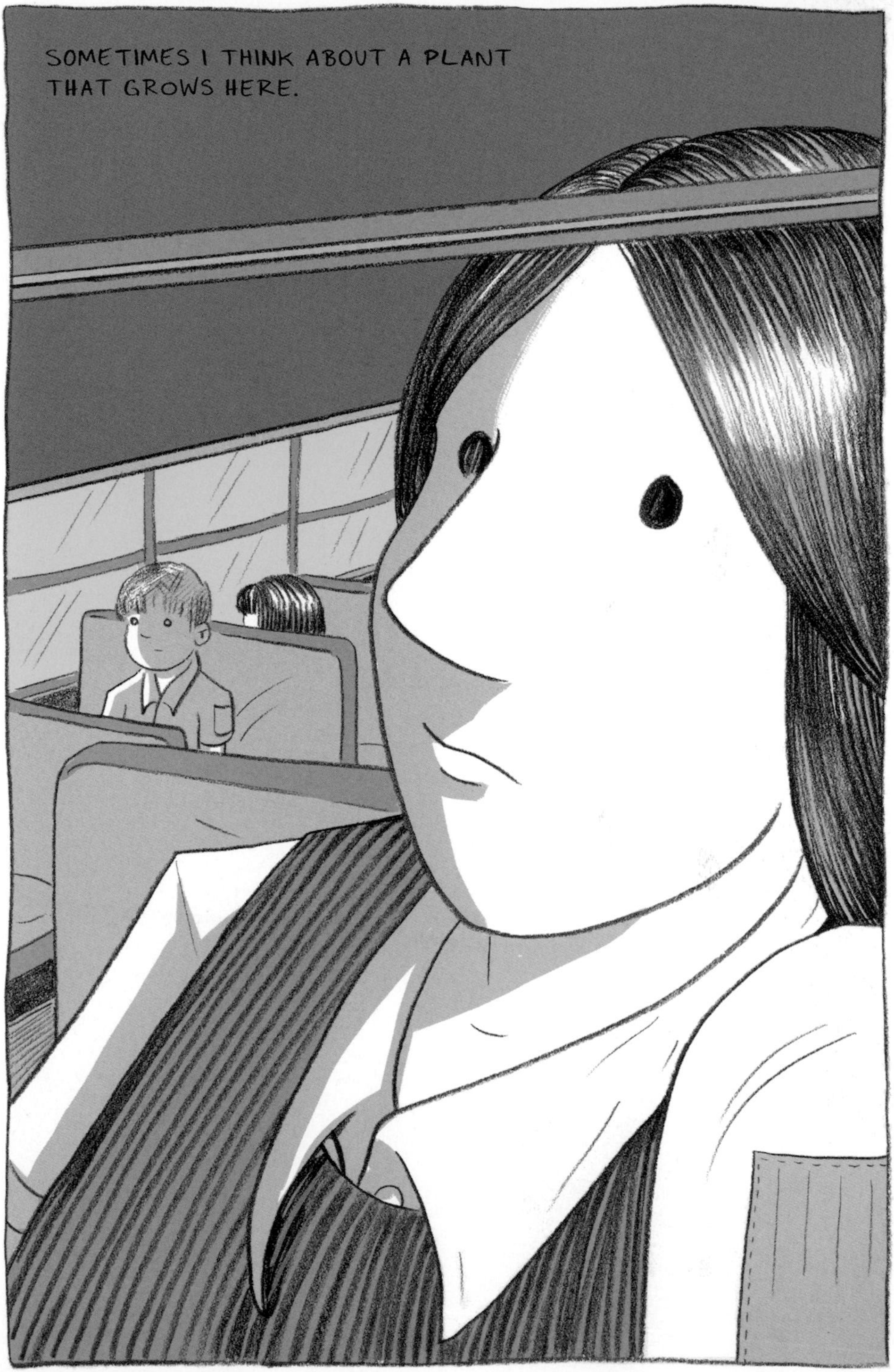
SOMETIMES I THINK ABOUT A PLANT THAT GROWS HERE.

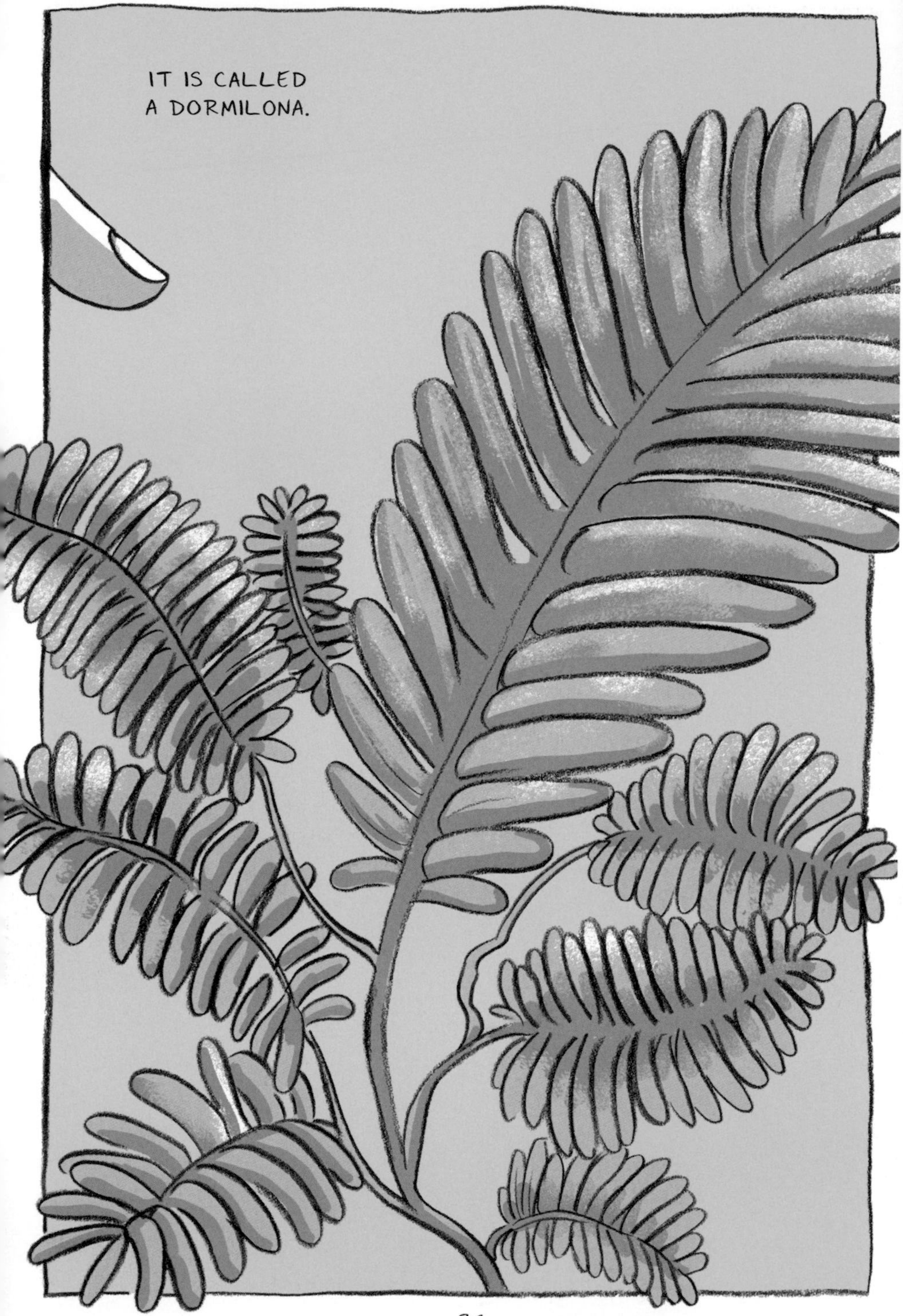
IT IS CALLED
A DORMILONA.

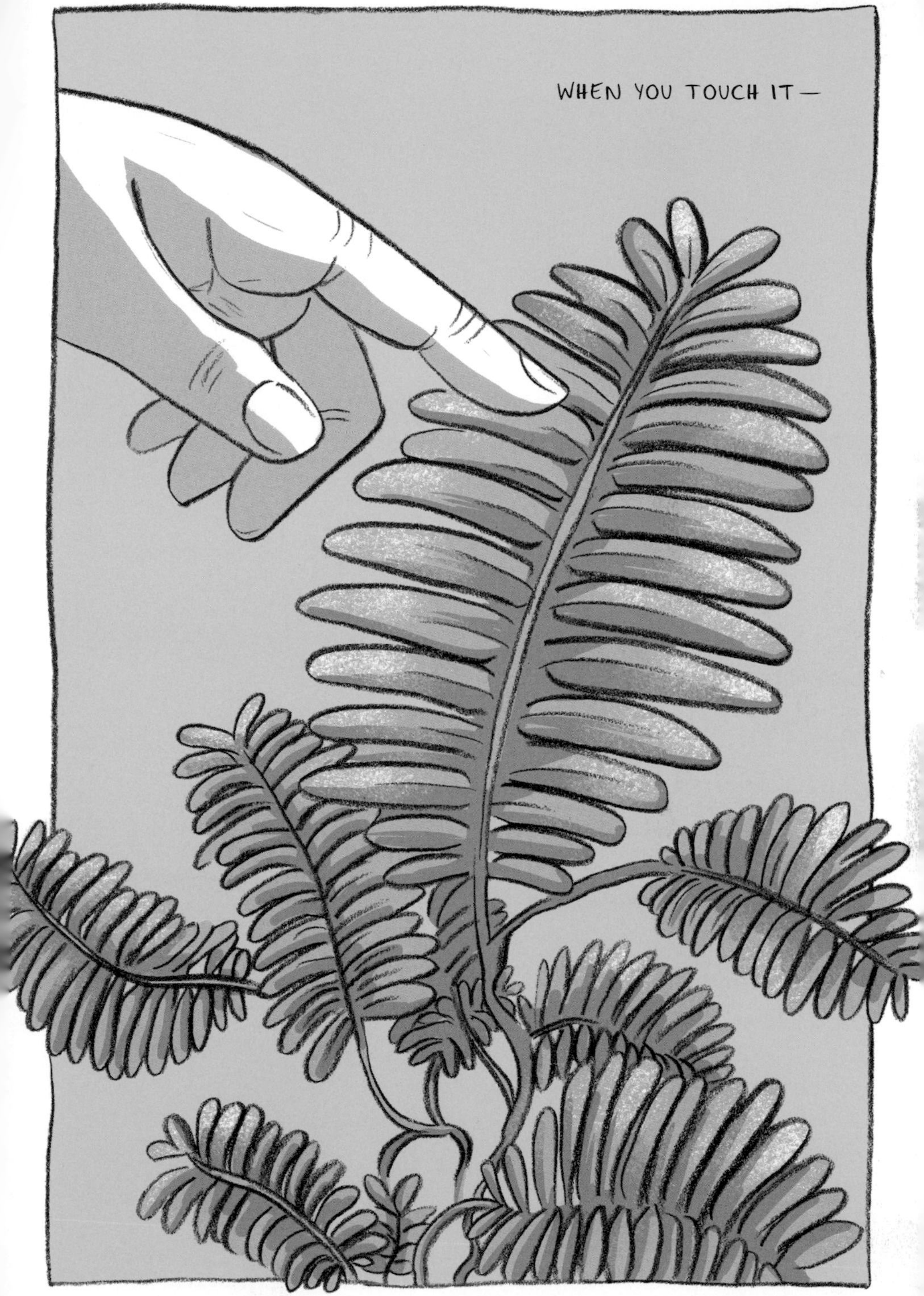
WHEN YOU TOUCH IT—

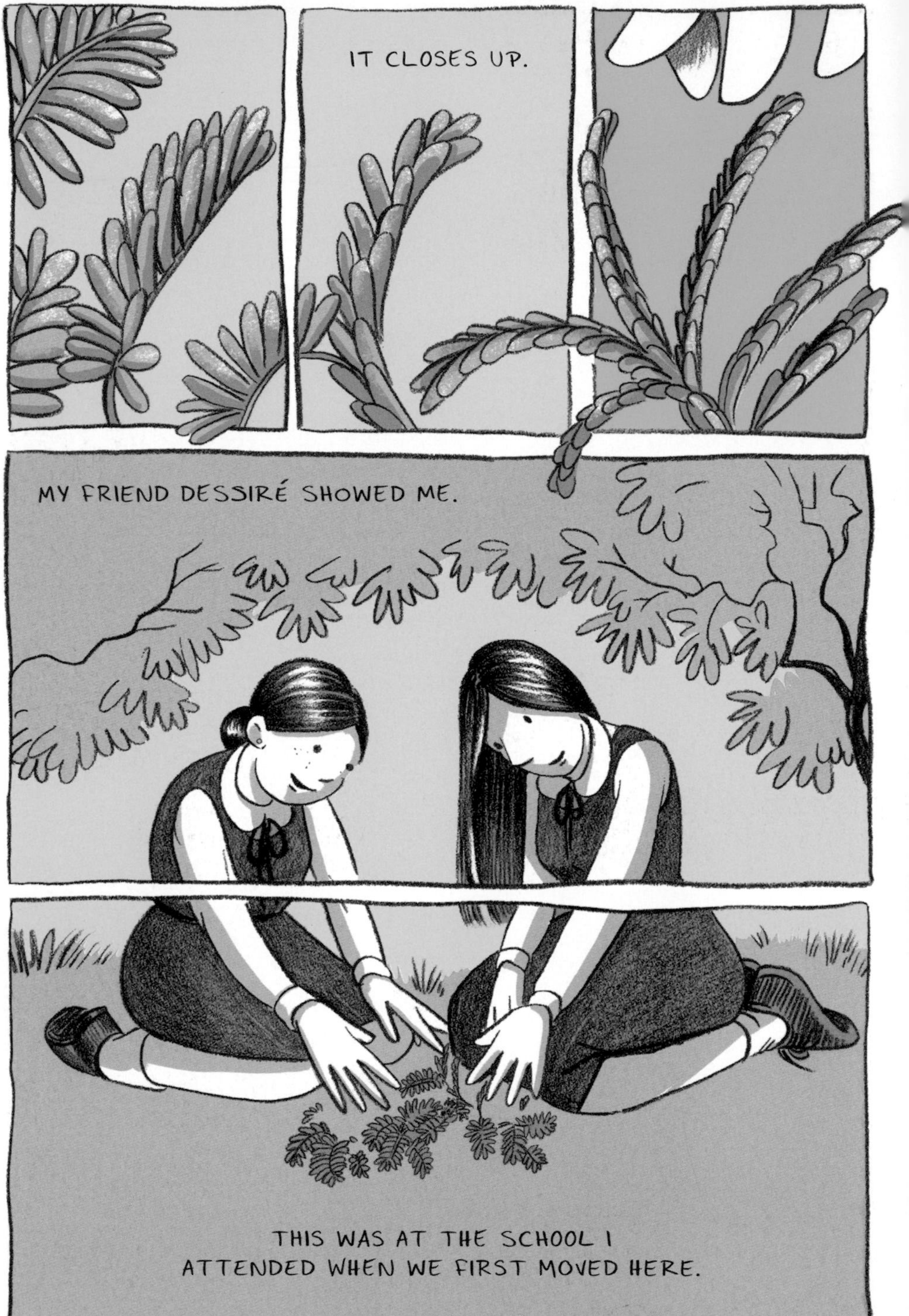
IT CLOSES UP.
MY FRIEND DESSIRÉ SHOWED ME.
THIS WAS AT THE SCHOOL I
ATTENDED WHEN WE FIRST MOVED HERE.

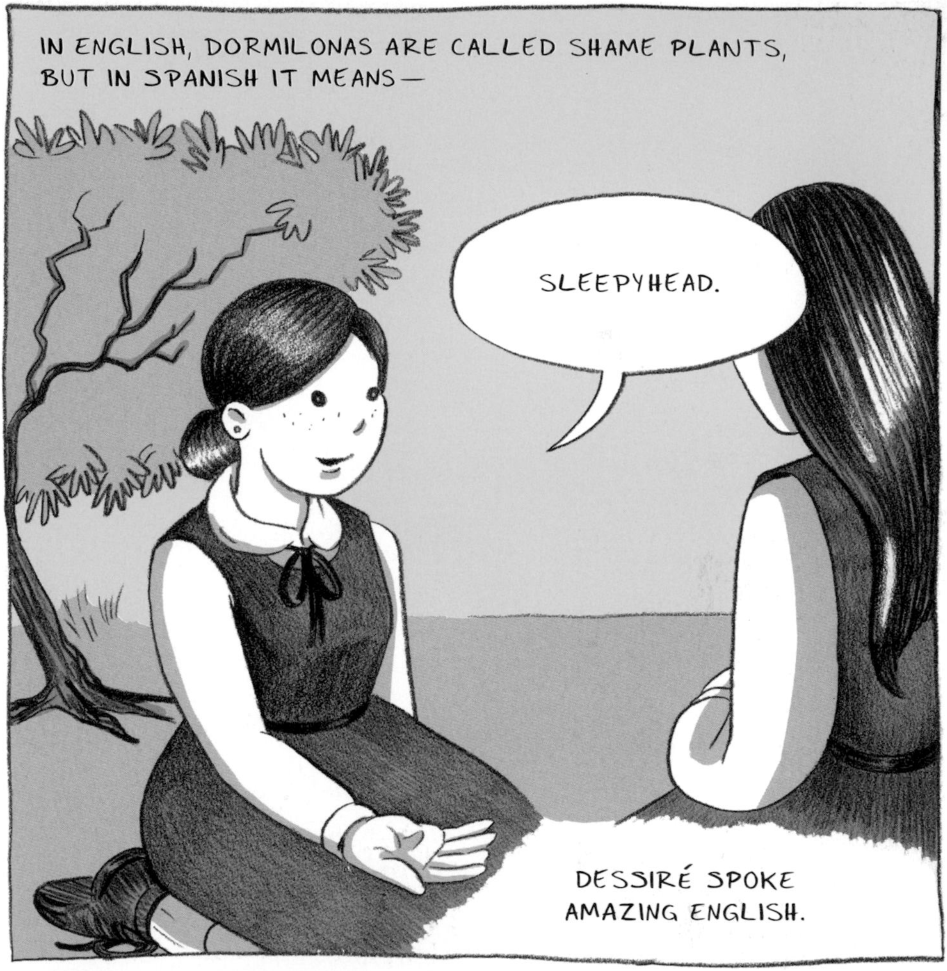
IN ENGLISH, DORMILONAS ARE CALLED SHAME PLANTS, BUT IN SPANISH IT MEANS—
SLEEPYHEAD.
DESSIRÉ SPOKE AMAZING ENGLISH.

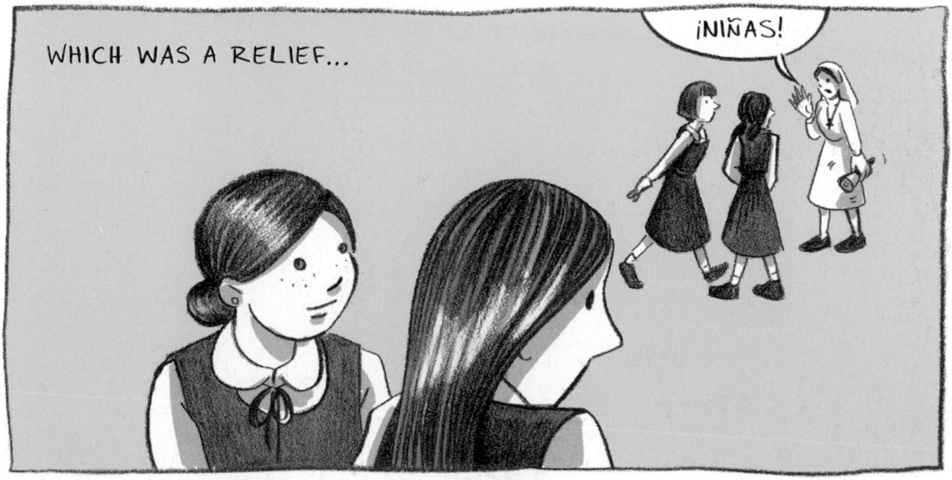
WHICH WAS A RELIEF...
¡NIÑAS!

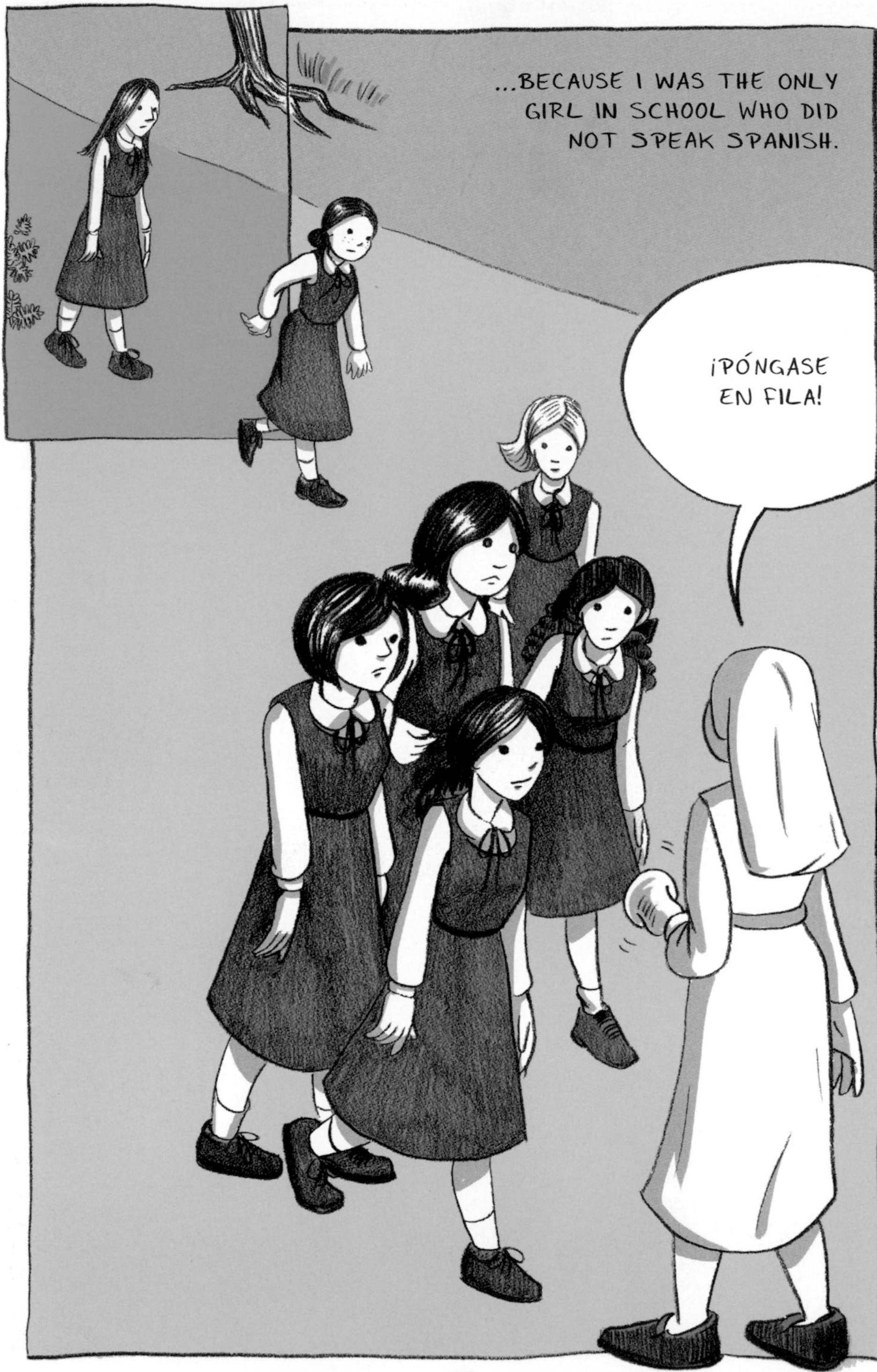
...BECAUSE I WAS THE ONLY GIRL IN SCHOOL WHO DID NOT SPEAK SPANISH.
¡PÓNGASE EN FILA!

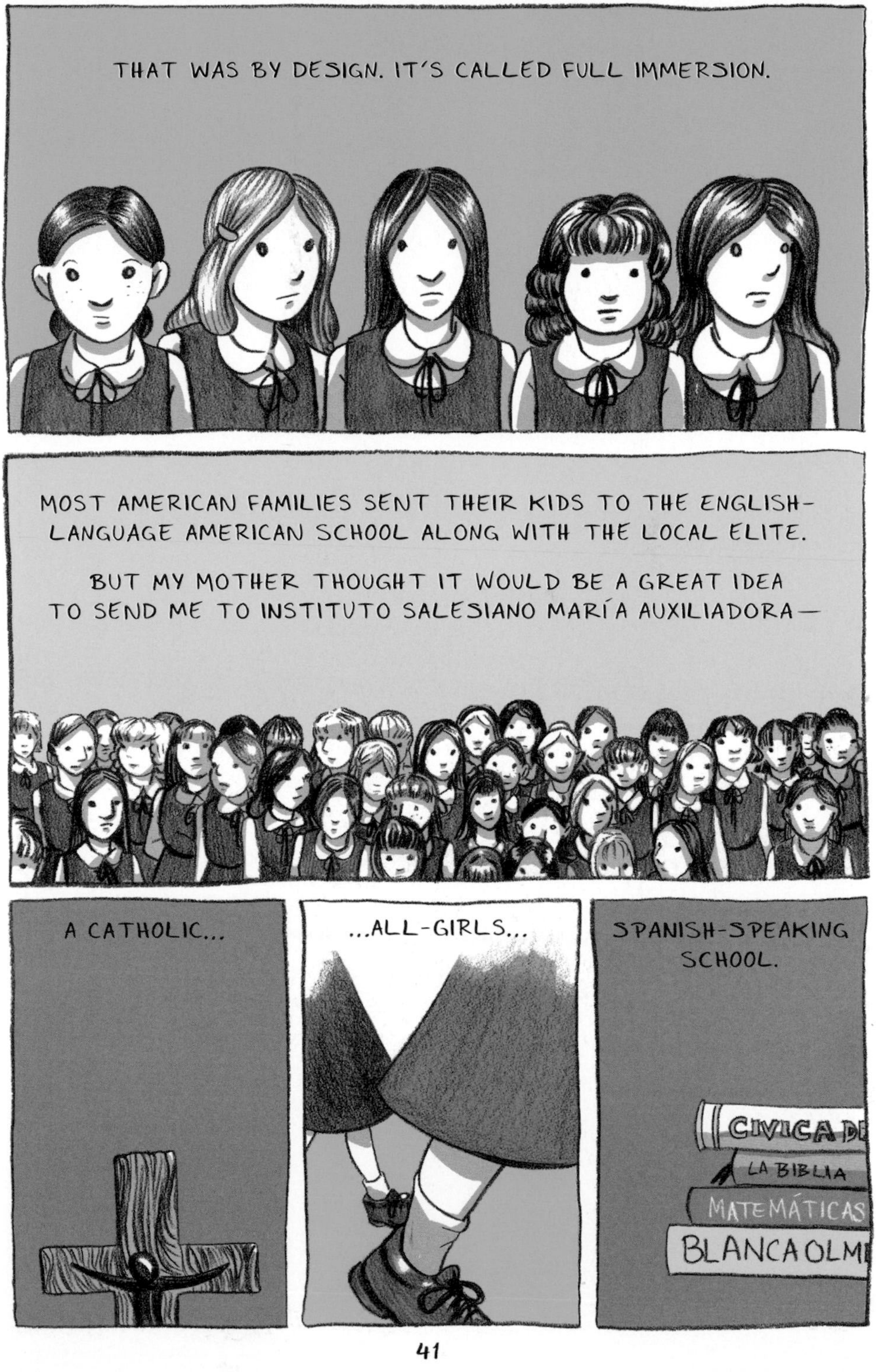
THAT WAS BY DESIGN. IT'S CALLED FULL IMMERSION.
MOST AMERICAN FAMILIES SENT THEIR KIDS TO THE ENGLISH-LANGUAGE AMERICAN SCHOOL ALONG WITH THE LOCAL ELITE.
BUT MY MOTHER THOUGHT IT WOULD BE A GREAT IDEA TO SEND ME TO INSTITUTO SALESIANO MARÍA AUXILIADORA—
A CATHOLIC...
...ALL-GIRLS...
SPANISH-SPEAKING SCHOOL.
CIVICA
LA BIBLIA
MATEMÁTICAS
BLANCA OLM

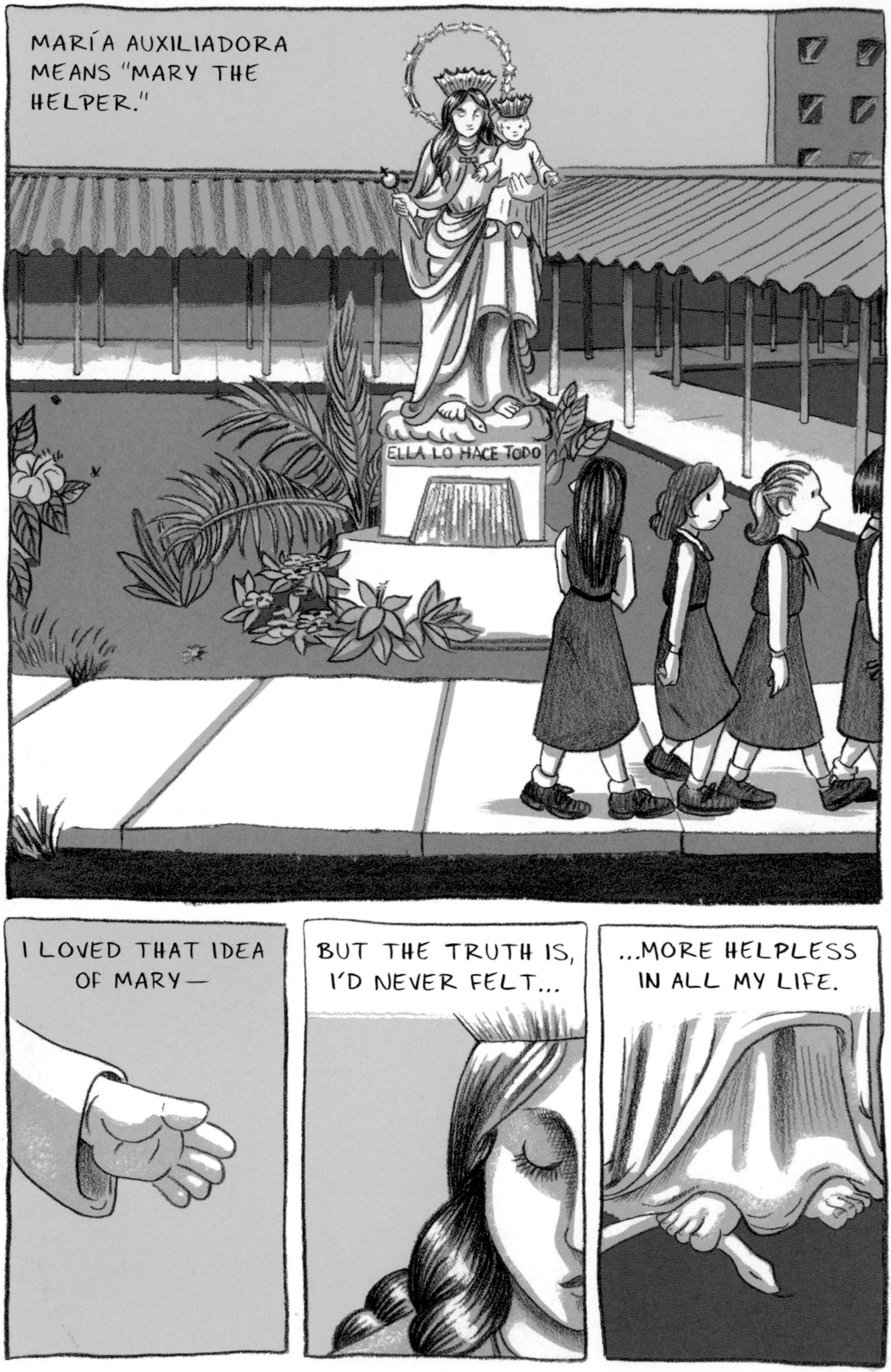
MARÍA AUXILIADORA MEANS "MARY THE HELPER."
ELLA LO HACE TODO
I LOVED THAT IDEA OF MARY—
BUT THE TRUTH IS, I'D NEVER FELT...
...MORE HELPLESS IN ALL MY LIFE.

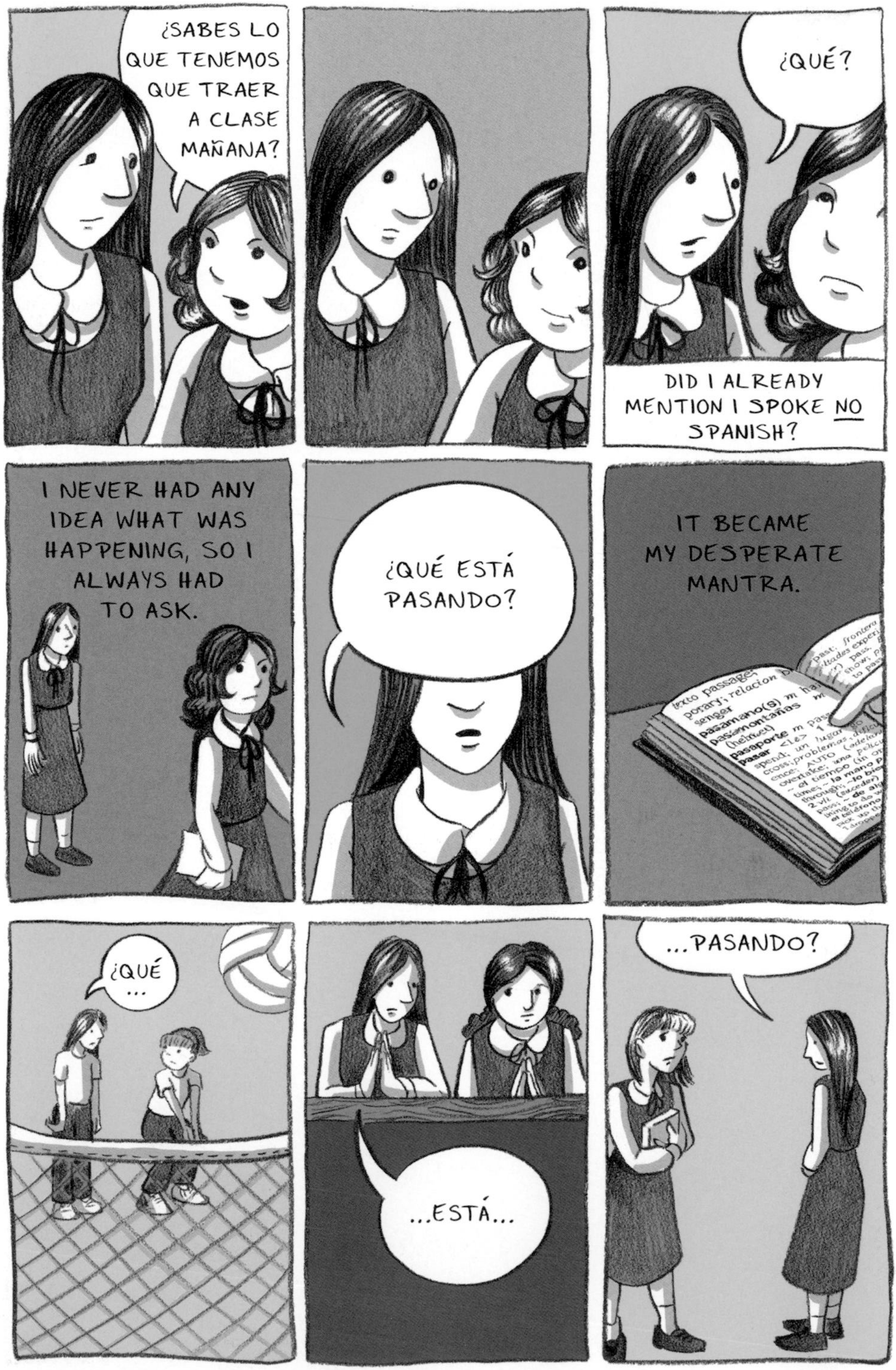
¿SABES LO QUE TENEMOS QUE TRAER A CLASE MAÑANA?
¿QUÉ?
DID I ALREADY MENTION I SPOKE NO SPANISH?
I NEVER HAD ANY IDEA WHAT WAS HAPPENING, SO I ALWAYS HAD TO ASK.
¿QUÉ ESTÁ PASANDO?
IT BECAME MY DESPERATE MANTRA.
¿QUÉ ...
...ESTÁ...
...PASANDO?

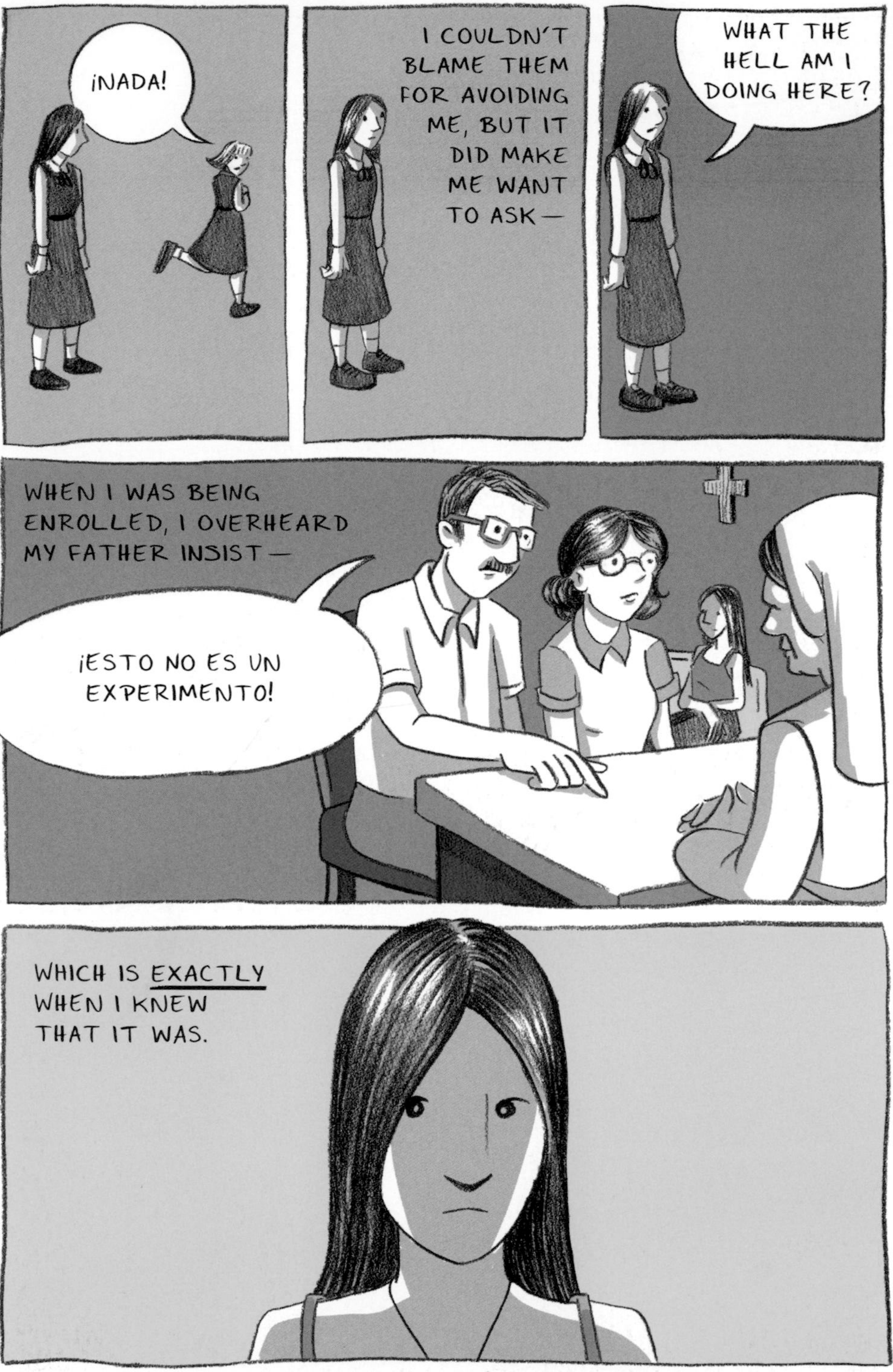
¡NADA!
I COULDN'T BLAME THEM FOR AVOIDING ME, BUT IT DID MAKE ME WANT TO ASK—
WHAT THE HELL AM I DOING HERE?
WHEN I WAS BEING ENROLLED, I OVERHEARD MY FATHER INSIST—
¡ESTO NO ES UN EXPERIMENTO!
WHICH IS EXACTLY WHEN I KNEW THAT IT WAS.

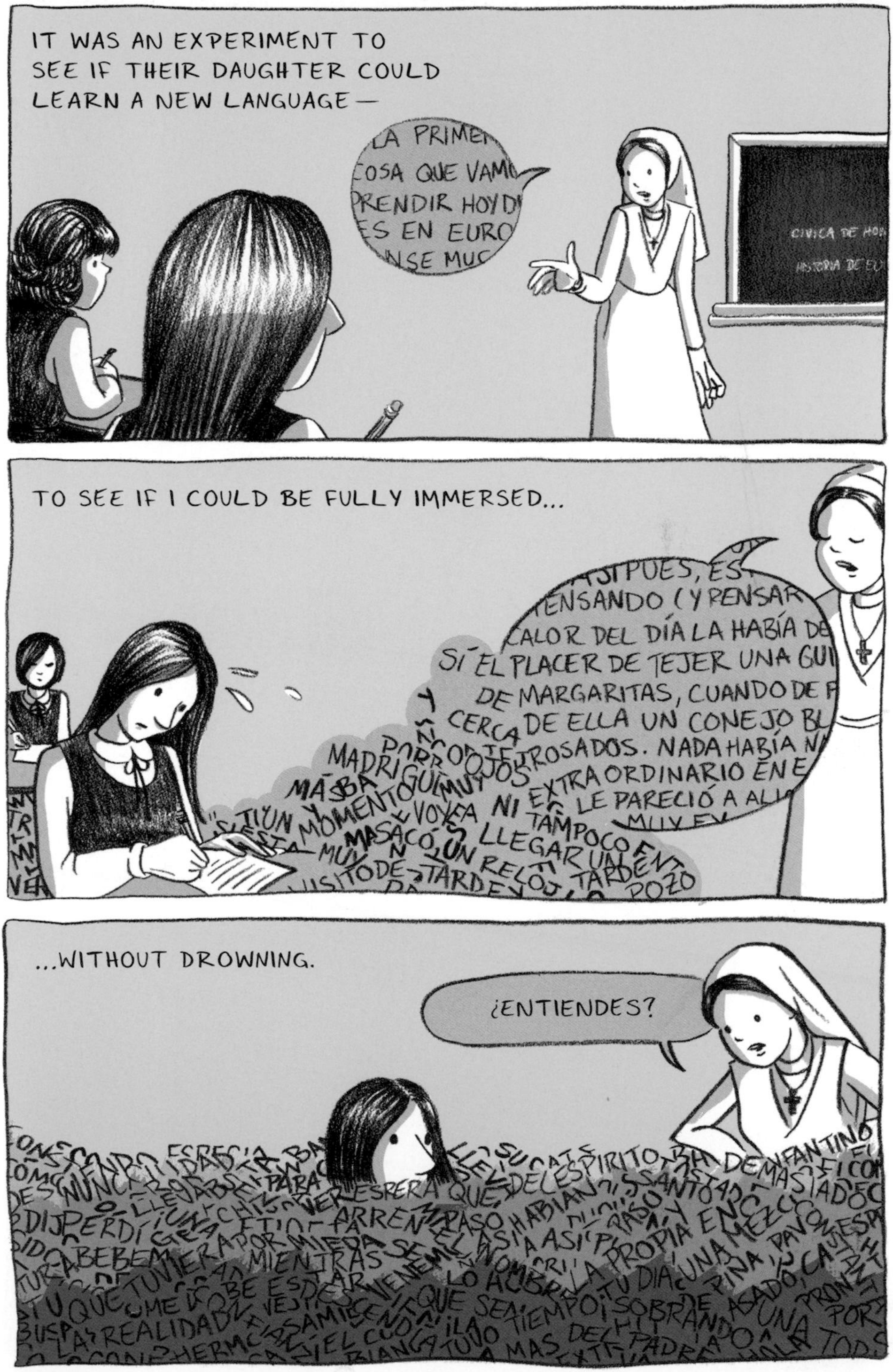
IT WAS AN EXPERIMENT TO SEE IF THEIR DAUGHTER COULD LEARN A NEW LANGUAGE—
LA PRIME
COSA QUE VAMO
PRENDIR HOY D
ES EN EURO
NSE MUC
CIVICA DE HO
HISTORIA DE EU
TO SEE IF I COULD BE FULLY IMMERSED...
PENSANDO (Y PENSAR
CALOR DEL DÍA LA HABÍA DE
SÍ EL PLACER DE TEJER UNA GU
DE MARGARITAS, CUANDO DE
DE ELLA UN CONEJO B
ROSADOS. NADA HABÍA N
EXTRA ORDINARIO EN E
LE PARECIÓ A AL
...WITHOUT DROWNING.
¿ENTIENDES?

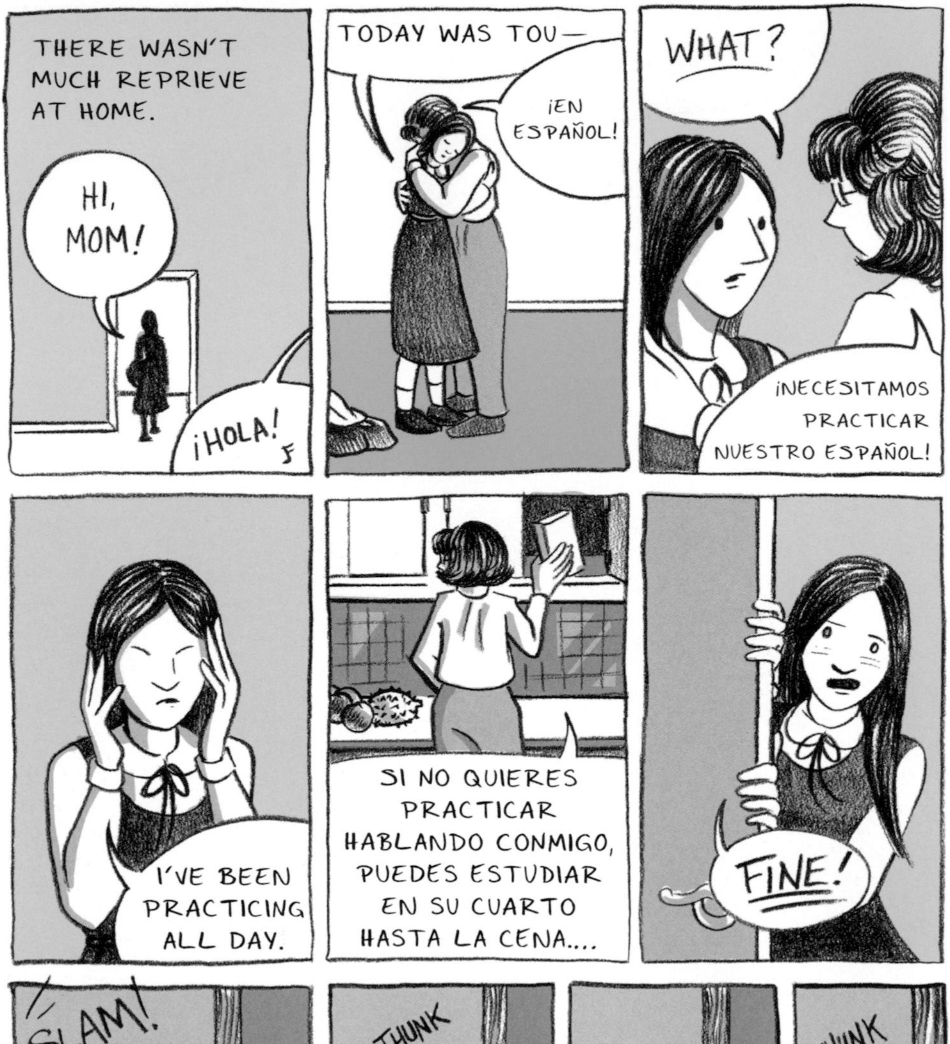

THERE WASN'T MUCH REPRIEVE AT HOME.
HI, MOM!
¡HOLA!
TODAY WAS TOU—
¡EN ESPAÑOL!
WHAT?
¡NECESITAMOS PRACTICAR NUESTRO ESPAÑOL!
I'VE BEEN PRACTICING ALL DAY.
SI NO QUIERES PRACTICAR HABLANDO CONMIGO, PUEDES ESTUDIAR EN SU CUARTO HASTA LA CENA....
FINE!
SLAM!
THUNK
THUNK

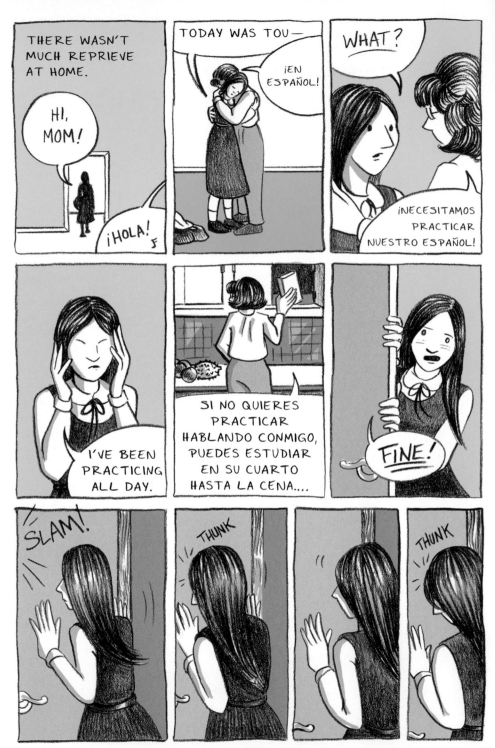

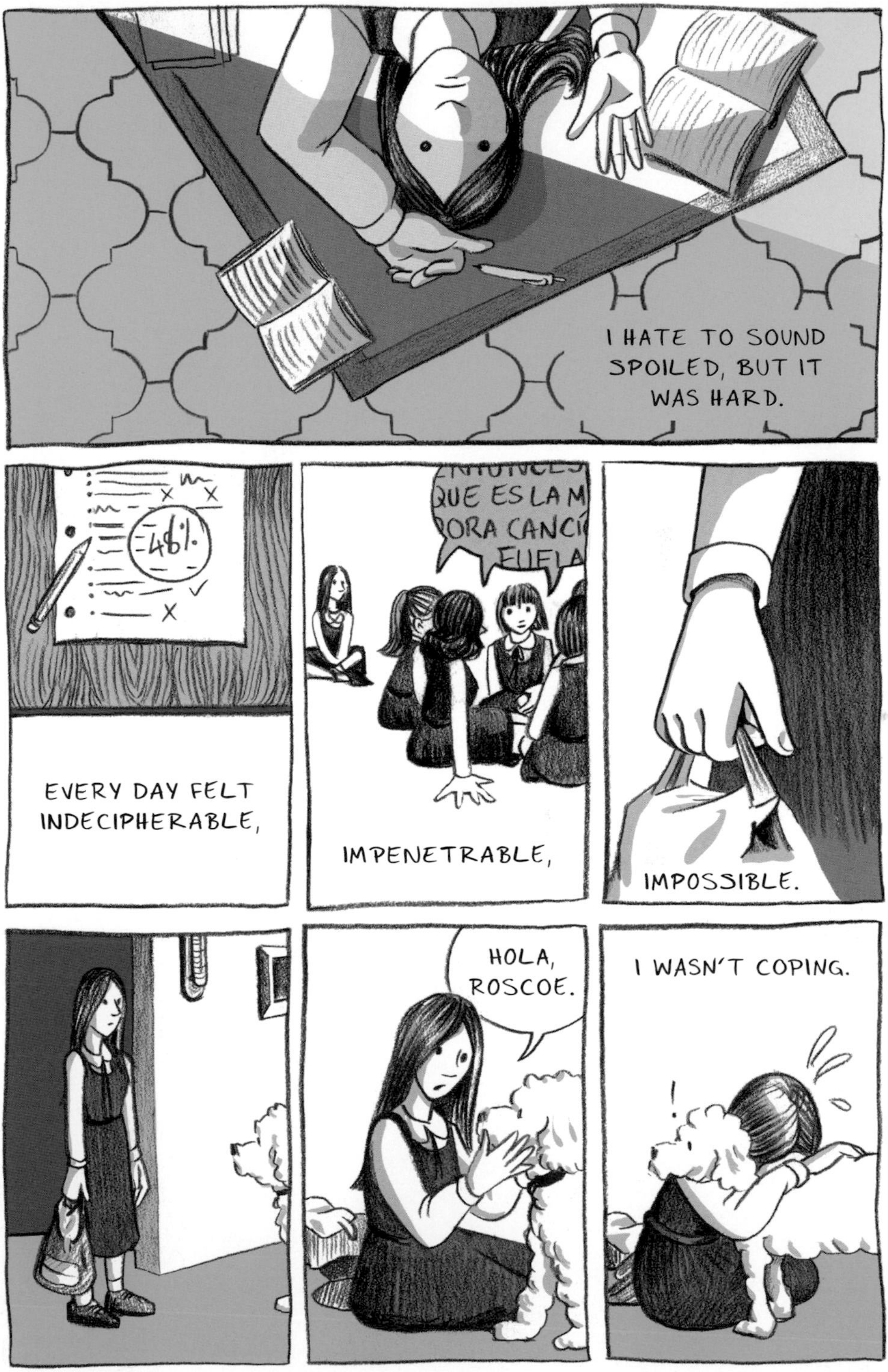
I HATE TO SOUND SPOILED, BUT IT WAS HARD.
48%
EVERY DAY FELT INDECIPHERABLE,
IMPENETRABLE,
IMPOSSIBLE.
HOLA, ROSCOE.
I WASN'T COPING.
!

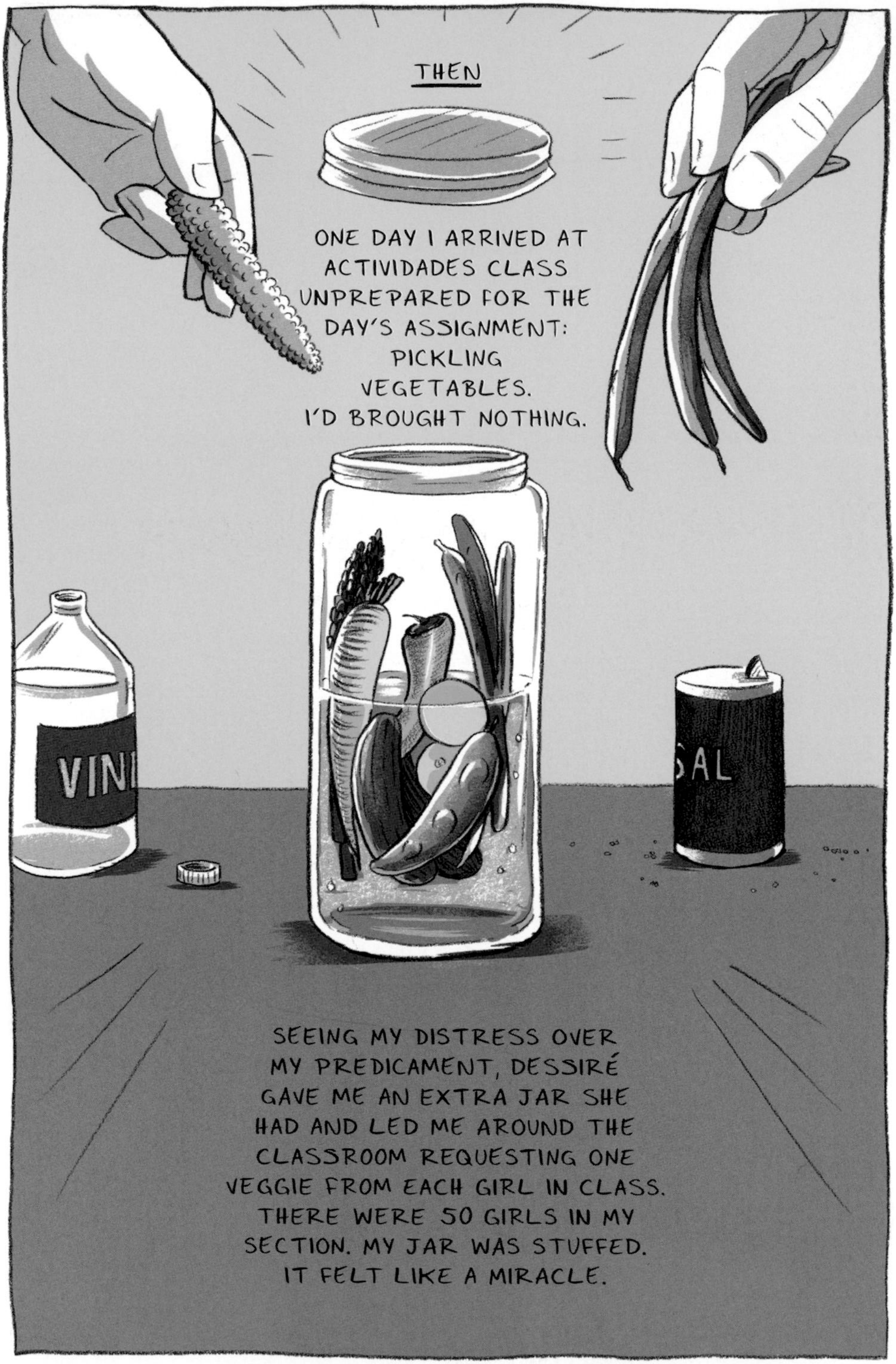
THEN
ONE DAY I ARRIVED AT ACTIVIDADES CLASS UNPREPARED FOR THE DAY'S ASSIGNMENT: PICKLING VEGETABLES. I'D BROUGHT NOTHING.
VIN
SAL
SEEING MY DISTRESS OVER MY PREDICAMENT, DESSIRÉ GAVE ME AN EXTRA JAR SHE HAD AND LED ME AROUND THE CLASSROOM REQUESTING ONE VEGGIE FROM EACH GIRL IN CLASS. THERE WERE 50 GIRLS IN MY SECTION. MY JAR WAS STUFFED. IT FELT LIKE A MIRACLE.

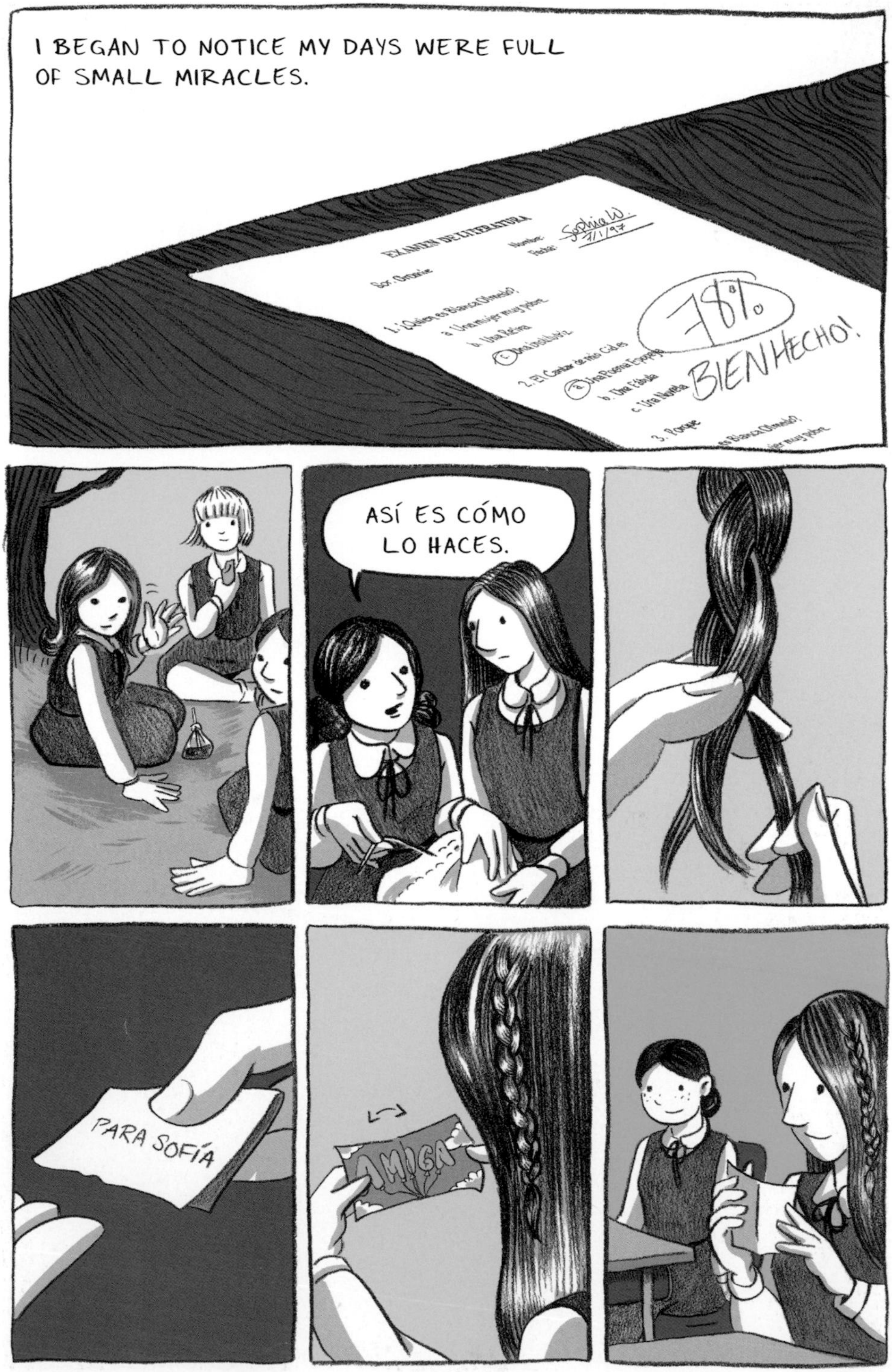
I BEGAN TO NOTICE MY DAYS WERE FULL OF SMALL MIRACLES.
EXAMEN DE LITERATURA
Sophia W.
7/1/97
78%
BIEN HECHO!
ASÍ ES CÓMO LO HACES.
PARA SOFÍA
AMIGA

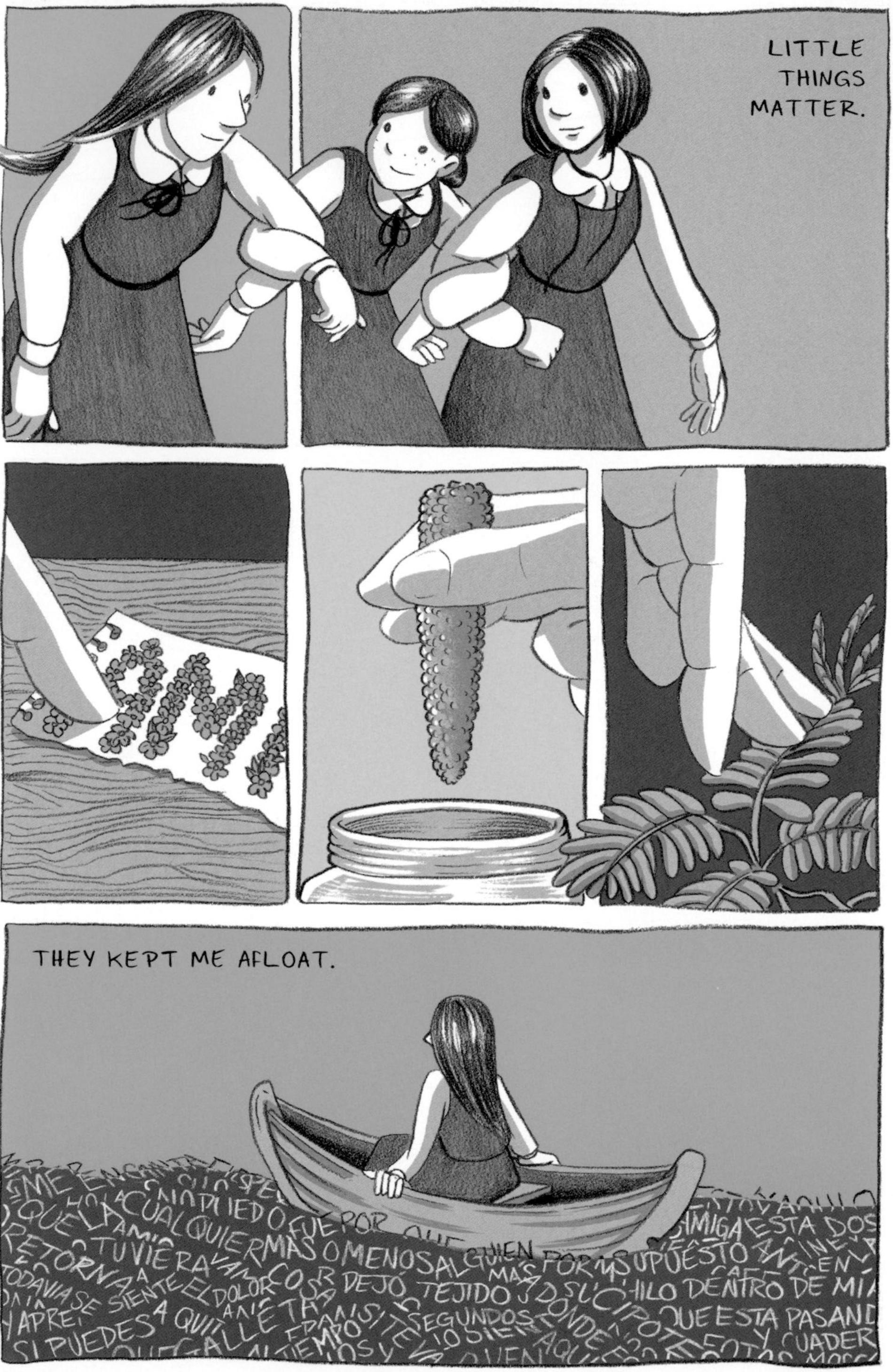
LITTLE THINGS MATTER.
THEY KEPT ME AFLOAT.

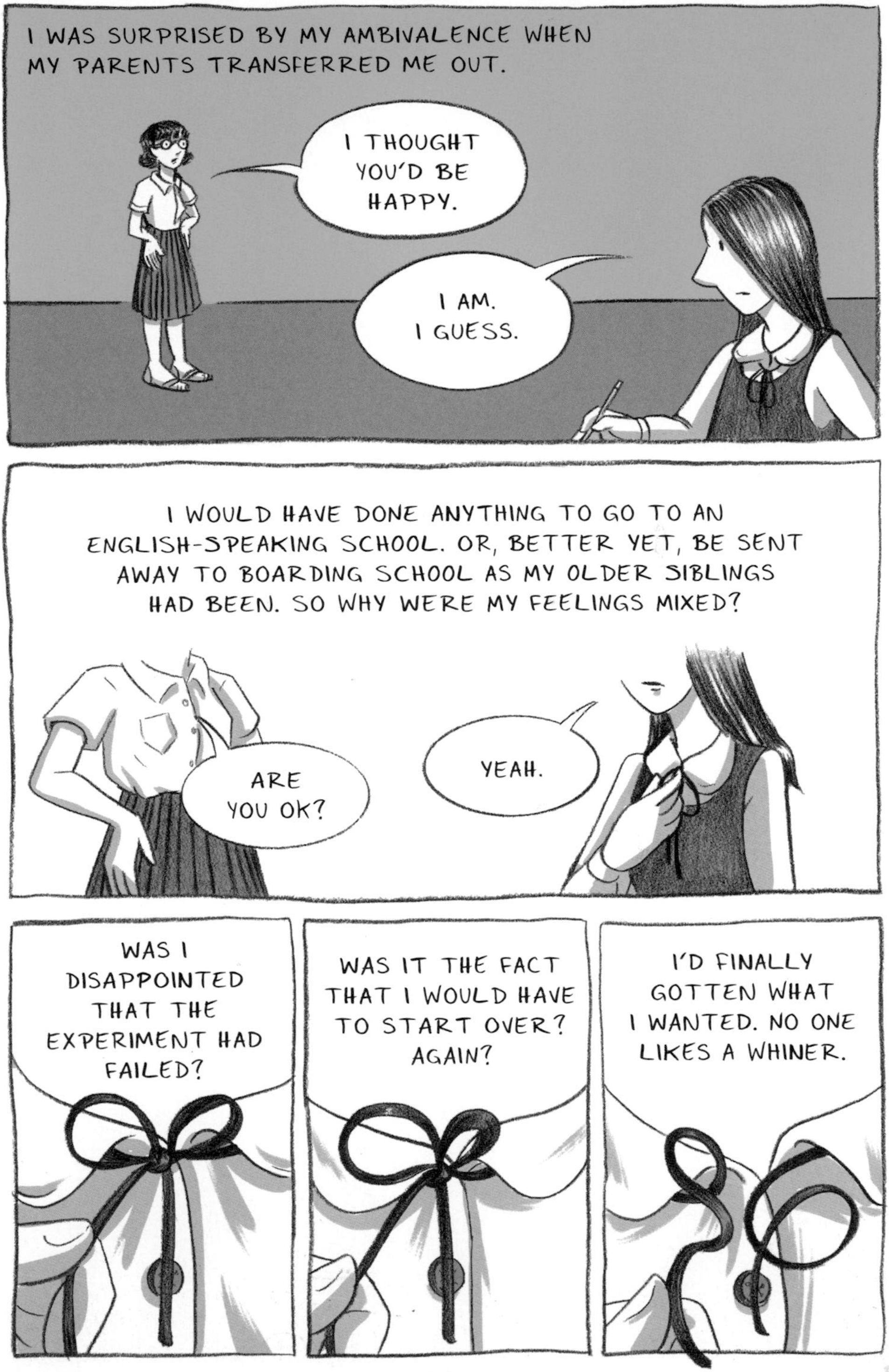
I WAS SURPRISED BY MY AMBIVALENCE WHEN MY PARENTS TRANSFERRED ME OUT.
I THOUGHT YOU'D BE HAPPY.
I AM. I GUESS.
I WOULD HAVE DONE ANYTHING TO GO TO AN ENGLISH-SPEAKING SCHOOL. OR, BETTER YET, BE SENT AWAY TO BOARDING SCHOOL AS MY OLDER SIBLINGS HAD BEEN. SO WHY WERE MY FEELINGS MIXED?
ARE YOU OK?
YEAH.
WAS I DISAPPOINTED THAT THE EXPERIMENT HAD FAILED?
WAS IT THE FACT THAT I WOULD HAVE TO START OVER? AGAIN?
I'D FINALLY GOTTEN WHAT I WANTED. NO ONE LIKES A WHINER.

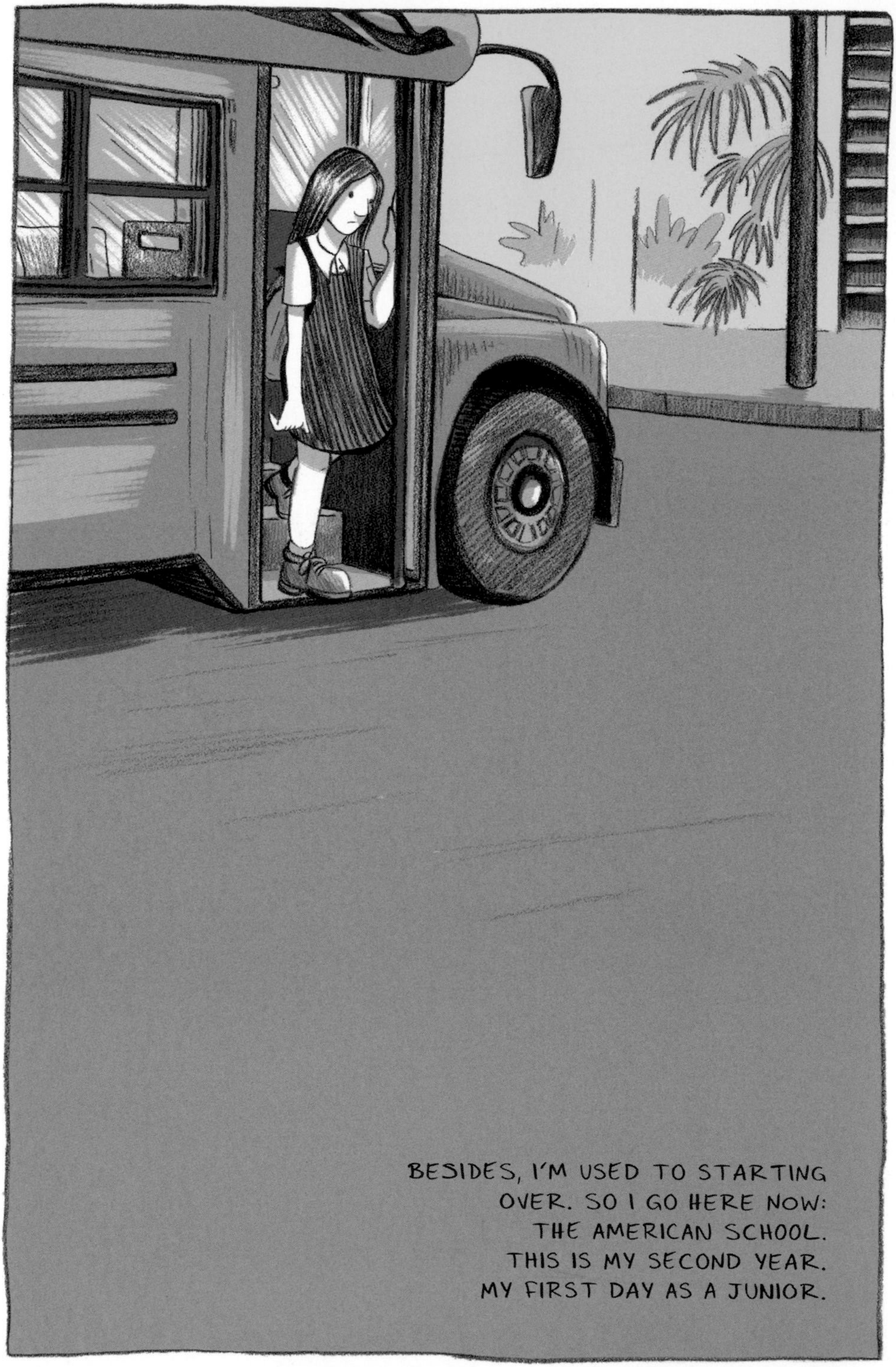
BESIDES, I'M USED TO STARTING OVER. SO I GO HERE NOW: THE AMERICAN SCHOOL. THIS IS MY SECOND YEAR. MY FIRST DAY AS A JUNIOR.

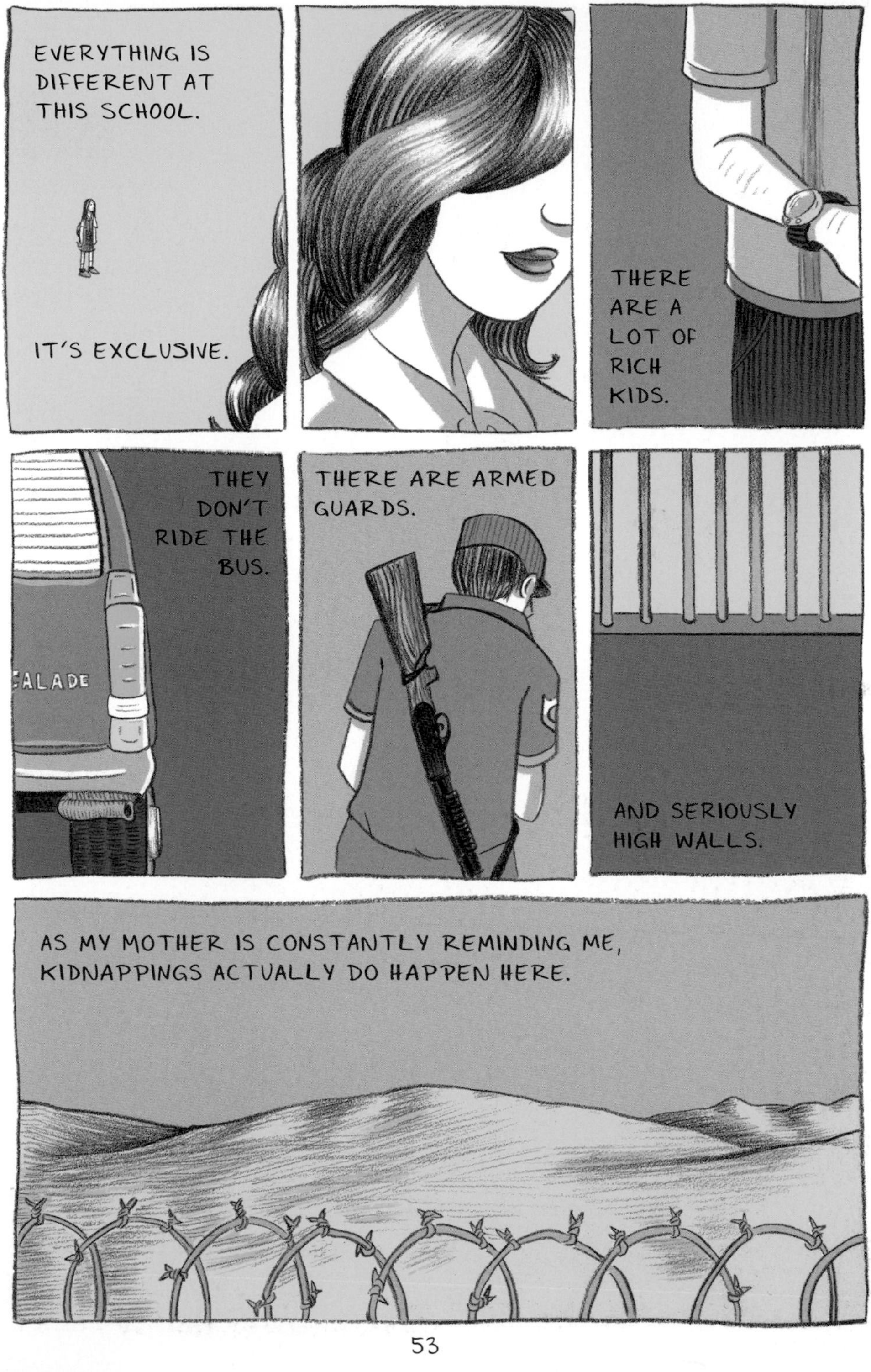
EVERYTHING IS DIFFERENT AT THIS SCHOOL.
IT'S EXCLUSIVE.
THERE ARE A LOT OF RICH KIDS.
THEY DON'T RIDE THE BUS.
CALADE
THERE ARE ARMED GUARDS.
AND SERIOUSLY HIGH WALLS.
AS MY MOTHER IS CONSTANTLY REMINDING ME, KIDNAPPINGS ACTUALLY DO HAPPEN HERE.

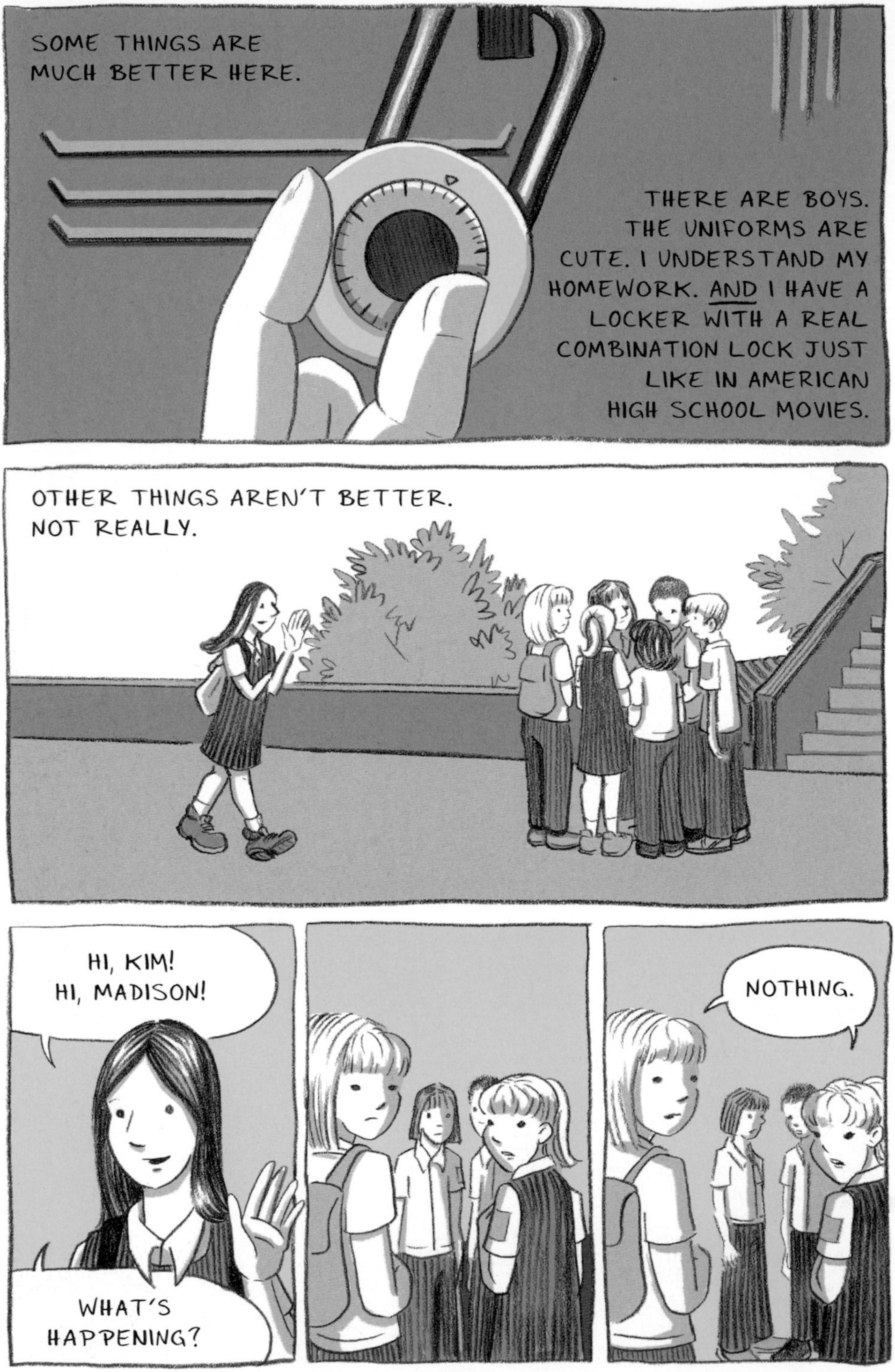
SOME THINGS ARE MUCH BETTER HERE.
THERE ARE BOYS. THE UNIFORMS ARE CUTE. I UNDERSTAND MY HOMEWORK. AND I HAVE A LOCKER WITH A REAL COMBINATION LOCK JUST LIKE IN AMERICAN HIGH SCHOOL MOVIES.
OTHER THINGS AREN'T BETTER. NOT REALLY.
HI, KIM! HI, MADISON!
WHAT'S HAPPENING?
NOTHING.

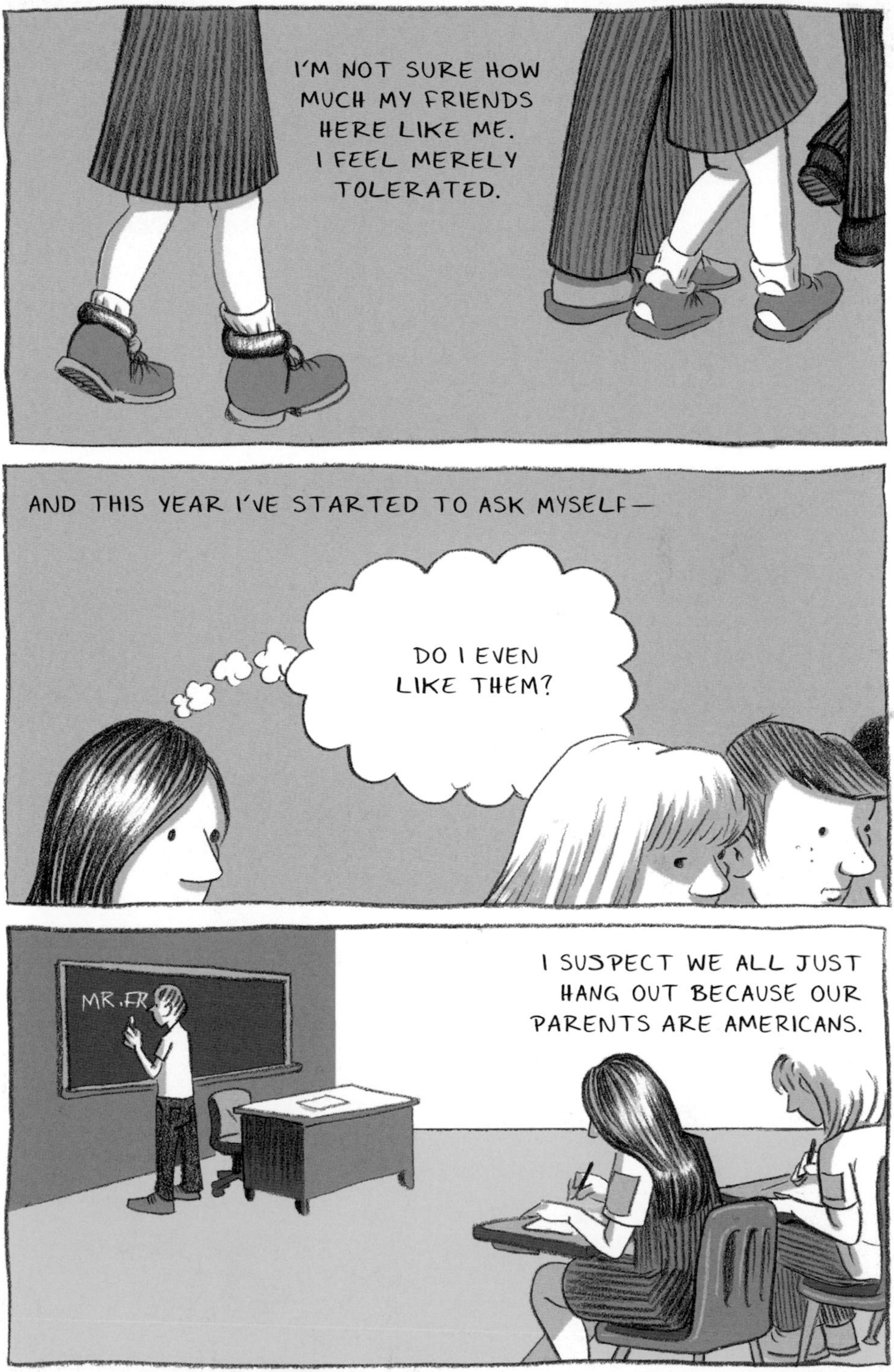
I'M NOT SURE HOW MUCH MY FRIENDS HERE LIKE ME. I FEEL MERELY TOLERATED.
AND THIS YEAR I'VE STARTED TO ASK MYSELF—
DO I EVEN LIKE THEM?
MR. FR
I SUSPECT WE ALL JUST HANG OUT BECAUSE OUR PARENTS ARE AMERICANS.

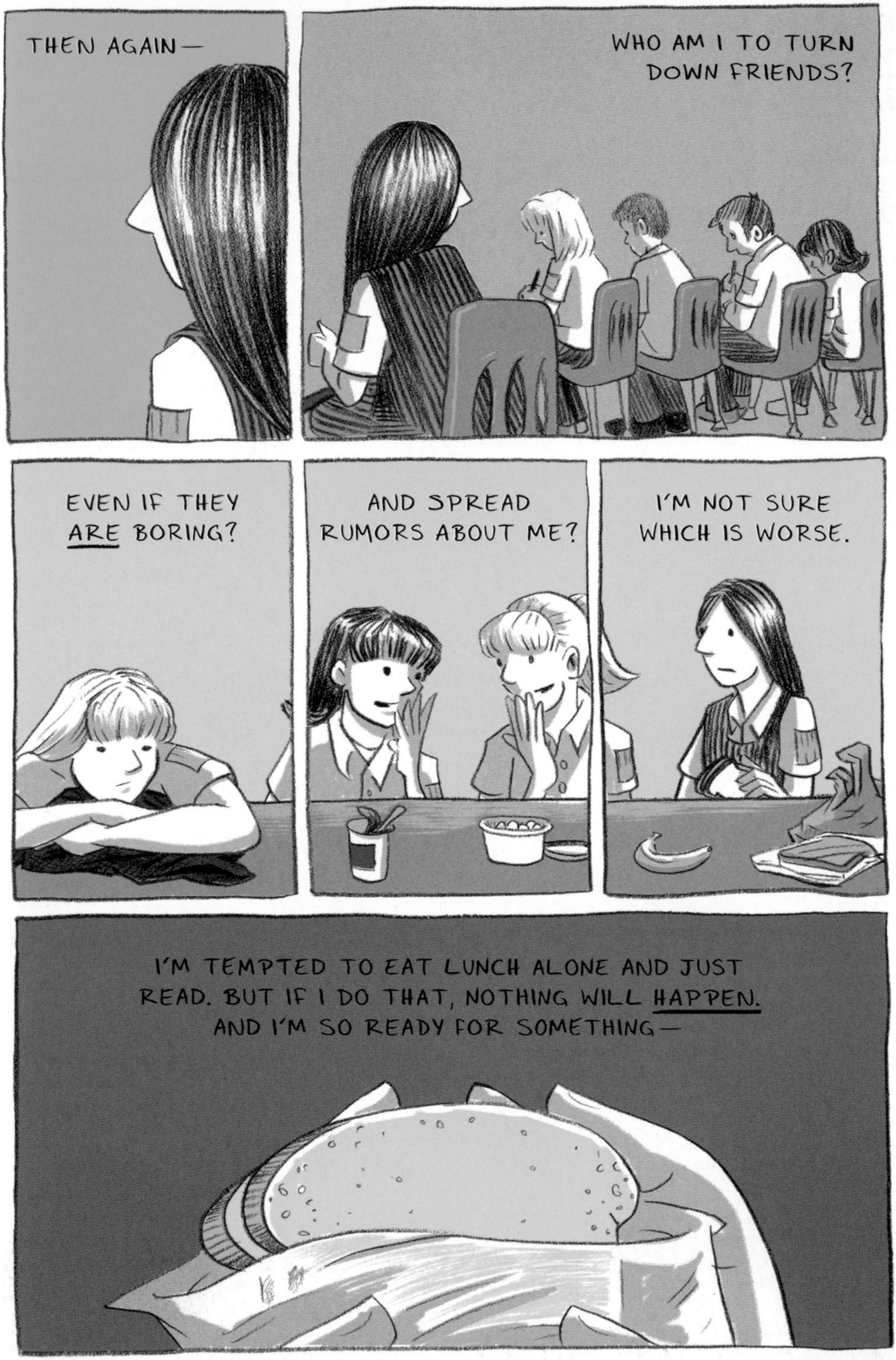
THEN AGAIN—
WHO AM I TO TURN DOWN FRIENDS?
EVEN IF THEY ARE BORING?
AND SPREAD RUMORS ABOUT ME?
I'M NOT SURE WHICH IS WORSE.
I'M TEMPTED TO EAT LUNCH ALONE AND JUST READ. BUT IF I DO THAT, NOTHING WILL HAPPEN. AND I'M SO READY FOR SOMETHING—

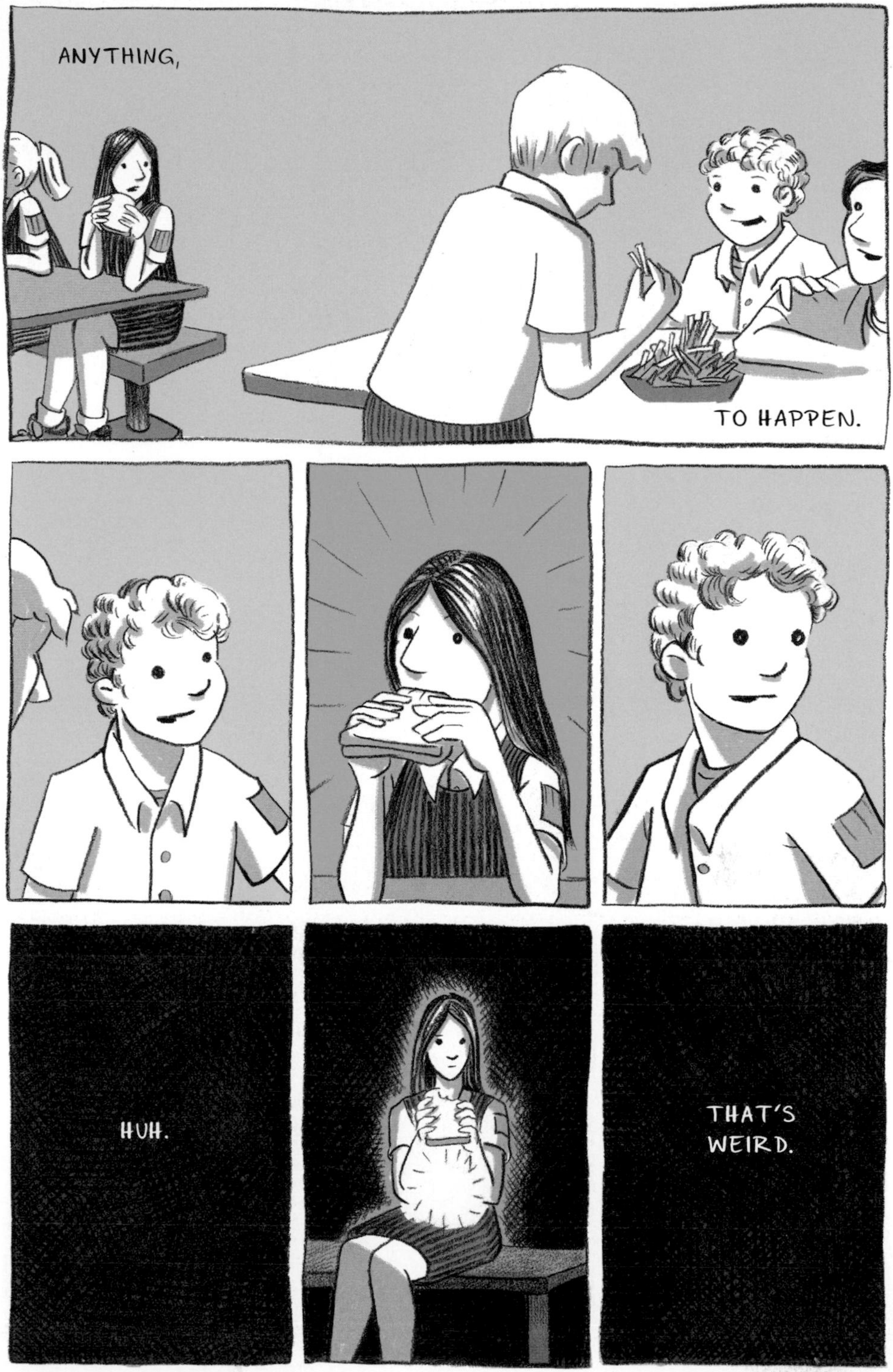
ANYTHING,
TO HAPPEN.
HUH.
THAT'S WEIRD.

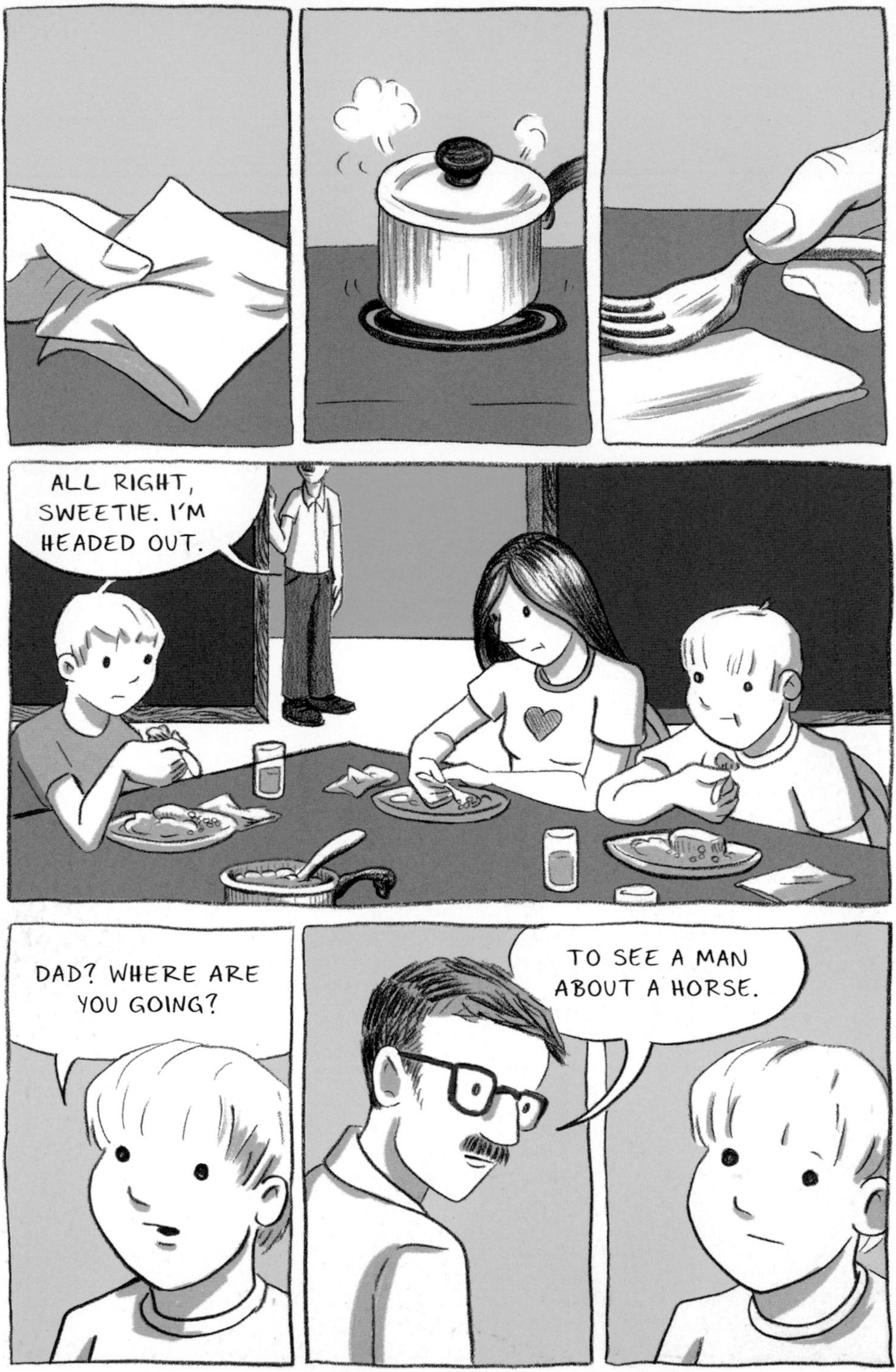
ALL RIGHT, SWEETIE. I'M HEADED OUT.
DAD? WHERE ARE YOU GOING?
TO SEE A MAN ABOUT A HORSE.

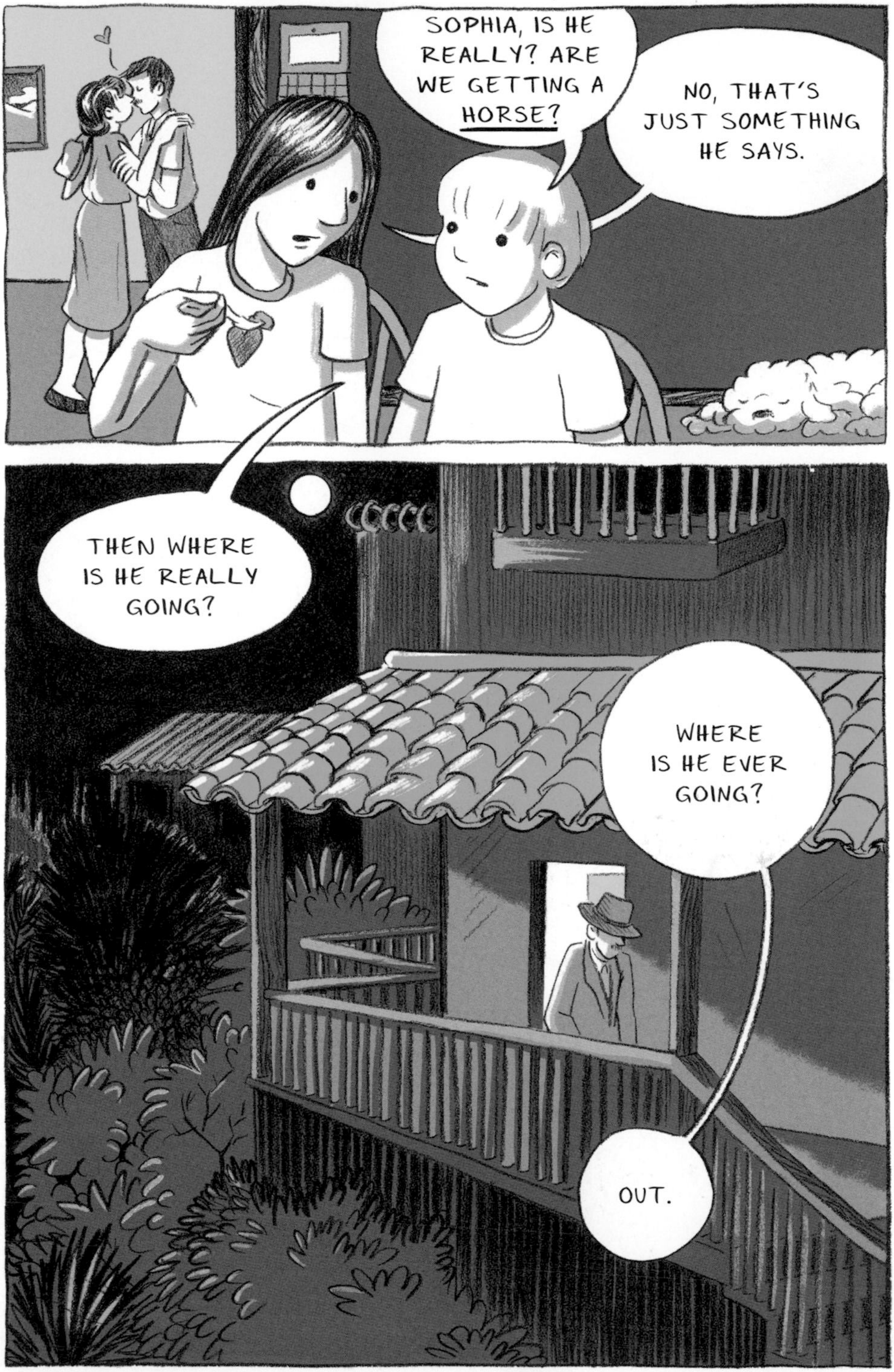
SOPHIA, IS HE REALLY? ARE WE GETTING A HORSE?
NO, THAT'S JUST SOMETHING HE SAYS.
THEN WHERE IS HE REALLY GOING?
WHERE IS HE EVER GOING?
OUT.

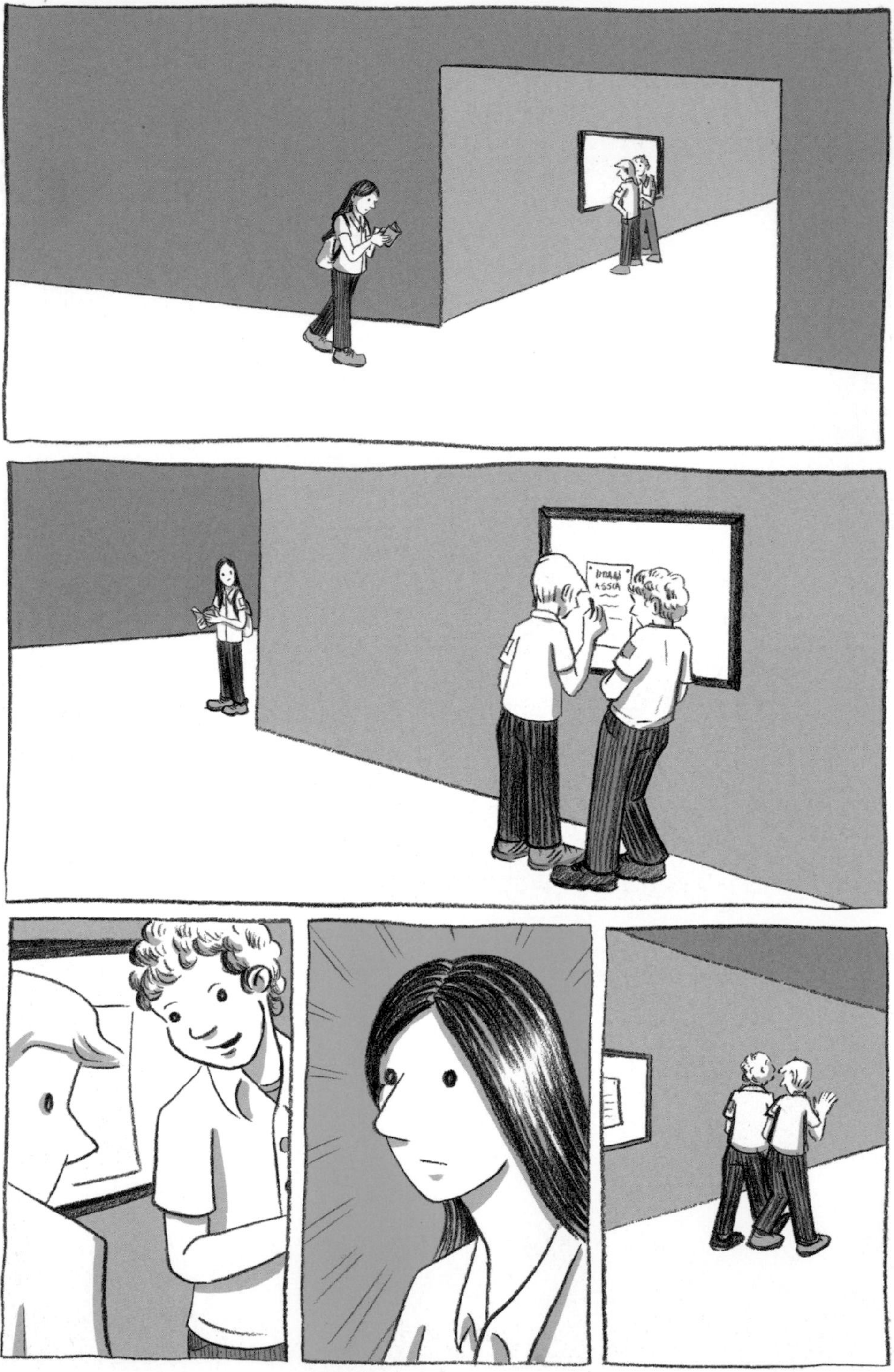

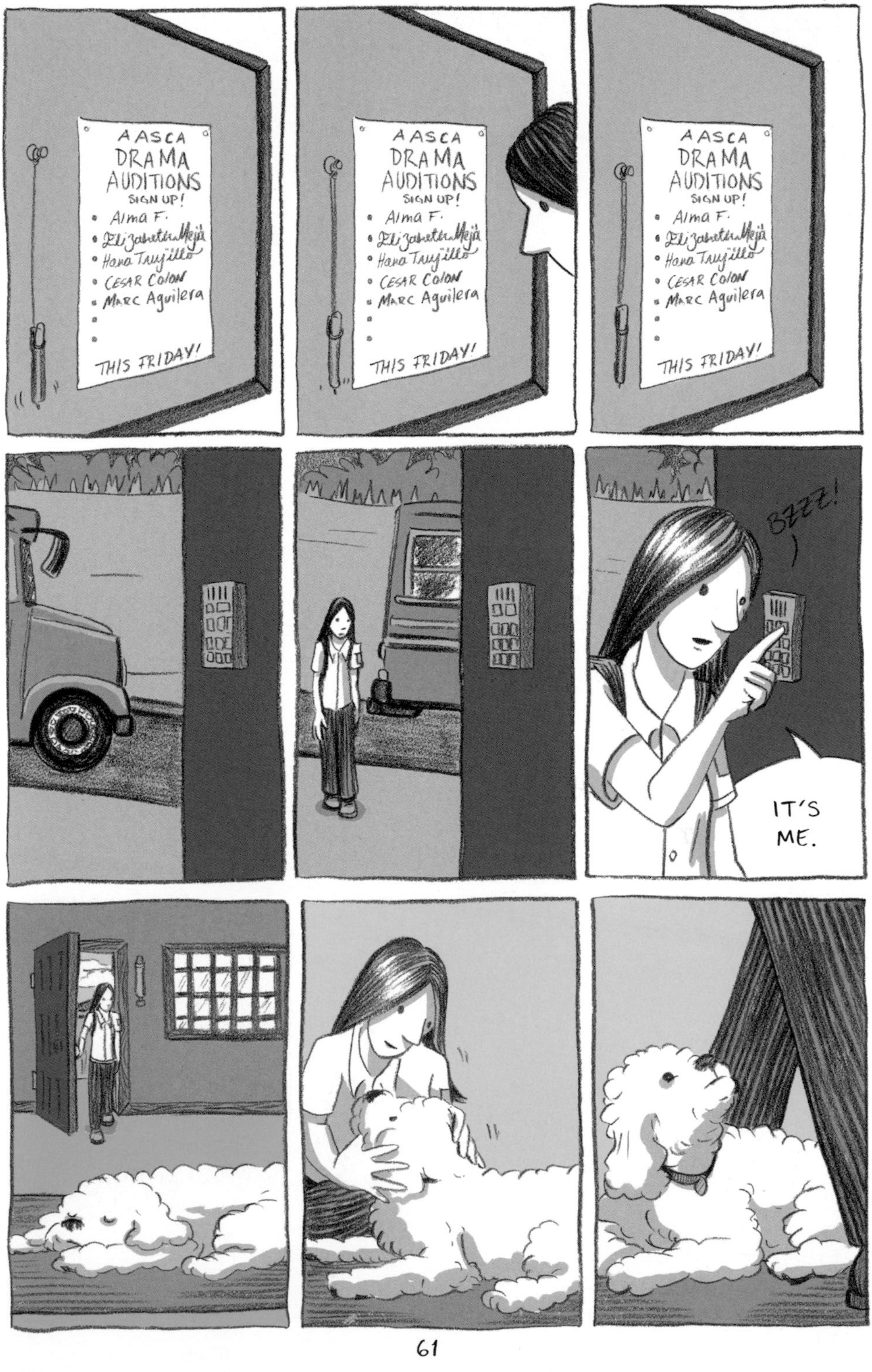
AASCA
DRAMA
AUDITIONS
SIGN UP!
Alma F.
Elizabeth Mejía
Hana Trujillo
CESAR Colon
Marc Aguilera
THIS FRIDAY!
BZZZ!
IT'S ME.

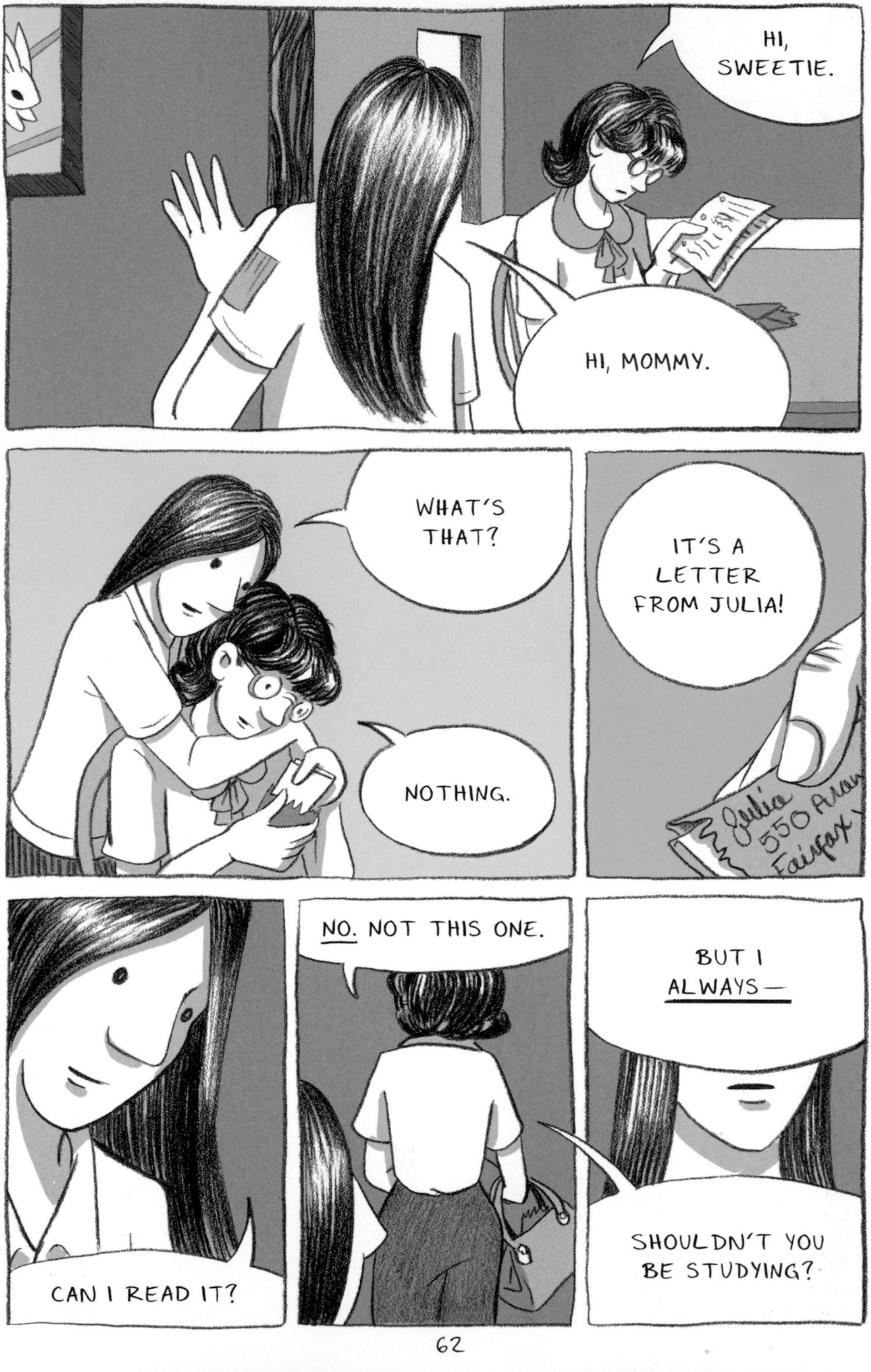
HI, SWEETIE.
HI, MOMMY.
WHAT'S THAT?
NOTHING.
IT'S A LETTER FROM JULIA!
Julia
550
Fairfax
CAN I READ IT?
NO. NOT THIS ONE.
BUT I ALWAYS—
SHOULDN'T YOU BE STUDYING?

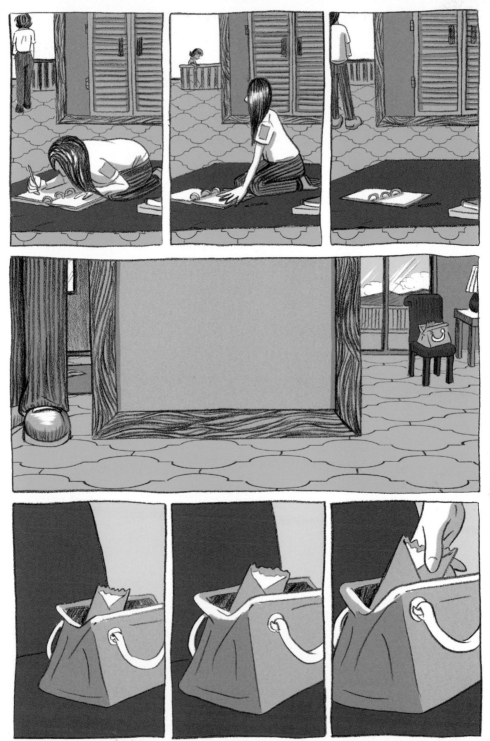

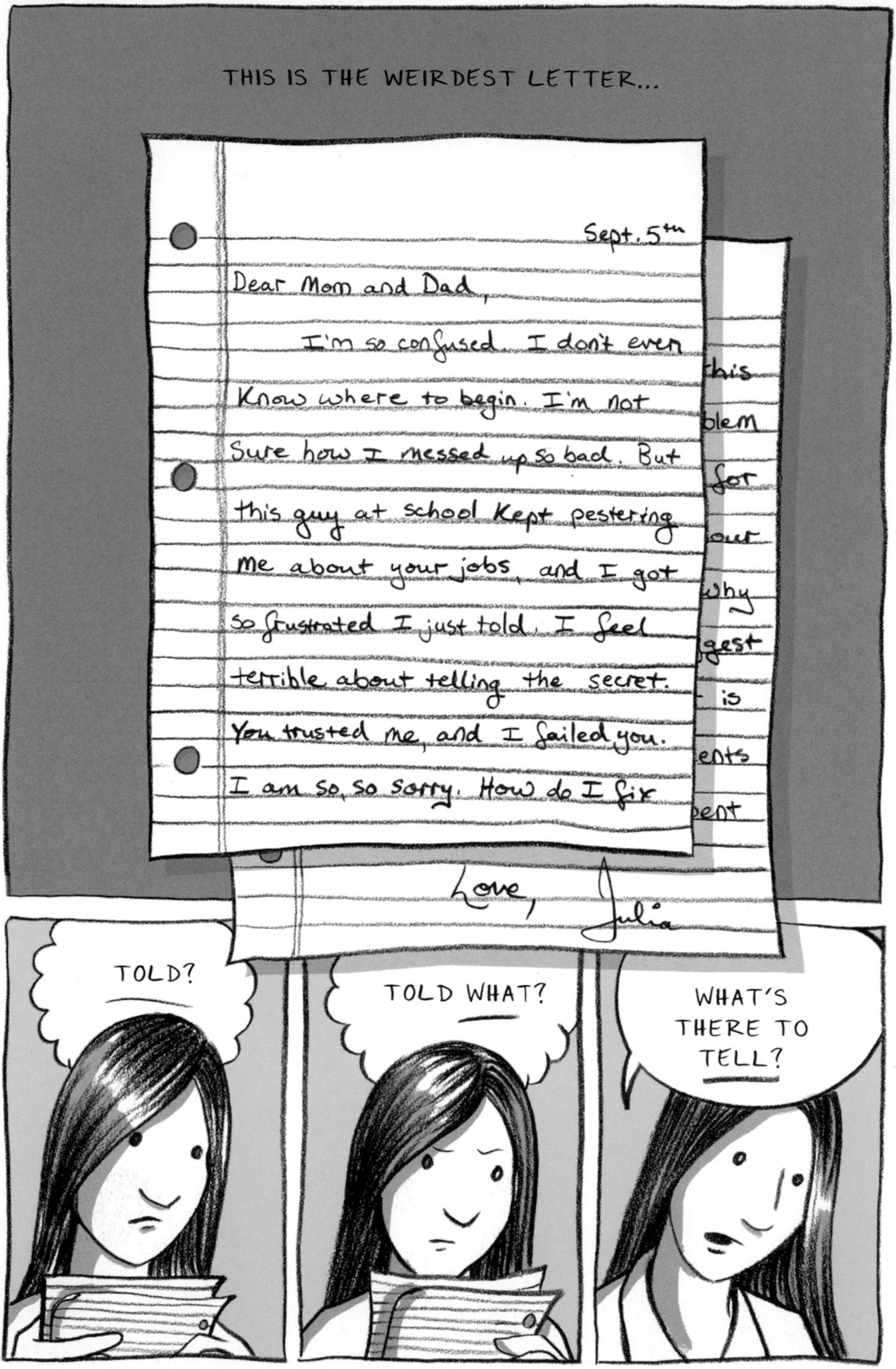
THIS IS THE WEIRDEST LETTER...
Sept. 5th
Dear Mom and Dad,
I'm so confused. I don't even Know where to begin. I'm not Sure how I messed up so bad. But this guy at school Kept pestering me about your jobs, and I got so frustrated I just told. I feel terrible about telling the secret. You trusted me, and I failed you. I am so, so sorry. How do I fix
Love, Julia
TOLD?
TOLD WHAT?
WHAT'S THERE TO TELL?

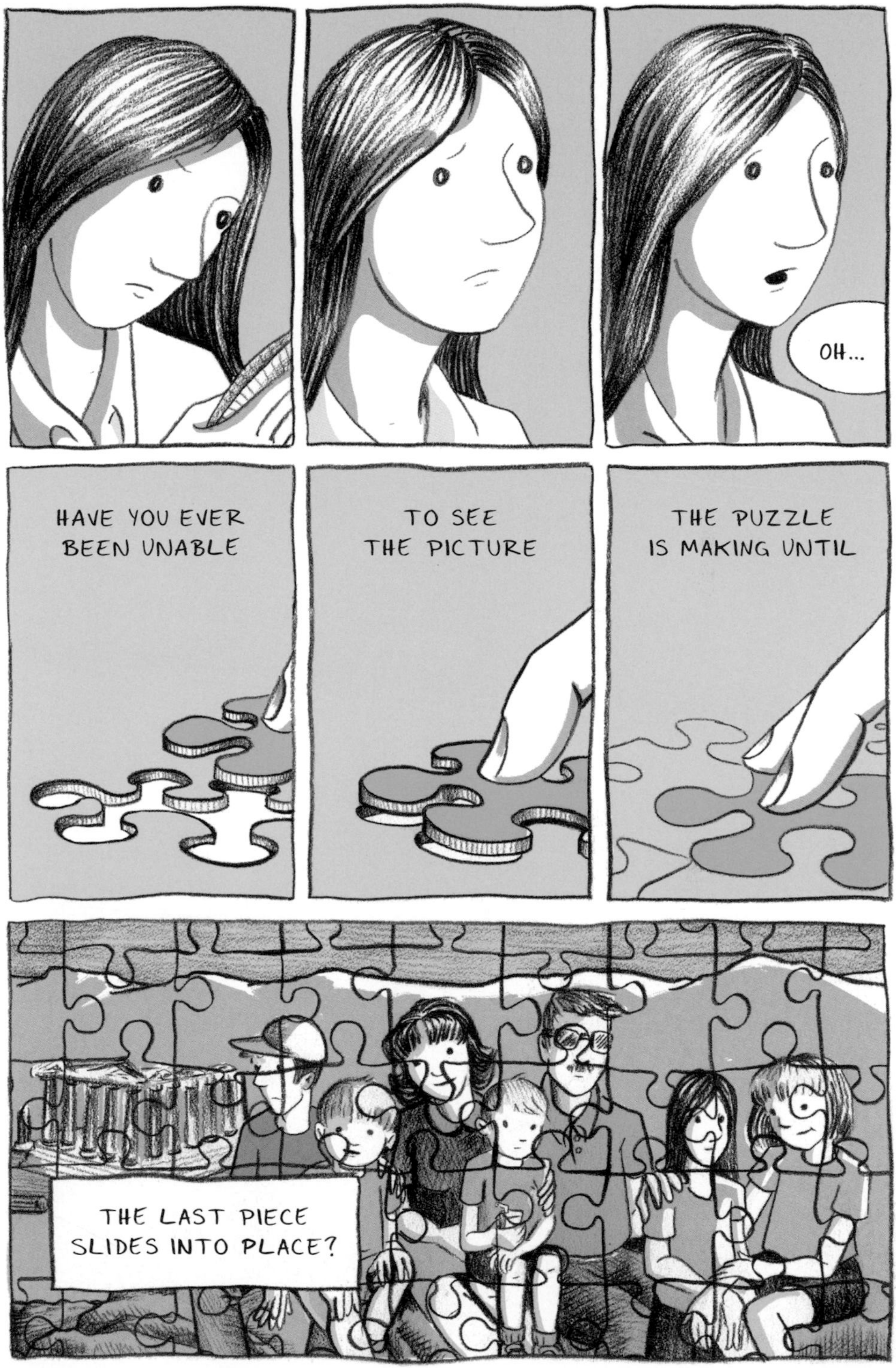
OH...
HAVE YOU EVER BEEN UNABLE
TO SEE THE PICTURE
THE PUZZLE IS MAKING UNTIL
THE LAST PIECE SLIDES INTO PLACE?

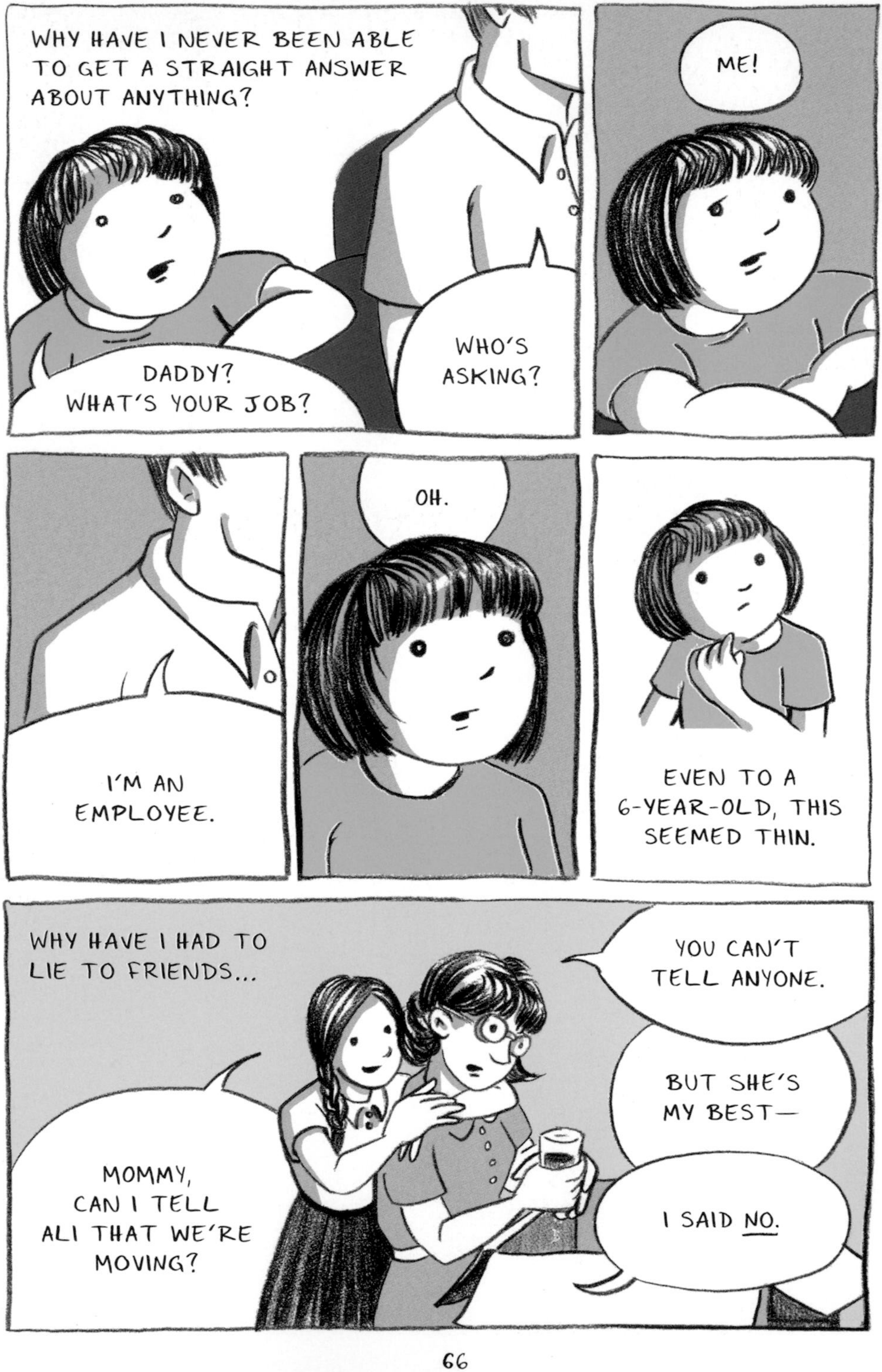
WHY HAVE I NEVER BEEN ABLE TO GET A STRAIGHT ANSWER ABOUT ANYTHING?
DADDY? WHAT'S YOUR JOB?
WHO'S ASKING?
ME!
I'M AN EMPLOYEE.
OH.
EVEN TO A 6-YEAR-OLD, THIS SEEMED THIN.
WHY HAVE I HAD TO LIE TO FRIENDS...
MOMMY, CAN I TELL ALI THAT WE'RE MOVING?
YOU CAN'T TELL ANYONE.
BUT SHE'S MY BEST—
I SAID NO.

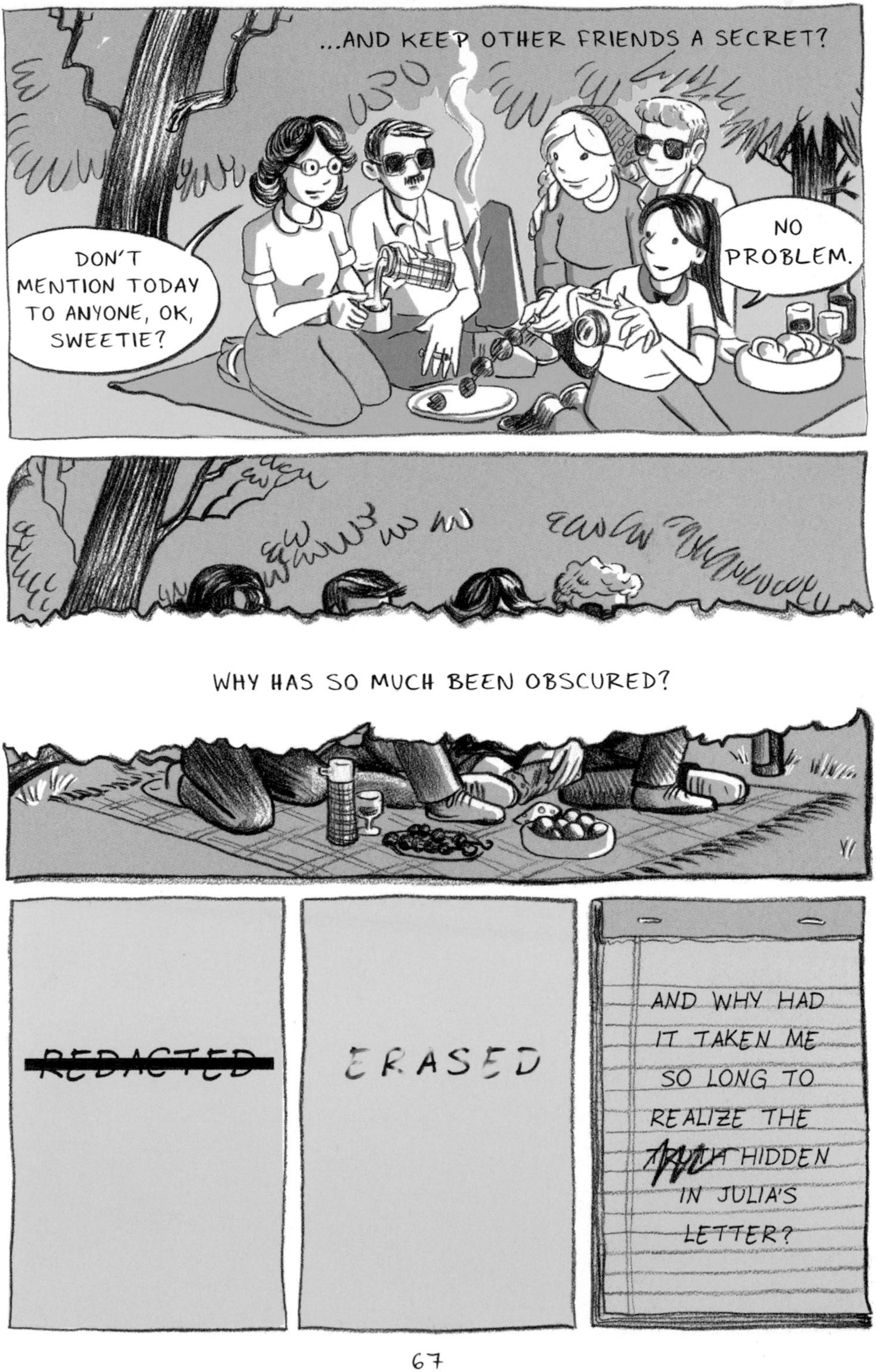

...AND KEEP OTHER FRIENDS A SECRET?
DON'T MENTION TODAY TO ANYONE, OK, SWEETIE?
NO PROBLEM.
WHY HAS SO MUCH BEEN OBSCURED?
~~REDACTED~~
ERASED
AND WHY HAD IT TAKEN ME SO LONG TO REALIZE THE ~~TRUTH~~ HIDDEN IN JULIA'S LETTER?

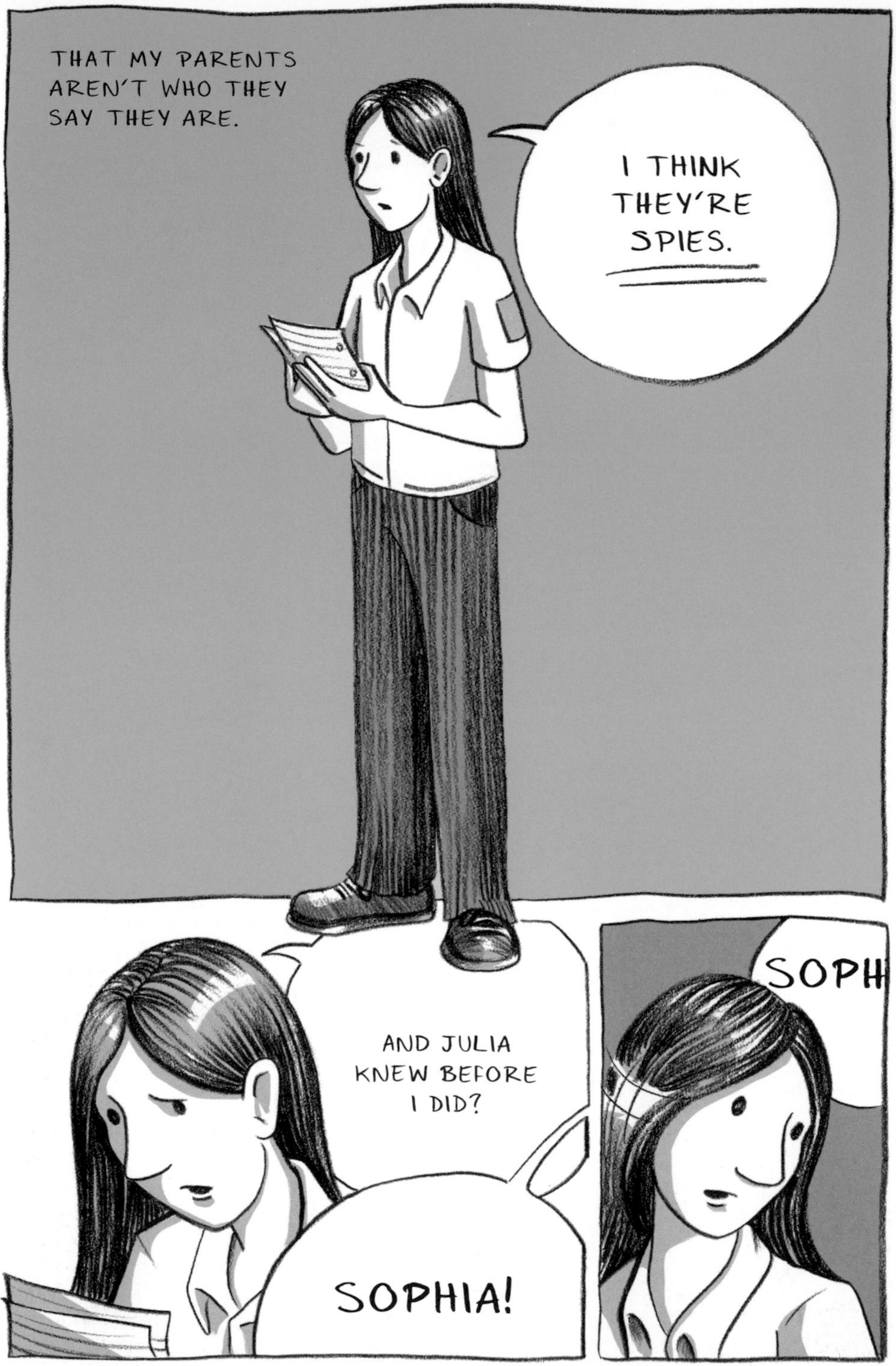
THAT MY PARENTS AREN'T WHO THEY SAY THEY ARE.
I THINK THEY'RE SPIES.
AND JULIA KNEW BEFORE I DID?
SOPHIA!
SOPH

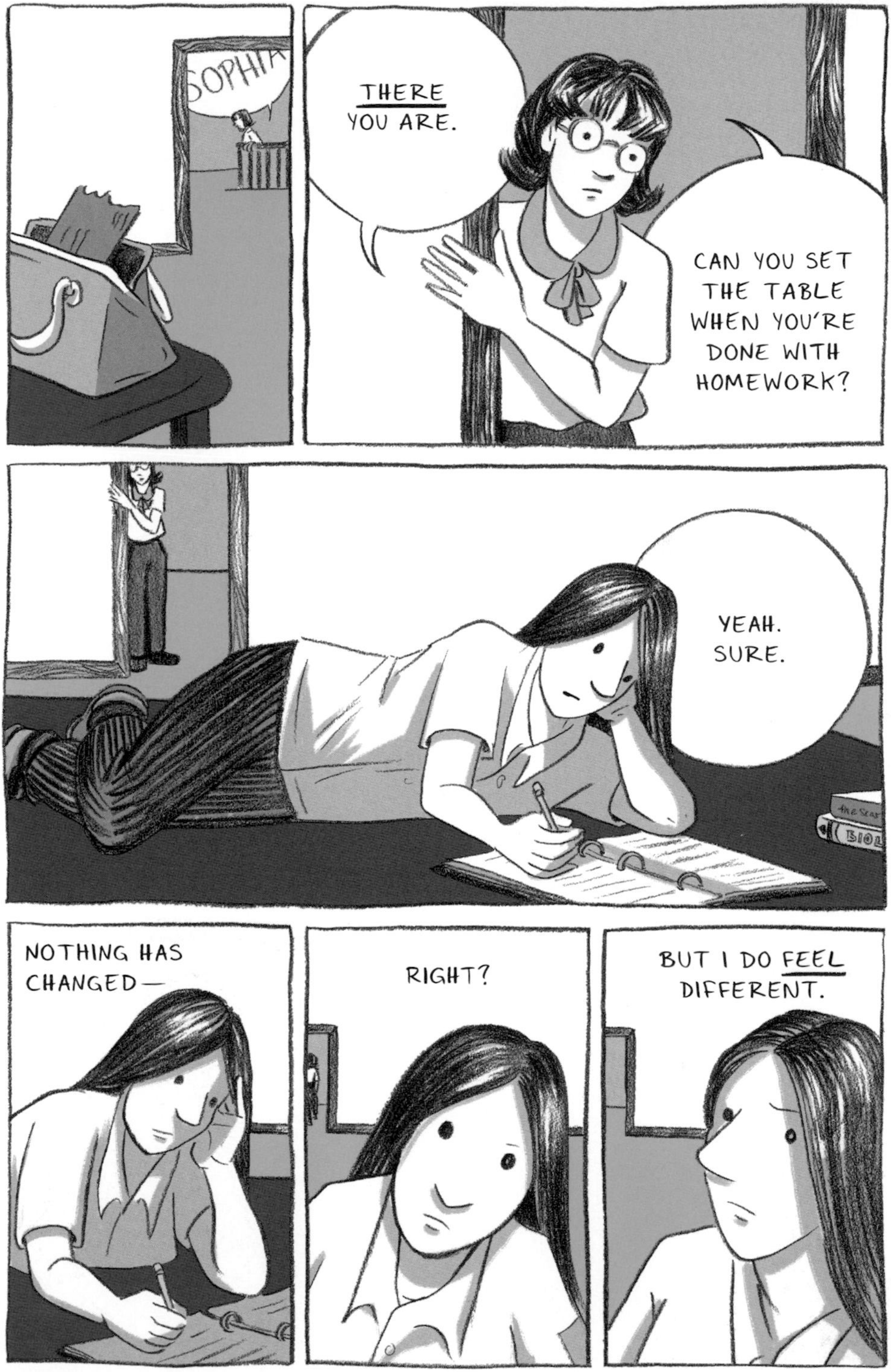
SOPHIA
THERE YOU ARE.
CAN YOU SET THE TABLE WHEN YOU'RE DONE WITH HOMEWORK?
YEAH. SURE.
NOTHING HAS CHANGED—
RIGHT?
BUT I DO FEEL DIFFERENT.

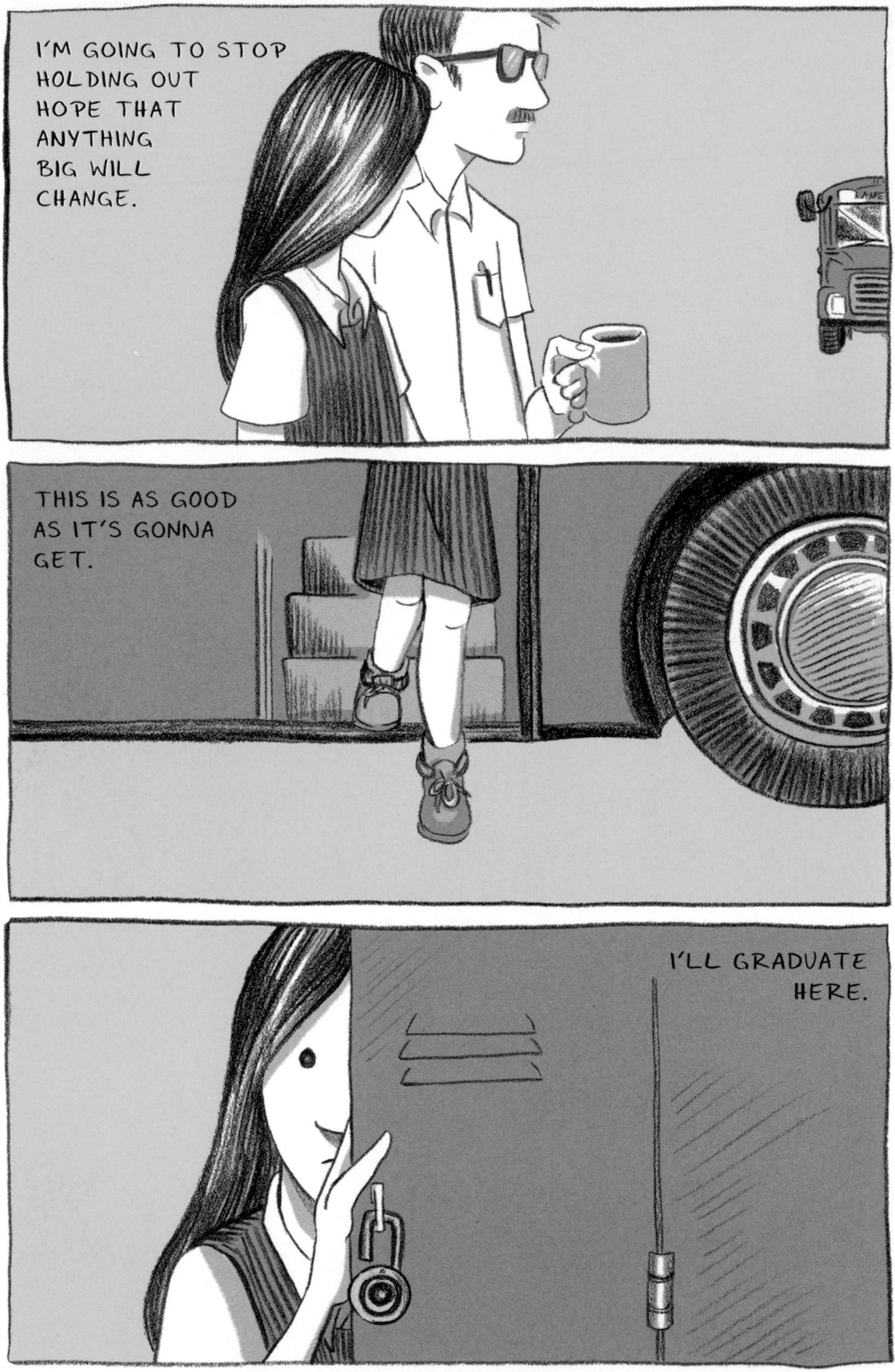
I'M GOING TO STOP HOLDING OUT HOPE THAT ANYTHING BIG WILL CHANGE.
THIS IS AS GOOD AS IT'S GONNA GET.
I'LL GRADUATE HERE.

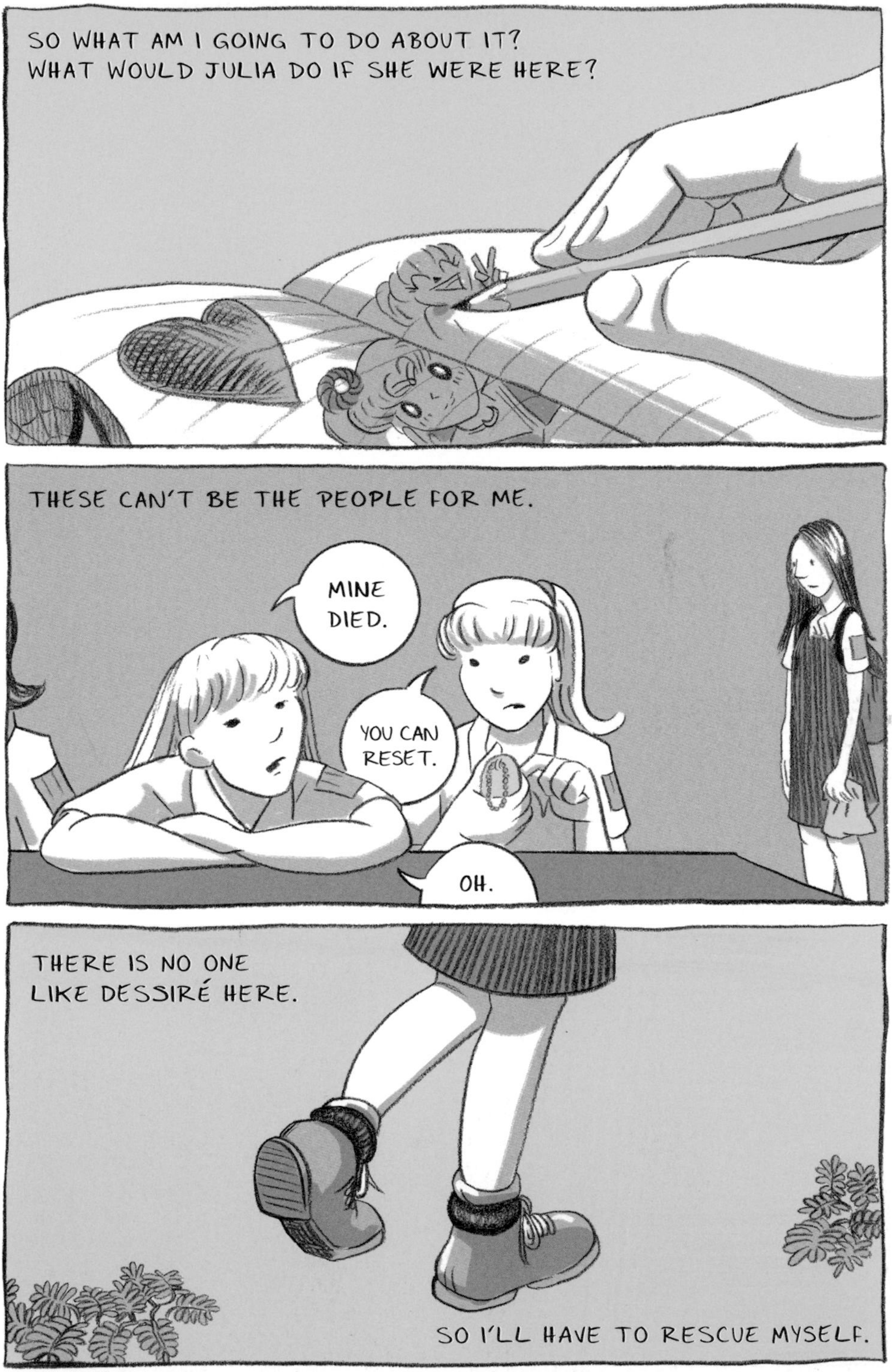
SO WHAT AM I GOING TO DO ABOUT IT?
WHAT WOULD JULIA DO IF SHE WERE HERE?
THESE CAN'T BE THE PEOPLE FOR ME.
MINE DIED.
YOU CAN RESET.
OH.
THERE IS NO ONE LIKE DESSIRÉ HERE.
SO I'LL HAVE TO RESCUE MYSELF.

AND THE ONLY WAY OUT
IS THROUGH.

AASCA
DRAMA
AUDITIONS
SIGN UP
○ Alma F.
○ Elizabeth Mejía
○ HANA Trujillo
○ CESAR COLON
○ MARC Aguilera
○
THIS FRIDAY!

AASCA
DRAMA
AUDITIONS
SIGN UP
○ Alma F.
○ Elizabeth Mejía
○ HANA Trujillo
○ CESAR COLON
○ MARC Aguilera
○
THIS FRIDAY!

○ Alma F
○ Elizabeth
○ Hana Truj
○ CESAR COL
○ Marc Aguile
○ Sophiea W
○
THIS FRID

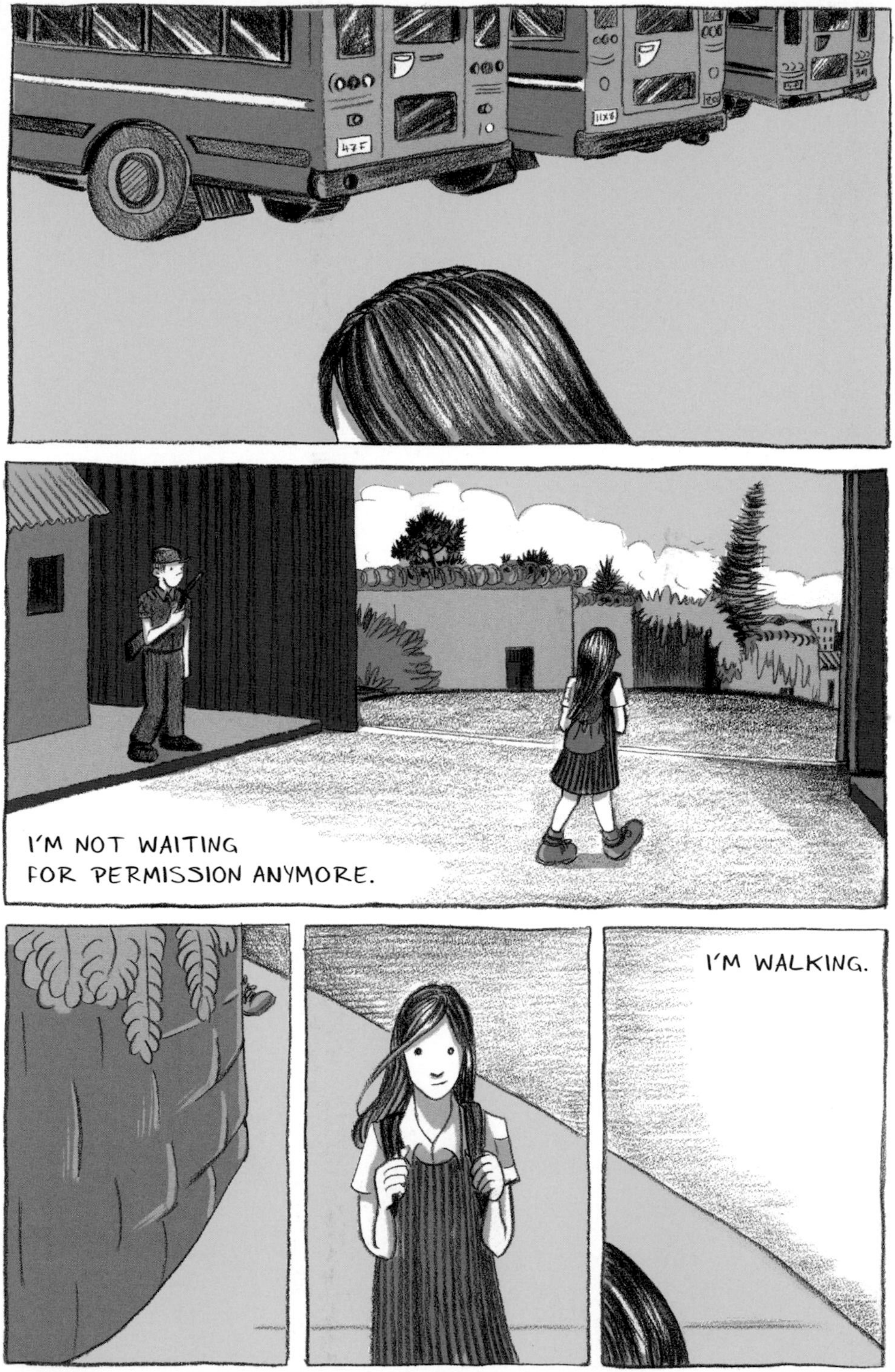
I'M NOT WAITING
FOR PERMISSION ANYMORE.
I'M WALKING.

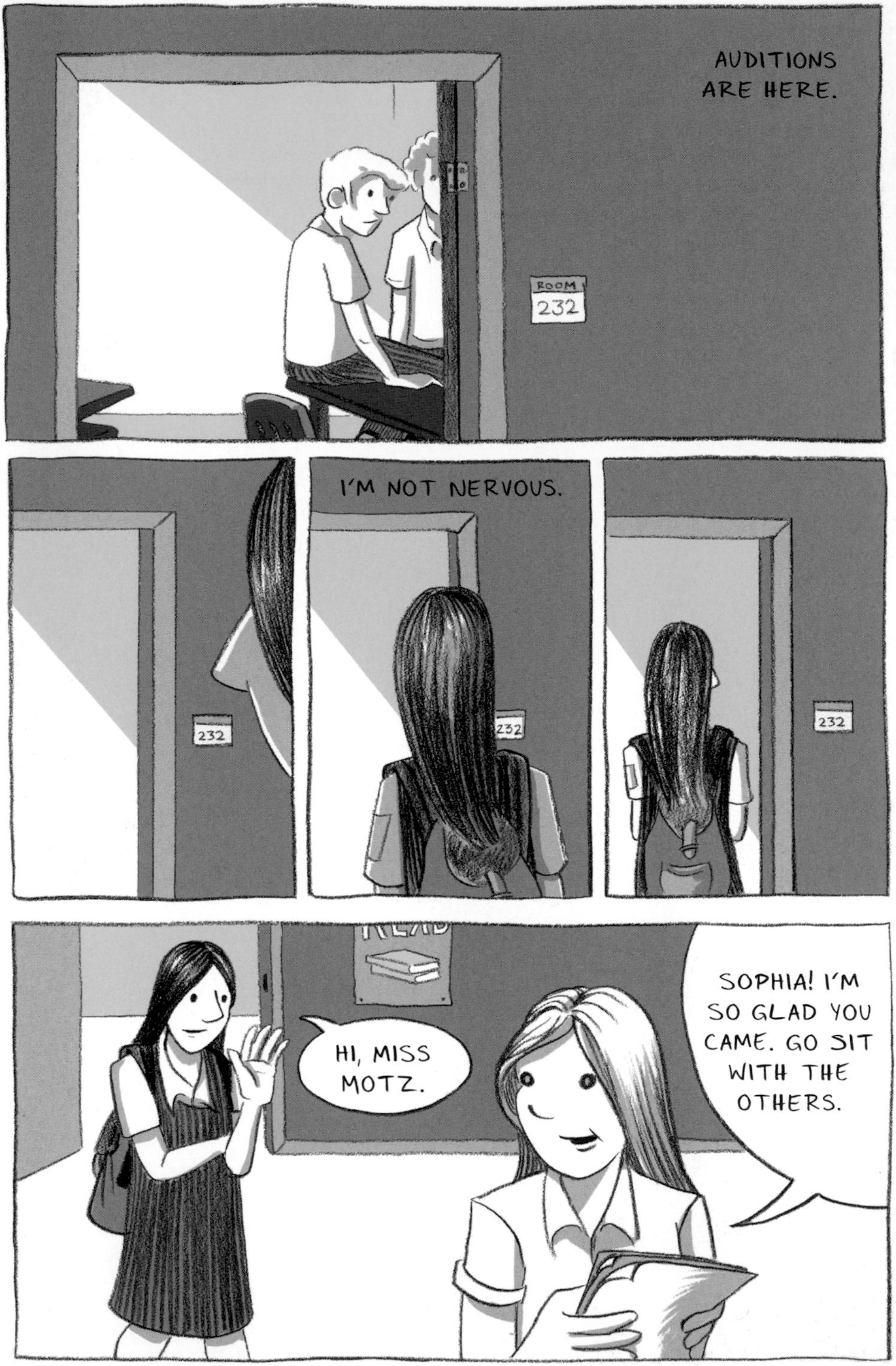
AUDITIONS ARE HERE.
ROOM 232
232
I'M NOT NERVOUS.
232
232
HI, MISS MOTZ.
SOPHIA! I'M SO GLAD YOU CAME. GO SIT WITH THE OTHERS.

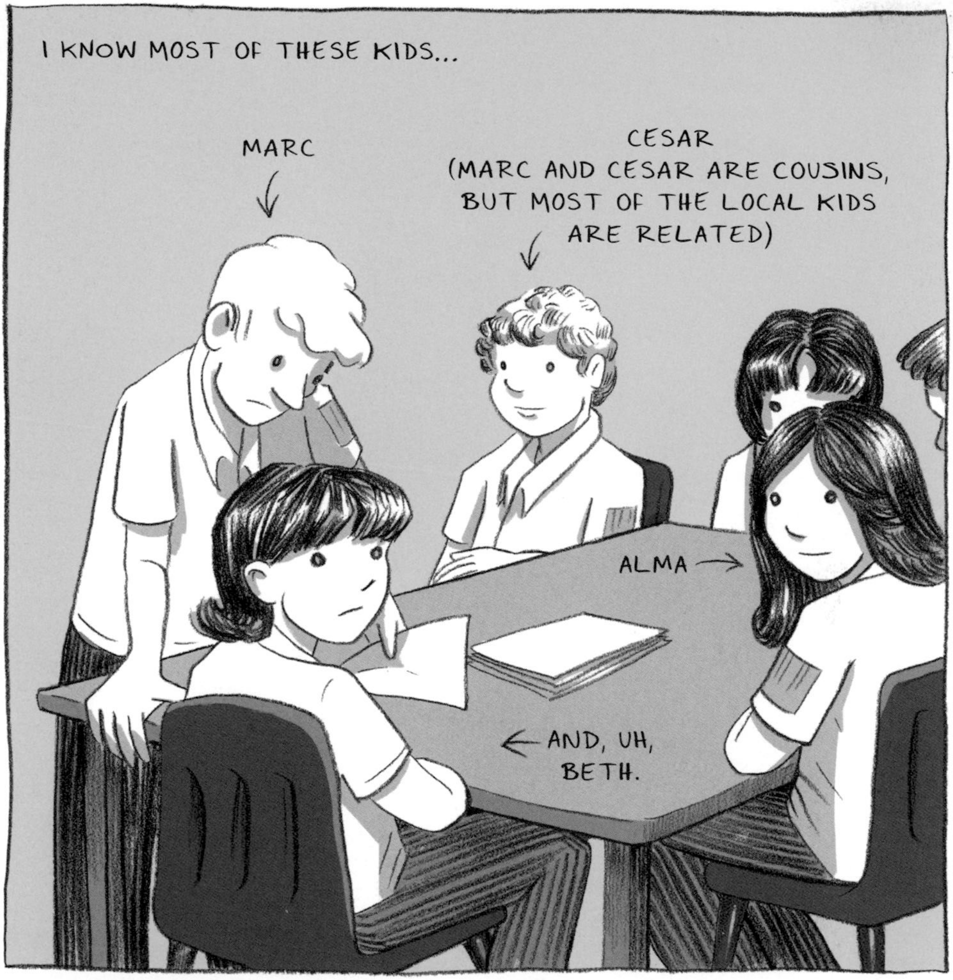
I KNOW MOST OF THESE KIDS...
MARC
CESAR
(MARC AND CESAR ARE COUSINS, BUT MOST OF THE LOCAL KIDS ARE RELATED)
ALMA
AND, UH, BETH.

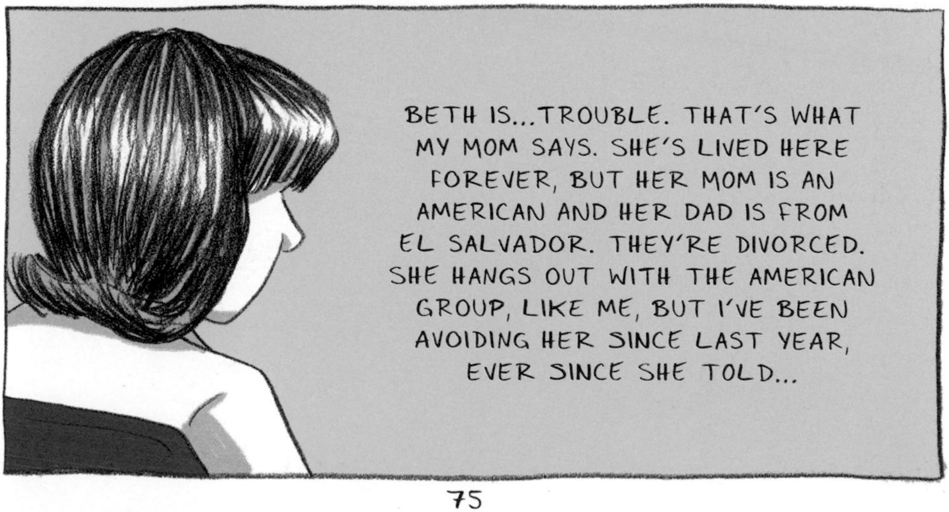
BETH IS...TROUBLE. THAT'S WHAT MY MOM SAYS. SHE'S LIVED HERE FOREVER, BUT HER MOM IS AN AMERICAN AND HER DAD IS FROM EL SALVADOR. THEY'RE DIVORCED. SHE HANGS OUT WITH THE AMERICAN GROUP, LIKE ME, BUT I'VE BEEN AVOIDING HER SINCE LAST YEAR, EVER SINCE SHE TOLD...

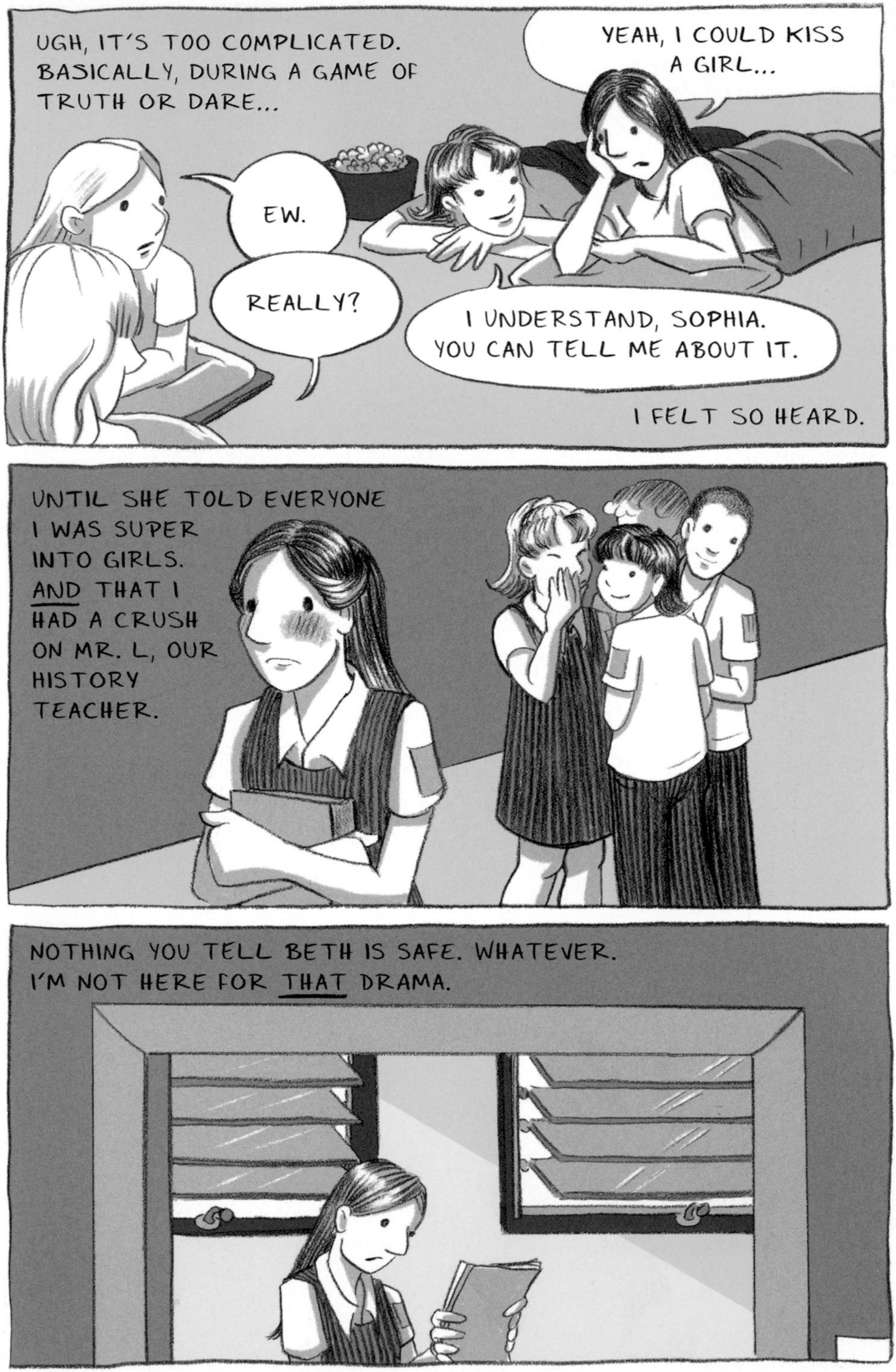
UGH, IT'S TOO COMPLICATED. BASICALLY, DURING A GAME OF TRUTH OR DARE...
YEAH, I COULD KISS A GIRL...
EW.
REALLY?
I UNDERSTAND, SOPHIA. YOU CAN TELL ME ABOUT IT.
I FELT SO HEARD.
UNTIL SHE TOLD EVERYONE I WAS SUPER INTO GIRLS. AND THAT I HAD A CRUSH ON MR. L, OUR HISTORY TEACHER.
NOTHING YOU TELL BETH IS SAFE. WHATEVER. I'M NOT HERE FOR THAT DRAMA.

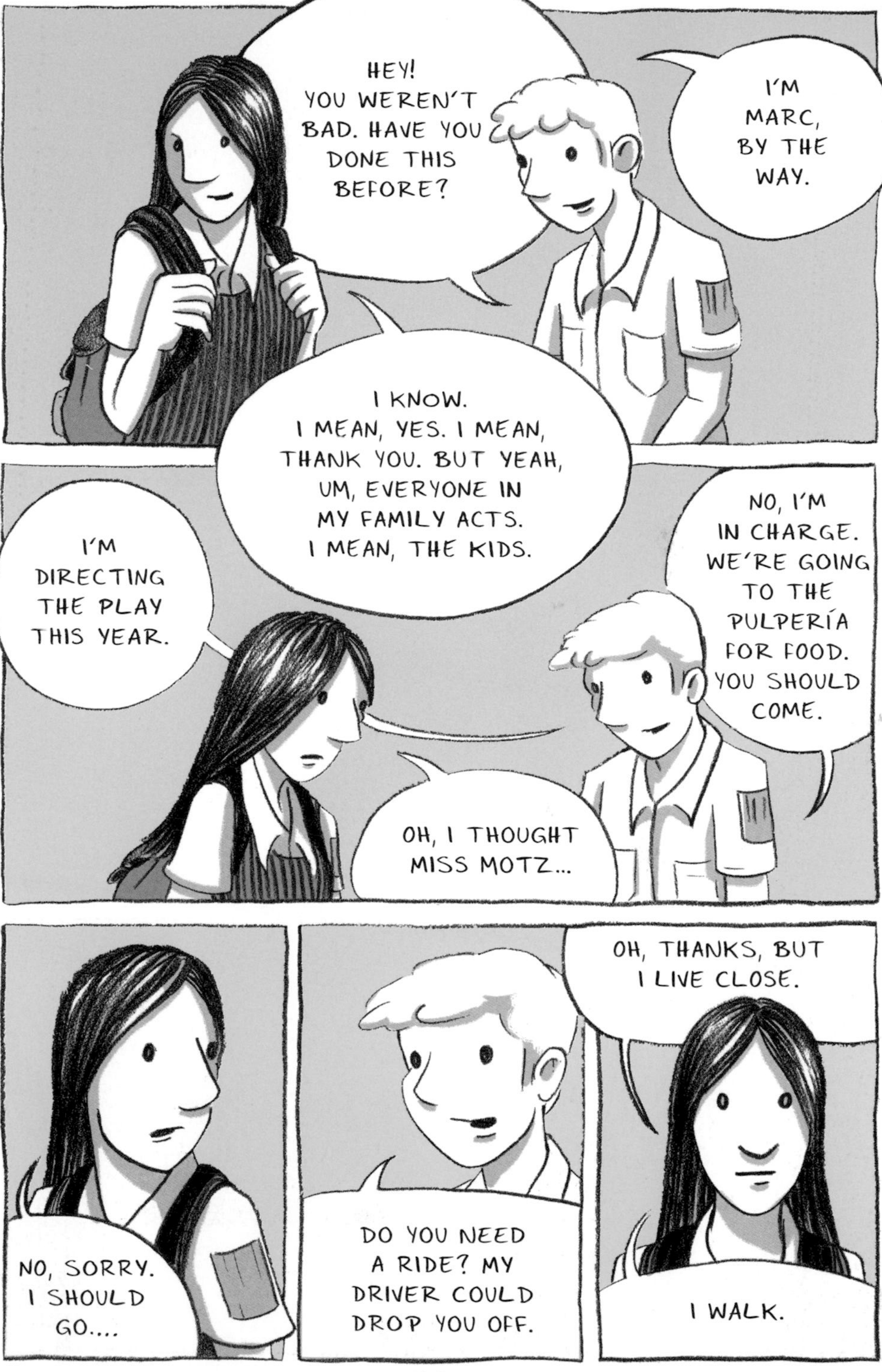
HEY! YOU WEREN'T BAD. HAVE YOU DONE THIS BEFORE?
I'M MARC, BY THE WAY.
I KNOW. I MEAN, YES. I MEAN, THANK YOU. BUT YEAH, UM, EVERYONE IN MY FAMILY ACTS. I MEAN, THE KIDS.
I'M DIRECTING THE PLAY THIS YEAR.
OH, I THOUGHT MISS MOTZ...
NO, I'M IN CHARGE. WE'RE GOING TO THE PULPERÍA FOR FOOD. YOU SHOULD COME.
NO, SORRY. I SHOULD GO....
DO YOU NEED A RIDE? MY DRIVER COULD DROP YOU OFF.
OH, THANKS, BUT I LIVE CLOSE.
I WALK.

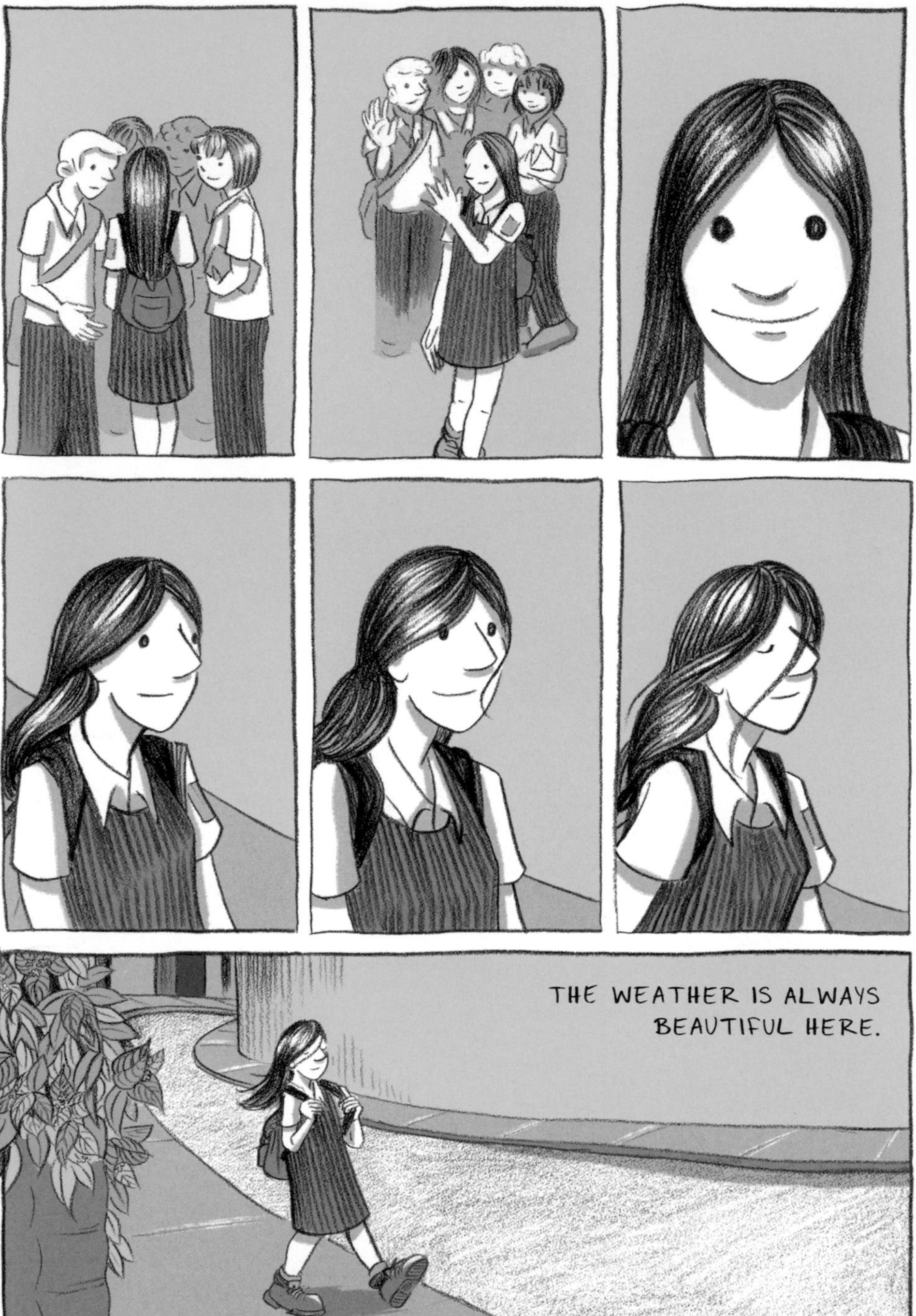
THE WEATHER IS ALWAYS BEAUTIFUL HERE.

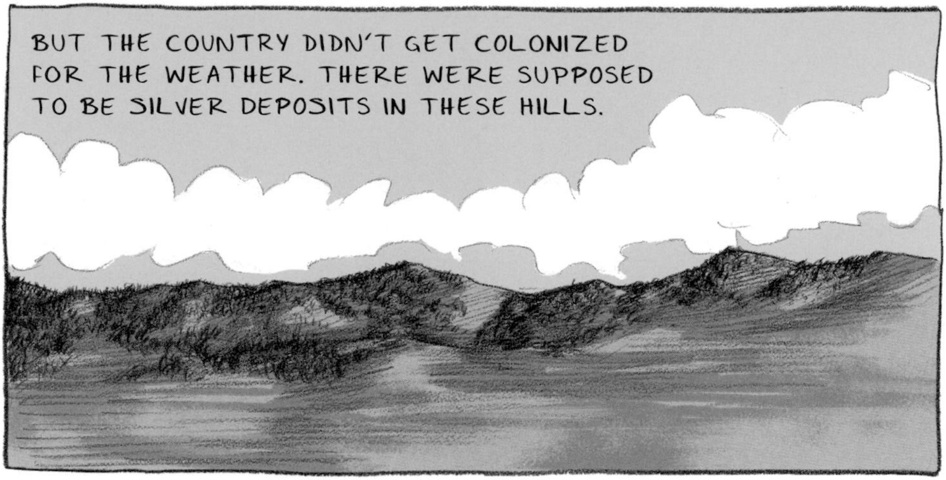
BUT THE COUNTRY DIDN'T GET COLONIZED FOR THE WEATHER. THERE WERE SUPPOSED TO BE SILVER DEPOSITS IN THESE HILLS.

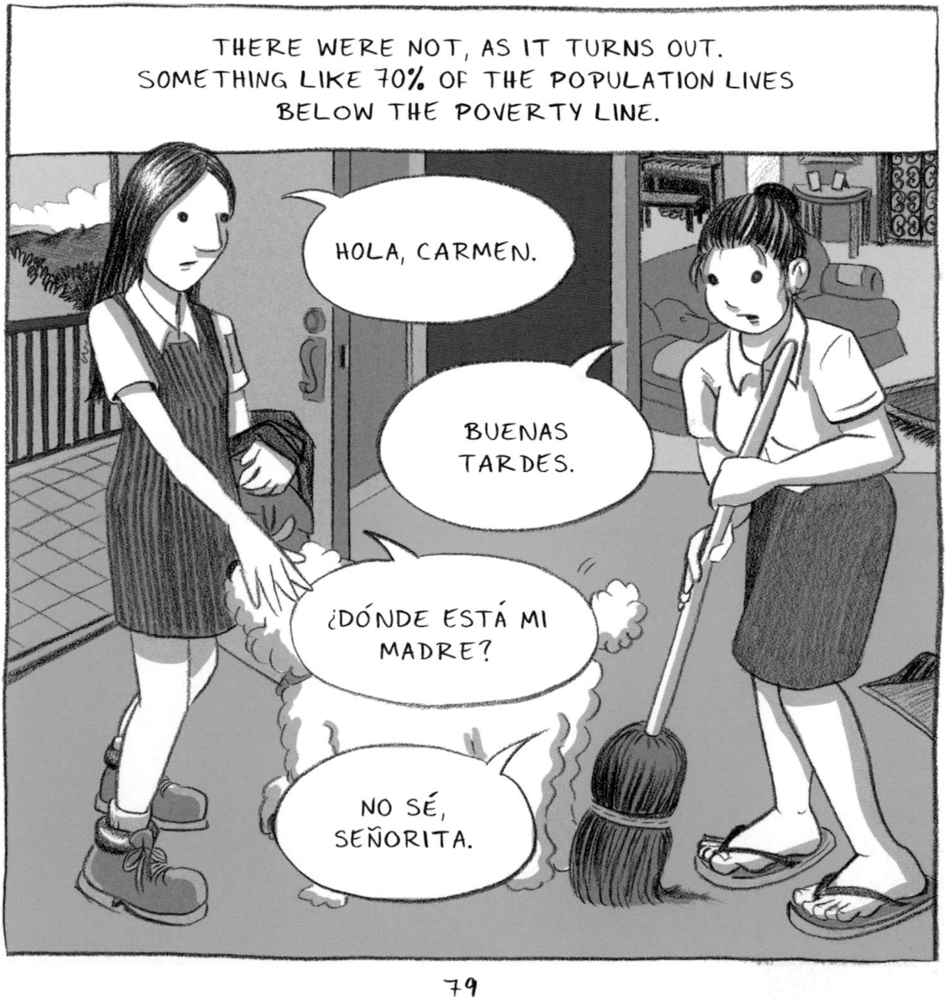
THERE WERE NOT, AS IT TURNS OUT. SOMETHING LIKE 70% OF THE POPULATION LIVES BELOW THE POVERTY LINE.
HOLA, CARMEN.
BUENAS TARDES.
¿DÓNDE ESTÁ MI MADRE?
NO SÉ, SEÑORITA.

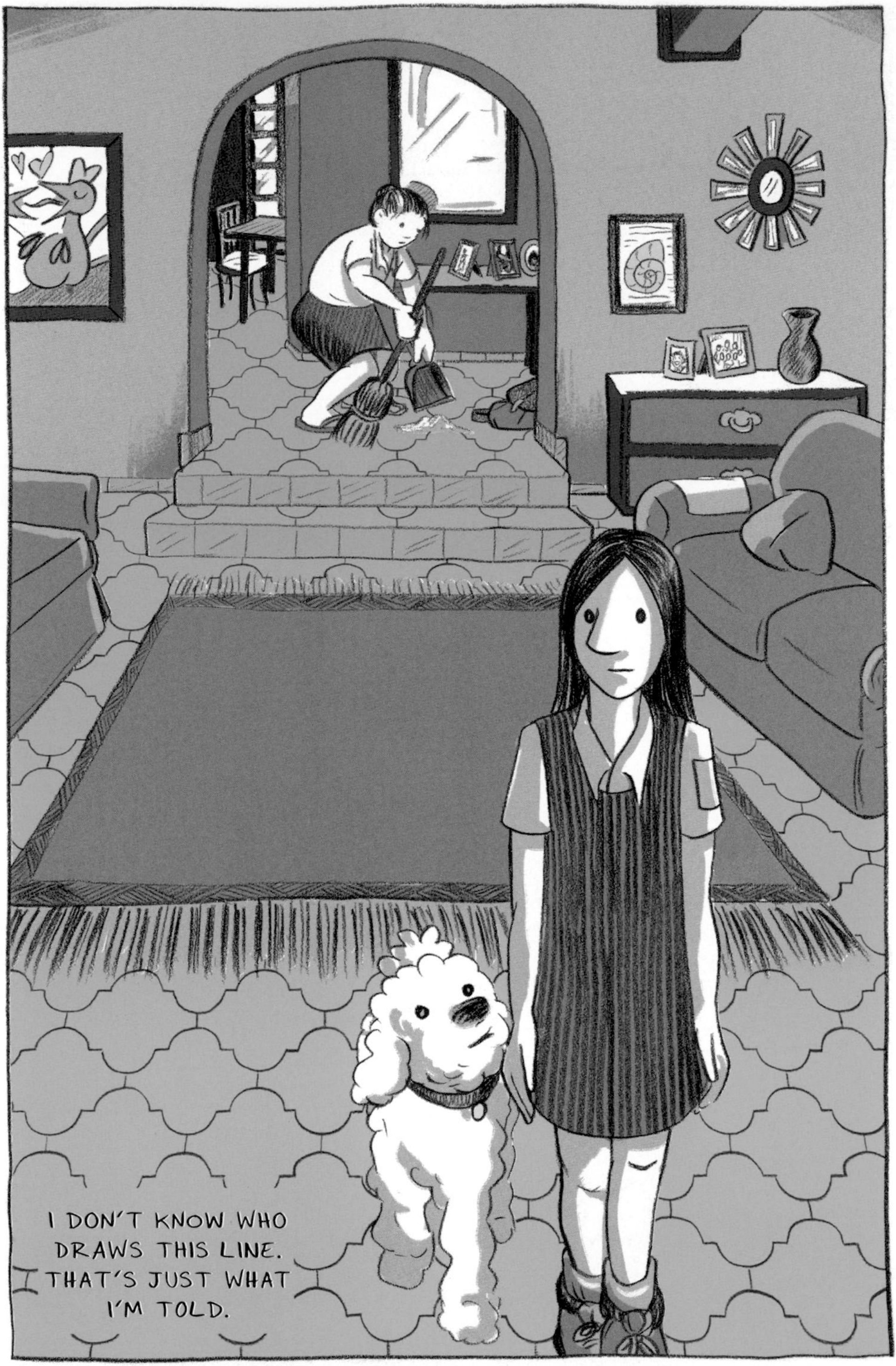
I DON'T KNOW WHO DRAWS THIS LINE. THAT'S JUST WHAT I'M TOLD.

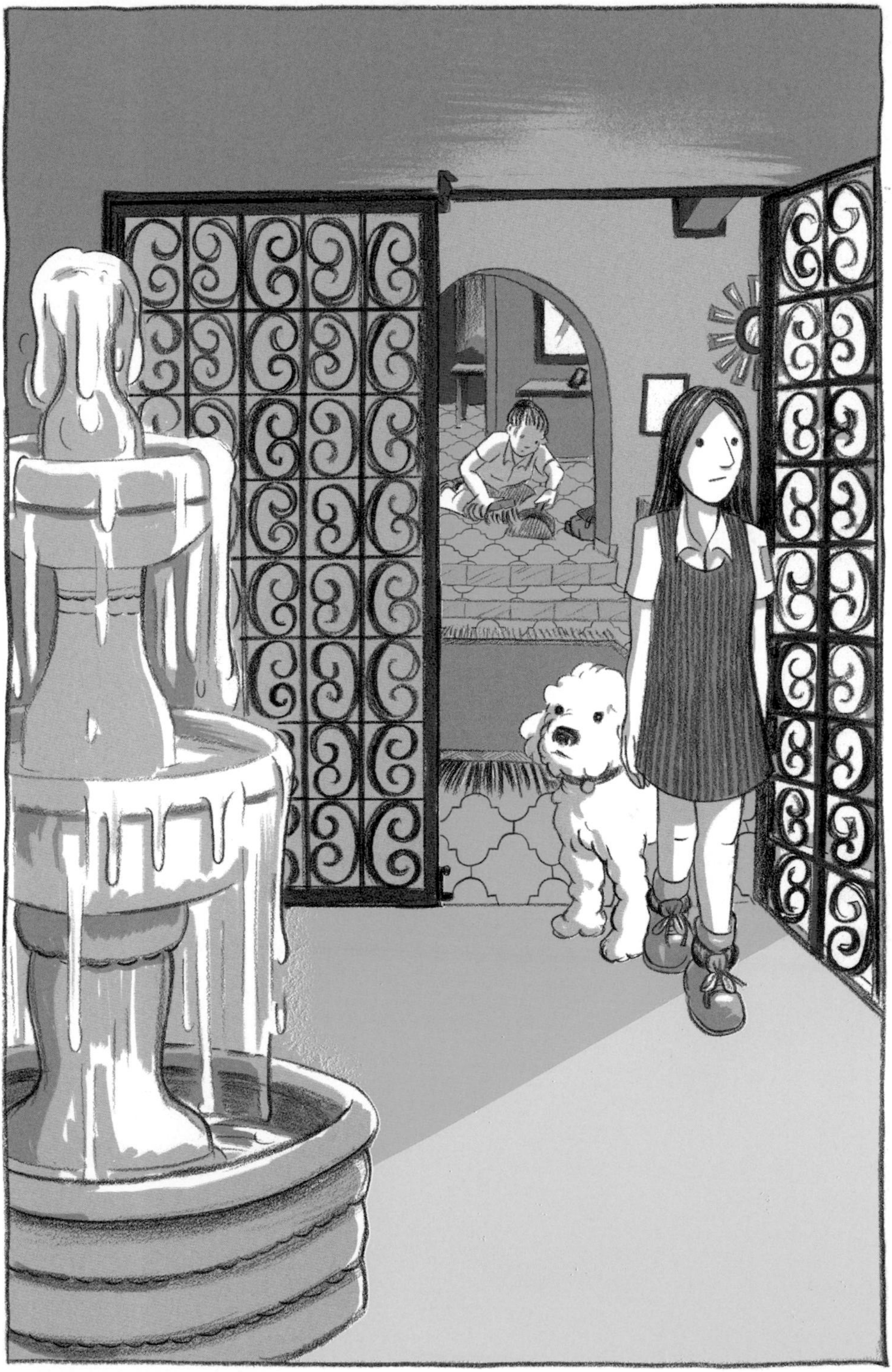

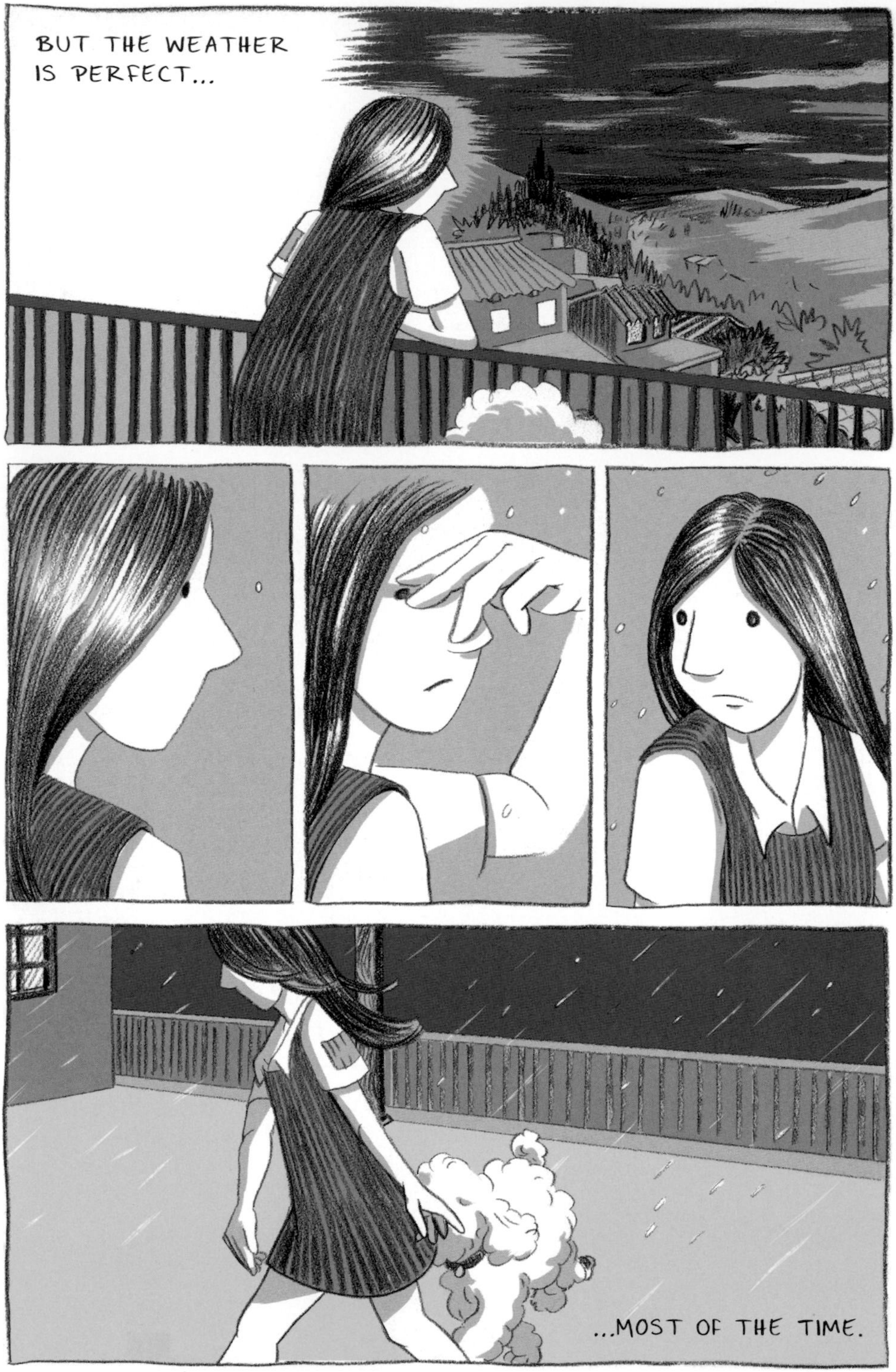
BUT THE WEATHER IS PERFECT...
...MOST OF THE TIME.

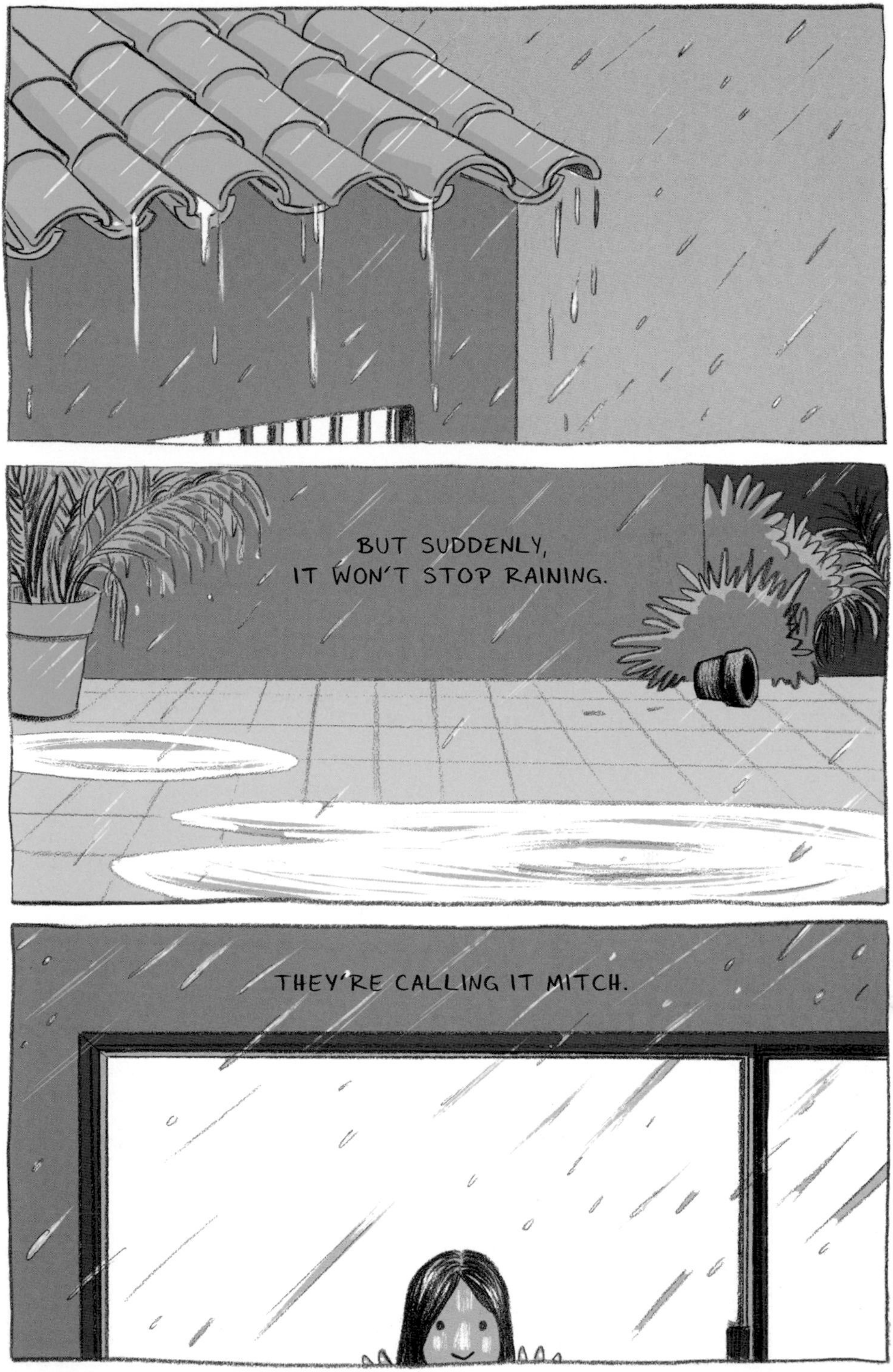
BUT SUDDENLY,
IT WON'T STOP RAINING.
THEY'RE CALLING IT MITCH.

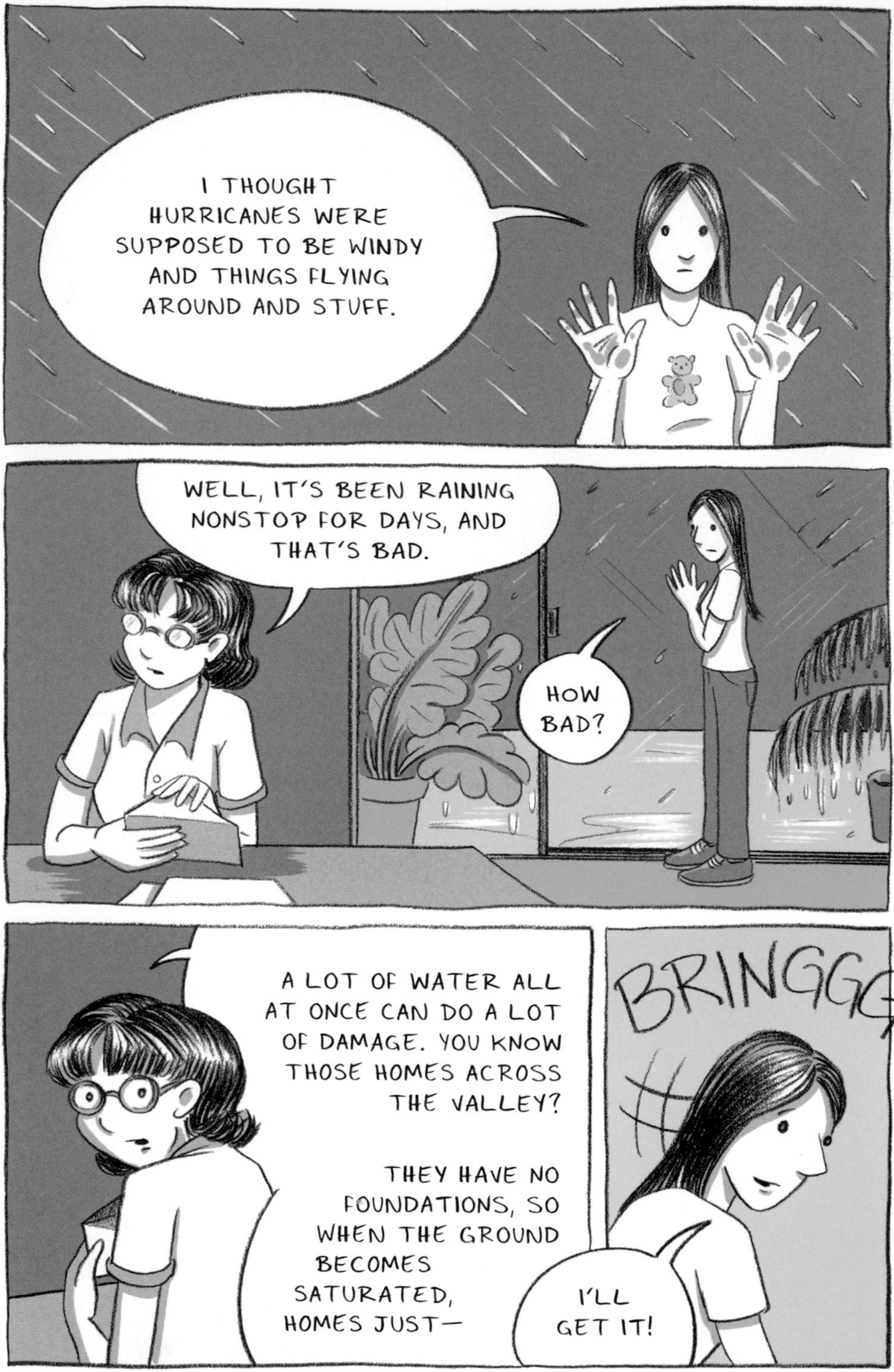
I THOUGHT HURRICANES WERE SUPPOSED TO BE WINDY AND THINGS FLYING AROUND AND STUFF.
WELL, IT'S BEEN RAINING NONSTOP FOR DAYS, AND THAT'S BAD.
HOW BAD?
A LOT OF WATER ALL AT ONCE CAN DO A LOT OF DAMAGE. YOU KNOW THOSE HOMES ACROSS THE VALLEY?
THEY HAVE NO FOUNDATIONS, SO WHEN THE GROUND BECOMES SATURATED, HOMES JUST—
BRINGGG
I'LL GET IT!

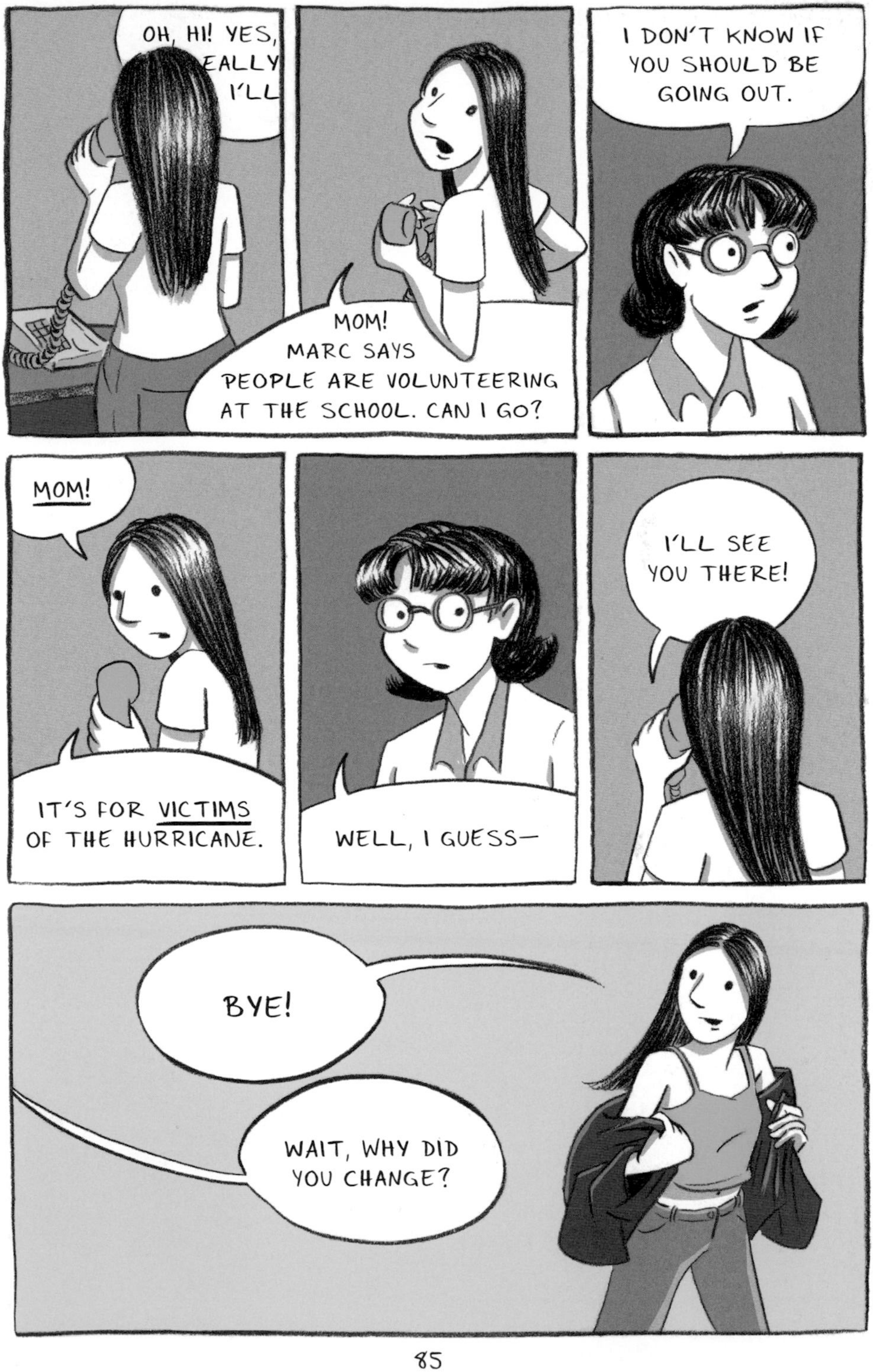
OH, HI! YES, EALLY I'LL
MOM! MARC SAYS PEOPLE ARE VOLUNTEERING AT THE SCHOOL. CAN I GO?
I DON'T KNOW IF YOU SHOULD BE GOING OUT.
MOM!
IT'S FOR VICTIMS OF THE HURRICANE.
WELL, I GUESS—
I'LL SEE YOU THERE!
BYE!
WAIT, WHY DID YOU CHANGE?

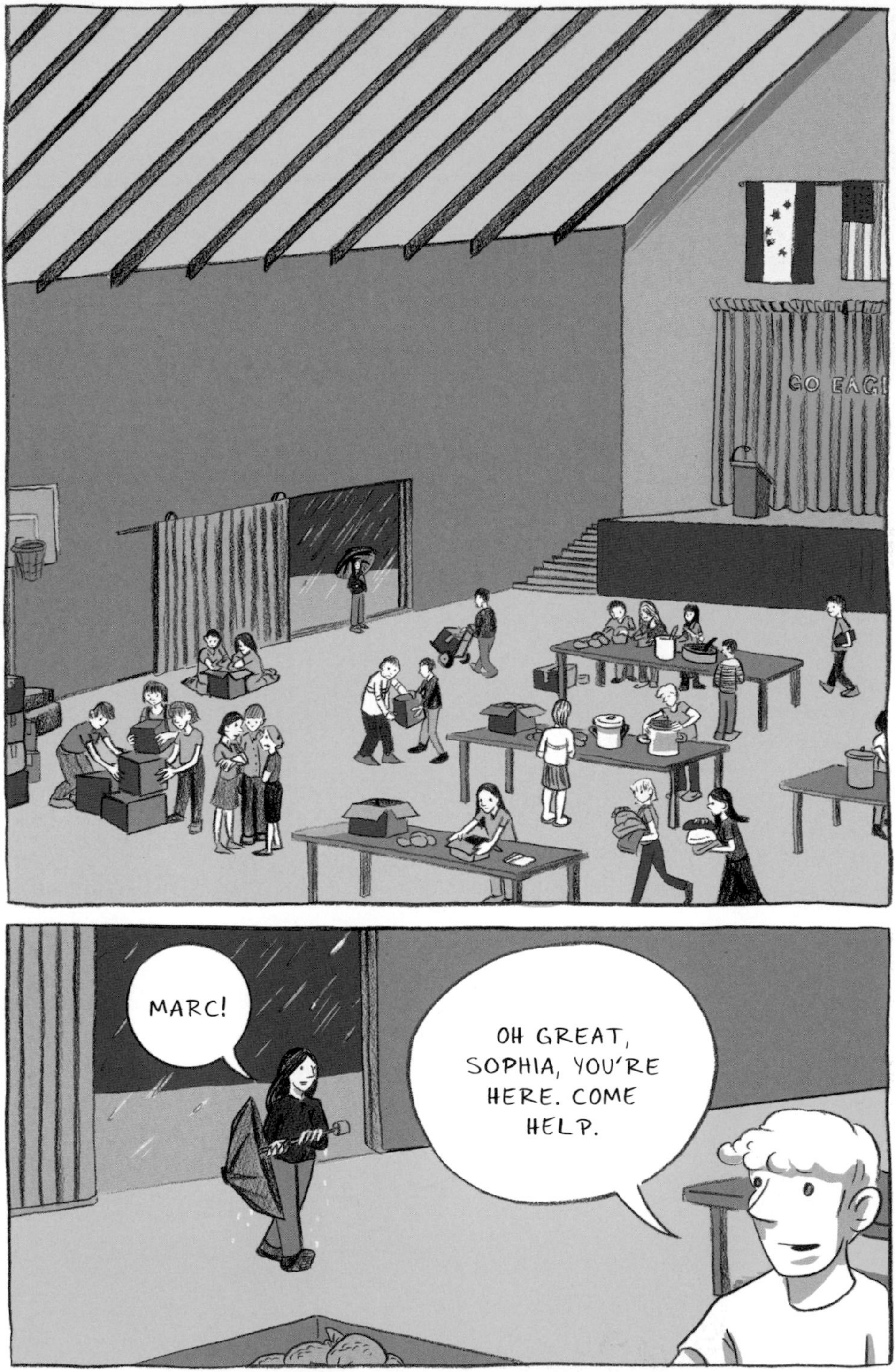
GO EAG
MARC!
OH GREAT, SOPHIA, YOU'RE HERE. COME HELP.

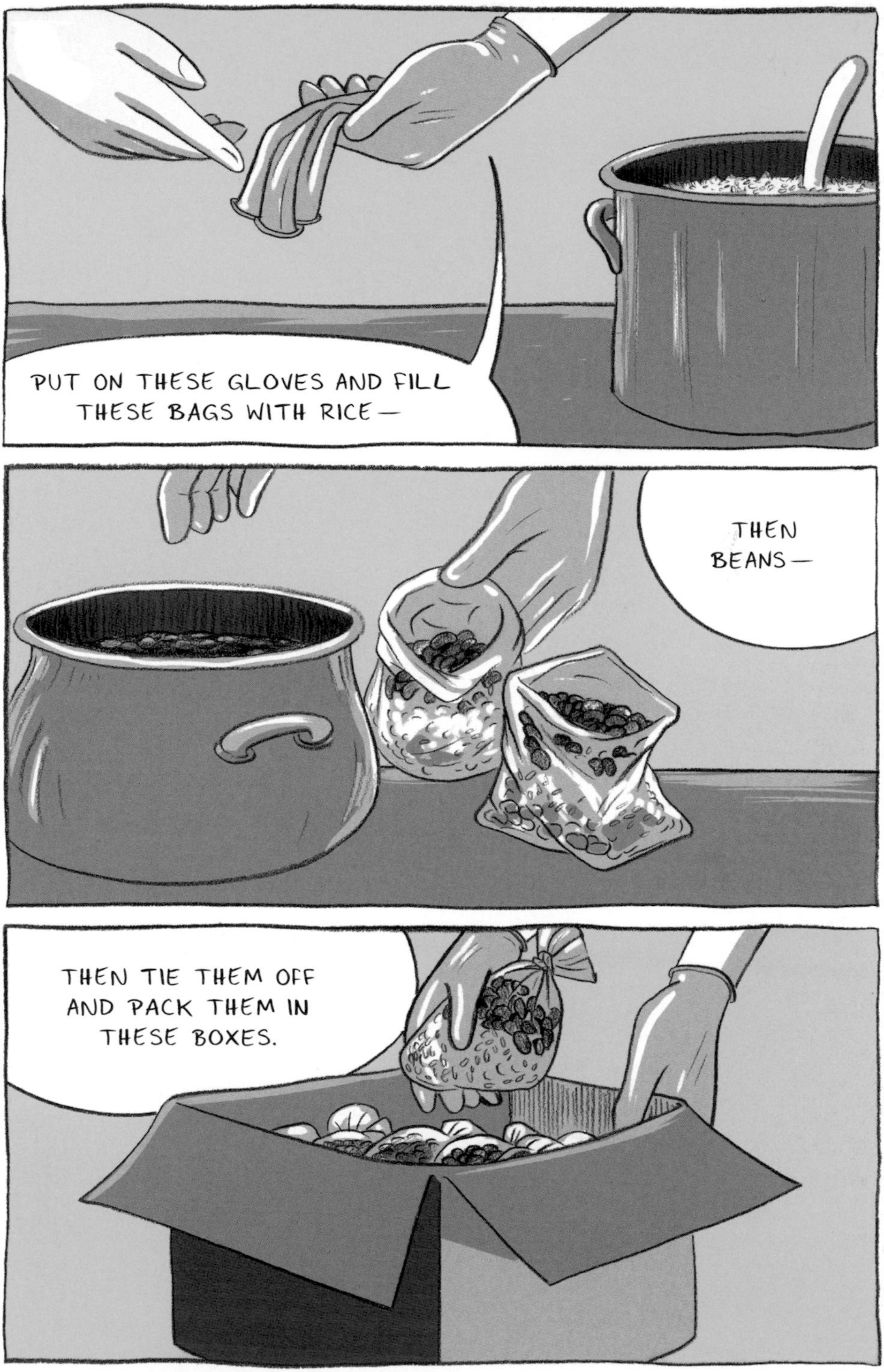
PUT ON THESE GLOVES AND FILL THESE BAGS WITH RICE—
THEN BEANS—
THEN TIE THEM OFF AND PACK THEM IN THESE BOXES.

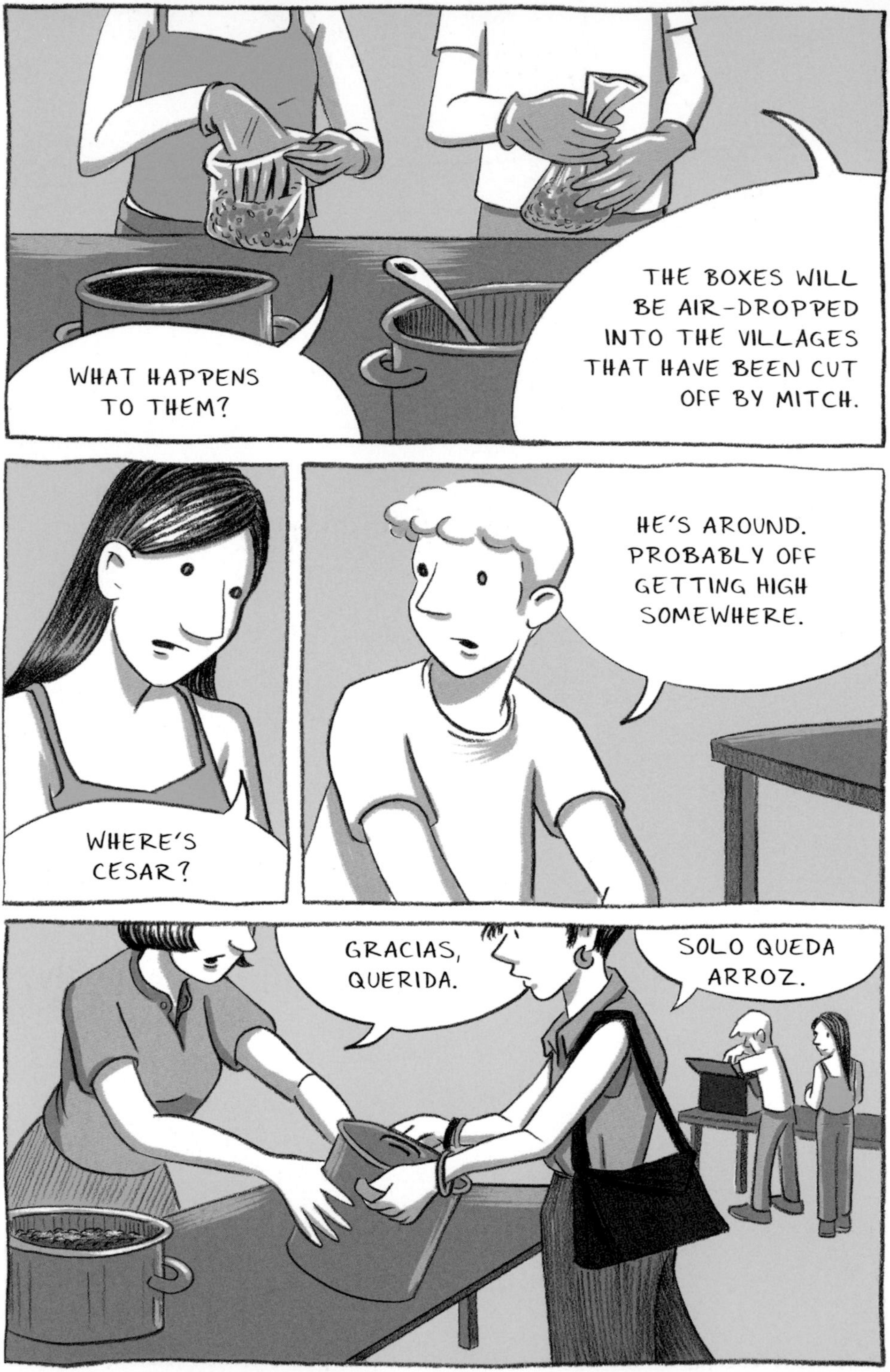
WHAT HAPPENS TO THEM?
THE BOXES WILL BE AIR-DROPPED INTO THE VILLAGES THAT HAVE BEEN CUT OFF BY MITCH.
WHERE'S CESAR?
HE'S AROUND. PROBABLY OFF GETTING HIGH SOMEWHERE.
GRACIAS, QUERIDA.
SOLO QUEDA ARROZ.

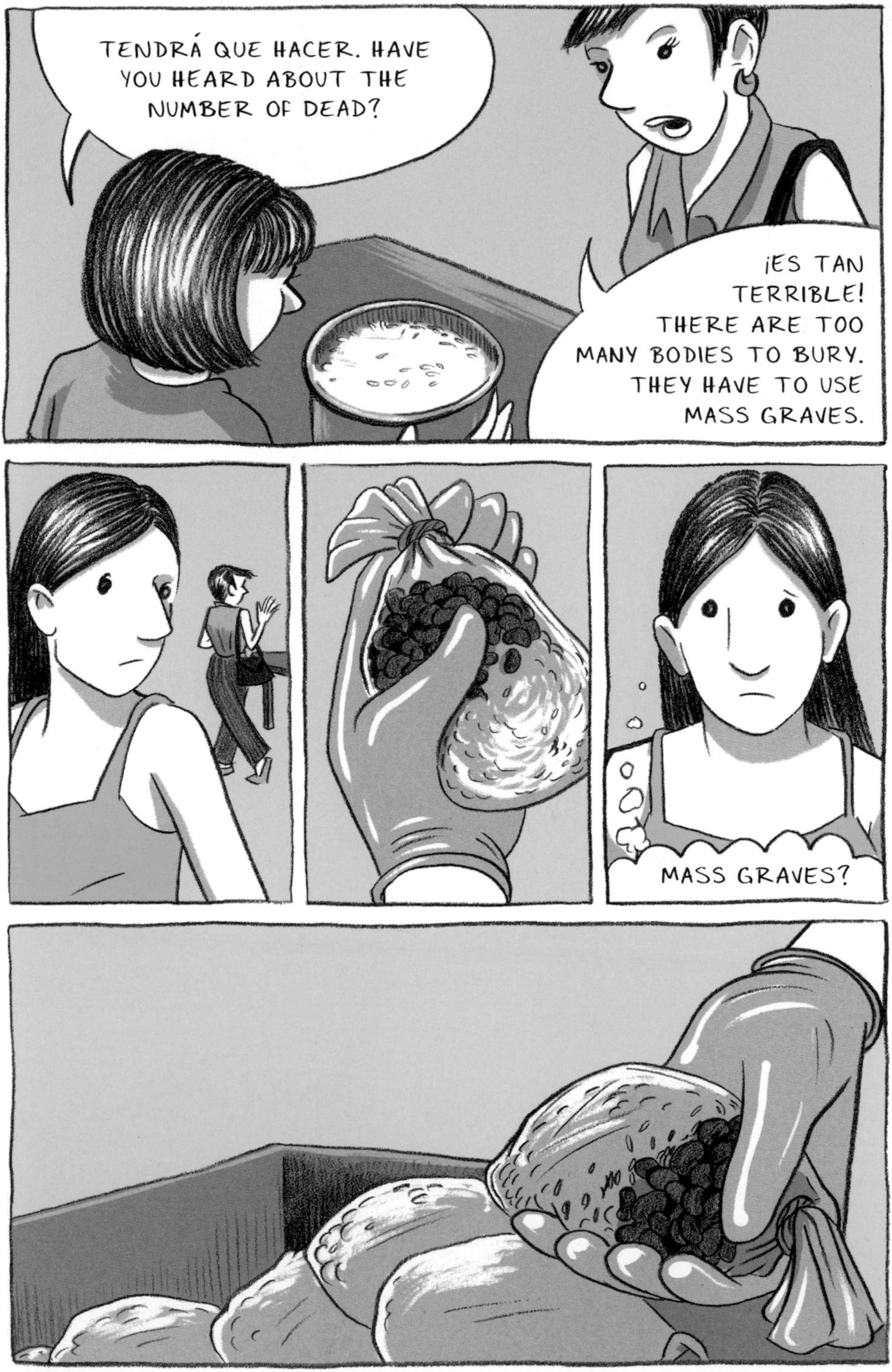
TENDRÁ QUE HACER. HAVE YOU HEARD ABOUT THE NUMBER OF DEAD?
¡ES TAN TERRIBLE! THERE ARE TOO MANY BODIES TO BURY. THEY HAVE TO USE MASS GRAVES.
MASS GRAVES?

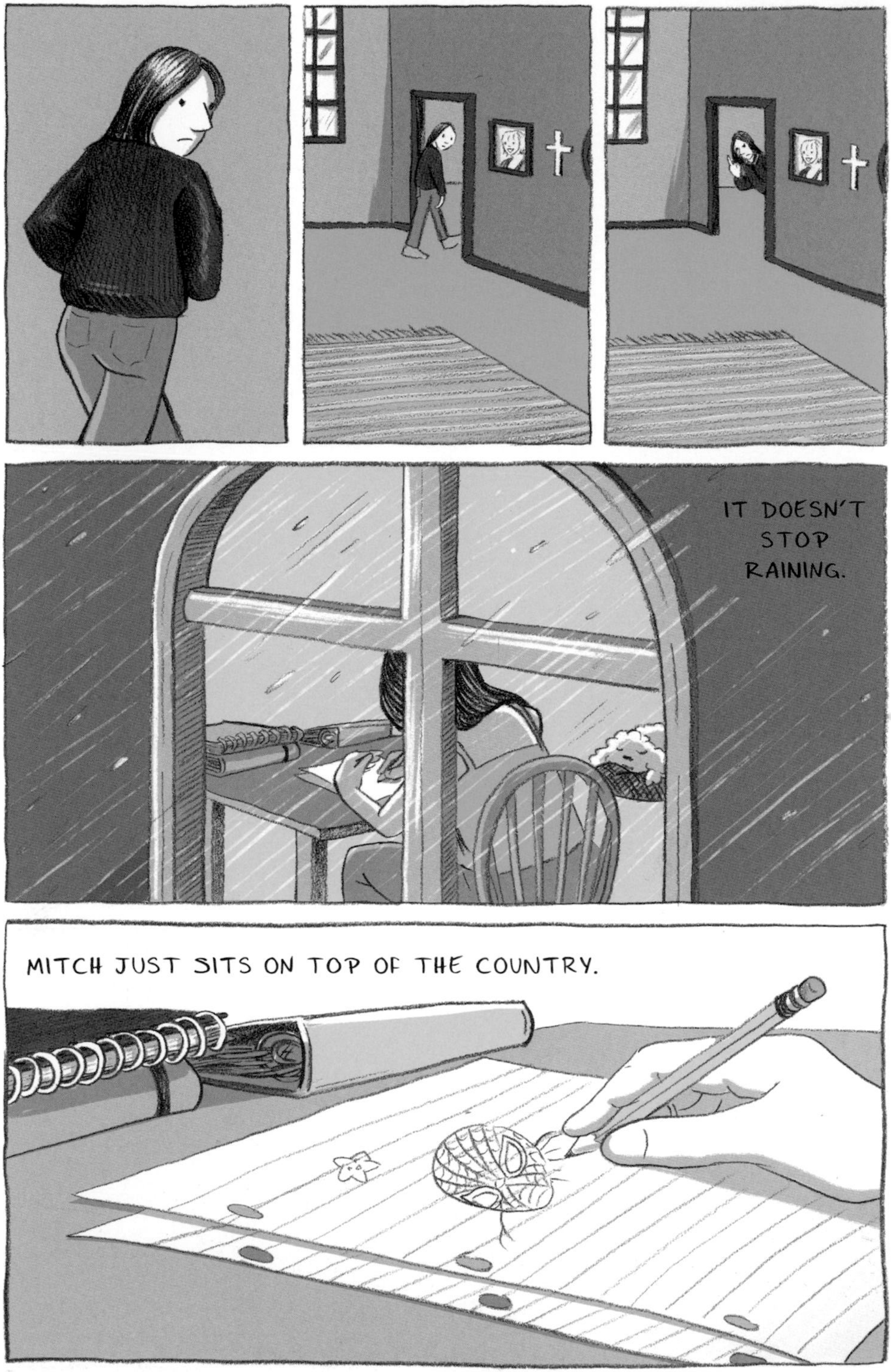
IT DOESN'T
STOP
RAINING.
MITCH JUST SITS ON TOP OF THE COUNTRY.

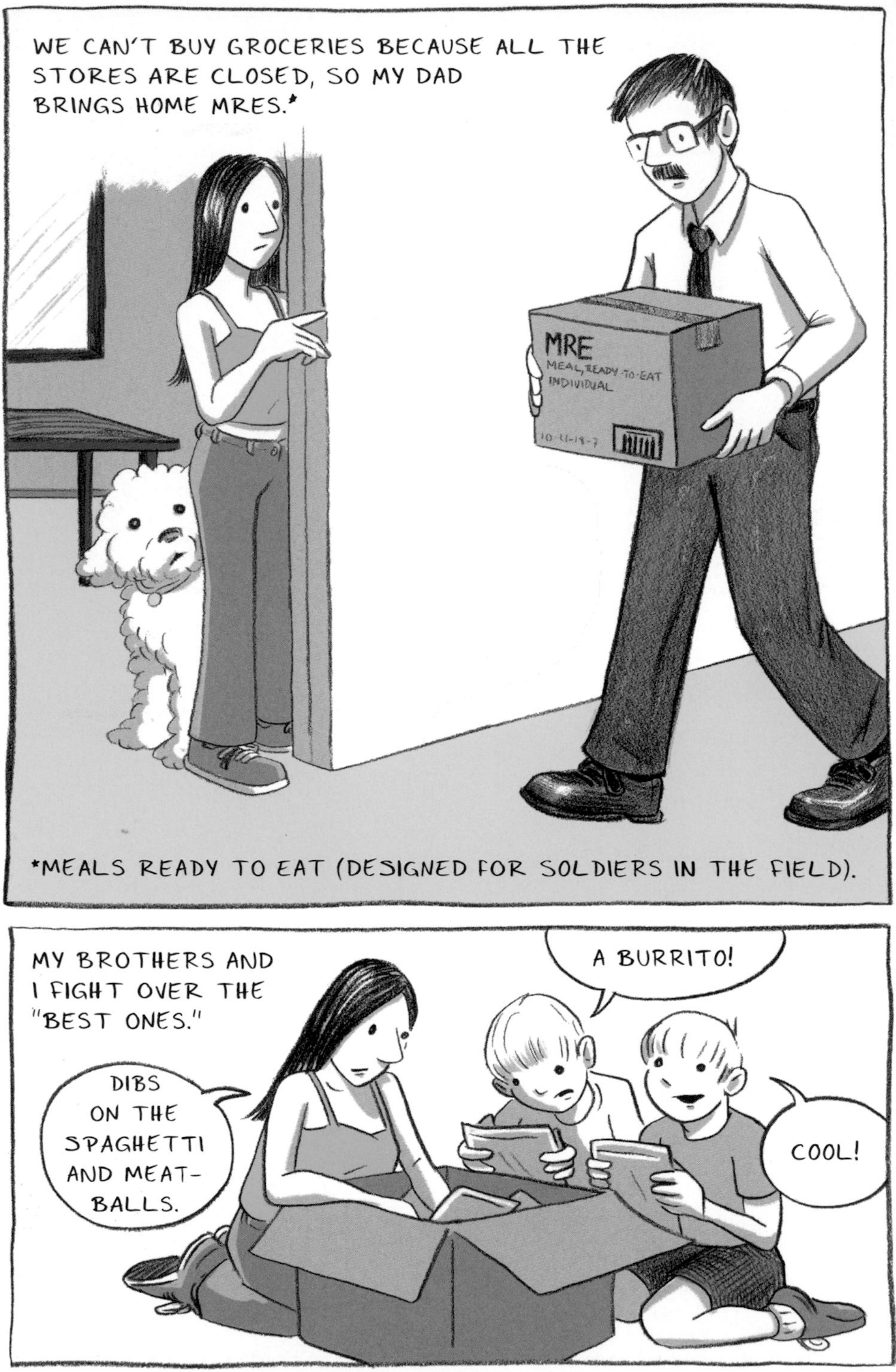
WE CAN'T BUY GROCERIES BECAUSE ALL THE STORES ARE CLOSED, SO MY DAD BRINGS HOME MRES.*
MRE
MEAL, READY-TO-EAT
INDIVIDUAL
*MEALS READY TO EAT (DESIGNED FOR SOLDIERS IN THE FIELD).
MY BROTHERS AND I FIGHT OVER THE "BEST ONES."
DIBS ON THE SPAGHETTI AND MEAT-BALLS.
A BURRITO!
COOL!

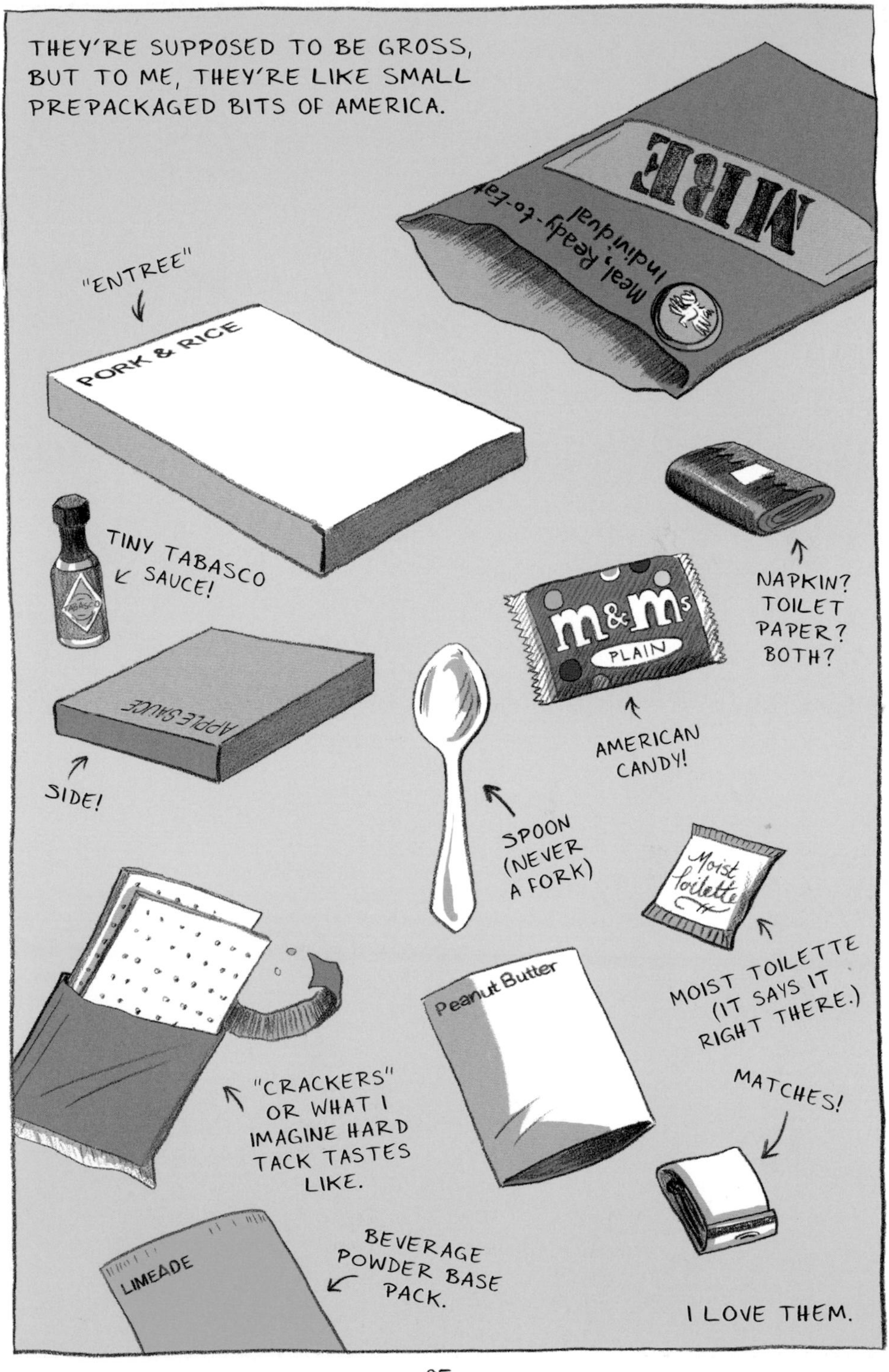
THEY'RE SUPPOSED TO BE GROSS, BUT TO ME, THEY'RE LIKE SMALL PREPACKAGED BITS OF AMERICA.
MRE
Meal, Ready-to-Eat
Individual
"ENTREE"
PORK & RICE
TINY TABASCO SAUCE!
APPLE SAUCE
SIDE!
m&m's
PLAIN
AMERICAN CANDY!
NAPKIN? TOILET PAPER? BOTH?
SPOON (NEVER A FORK)
Moist Toilette
MOIST TOILETTE (IT SAYS IT RIGHT THERE.)
Peanut Butter
"CRACKERS" OR WHAT I IMAGINE HARD TACK TASTES LIKE.
MATCHES!
LIMEADE
BEVERAGE POWDER BASE PACK.
I LOVE THEM.

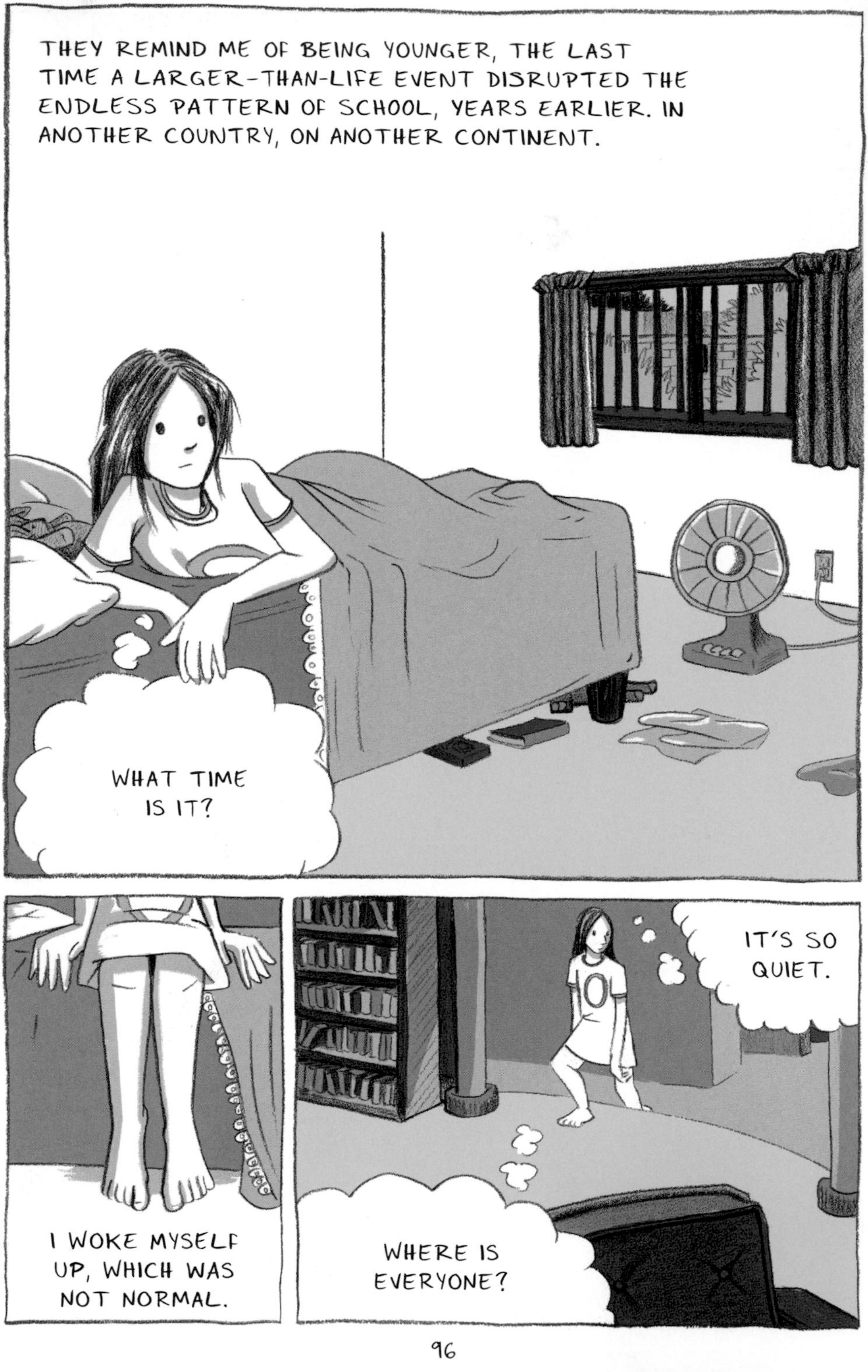
THEY REMIND ME OF BEING YOUNGER, THE LAST TIME A LARGER-THAN-LIFE EVENT DISRUPTED THE ENDLESS PATTERN OF SCHOOL, YEARS EARLIER. IN ANOTHER COUNTRY, ON ANOTHER CONTINENT.
WHAT TIME IS IT?
I WOKE MYSELF UP, WHICH WAS NOT NORMAL.
IT'S SO QUIET.
WHERE IS EVERYONE?

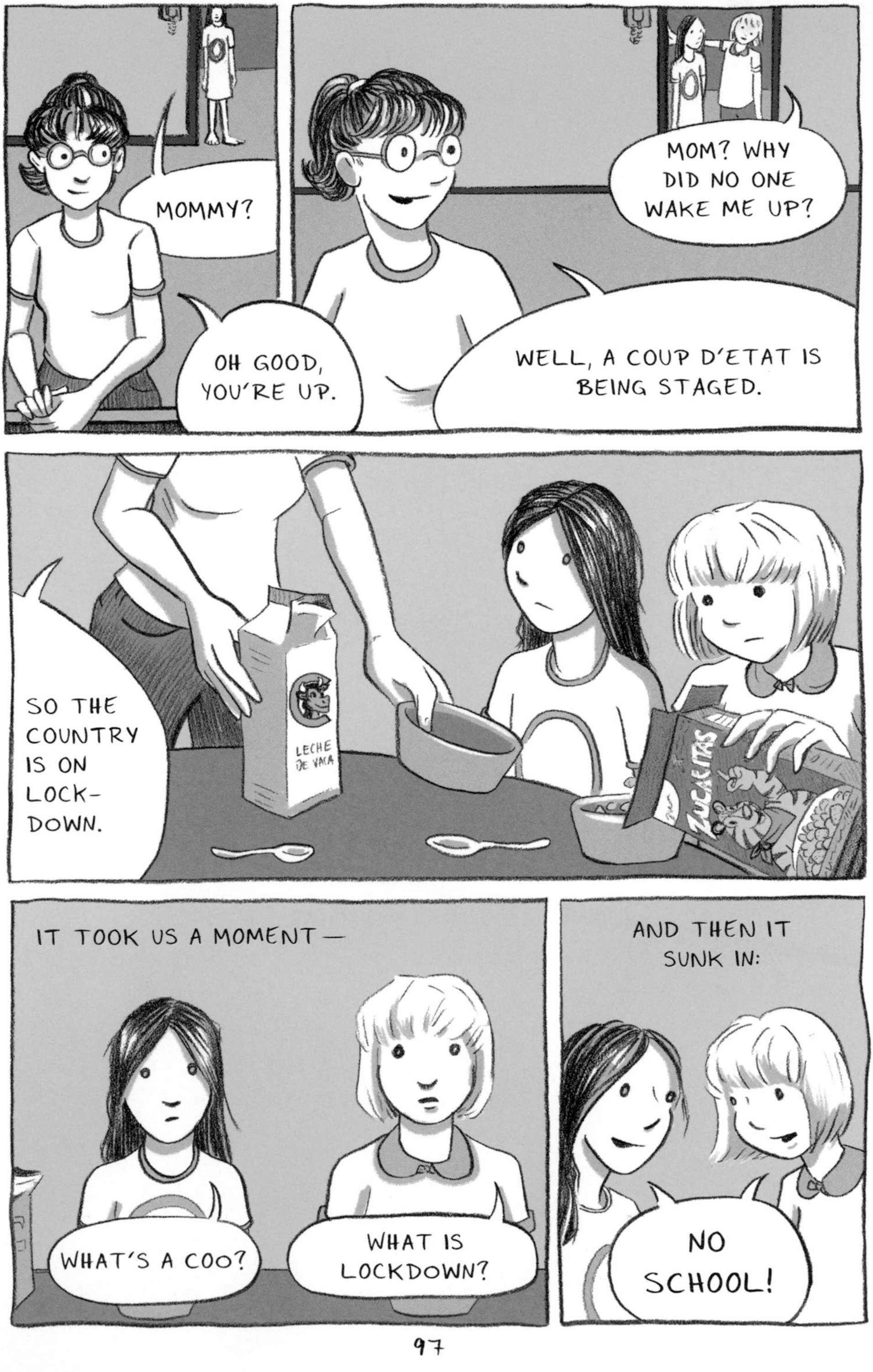
MOMMY?
MOM? WHY DID NO ONE WAKE ME UP?
OH GOOD, YOU'RE UP.
WELL, A COUP D'ETAT IS BEING STAGED.
SO THE COUNTRY IS ON LOCK-DOWN.
LECHE DE VACA
ZUCARITAS
IT TOOK US A MOMENT—
WHAT'S A COO?
WHAT IS LOCKDOWN?
AND THEN IT SUNK IN:
NO SCHOOL!

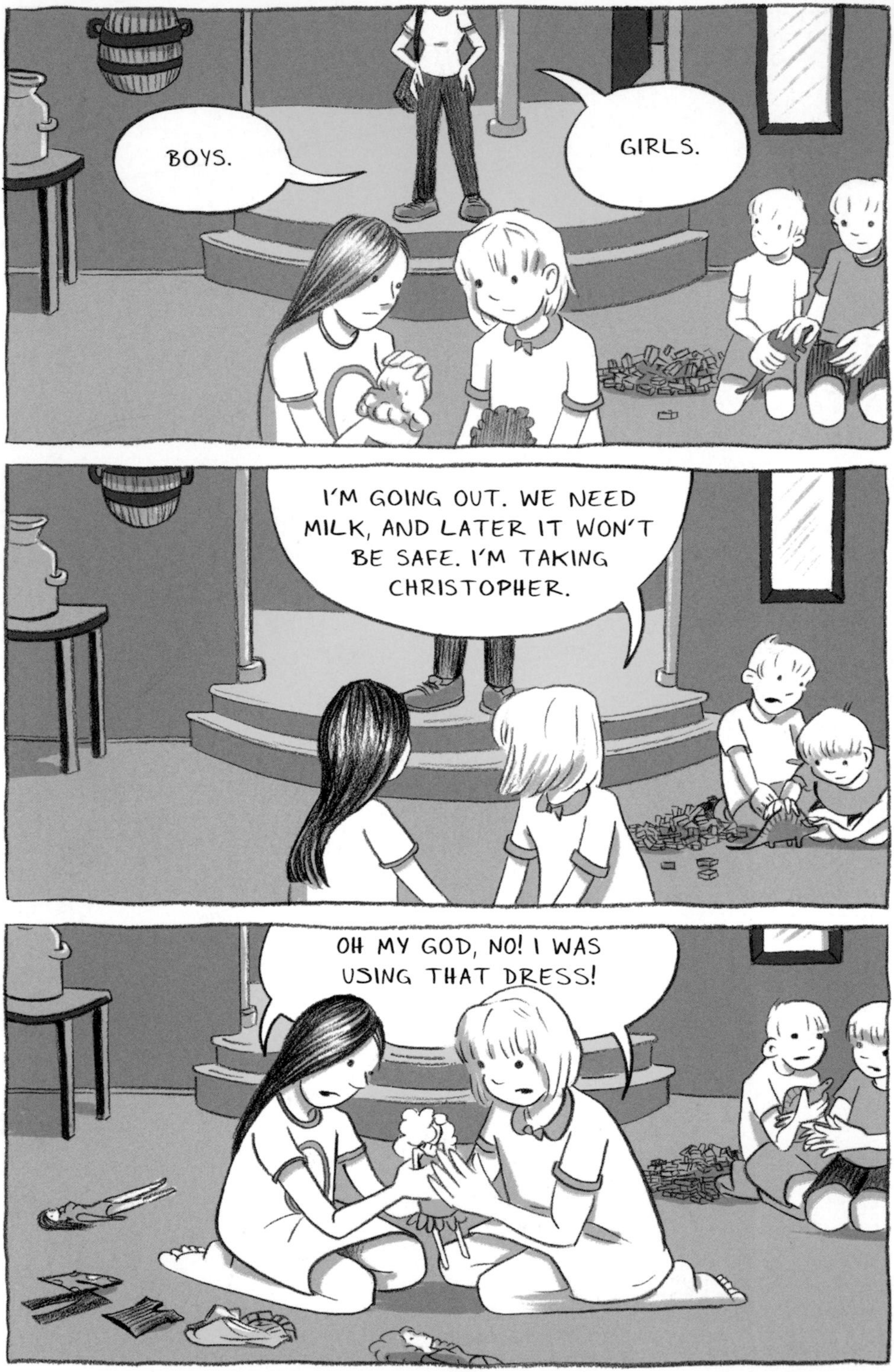
BOYS.
GIRLS.
I'M GOING OUT. WE NEED MILK, AND LATER IT WON'T BE SAFE. I'M TAKING CHRISTOPHER.
OH MY GOD, NO! I WAS USING THAT DRESS!

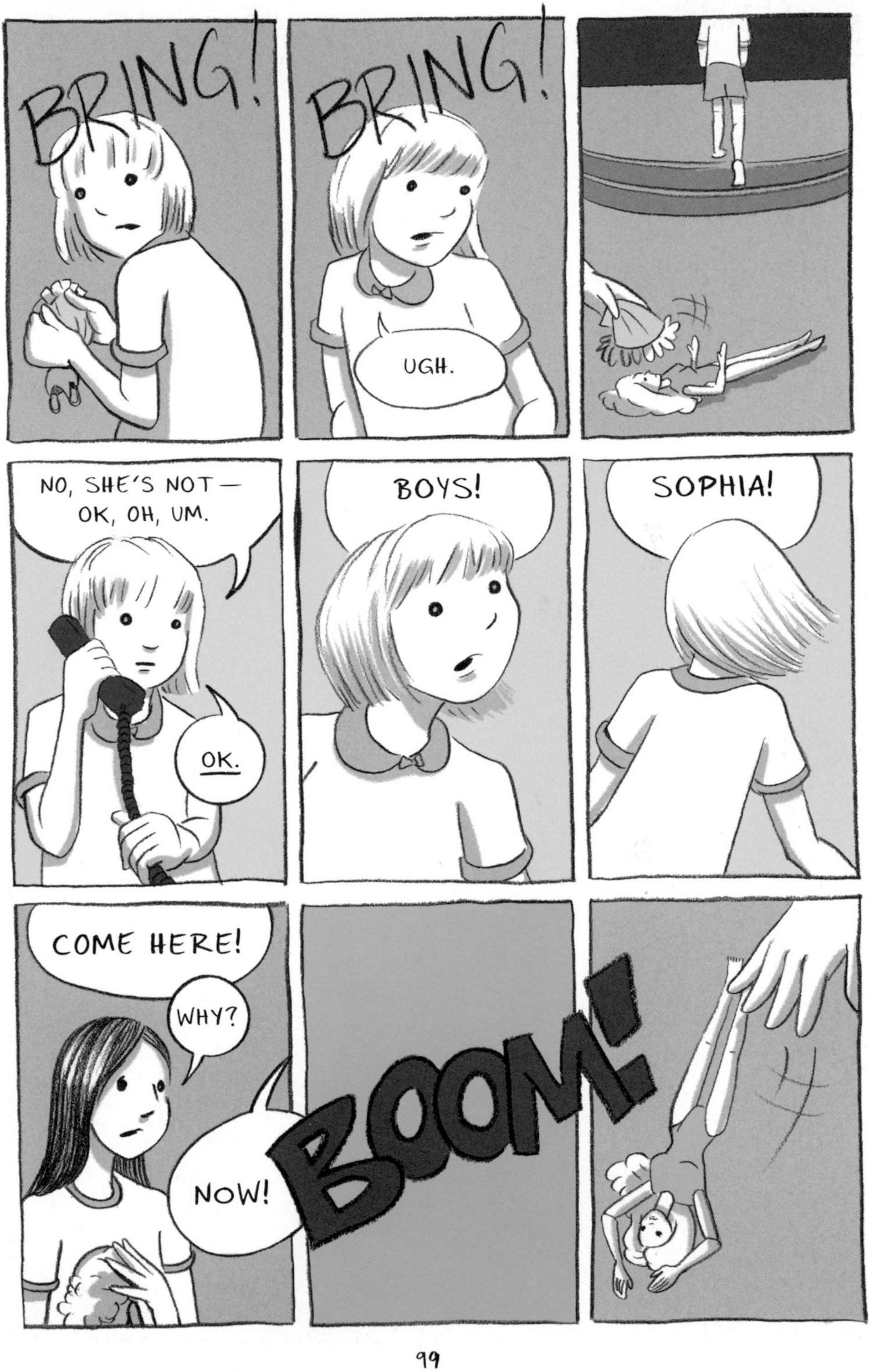
BRING!
BRING!
UGH.
NO, SHE'S NOT—
OK, OH, UM.
OK.
BOYS!
SOPHIA!
COME HERE!
WHY?
NOW!
BOOM!

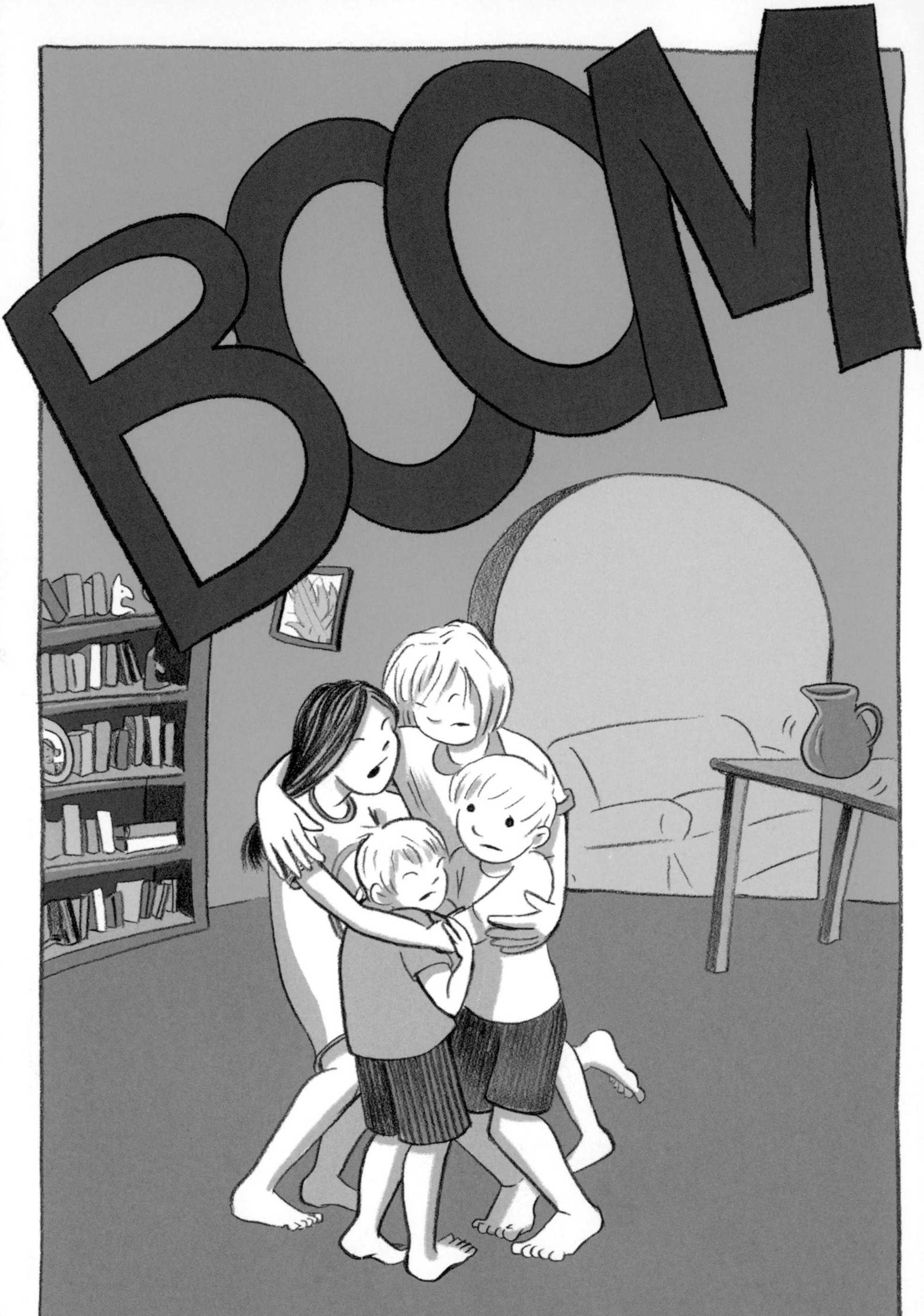
BOOM

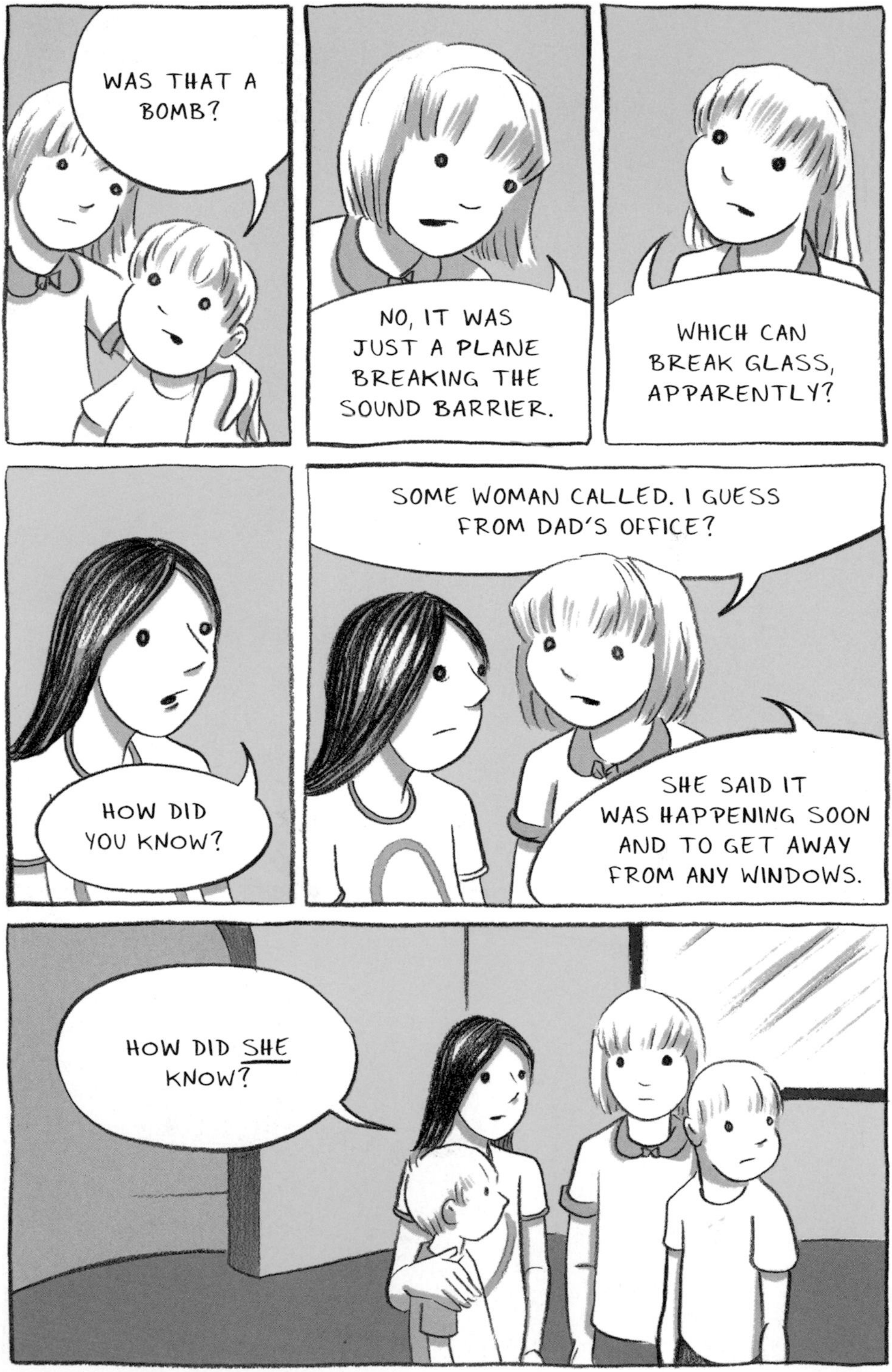
WAS THAT A BOMB?
NO, IT WAS JUST A PLANE BREAKING THE SOUND BARRIER.
WHICH CAN BREAK GLASS, APPARENTLY?
HOW DID YOU KNOW?
SOME WOMAN CALLED. I GUESS FROM DAD'S OFFICE?
SHE SAID IT WAS HAPPENING SOON AND TO GET AWAY FROM ANY WINDOWS.
HOW DID SHE KNOW?

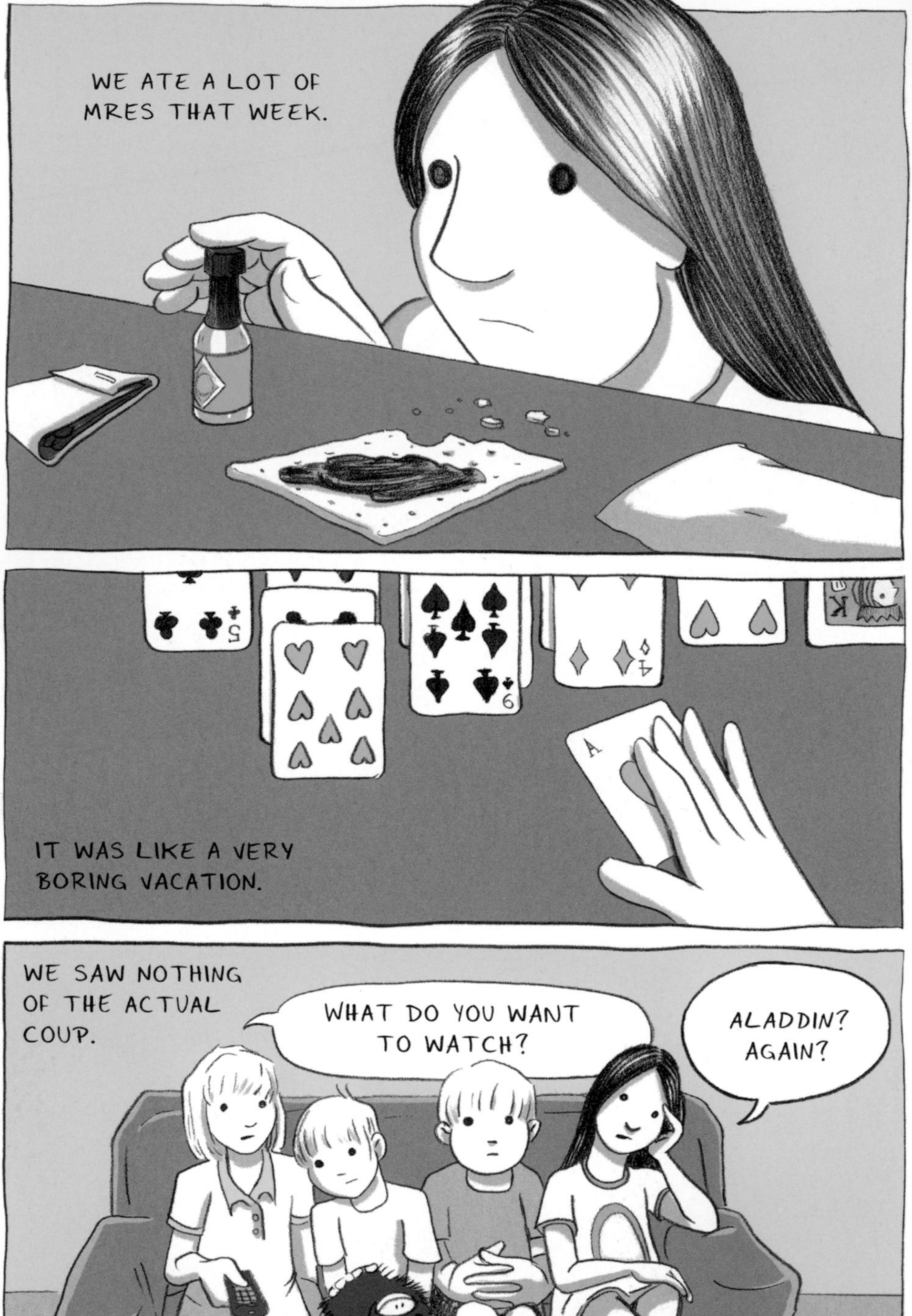
WE ATE A LOT OF MRES THAT WEEK.
IT WAS LIKE A VERY BORING VACATION.
WE SAW NOTHING OF THE ACTUAL COUP.
WHAT DO YOU WANT TO WATCH?
ALADDIN? AGAIN?

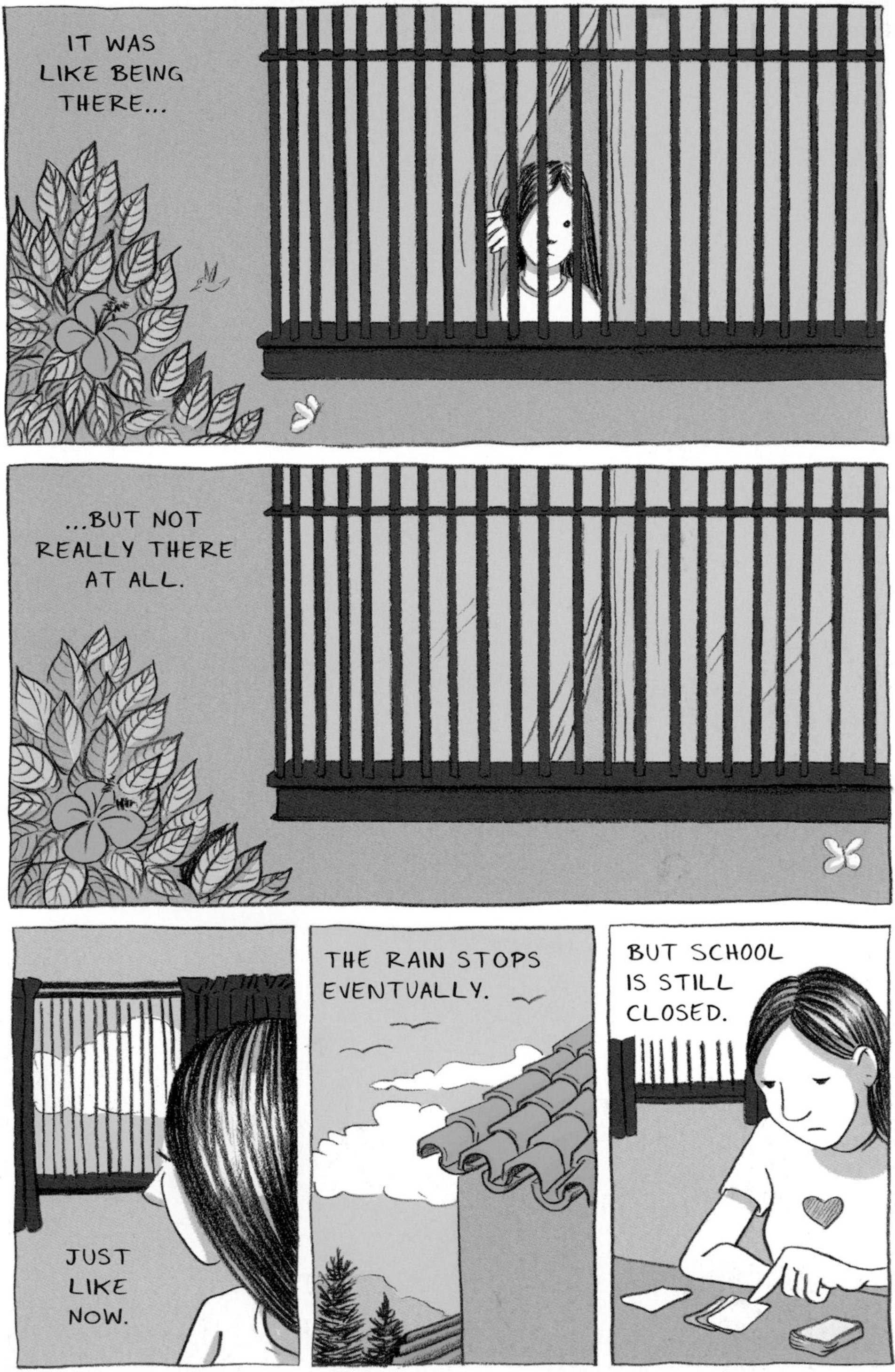
IT WAS LIKE BEING THERE...
...BUT NOT REALLY THERE AT ALL.
JUST LIKE NOW.
THE RAIN STOPS EVENTUALLY.
BUT SCHOOL IS STILL CLOSED.

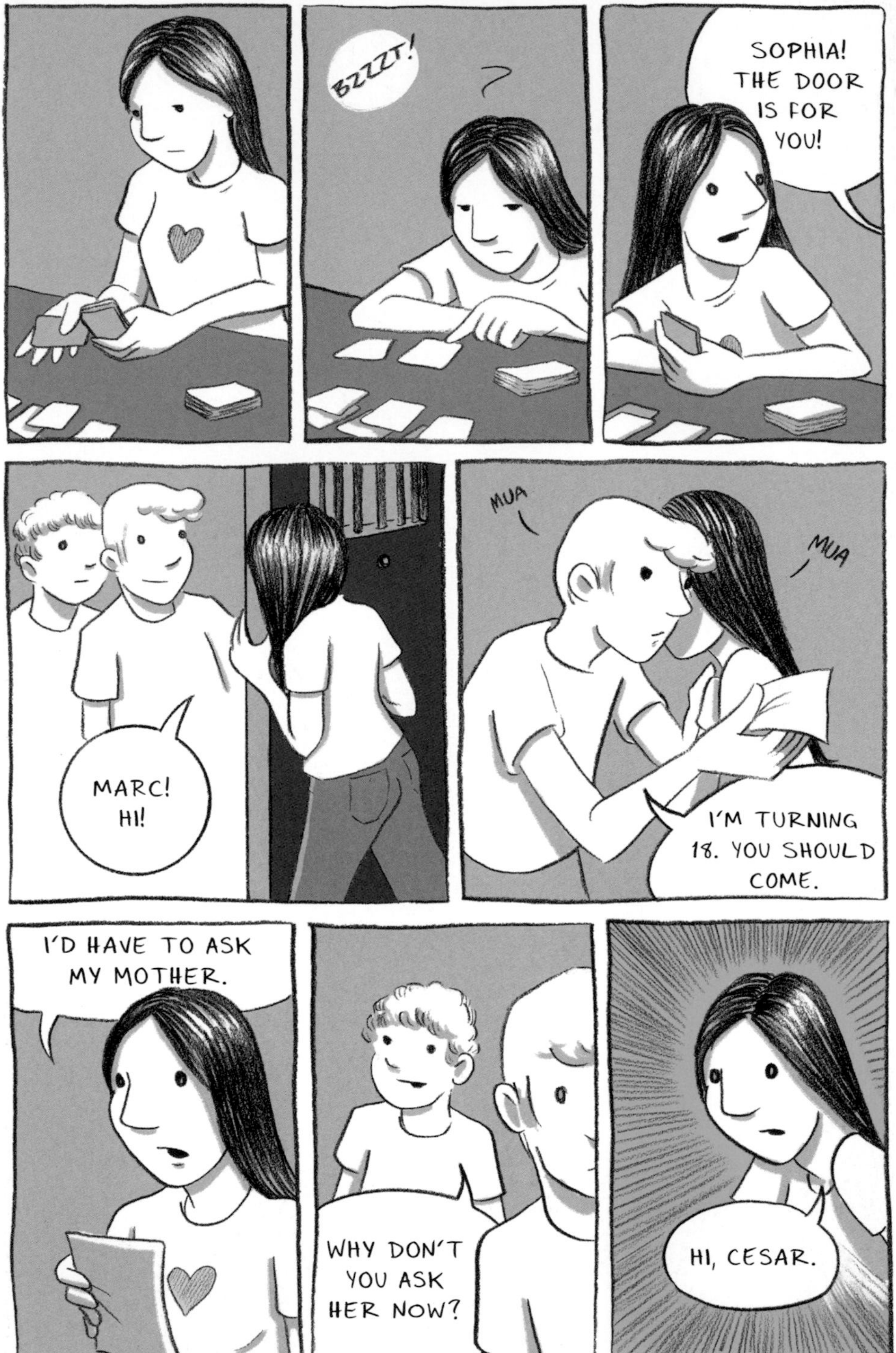
BZZZT!
?
SOPHIA! THE DOOR IS FOR YOU!
MARC! HI!
MUA
MUA
I'M TURNING 18. YOU SHOULD COME.
I'D HAVE TO ASK MY MOTHER.
WHY DON'T YOU ASK HER NOW?
HI, CESAR.

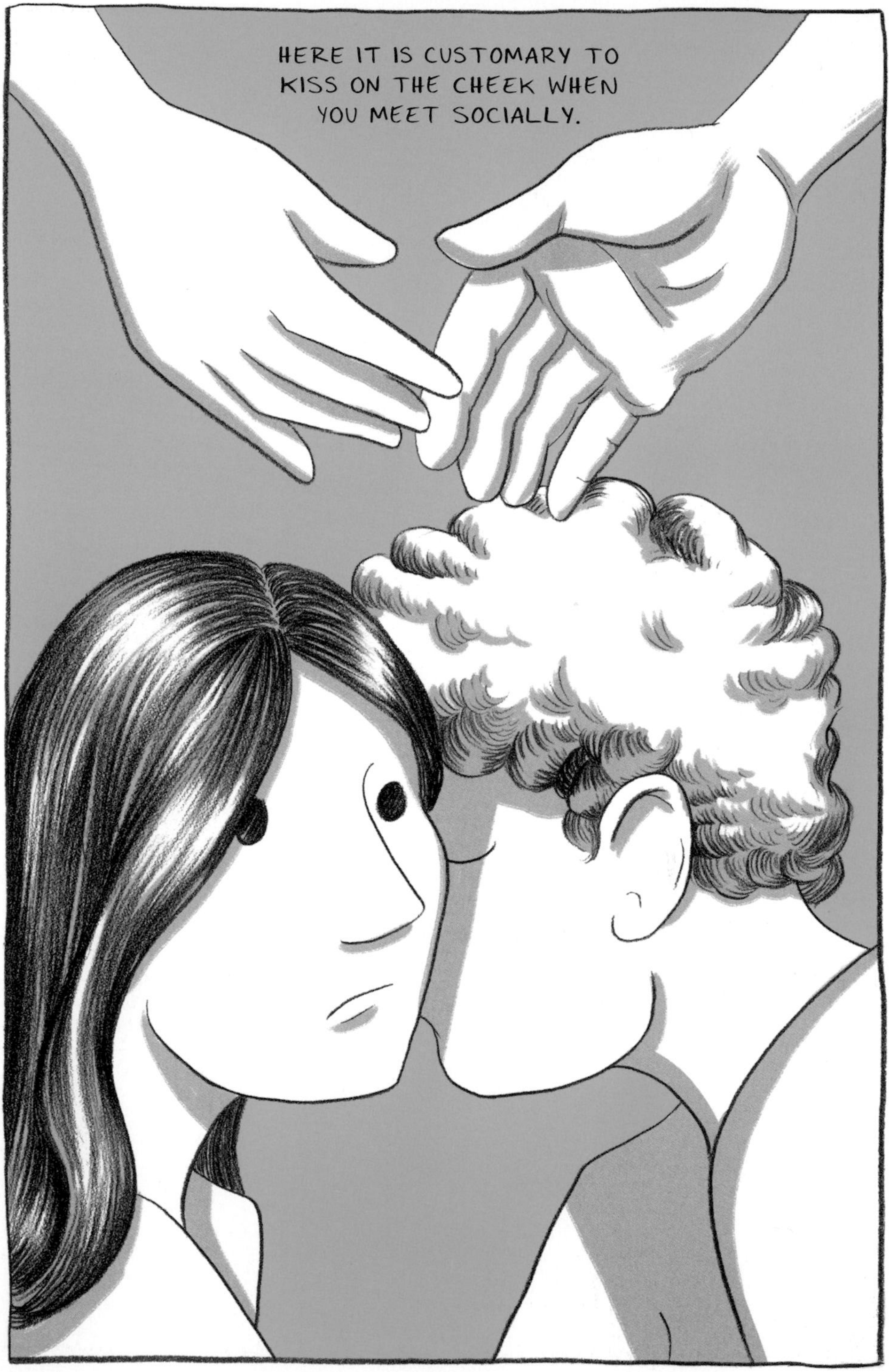
HERE IT IS CUSTOMARY TO KISS ON THE CHEEK WHEN YOU MEET SOCIALLY.

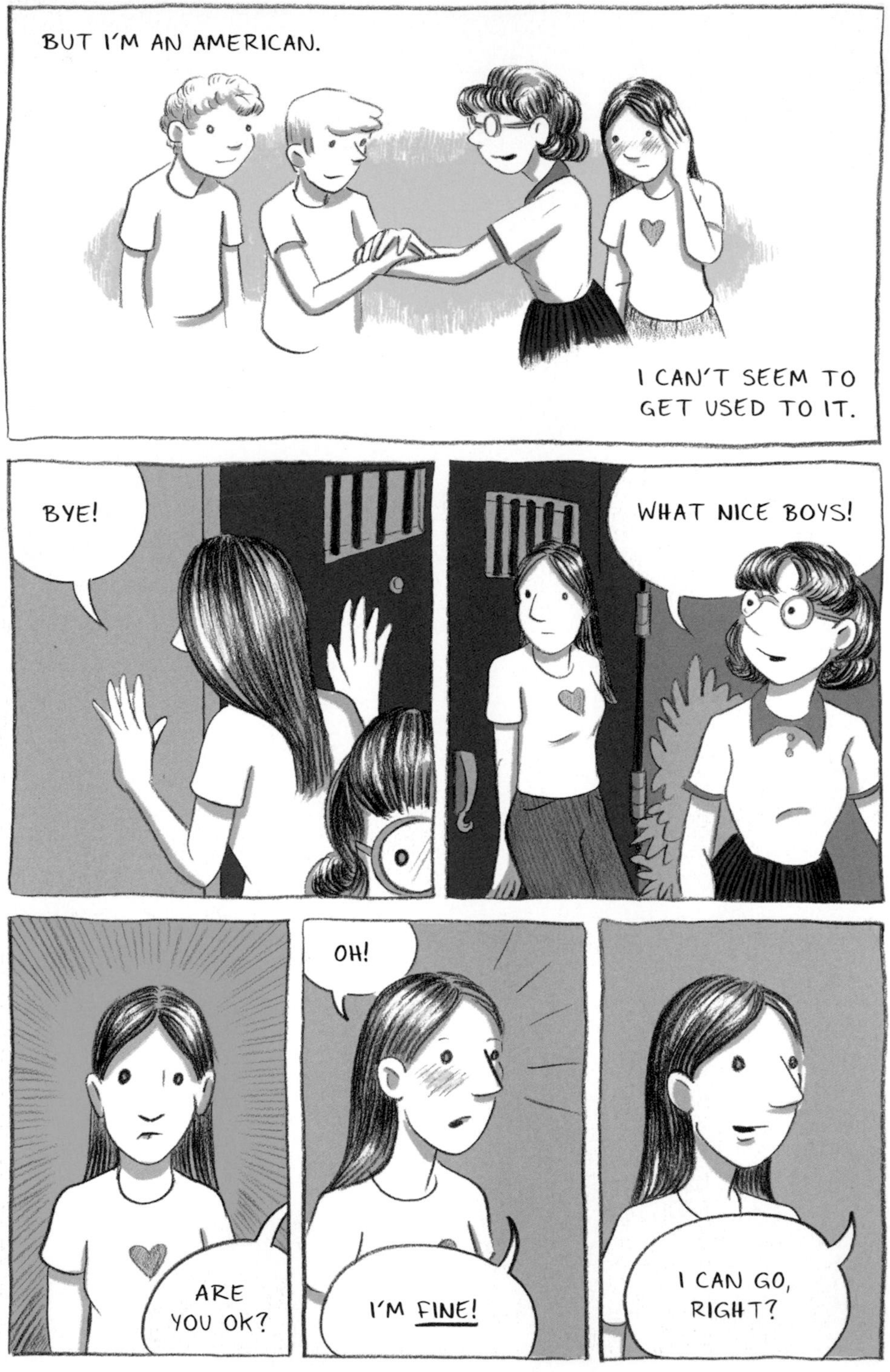
BUT I'M AN AMERICAN.
I CAN'T SEEM TO GET USED TO IT.
BYE!
WHAT NICE BOYS!
ARE YOU OK?
OH!
I'M FINE!
I CAN GO, RIGHT?

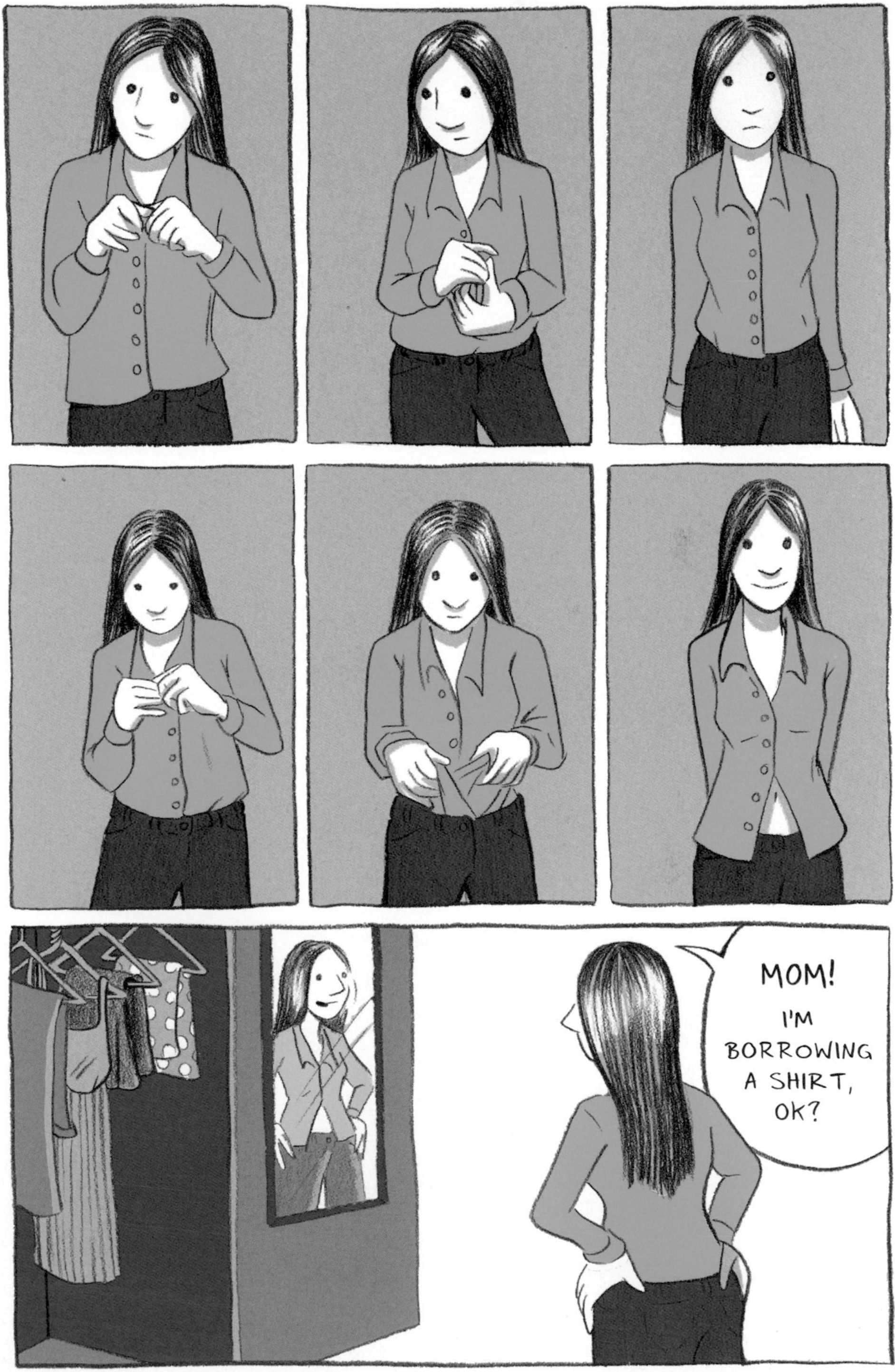
MOM!
I'M BORROWING A SHIRT, OK?

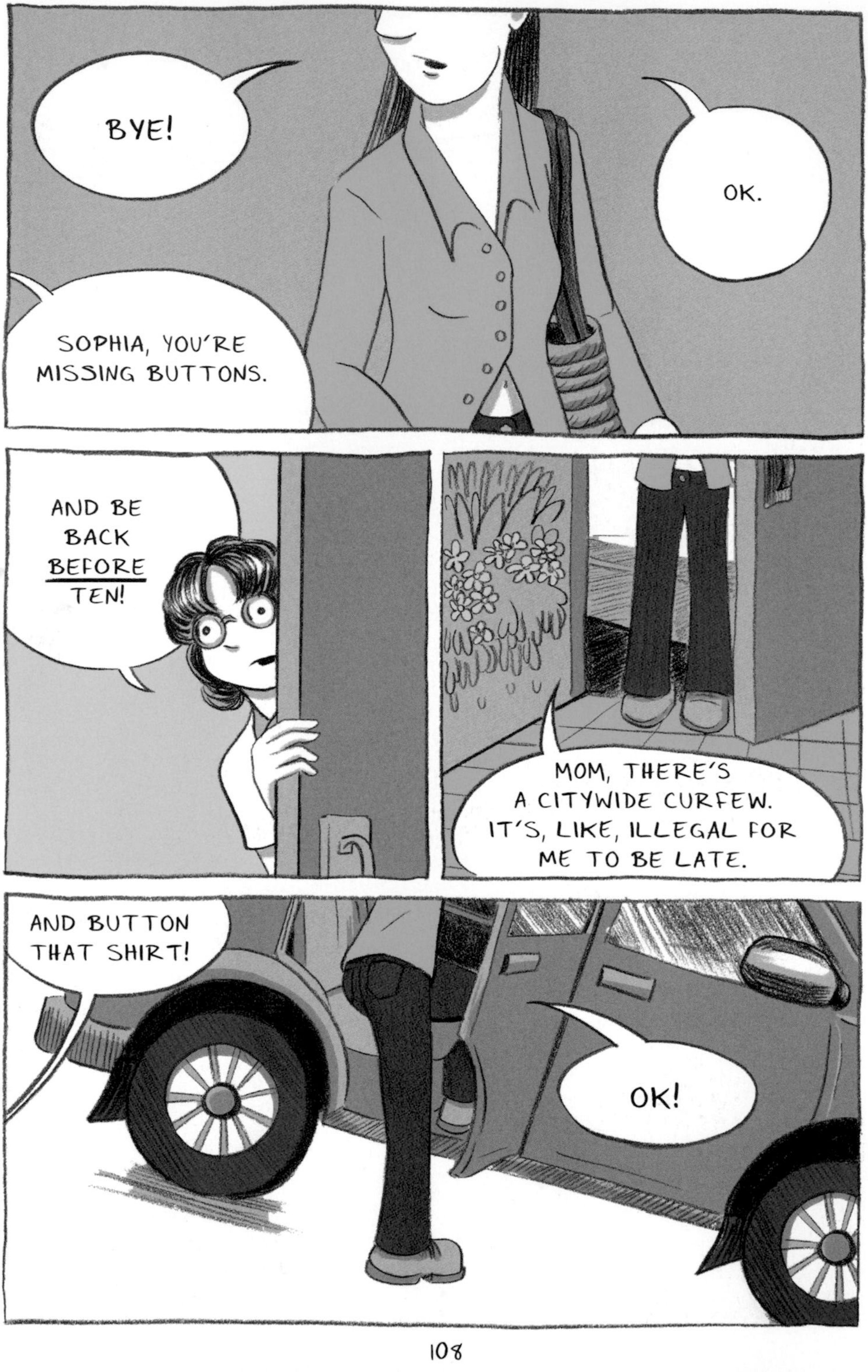
BYE!
OK.
SOPHIA, YOU'RE MISSING BUTTONS.
AND BE BACK BEFORE TEN!
MOM, THERE'S A CITYWIDE CURFEW. IT'S, LIKE, ILLEGAL FOR ME TO BE LATE.
AND BUTTON THAT SHIRT!
OK!

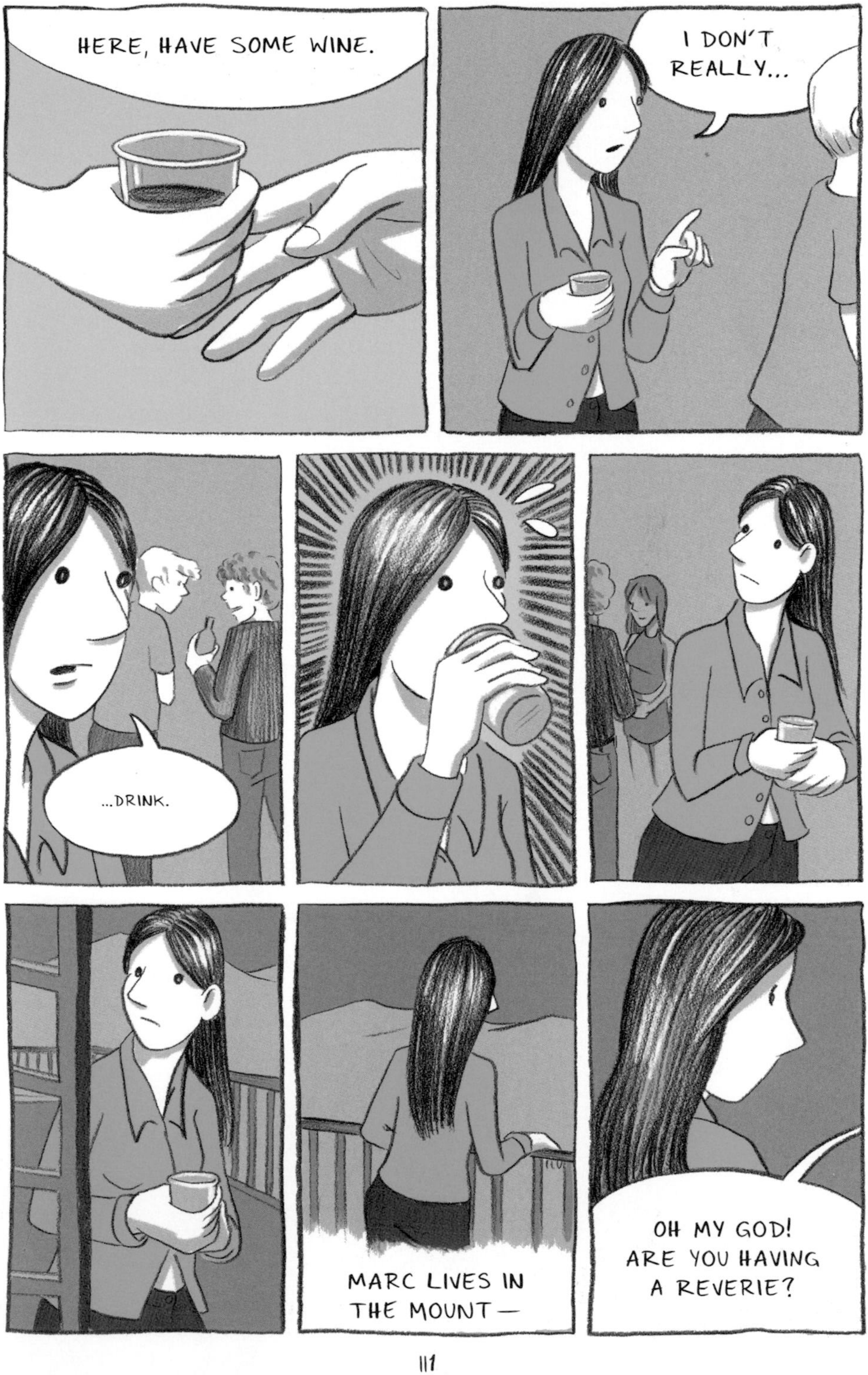
HERE, HAVE SOME WINE.
I DON'T REALLY...
...DRINK.
MARC LIVES IN THE MOUNT—
OH MY GOD! ARE YOU HAVING A REVERIE?

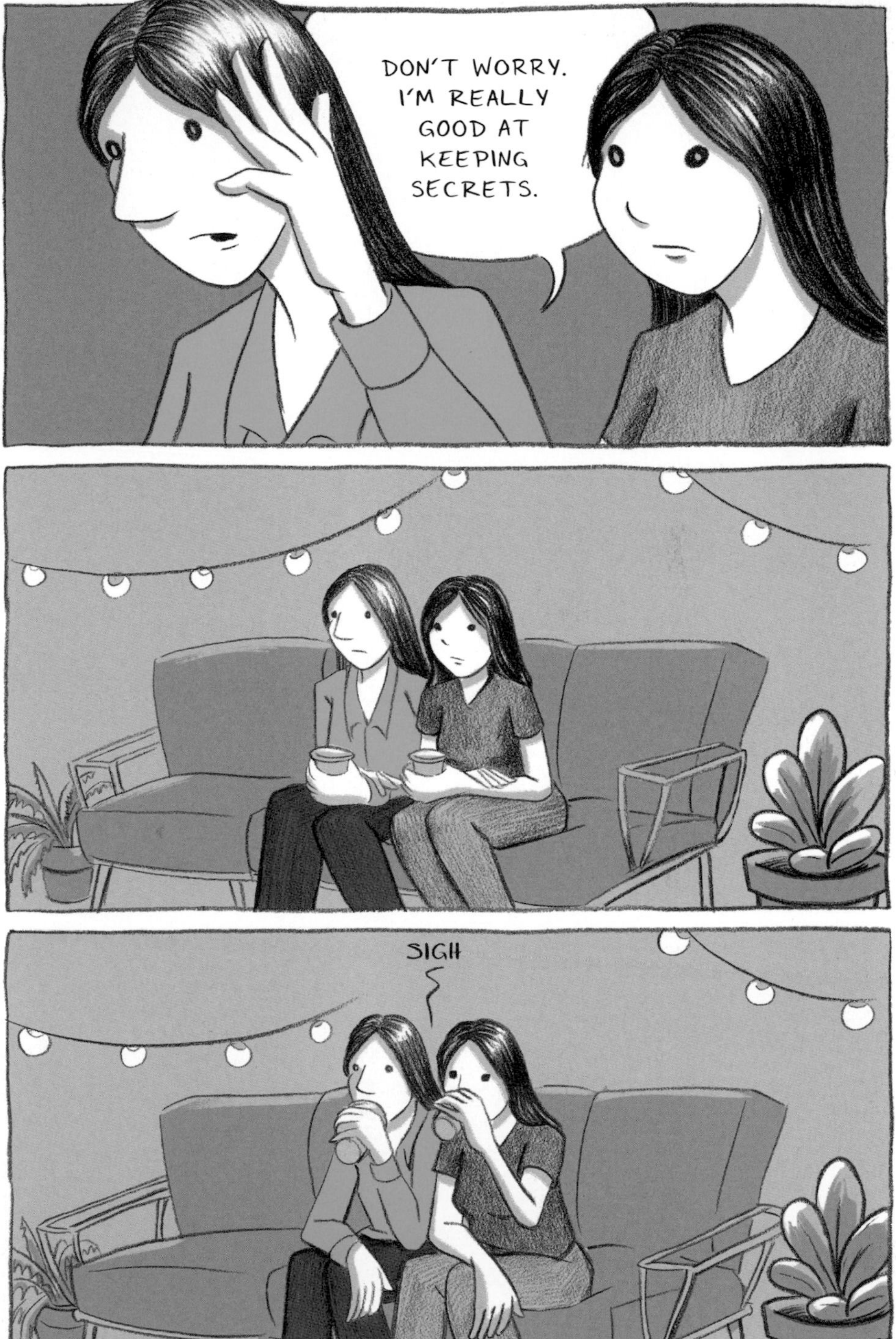
DON'T WORRY. I'M REALLY GOOD AT KEEPING SECRETS.
SIGH

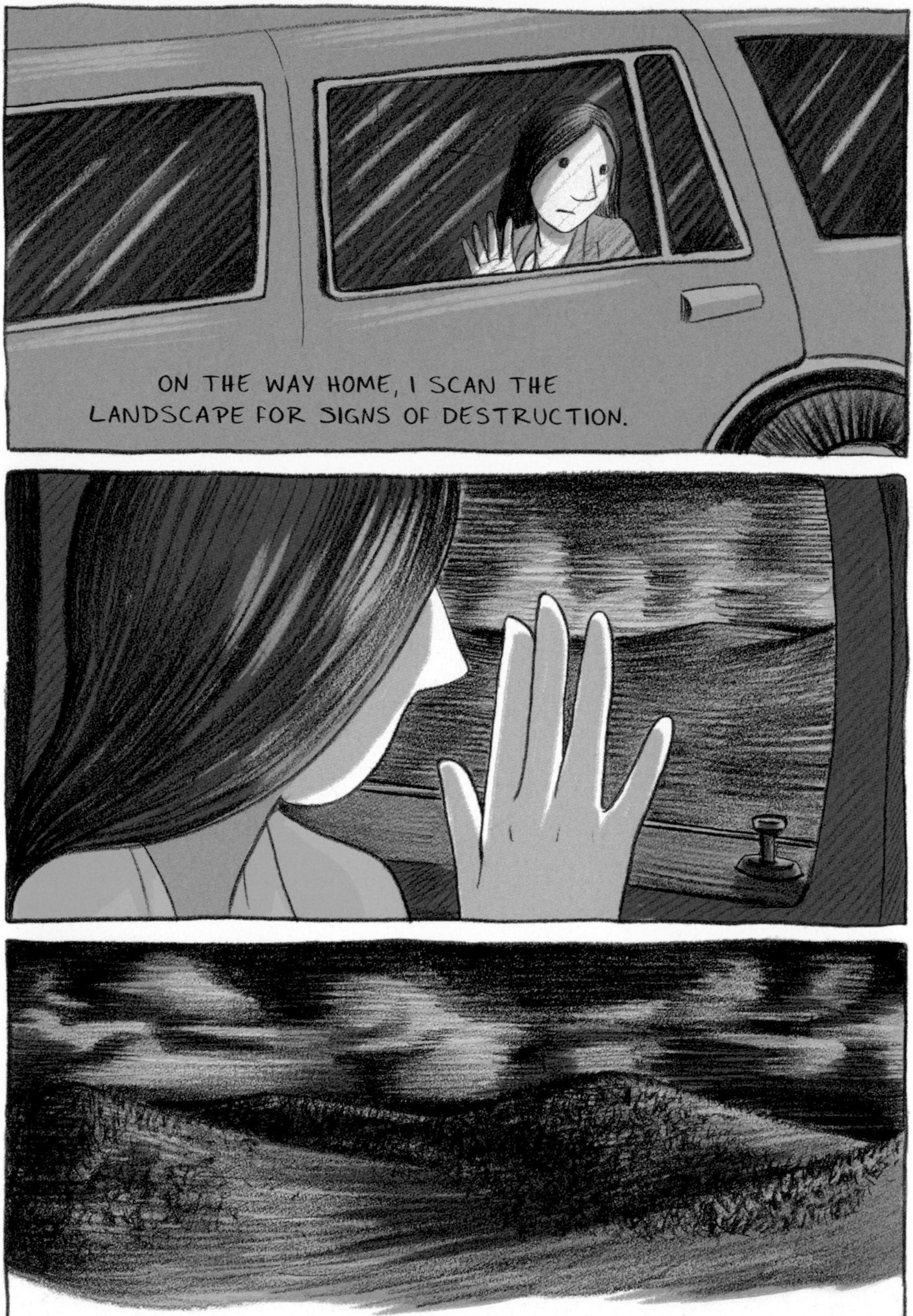
ON THE WAY HOME, I SCAN THE LANDSCAPE FOR SIGNS OF DESTRUCTION.
BUT IT'S SO DARK I CAN'T SEE ANYTHING.

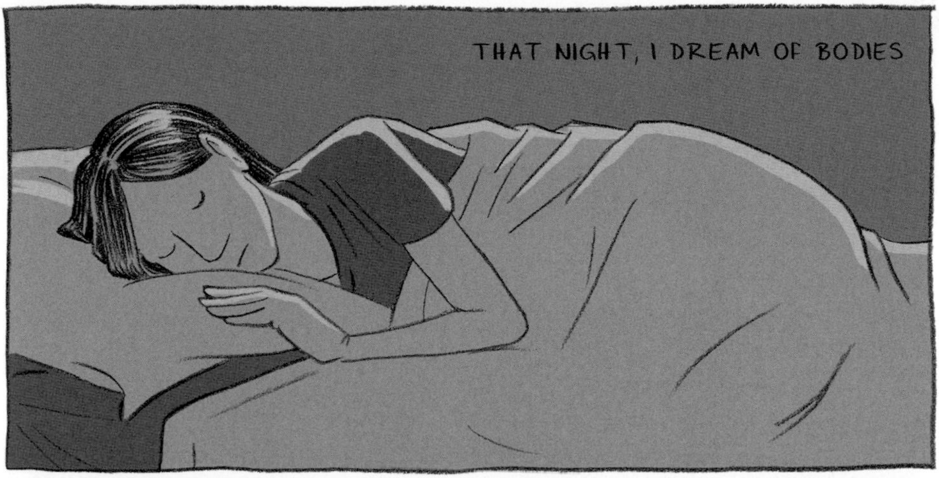
THAT NIGHT, I DREAM OF BODIES

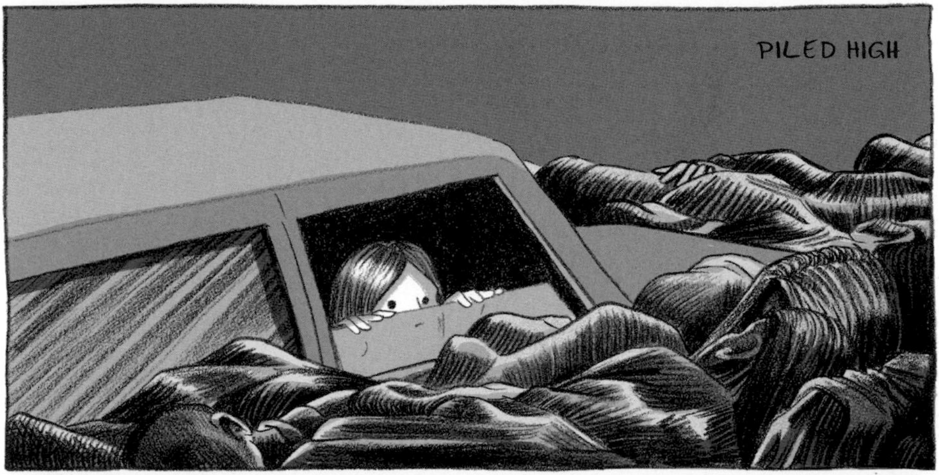
PILED HIGH

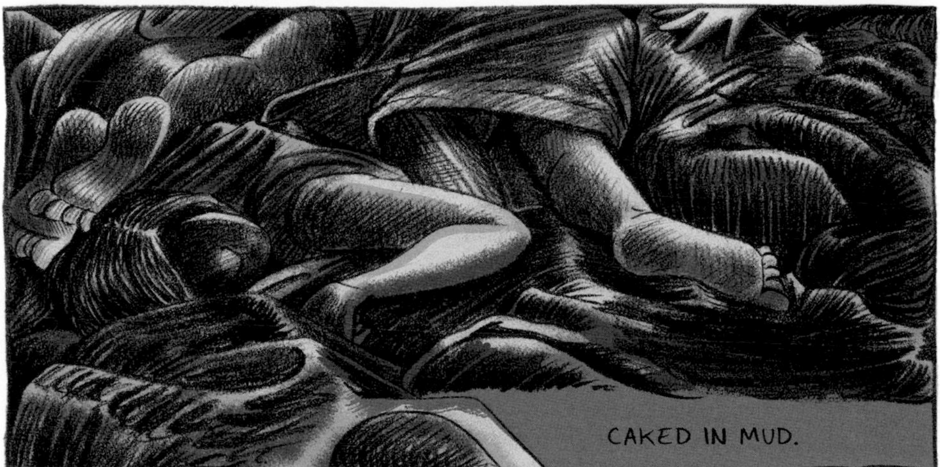
CAKED IN MUD.

120

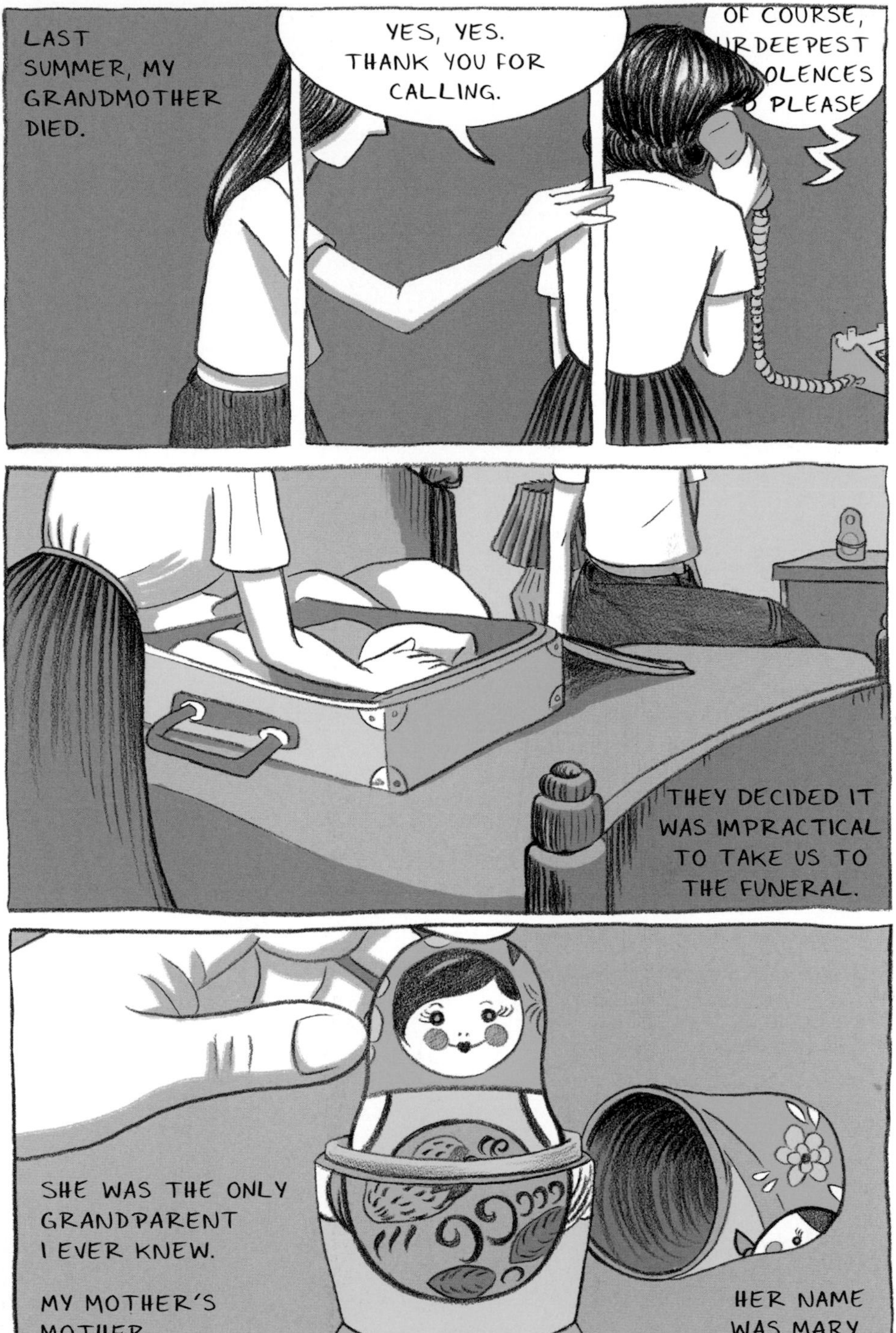
LAST SUMMER, MY GRANDMOTHER DIED.
YES, YES. THANK YOU FOR CALLING.
OF COURSE, RDEEPEST OLENCES PLEASE
THEY DECIDED IT WAS IMPRACTICAL TO TAKE US TO THE FUNERAL.
SHE WAS THE ONLY GRANDPARENT I EVER KNEW.
MY MOTHER'S MOTHER.
HER NAME WAS MARY.

11,000 PEOPLE DIE BECAUSE OF HURRICANE MITCH.

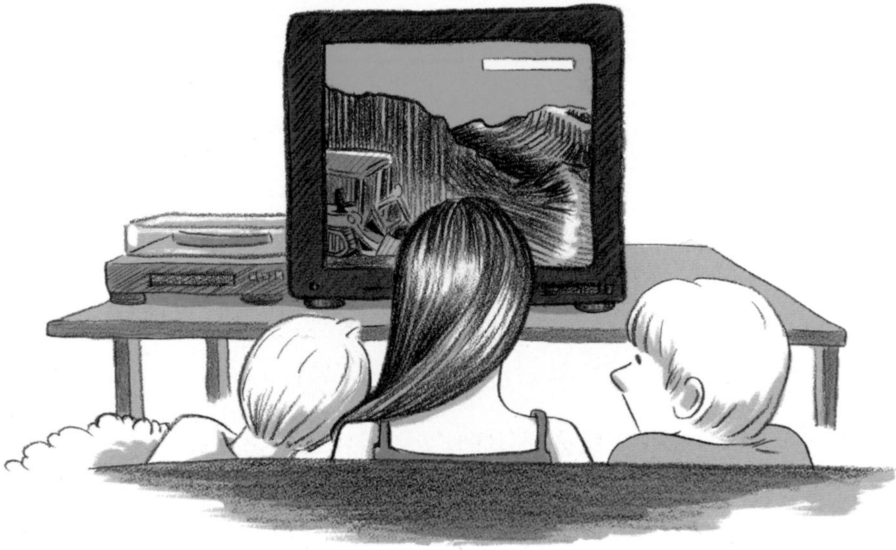

HUNDREDS OF THOUSANDS LOSE THEIR HOMES.
NO ONE I KNOW, THOUGH.

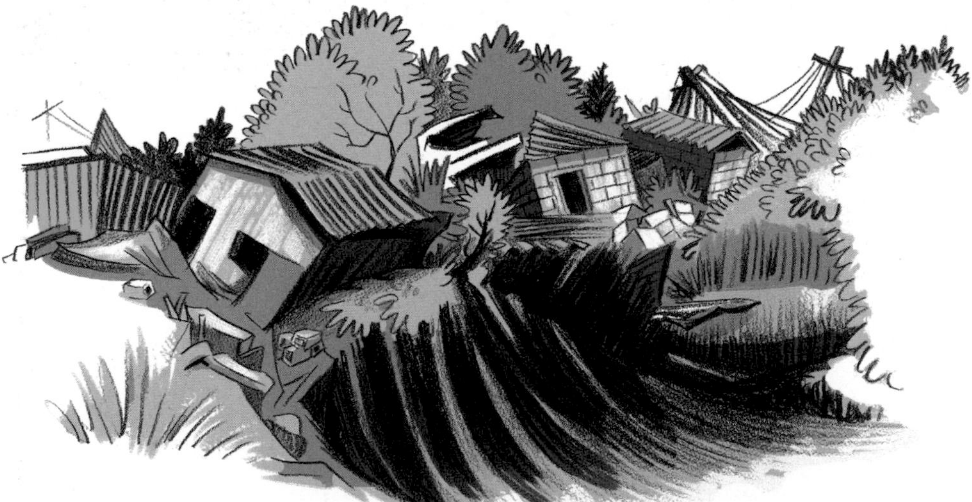

I WAS THERE. BUT AS USUAL,
I WASN'T ACTUALLY THERE.

DID I REALLY THINK
I'D MADE A DIFFERENCE
BY STUFFING RICE INTO
PLASTIC BAGS?

HOW DO YOU
COMPREHEND
IT?

HOW DOES
ANYTHING
GO BACK TO
NORMAL?

123

BUT IT DOES SOMEHOW.

SORT OF.

EXAM TODAY

A LOT OF AMERICAN FAMILIES ELECTED TO LEAVE DURING THE EVACUATION.

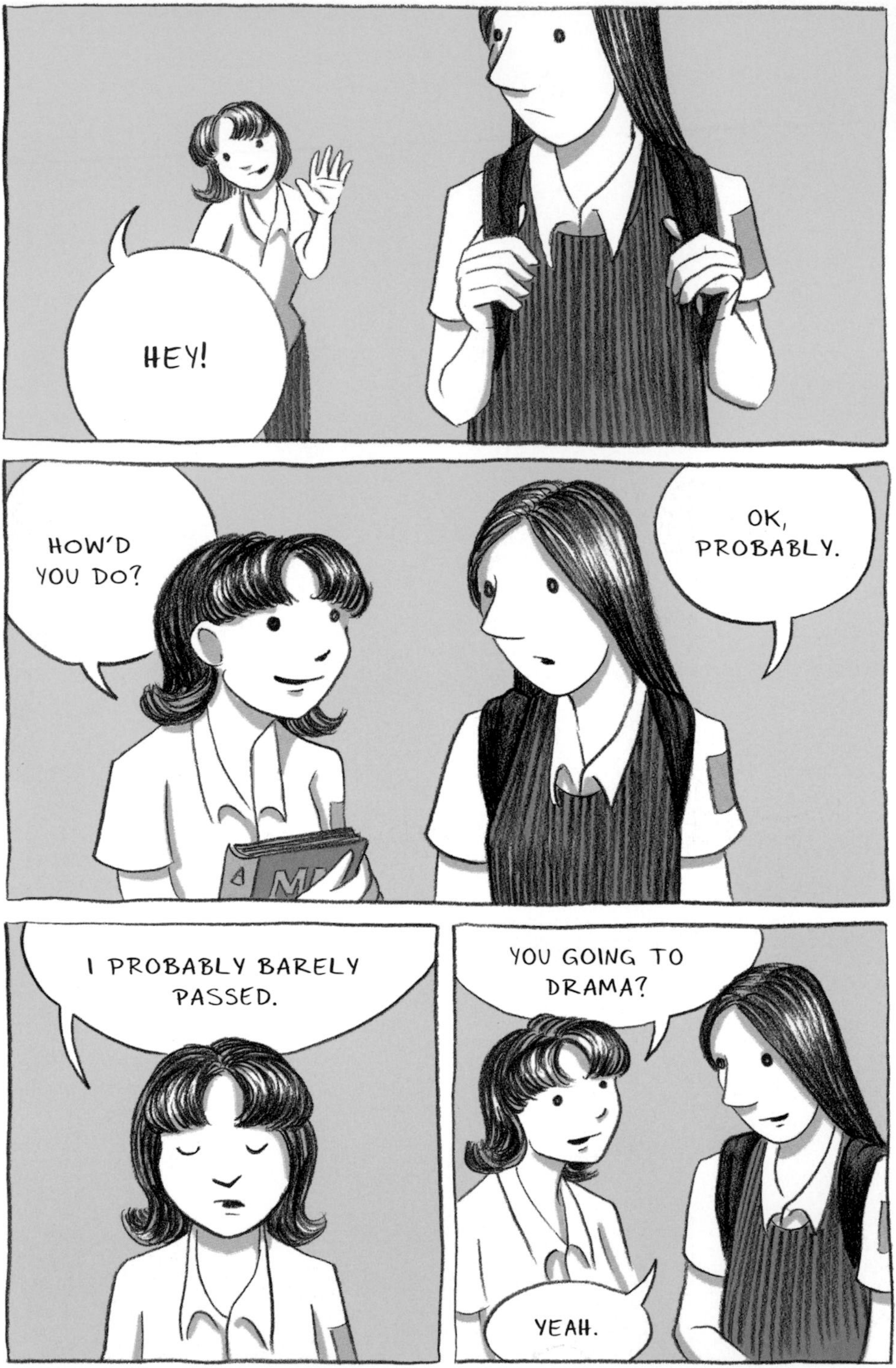
HEY!
HOW'D YOU DO?
OK, PROBABLY.
I PROBABLY BARELY PASSED.
YOU GOING TO DRAMA?
YEAH.

129

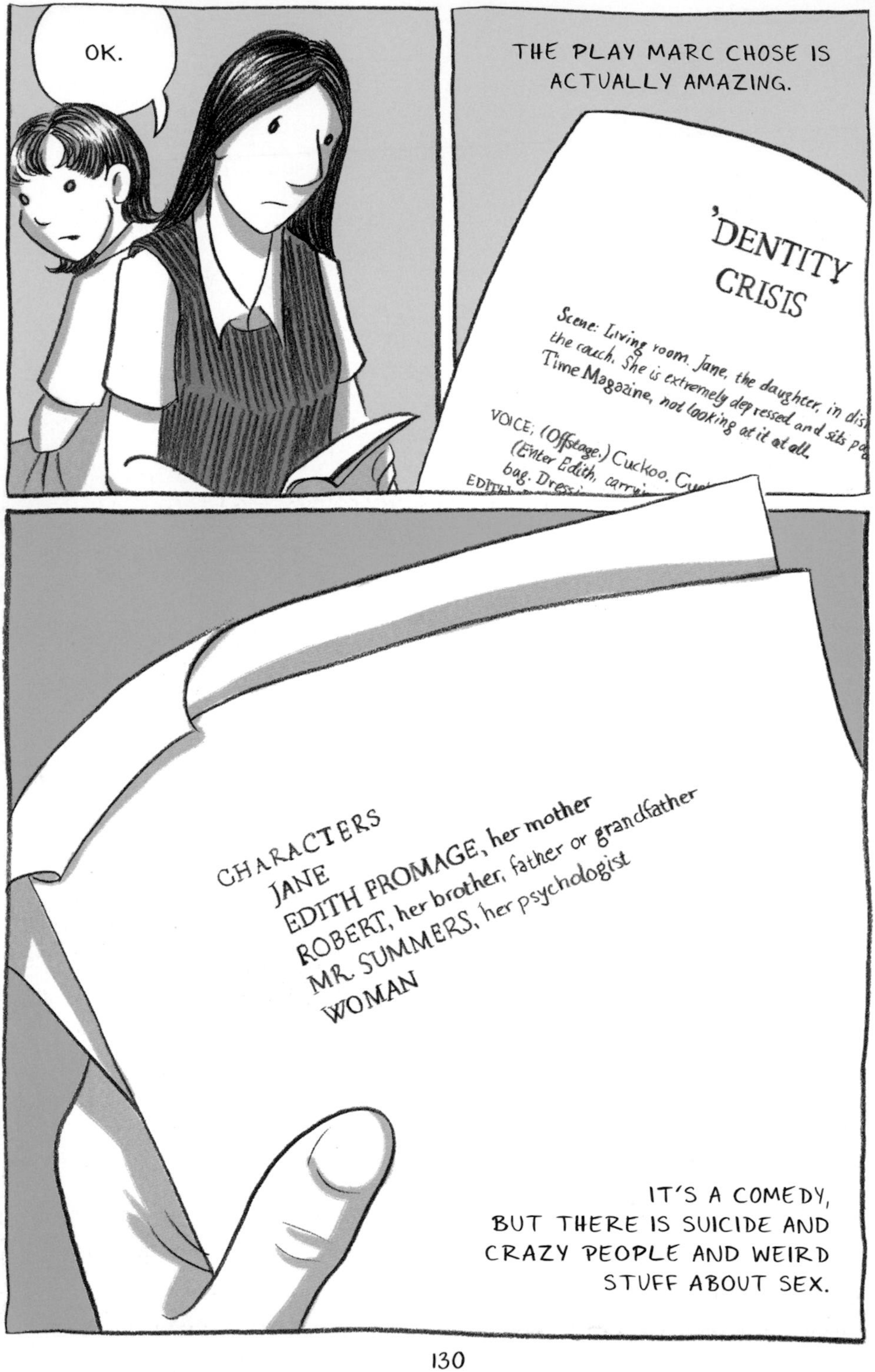
OK.
THE PLAY MARC CHOSE IS ACTUALLY AMAZING.
'DENTITY CRISIS
Scene: Living room. Jane, the daughter, in dis
the couch. She is extremely depressed and sits pa
Time Magazine, not looking at it at all.
VOICE; (Offstage.) Cuckoo. Cu
(Enter Edith, carry
CHARACTERS
JANE
EDITH FROMAGE, her mother
ROBERT, her brother, father or grandfather
MR. SUMMERS, her psychologist
WOMAN
IT'S A COMEDY, BUT THERE IS SUICIDE AND CRAZY PEOPLE AND WEIRD STUFF ABOUT SEX.

BETH GOT THE BEST PART: JANE. WHICH I GUESS IS BECAUSE SHE IS SO PRETTY... AND SMALL.

I'M CAST AS WOMAN. IT LOOKS LIKE I HAVE SOME GOOD LINES, THOUGH, AND A LOT OF MY SCENES ARE WITH CESAR, WHO PLAYS MR. SUMMERS...OH.

OH NO.

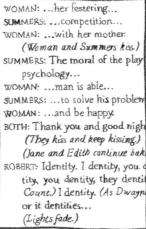

WOMAN: ...her festering...
SUMMERS: ...competition...
WOMAN: ...with her mother.
    (*Woman and Summers kiss.*)
SUMMERS: The moral of the play
    psychology...
WOMAN: ...man is able...
SUMMERS: ...to solve his problem
WOMAN: ...and be happy.
BOTH: Thank you and good nigh
    (*They kiss and keep kissing.*)
    (*Jane and Edith continue bak*
ROBERT: Identity. I dentity, you c
    tity, you dentity, they denti
    Count.) I dentity. (*As Dwayn*
    or it dentities...
    (*Lights fade.*)

MARC?

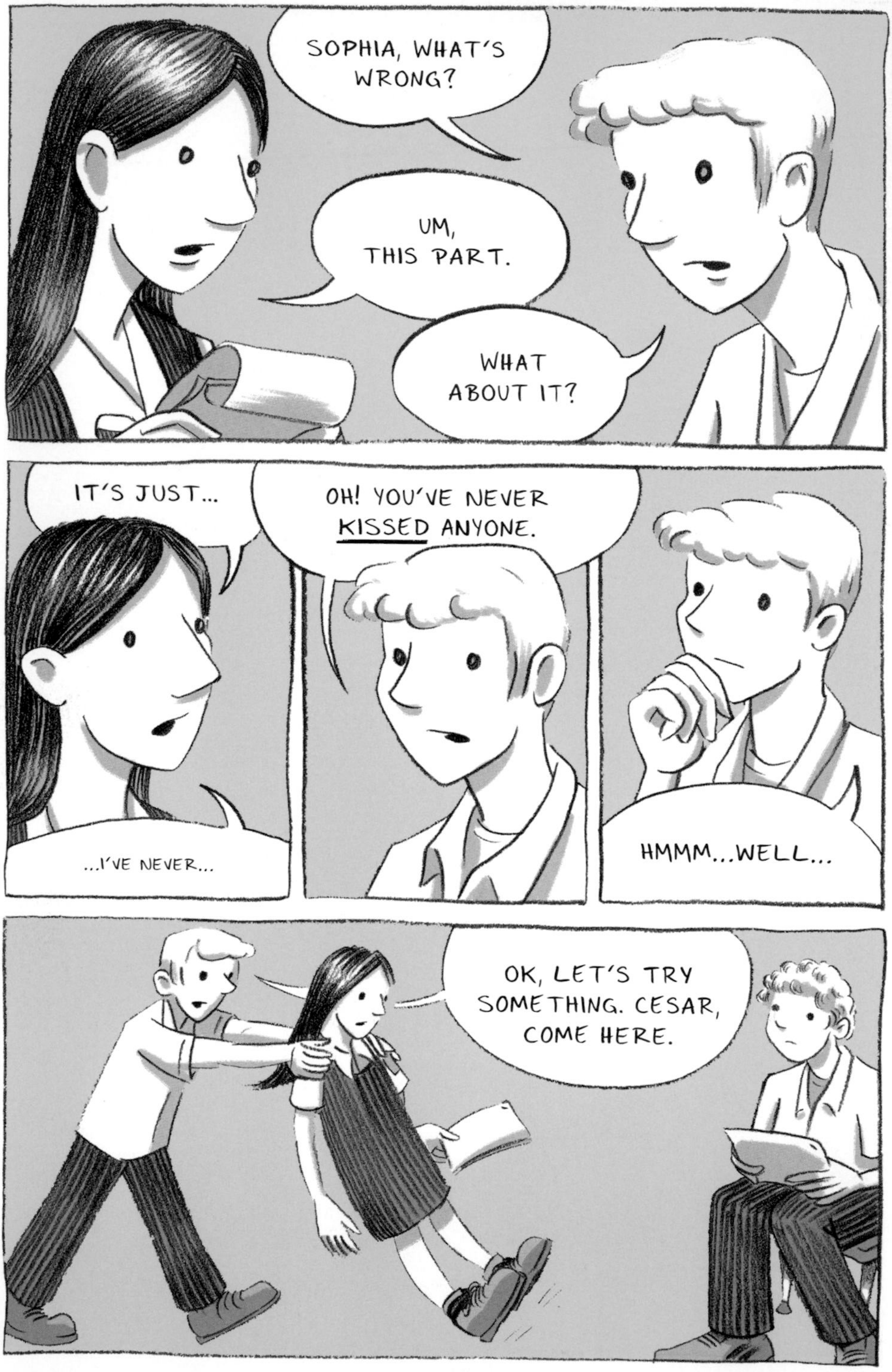
SOPHIA, WHAT'S WRONG?
UM, THIS PART.
WHAT ABOUT IT?
IT'S JUST...
OH! YOU'VE NEVER KISSED ANYONE.
...I'VE NEVER...
HMMM...WELL...
OK, LET'S TRY SOMETHING. CESAR, COME HERE.

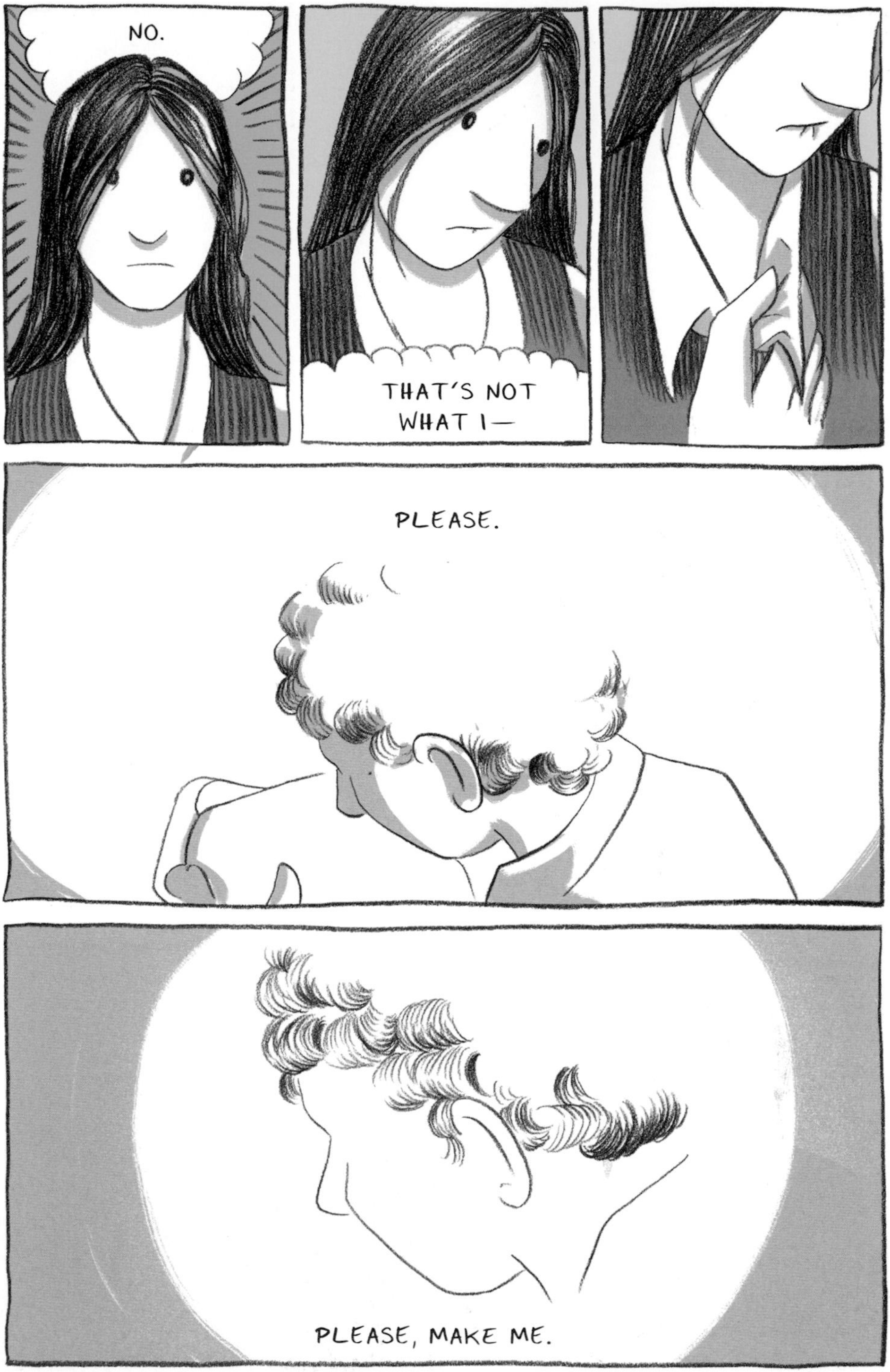
NO.
THAT'S NOT WHAT I—
PLEASE.
PLEASE, MAKE ME.

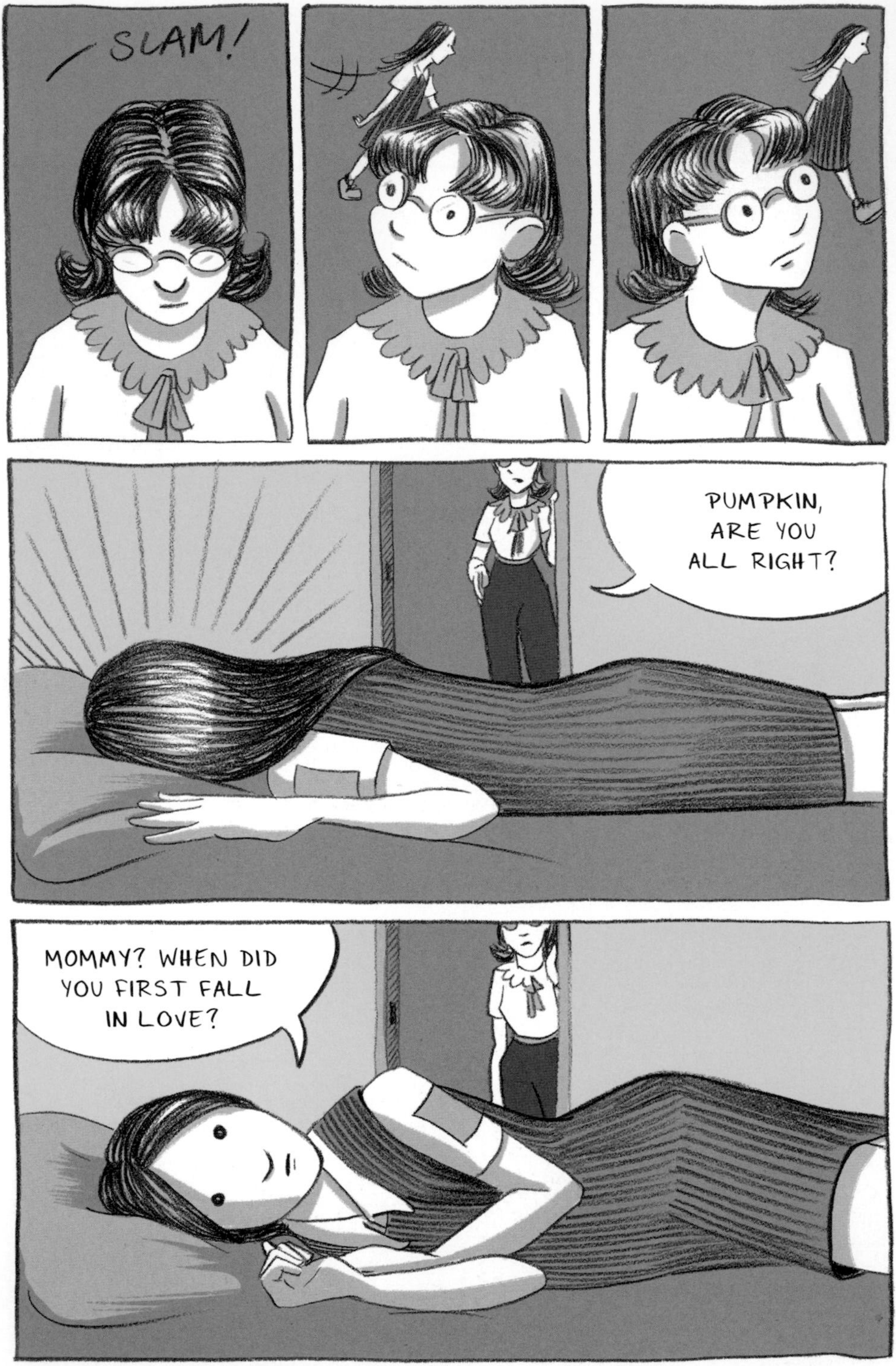
SLAM!
PUMPKIN, ARE YOU ALL RIGHT?
MOMMY? WHEN DID YOU FIRST FALL IN LOVE?

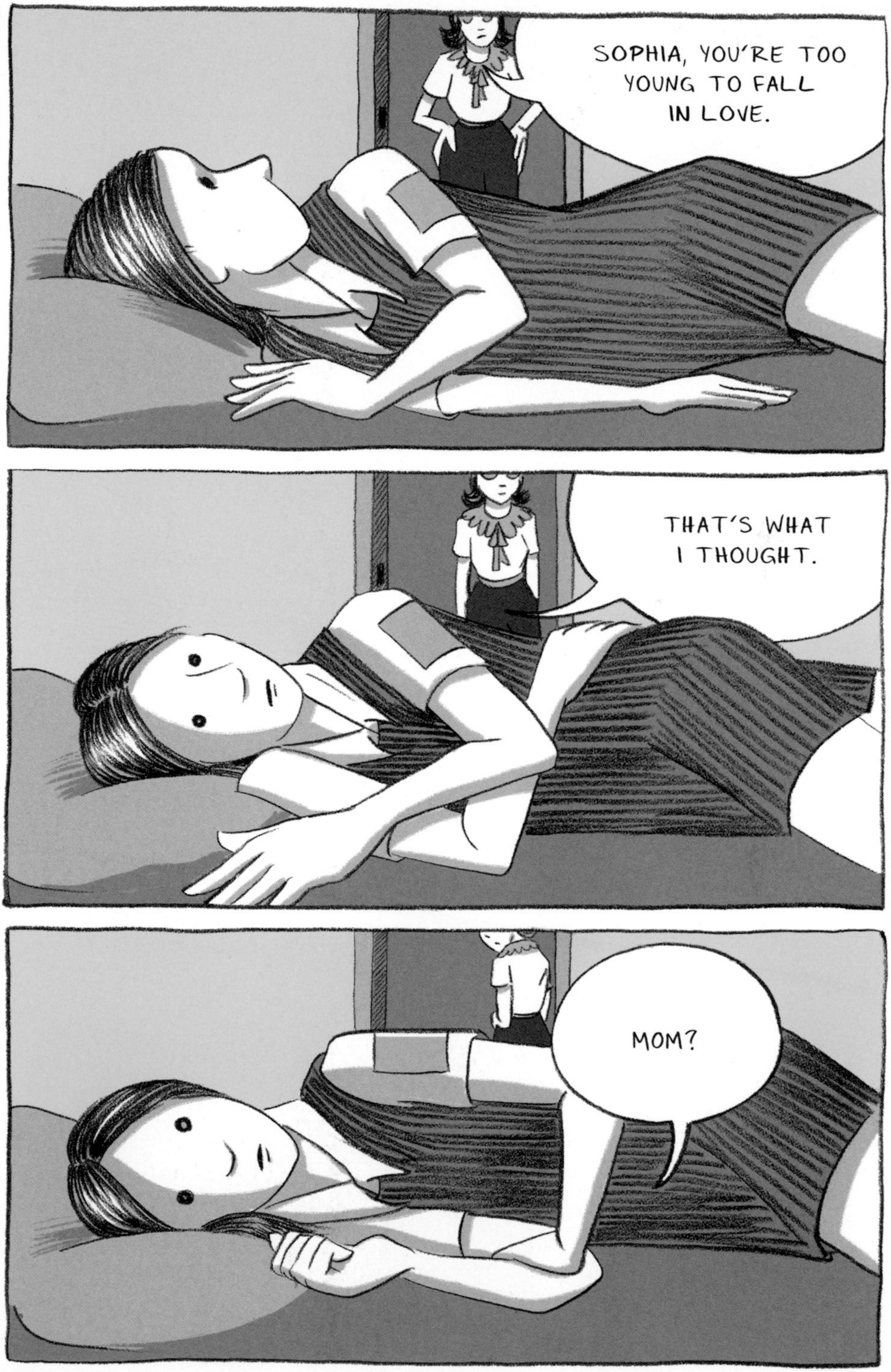
SOPHIA, YOU'RE TOO YOUNG TO FALL IN LOVE.
THAT'S WHAT I THOUGHT.
MOM?

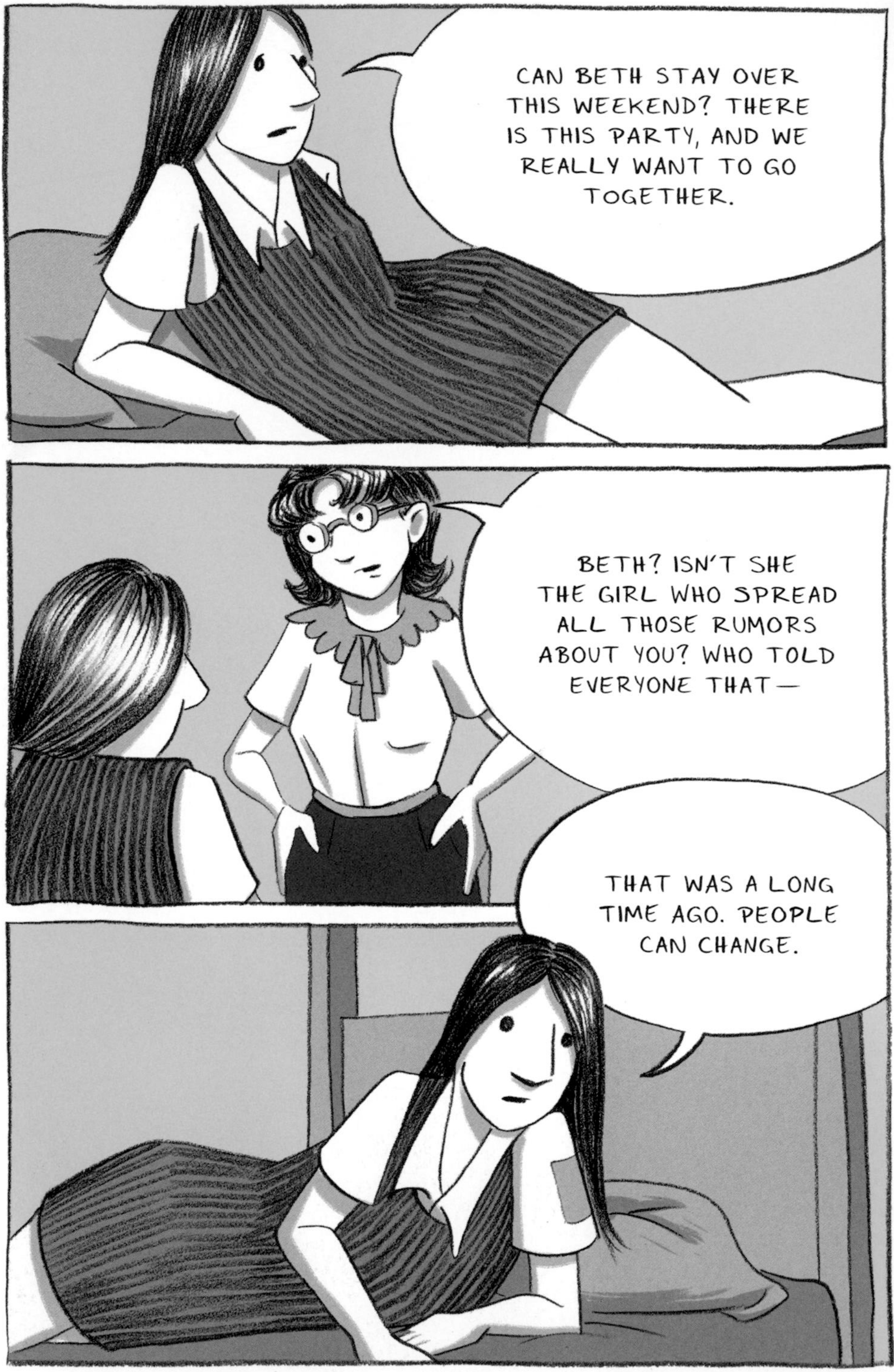
CAN BETH STAY OVER THIS WEEKEND? THERE IS THIS PARTY, AND WE REALLY WANT TO GO TOGETHER.
BETH? ISN'T SHE THE GIRL WHO SPREAD ALL THOSE RUMORS ABOUT YOU? WHO TOLD EVERYONE THAT—
THAT WAS A LONG TIME AGO. PEOPLE CAN CHANGE.

WHEN WE WERE LITTLE, MY SISTER WAS
THE CHAMPION OF SAVING HALLOWEEN CANDY.

I COULDN'T MAKE
MINE LAST MORE
THAN A WEEK, BUT
JULIA COULD SAVE
HERS FOR MONTHS.
ALMOST UNTIL IT
WENT STALE.

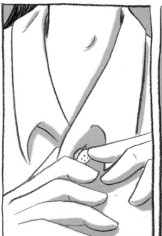

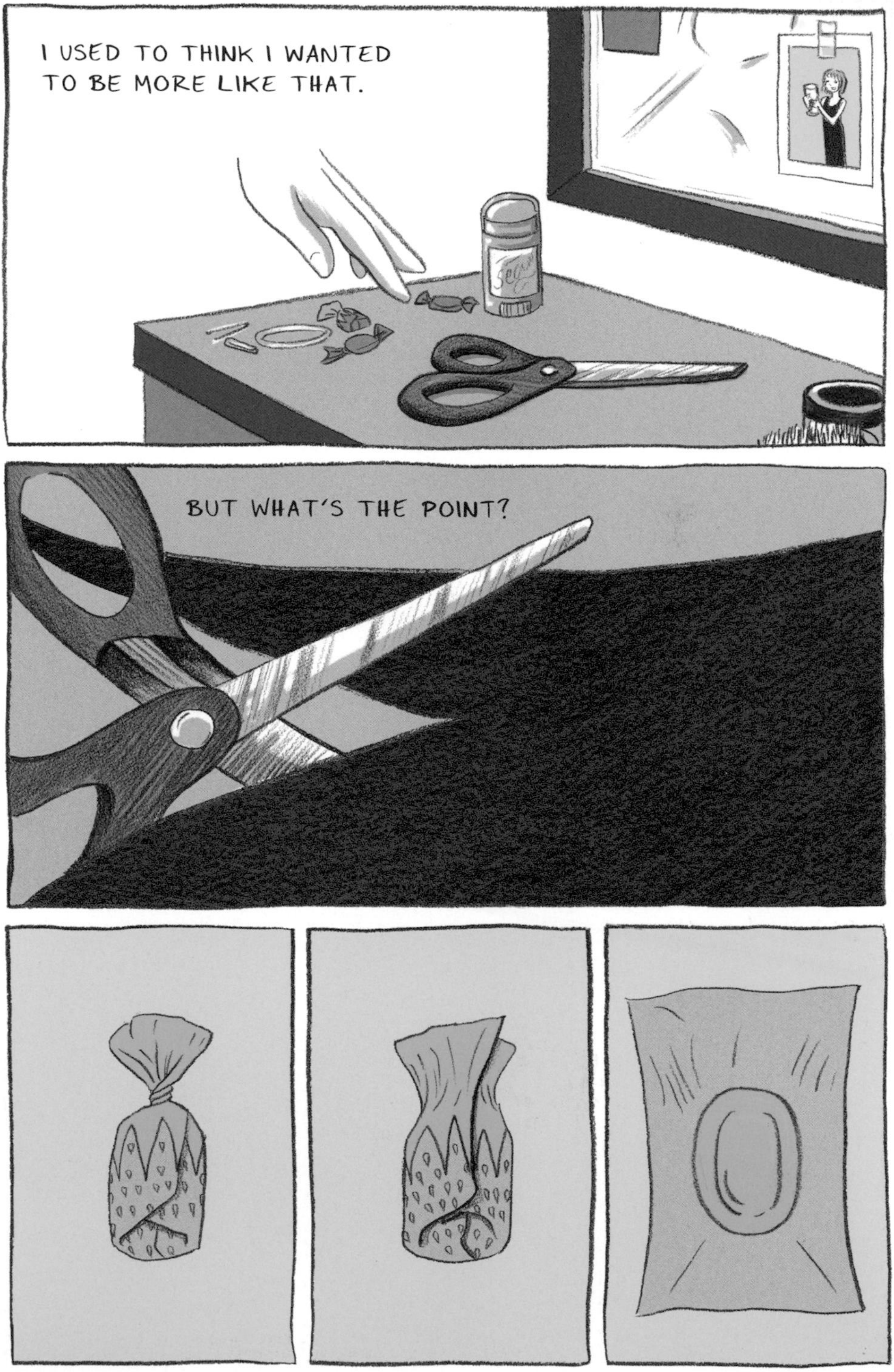
I USED TO THINK I WANTED TO BE MORE LIKE THAT.
BUT WHAT'S THE POINT?

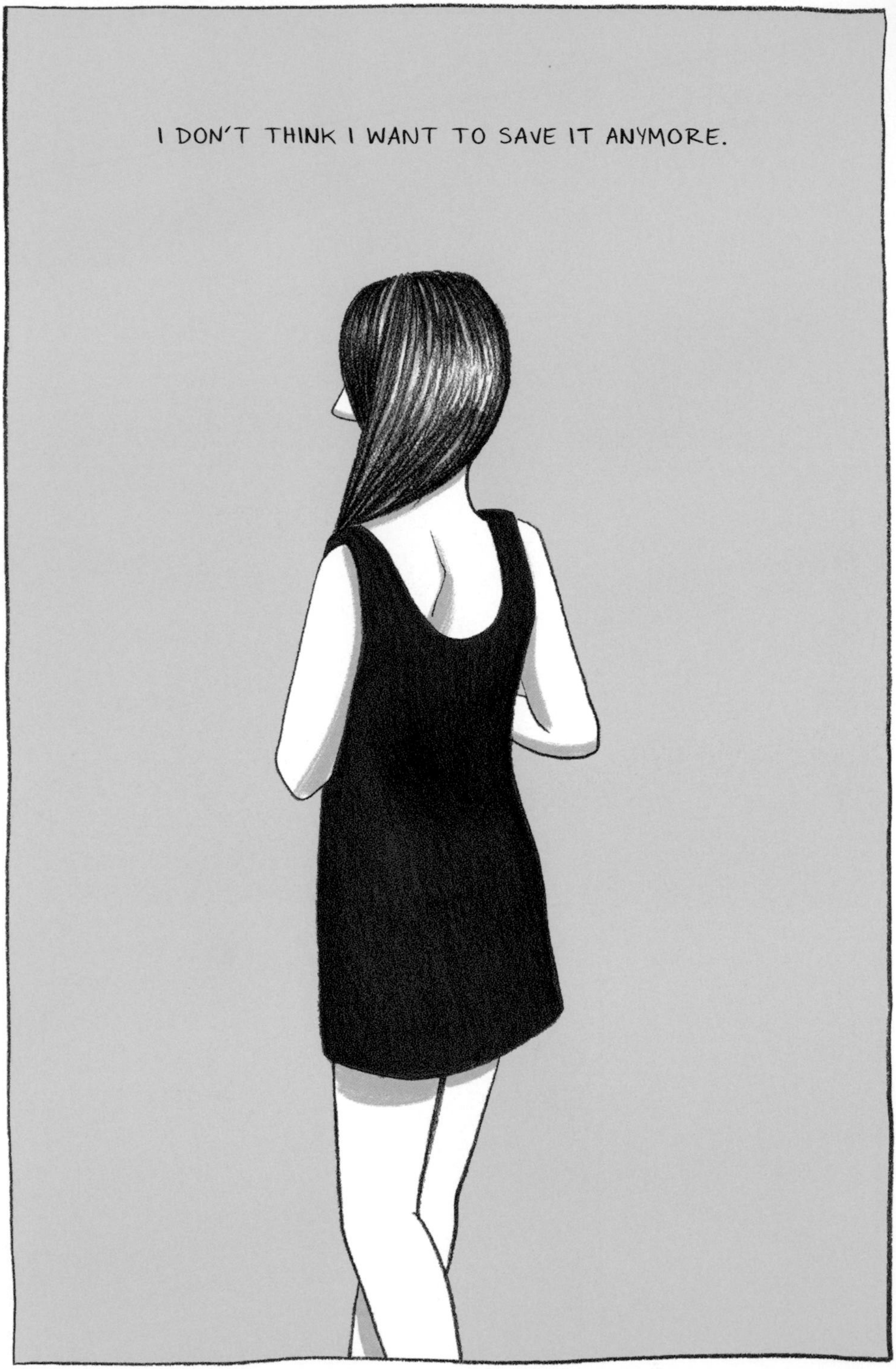
I DON'T THINK I WANT TO SAVE IT ANYMORE.

144

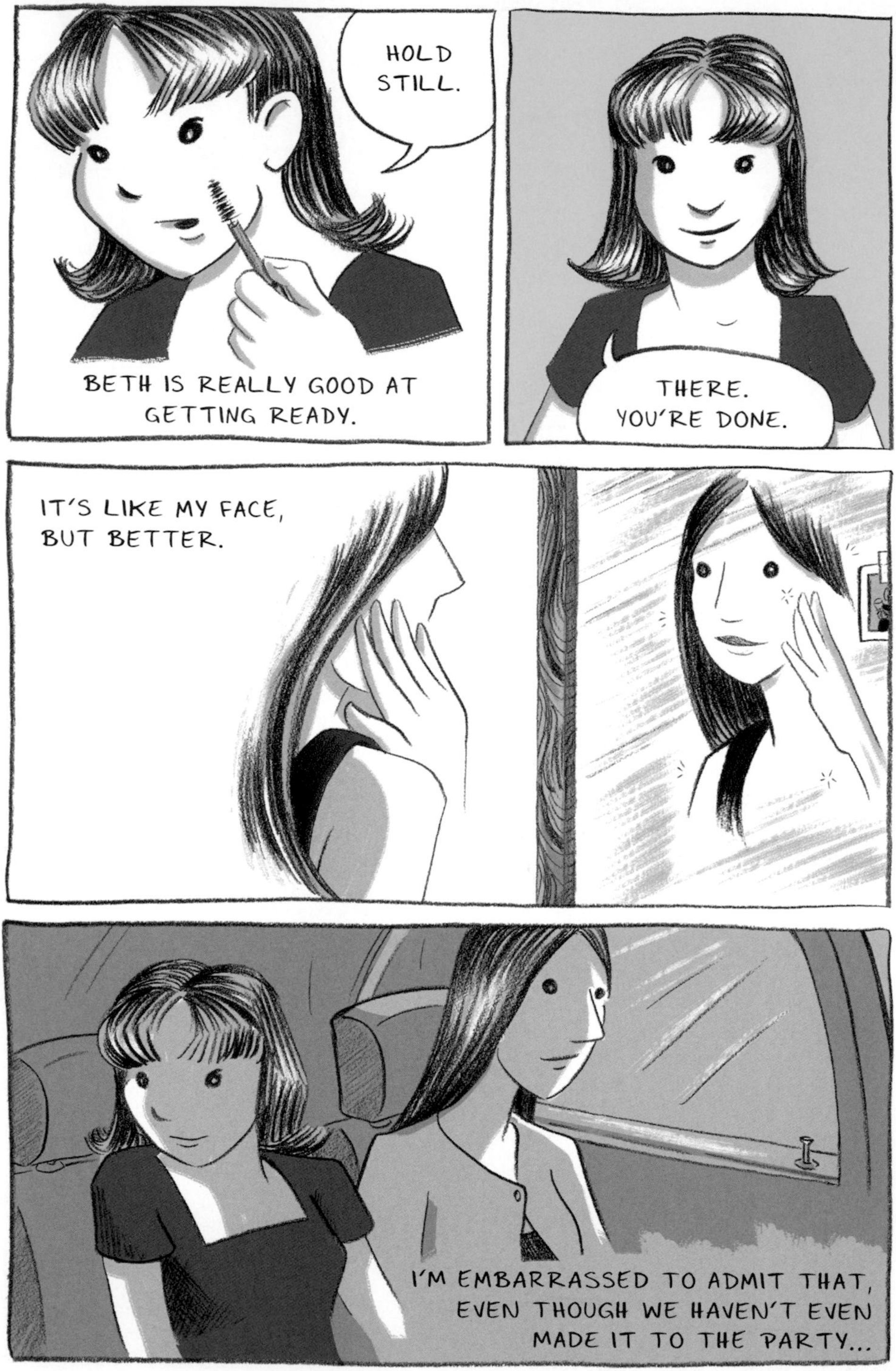
HOLD STILL.
BETH IS REALLY GOOD AT GETTING READY.
THERE. YOU'RE DONE.
IT'S LIKE MY FACE, BUT BETTER.
I'M EMBARRASSED TO ADMIT THAT, EVEN THOUGH WE HAVEN'T EVEN MADE IT TO THE PARTY...

147

148

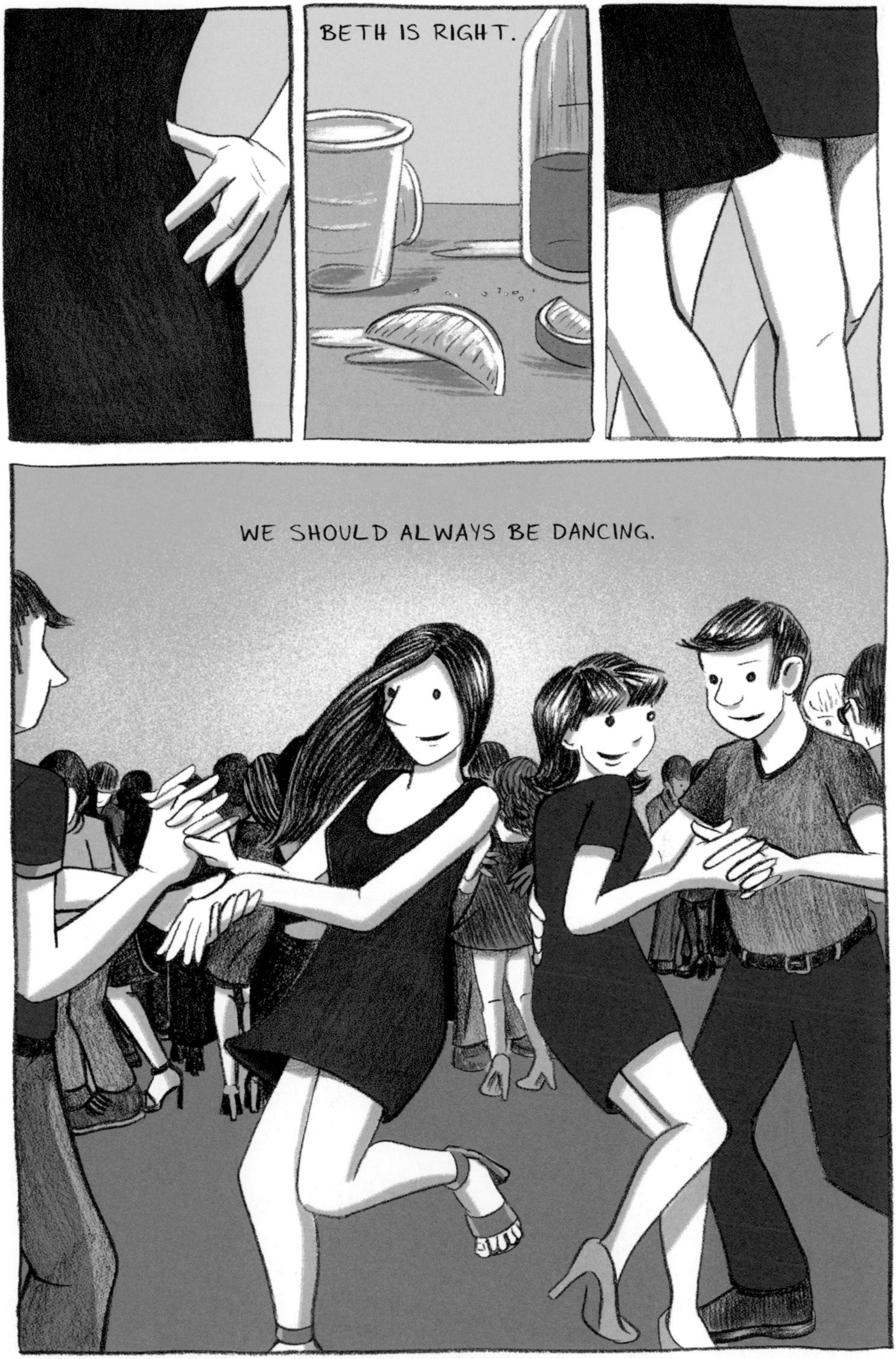
BETH IS RIGHT.
WE SHOULD ALWAYS BE DANCING.

153

154

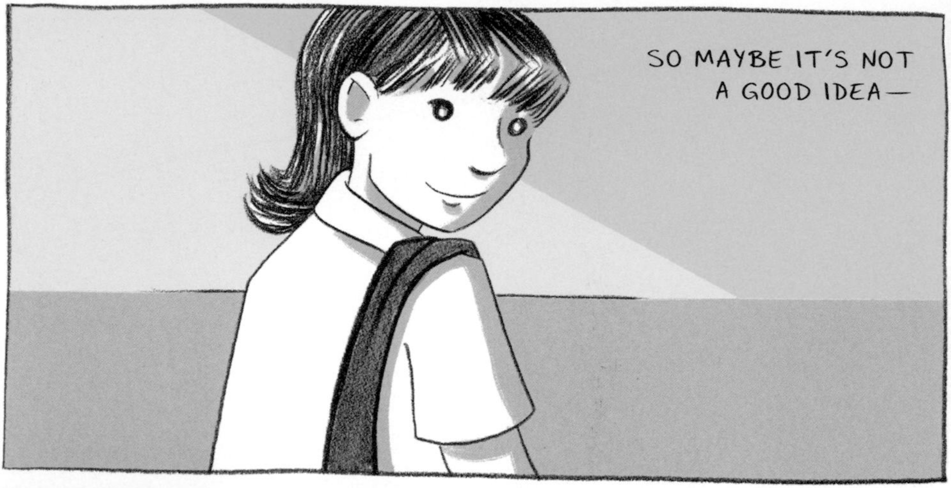
SO MAYBE IT'S NOT A GOOD IDEA—

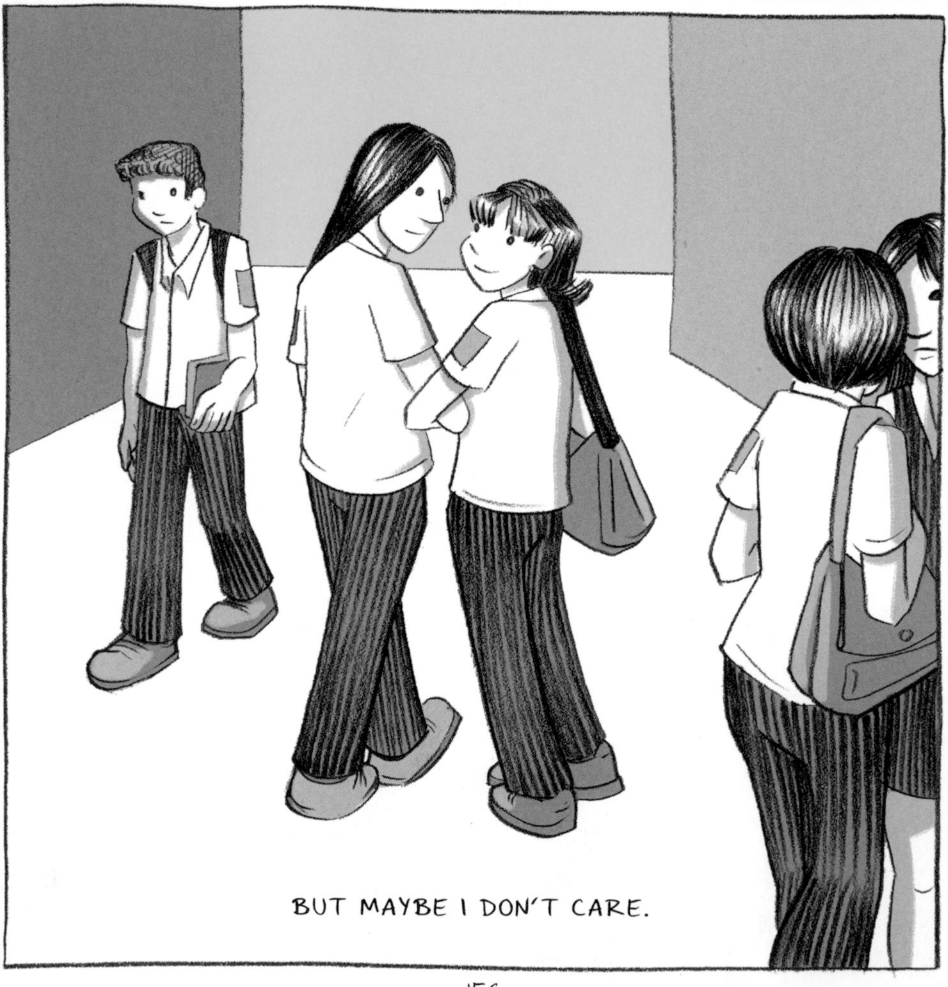
BUT MAYBE I DON'T CARE.

THINGS DO BEGIN TO HAPPEN.

MOSTLY PARTIES.

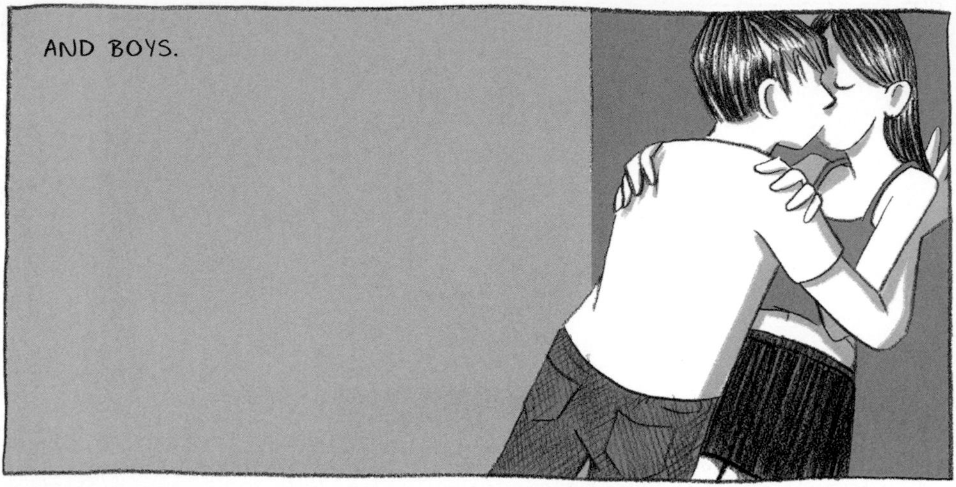
AND BOYS.

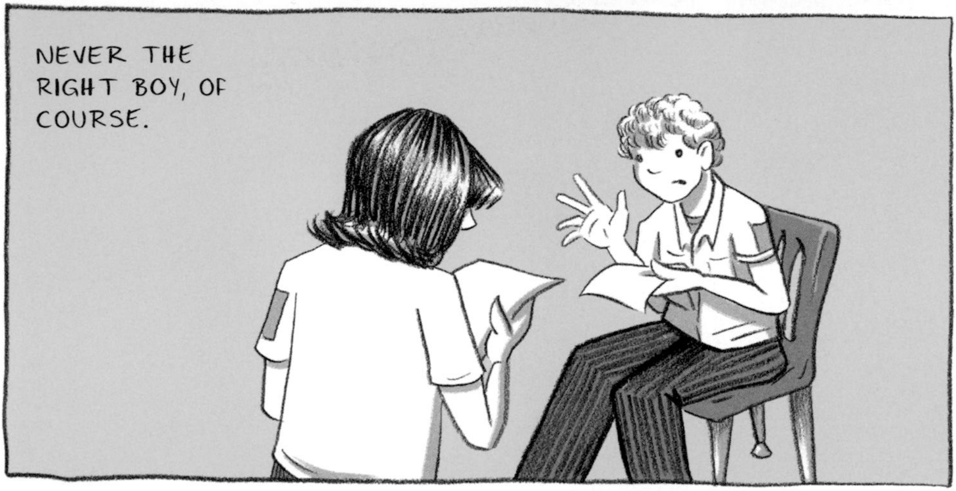
NEVER THE RIGHT BOY, OF COURSE.

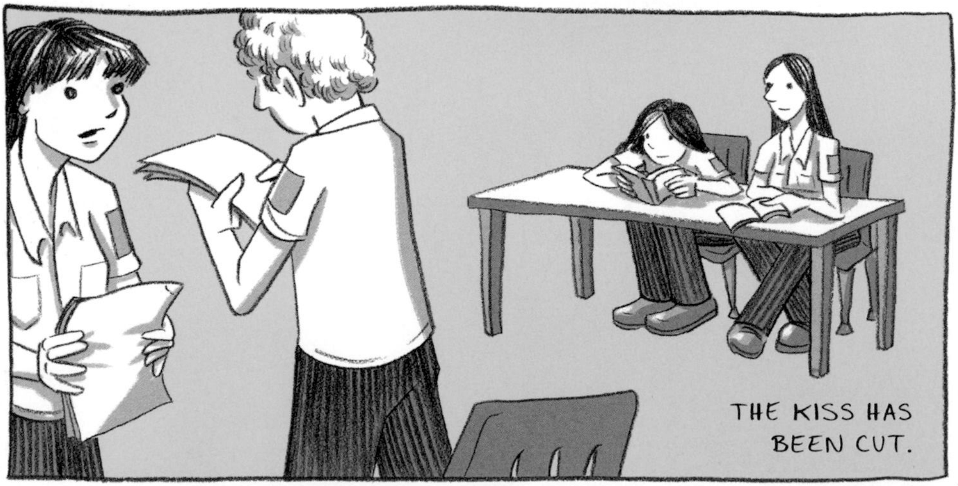
THE KISS HAS BEEN CUT.

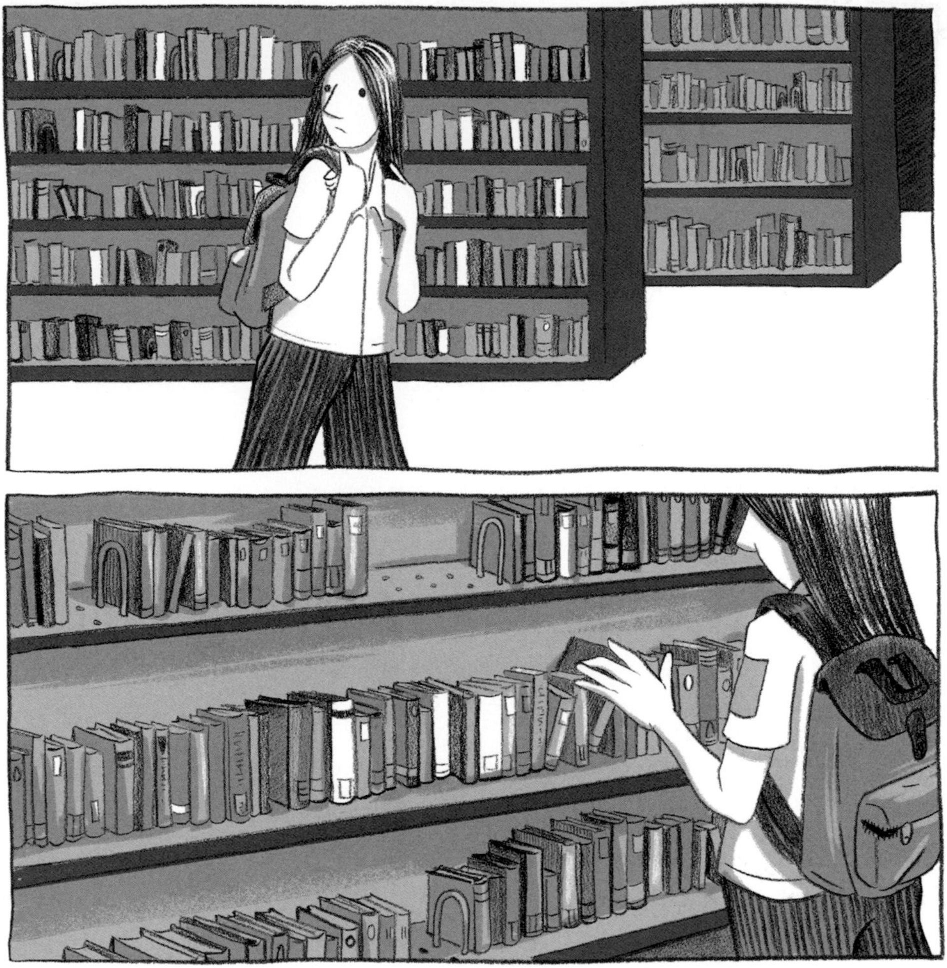
NINE STORIES
NAME
DUE
3/98 CARLA ESPINOSA 4/98
8/98 JORGE RODRIGUEZ 9/98
10/98 GABI FIGUEROA 11/98
2/99 CESAR COLON 3/99
3/99 MELISSA
4/99 LINDA
I'LL TAKE WHAT I CAN GET.

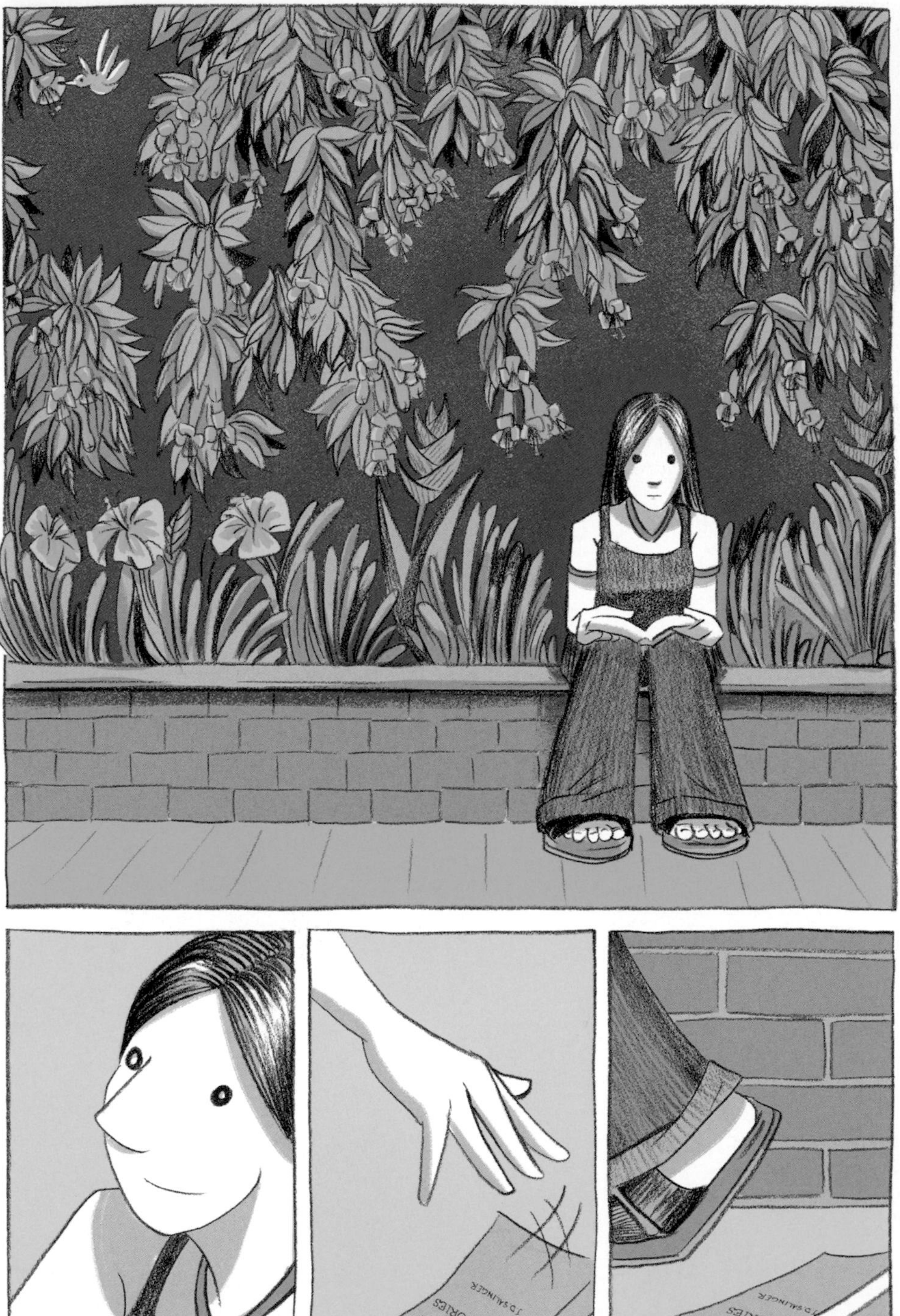
NINE STORIES
J.D. SALINGER

OH MAN! MAYBE YOU CAN DO MY MAKEUP FOR THE JUNIOR-SENIOR FAREWELL! IT'S THIS PARTY THE JUNIORS THROW THE SENIORS AND IT'S NEXT SATURDAY AND—

WHY'RE YOU SO EXCITED ABOUT THIS PARTY?

WELL—

I WANT TO TELL YOU ABOUT THIS BOY, BUT I DON'T WANT TO SOUND STUPID.

DO YOU HAVE A BOYFRIEND?

NO! NOT AT ALL! NO! NEVER!

BUT I THINK I MIGHT BE IN LOVE WITH HIM.

YOU'RE RIGHT.

YOU <u>DO</u> SOUND STUPID.

168

174

177

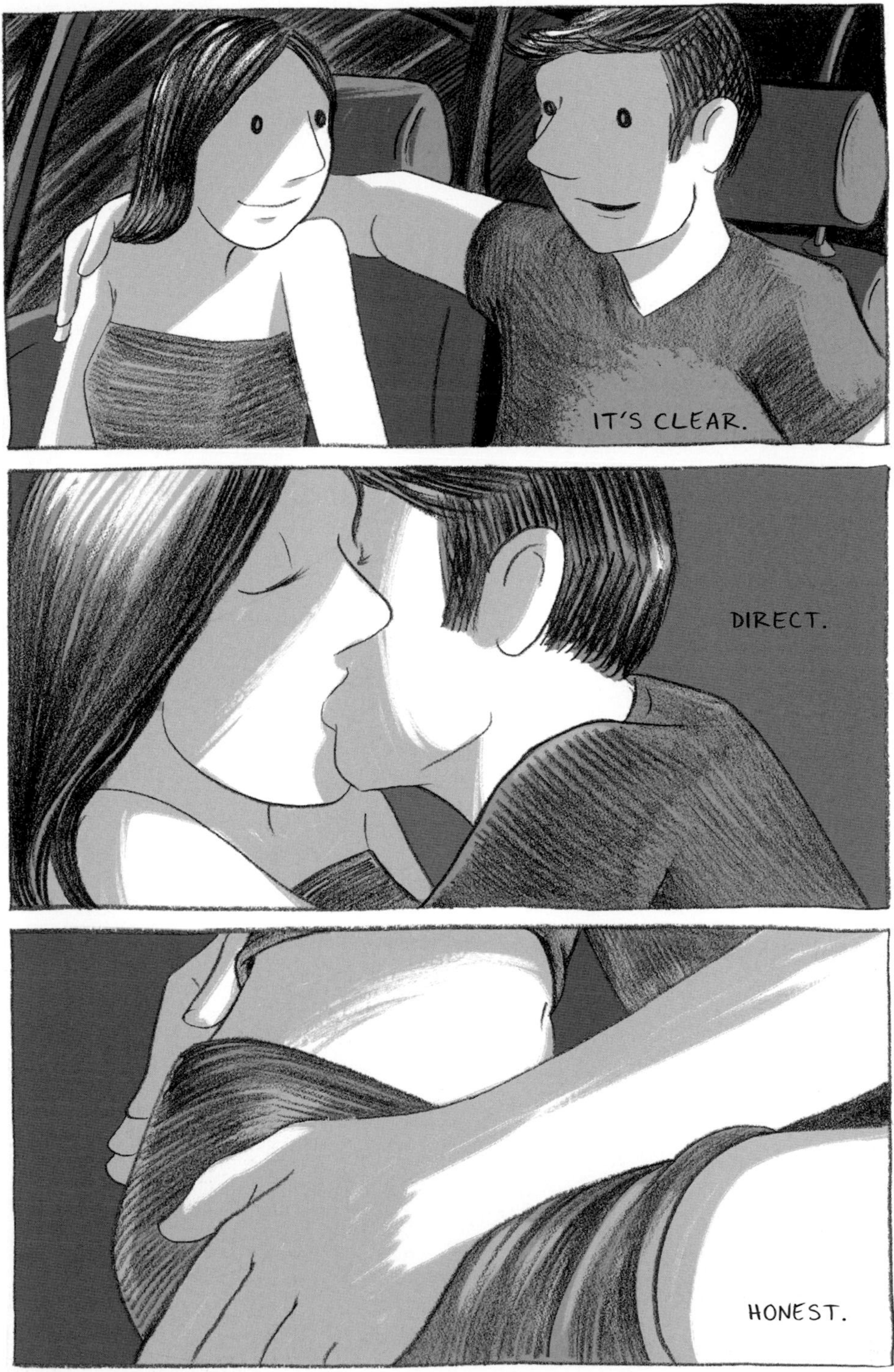
IT'S CLEAR.
DIRECT.
HONEST.

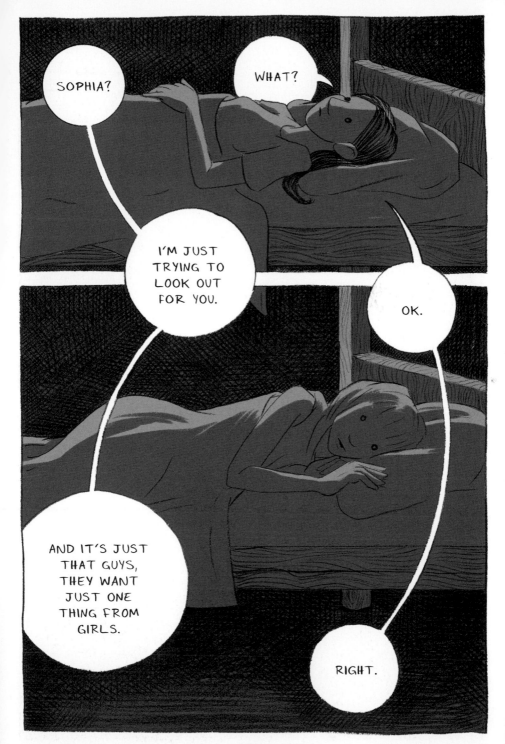

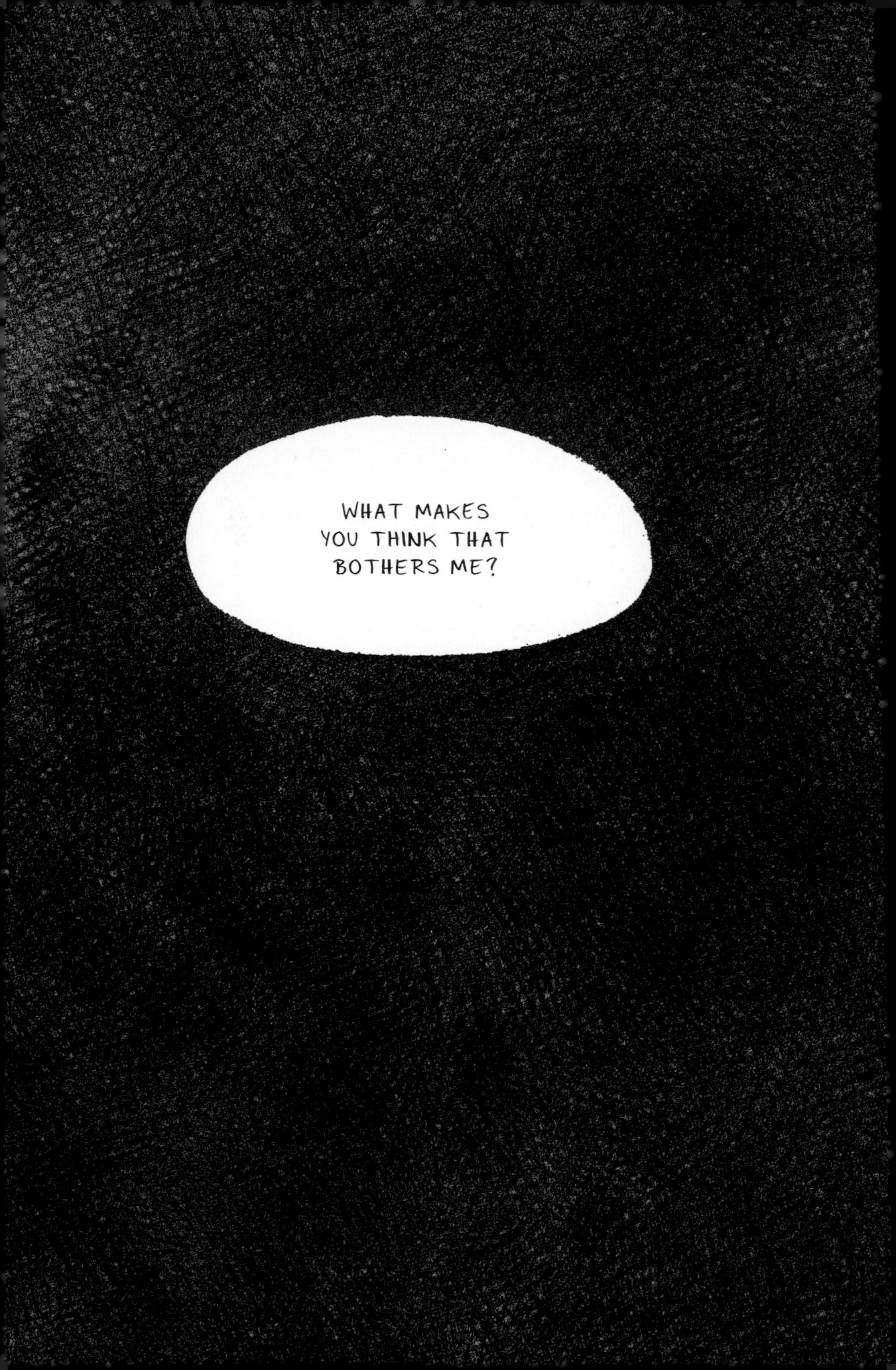
WHAT MAKES YOU THINK THAT BOTHERS ME?

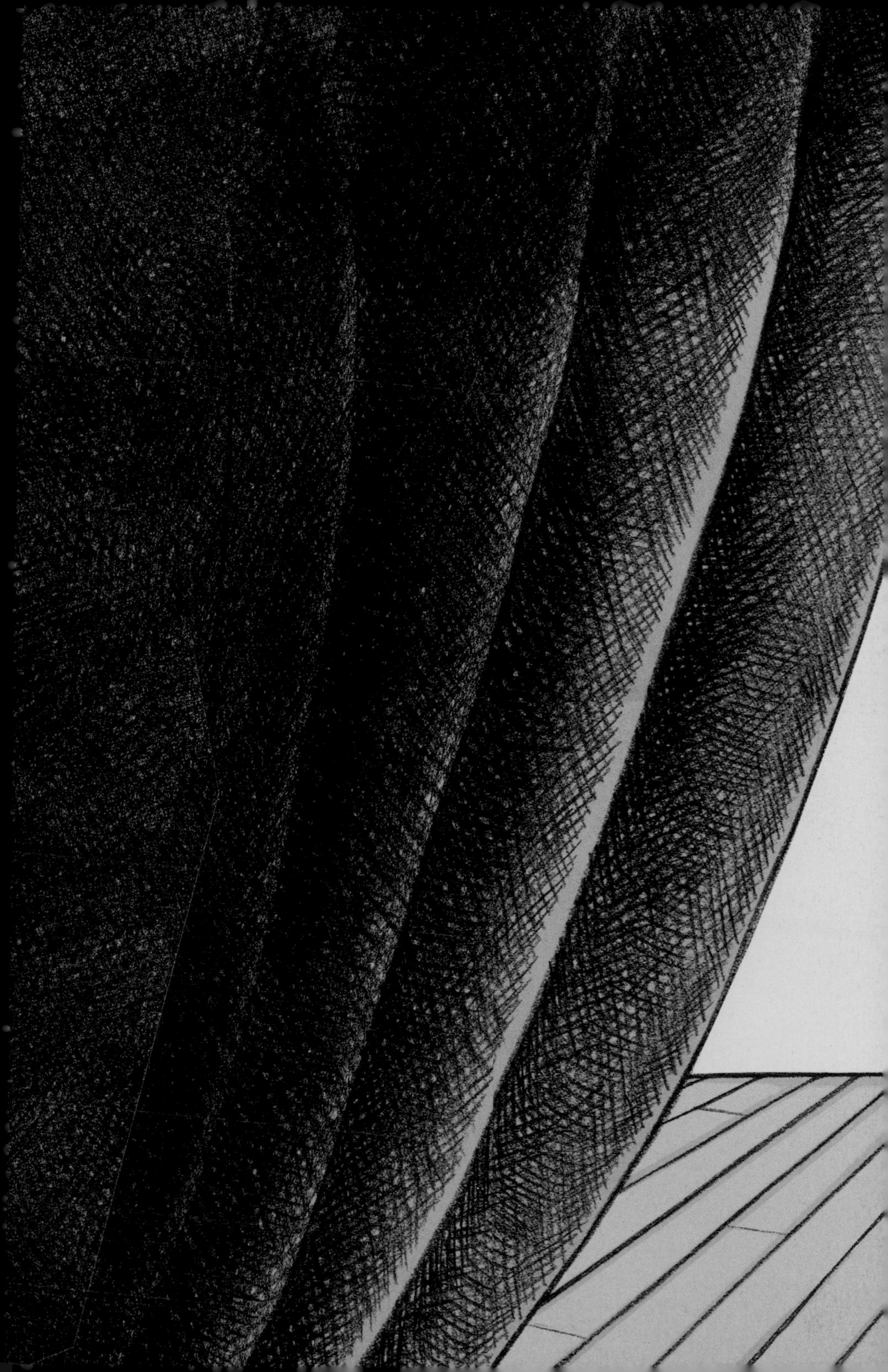

I LOVE THIS PLAY SO MUCH. AND I WANT MY FAMILY TO LOVE IT.... BUT THEN AGAIN, I SORT OF WANT THEM TO HATE IT, TOO.

WHAT IS THAT? THE NEED FOR THEIR AFFIRMATION ALL MIXED UP WITH A DESIRE TO REPULSE THEM.

185

188

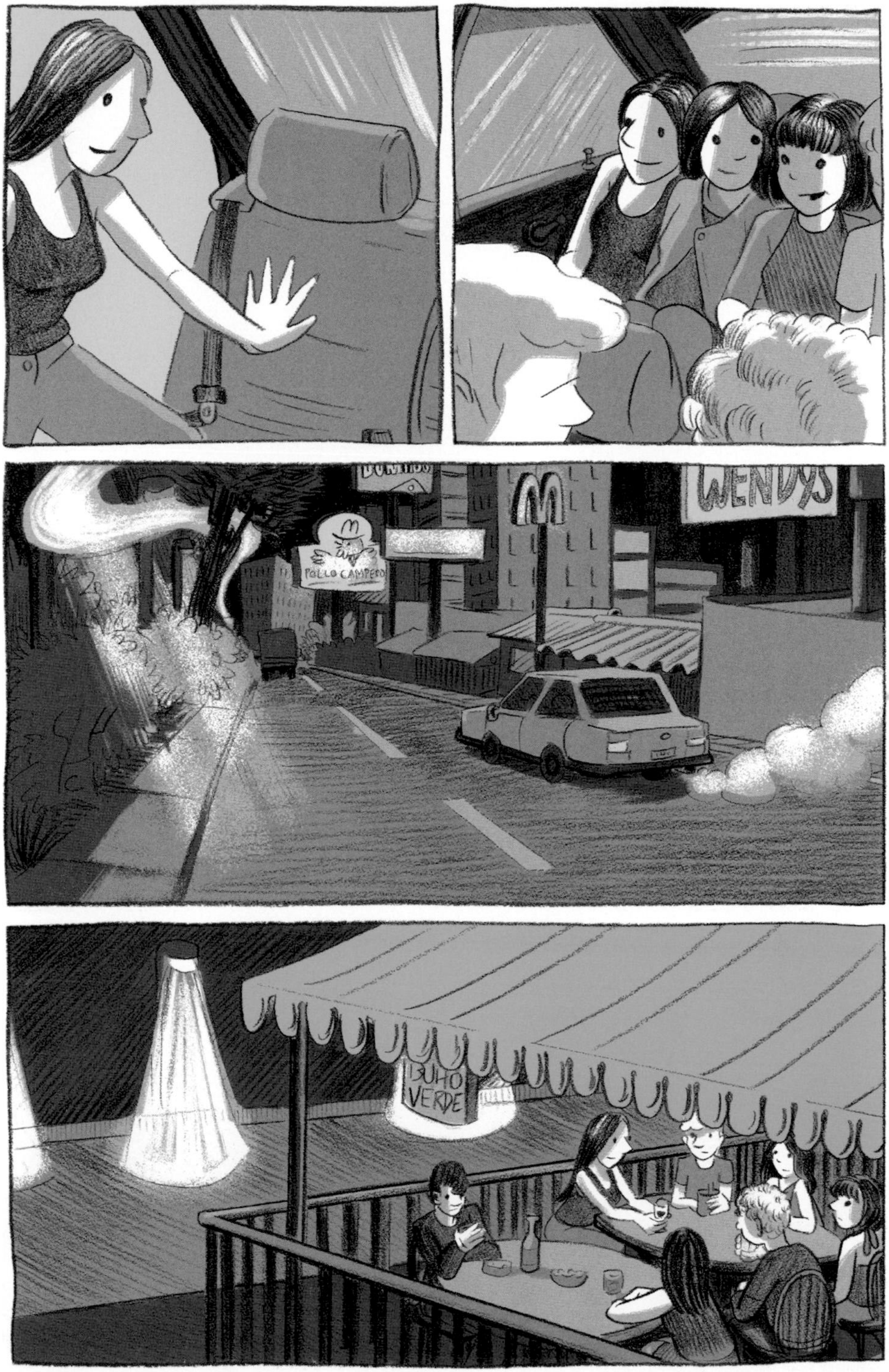

POLLO CAMPERO
WENDYS
BUHO VERDE

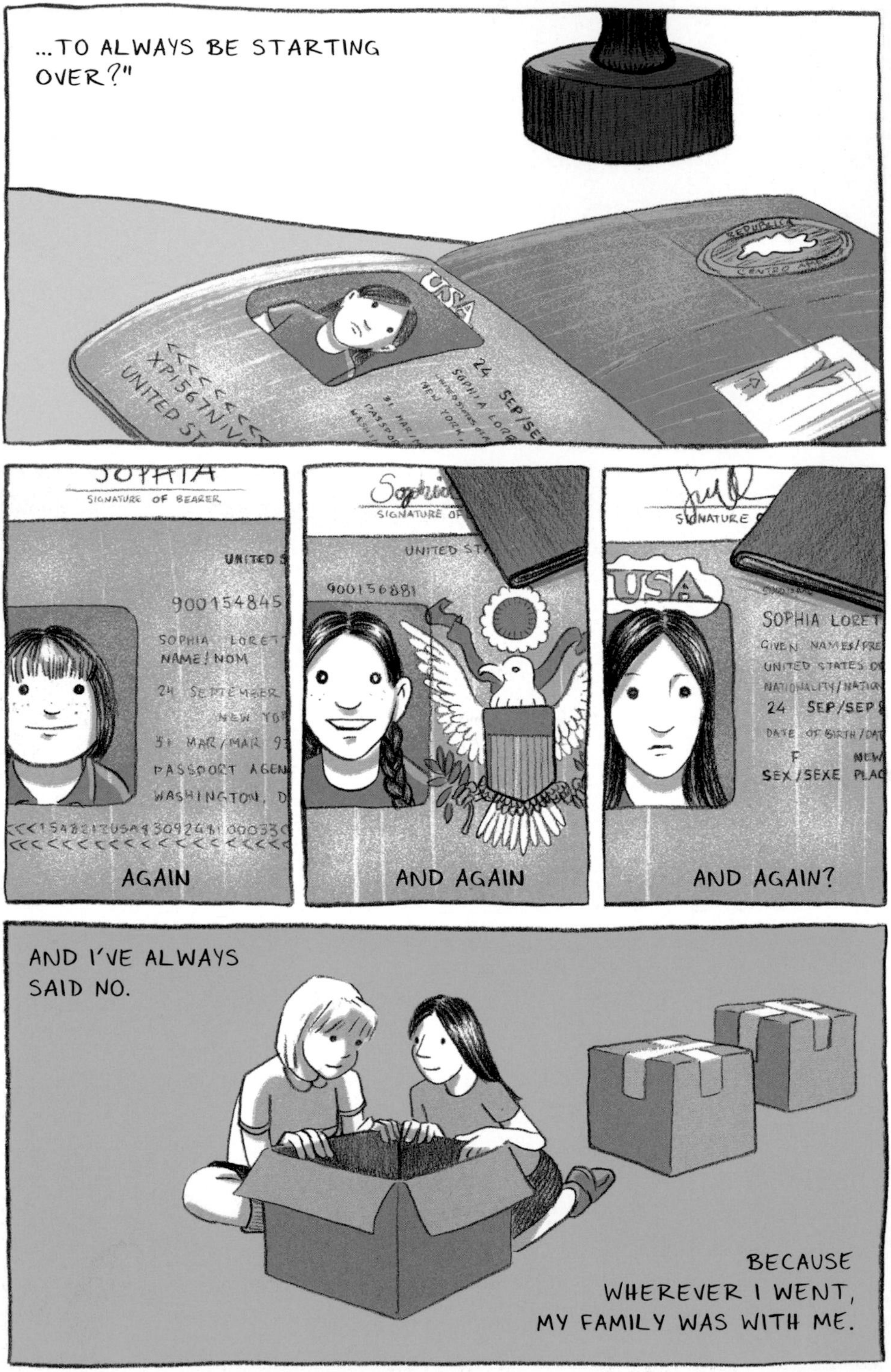
...TO ALWAYS BE STARTING OVER?"
AGAIN
AND AGAIN
AND AGAIN?
AND I'VE ALWAYS SAID NO.
BECAUSE WHEREVER I WENT, MY FAMILY WAS WITH ME.

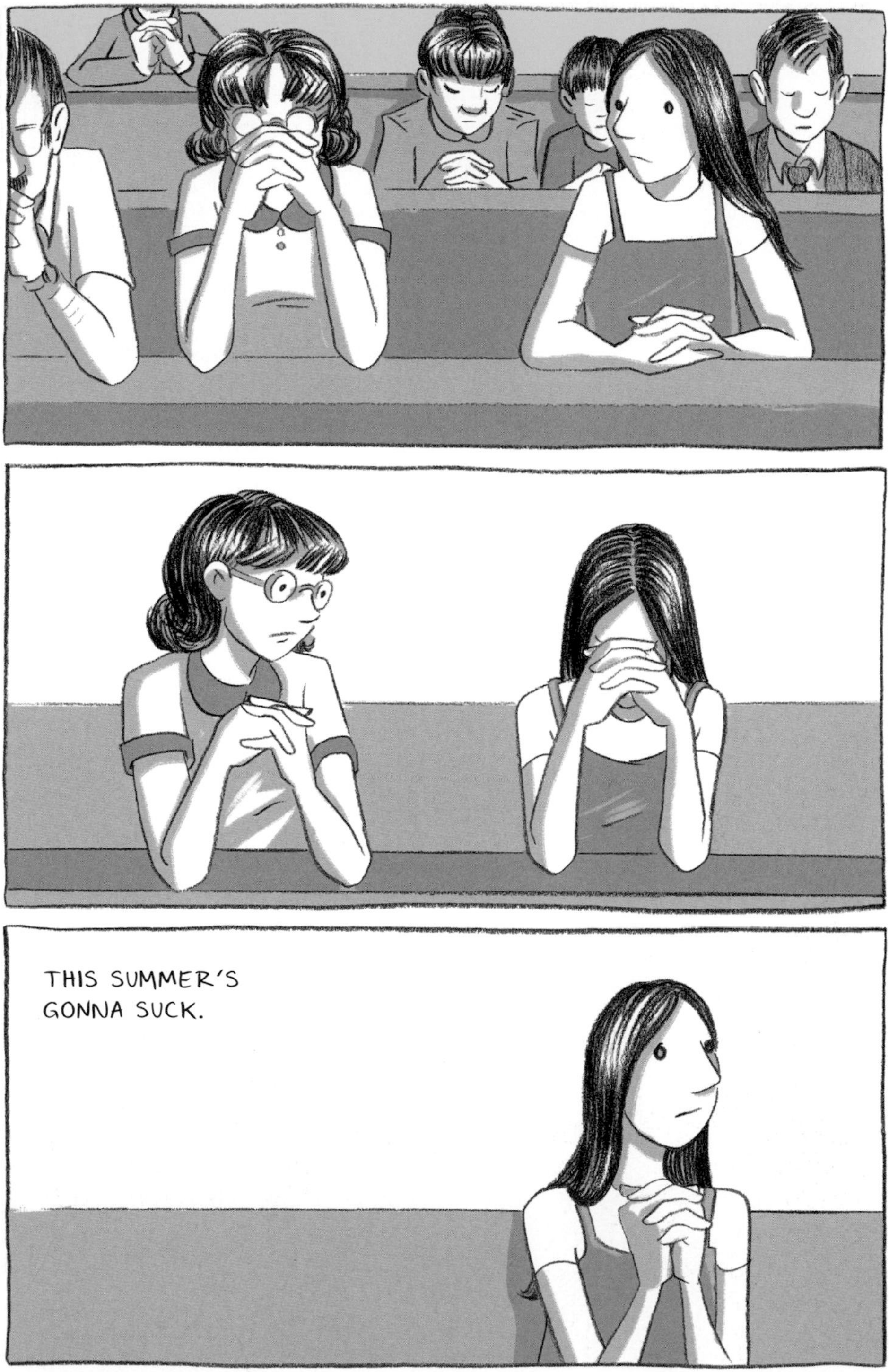
THIS SUMMER'S
GONNA SUCK.

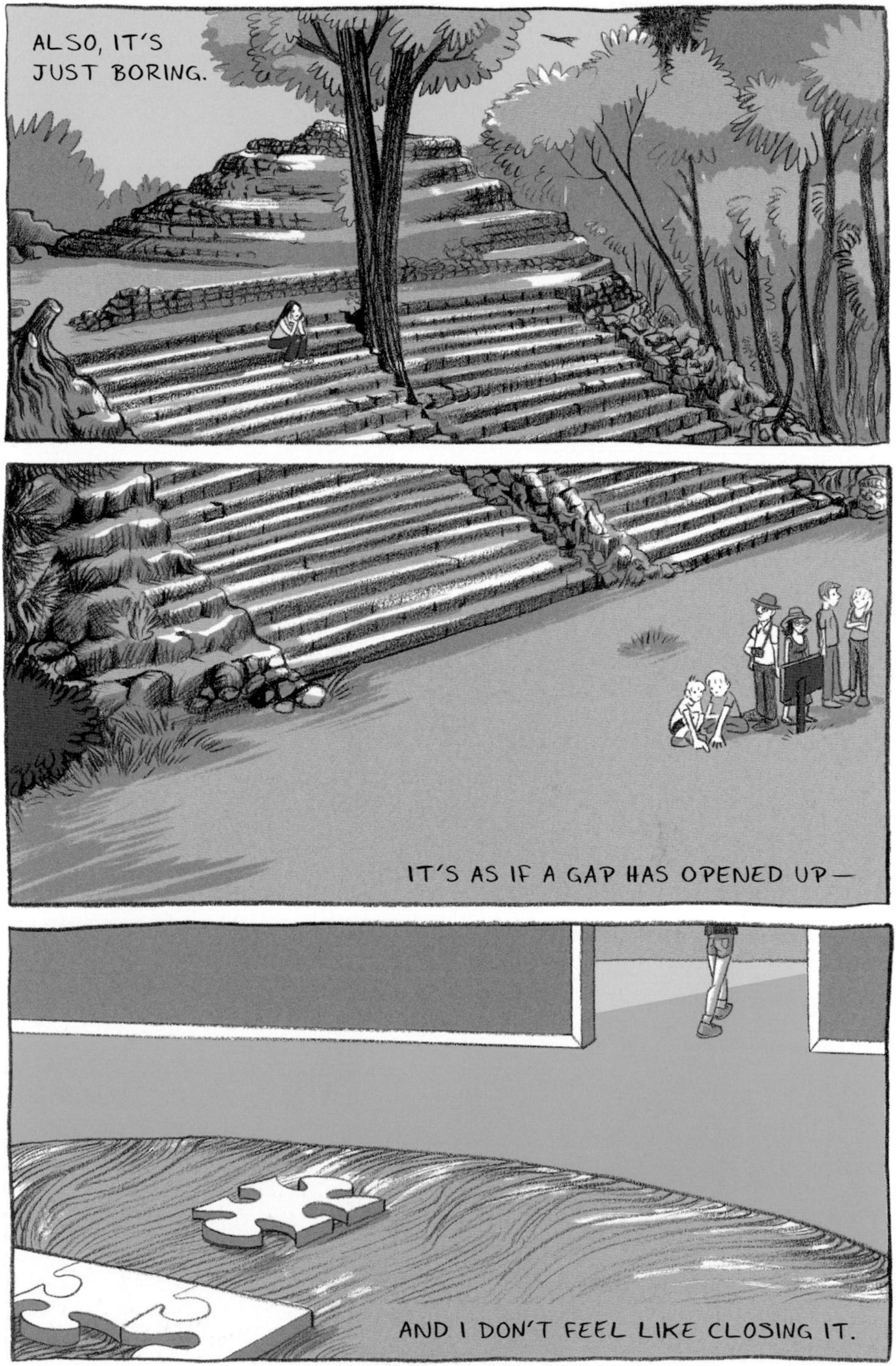
ALSO, IT'S JUST BORING.
IT'S AS IF A GAP HAS OPENED UP—
AND I DON'T FEEL LIKE CLOSING IT.

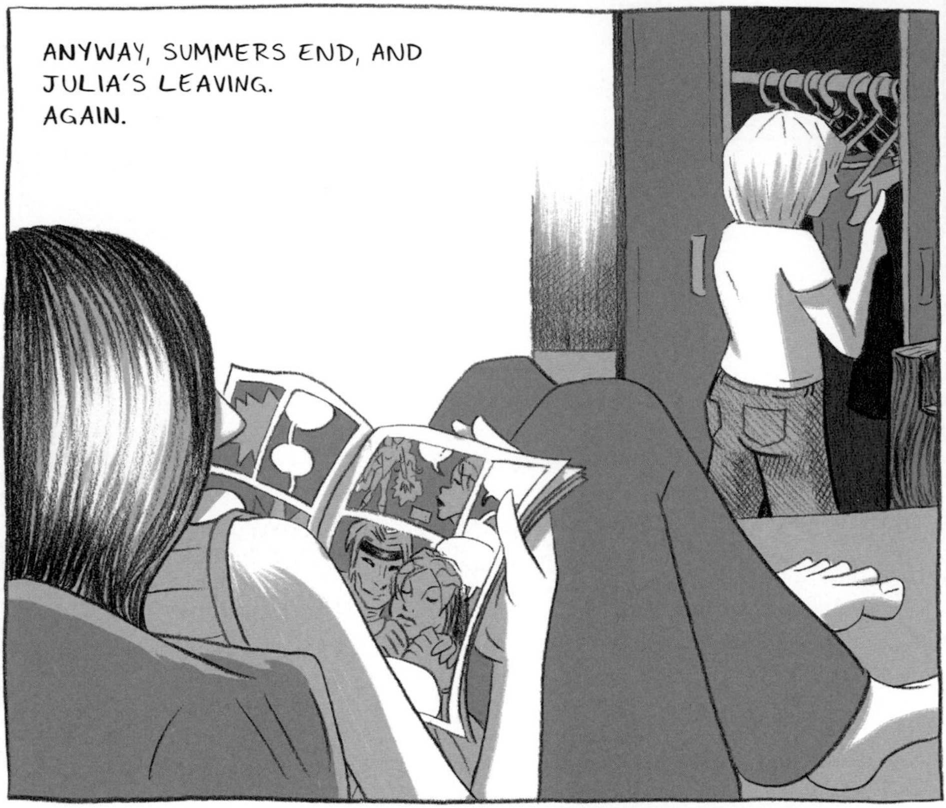
ANYWAY, SUMMERS END, AND JULIA'S LEAVING.
AGAIN.

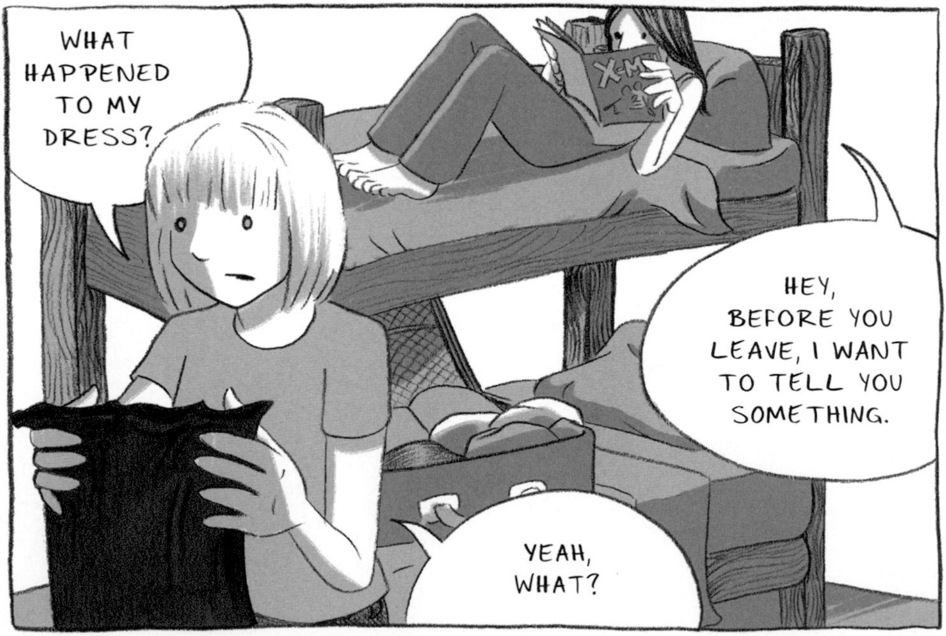
WHAT HAPPENED TO MY DRESS?
X-MEN
HEY, BEFORE YOU LEAVE, I WANT TO TELL YOU SOMETHING.
YEAH, WHAT?

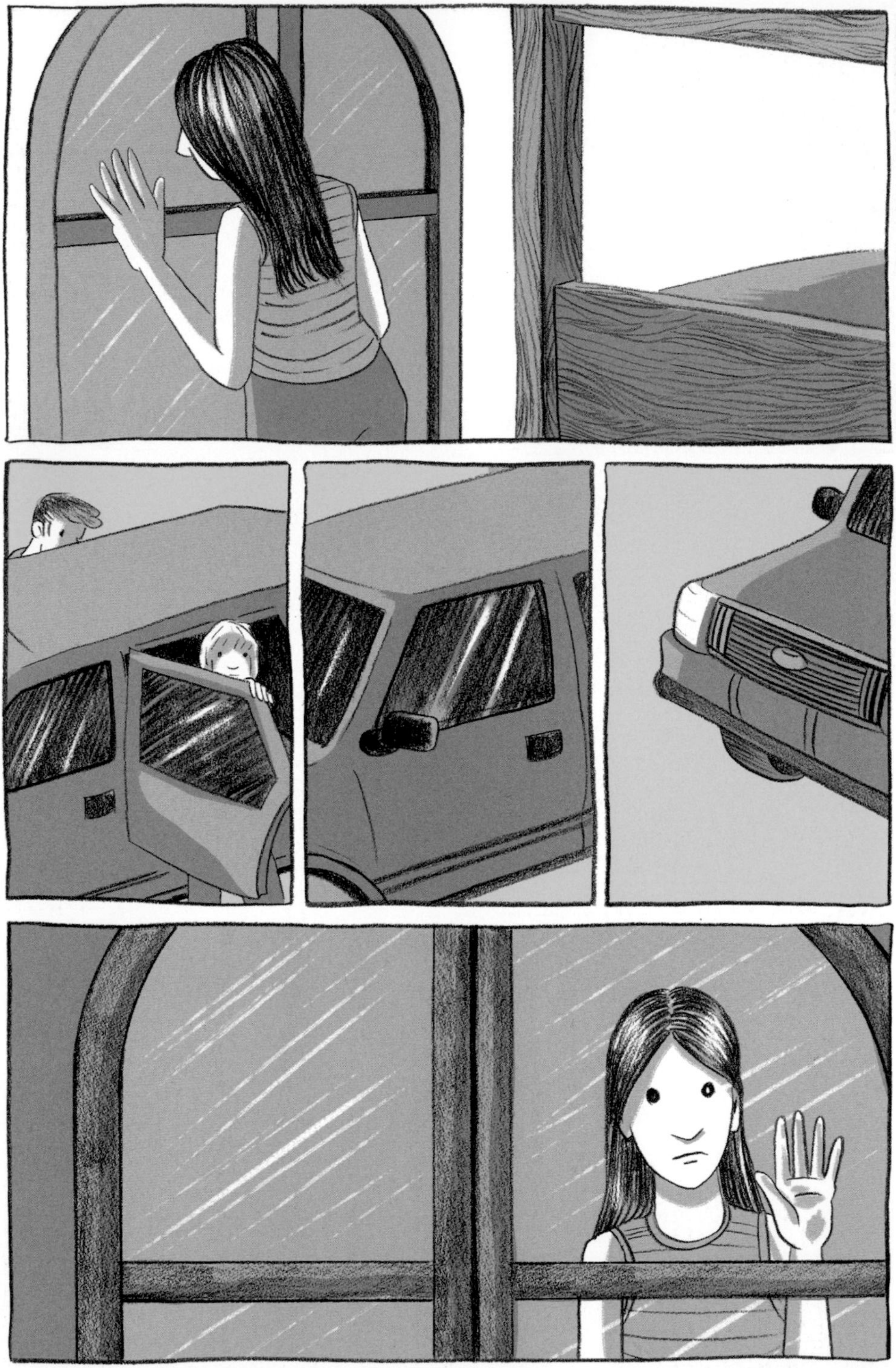

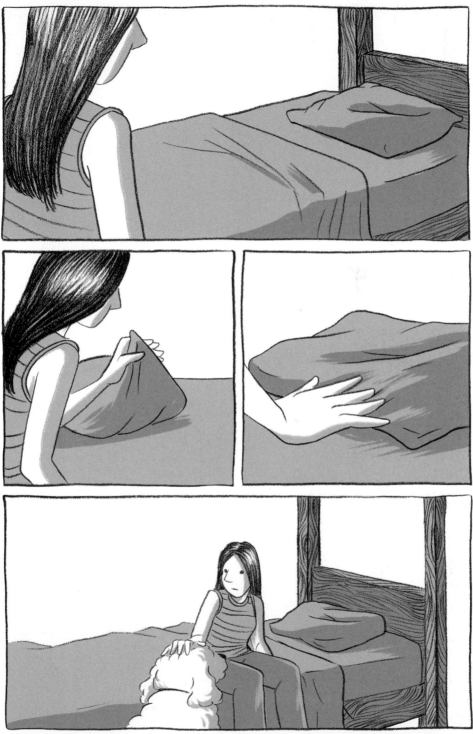

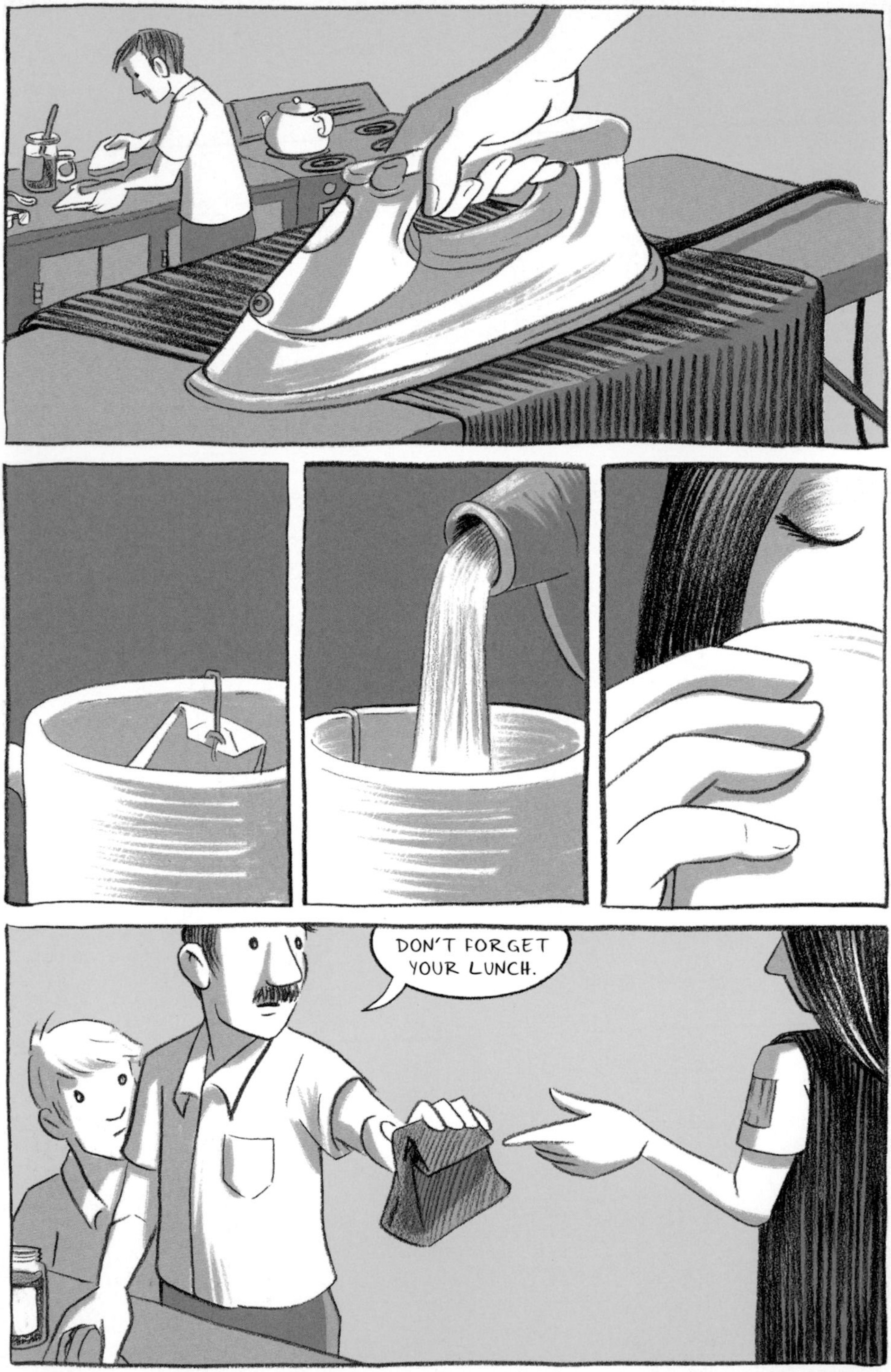
DON'T FORGET YOUR LUNCH.

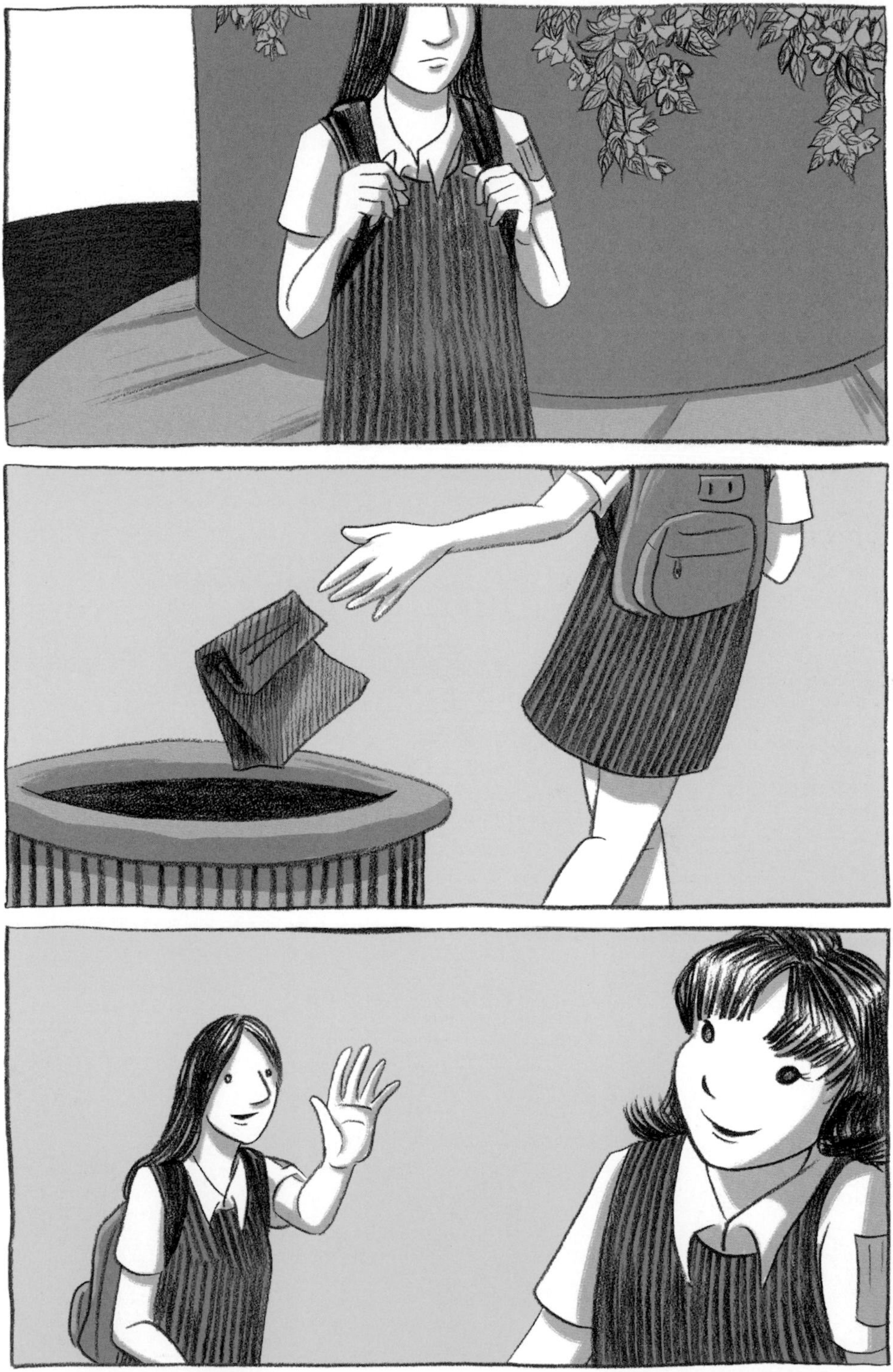

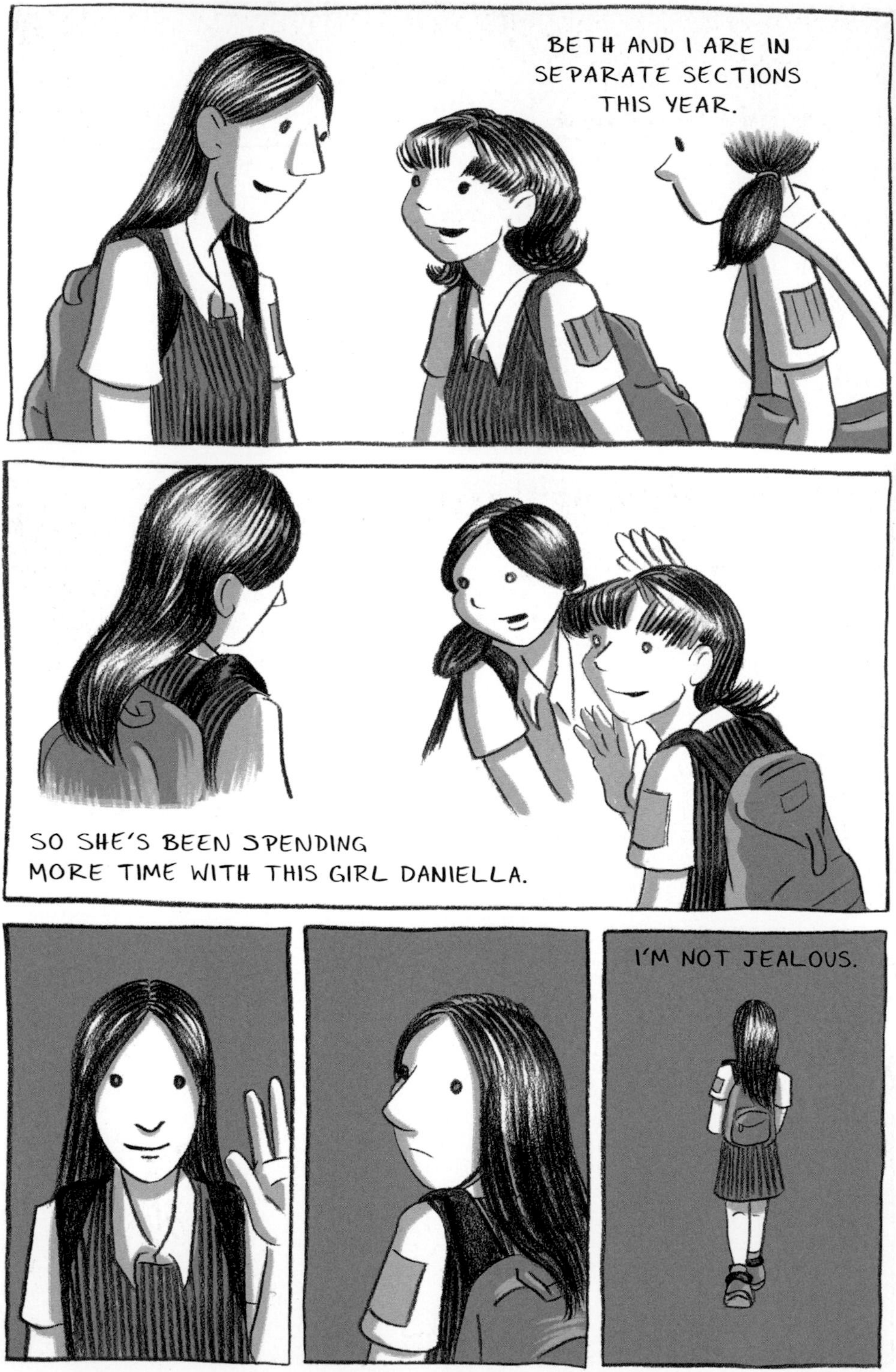
BETH AND I ARE IN SEPARATE SECTIONS THIS YEAR.
SO SHE'S BEEN SPENDING MORE TIME WITH THIS GIRL DANIELLA.
I'M NOT JEALOUS.

213

217

218

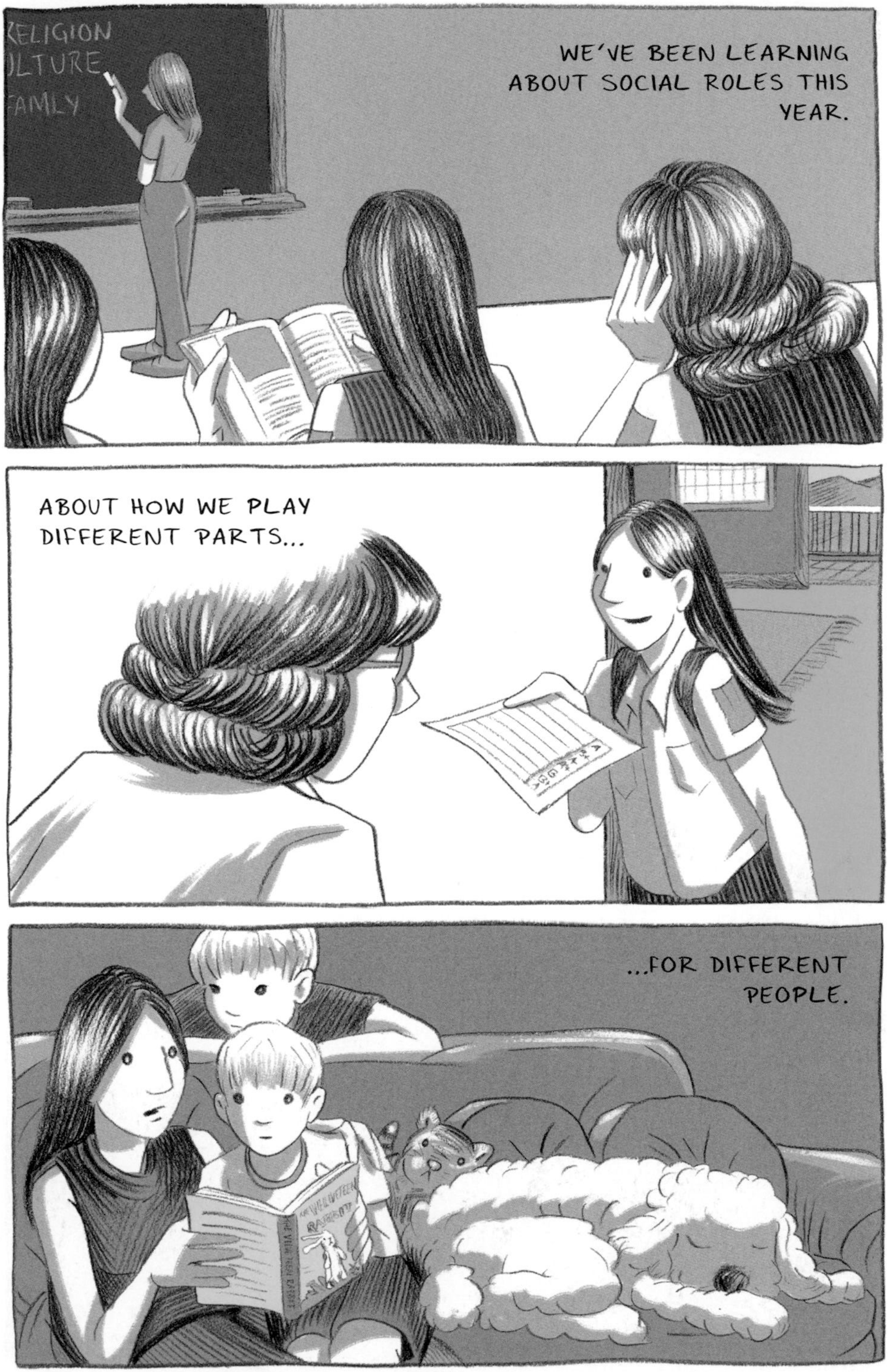
RELIGION
WE'VE BEEN LEARNING ABOUT SOCIAL ROLES THIS YEAR.
ABOUT HOW WE PLAY DIFFERENT PARTS...
...FOR DIFFERENT PEOPLE.

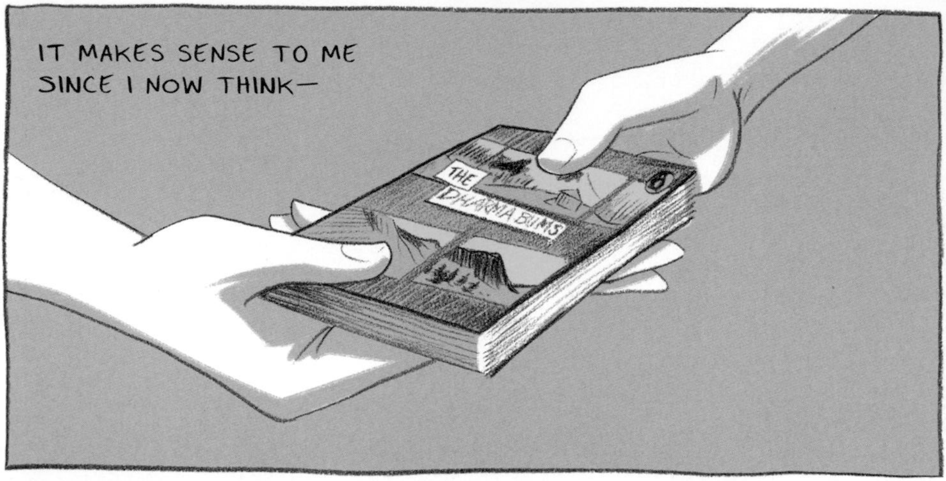
IT MAKES SENSE TO ME
SINCE I NOW THINK—
THE DHARMA BUMS

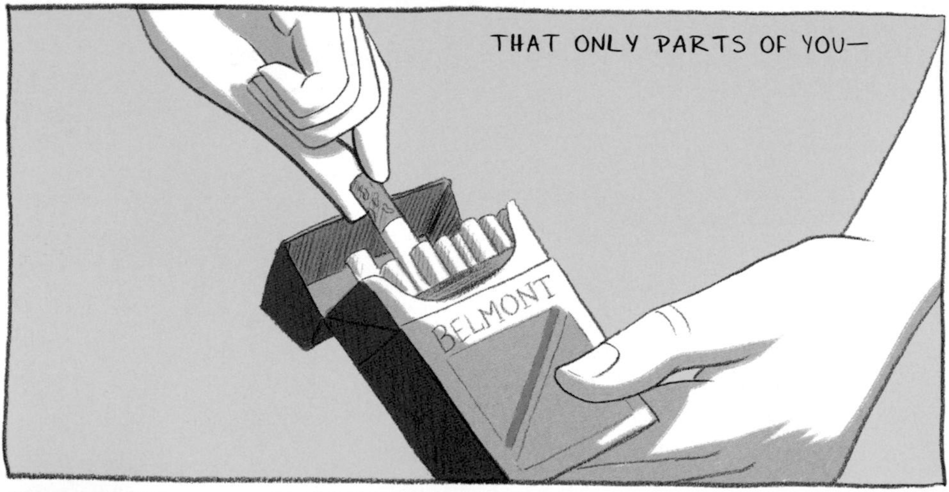
THAT ONLY PARTS OF YOU—
BELMONT

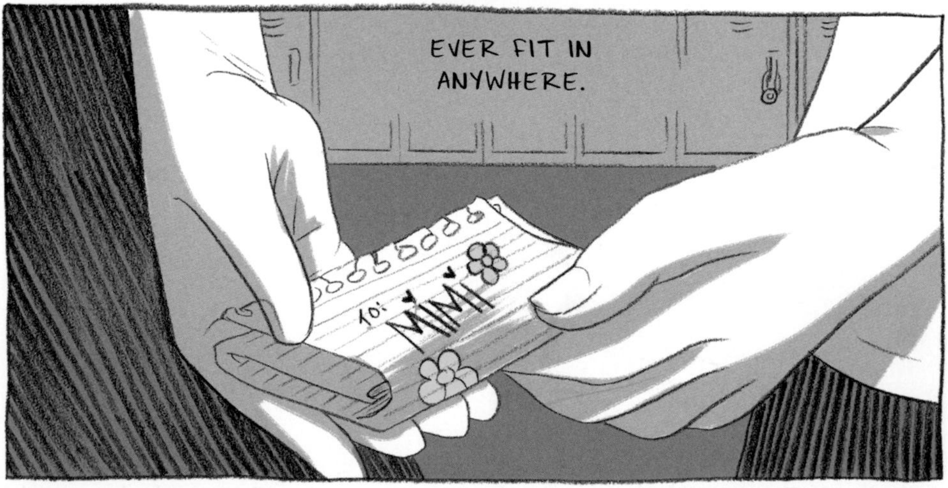
EVER FIT IN
ANYWHERE.
TO: MIMI

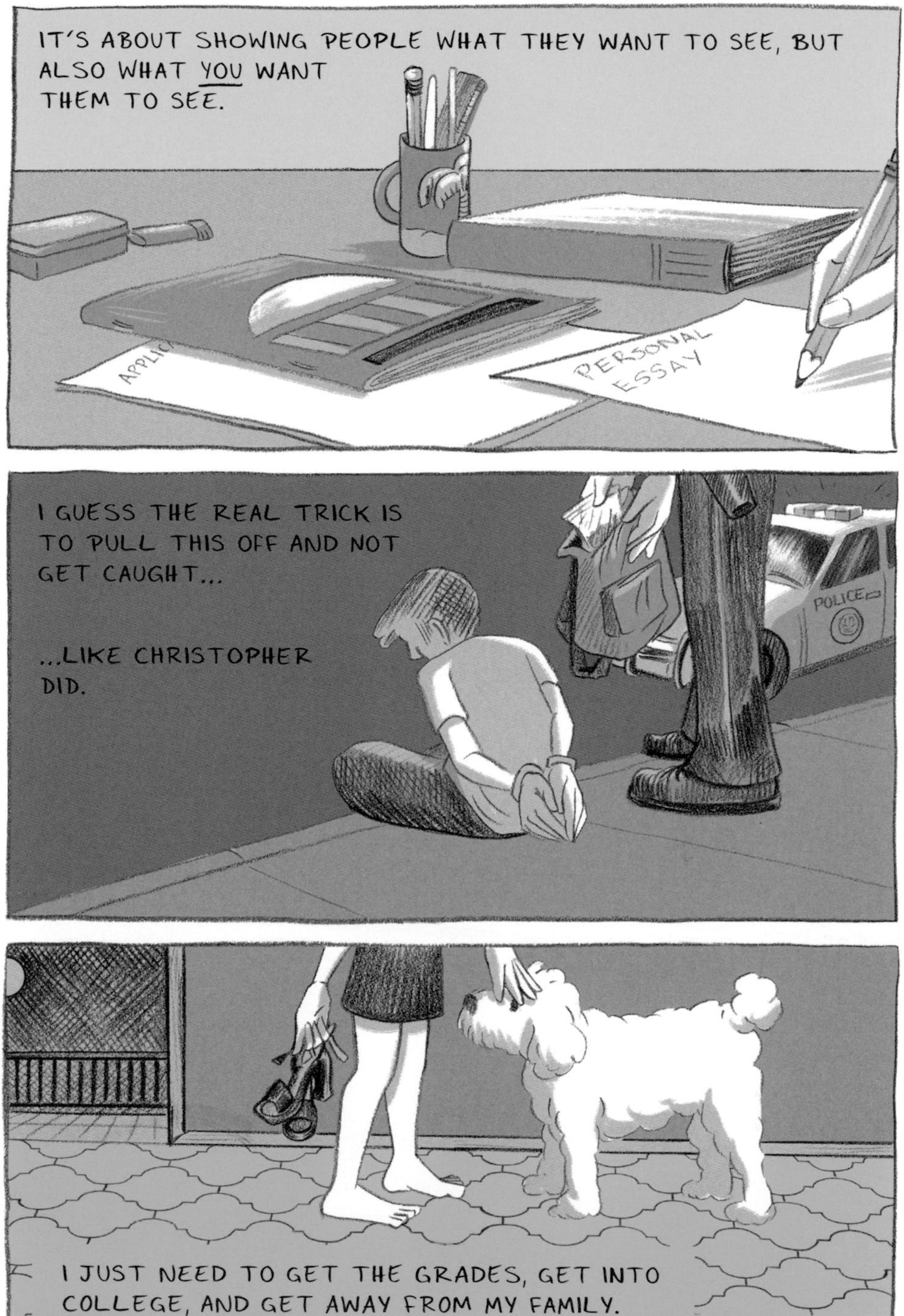
IT'S ABOUT SHOWING PEOPLE WHAT THEY WANT TO SEE, BUT ALSO WHAT YOU WANT THEM TO SEE.
PERSONAL ESSAY
I GUESS THE REAL TRICK IS TO PULL THIS OFF AND NOT GET CAUGHT...
...LIKE CHRISTOPHER DID.
POLICE
I JUST NEED TO GET THE GRADES, GET INTO COLLEGE, AND GET AWAY FROM MY FAMILY.
ALL WHILE HAVING AS MUCH FUN AS POSSIBLE.

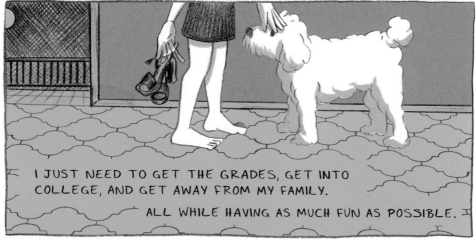

224

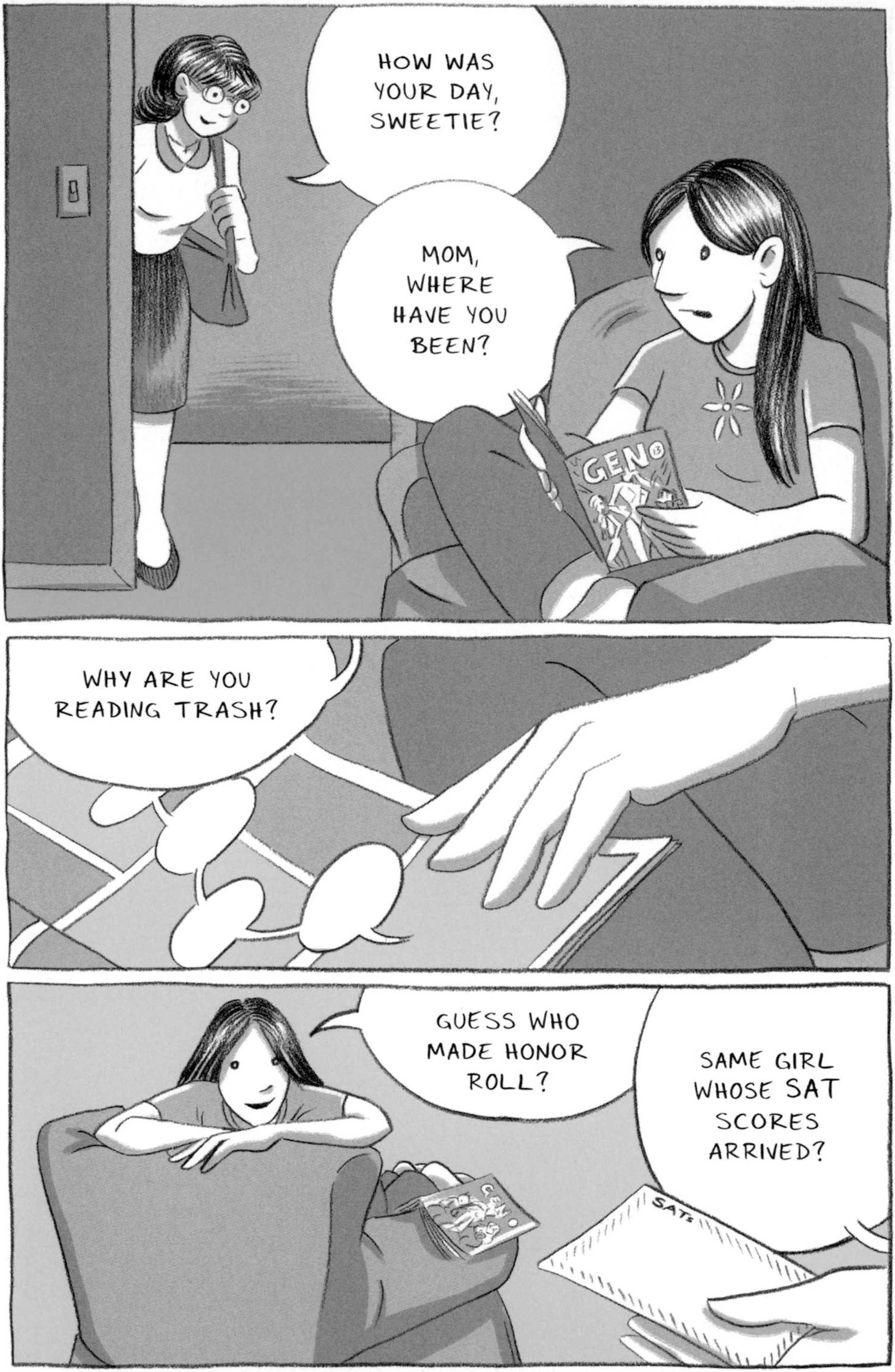
HOW WAS YOUR DAY, SWEETIE?
MOM, WHERE HAVE YOU BEEN?
GEN 13
WHY ARE YOU READING TRASH?
GUESS WHO MADE HONOR ROLL?
SAME GIRL WHOSE SAT SCORES ARRIVED?
SATs

229

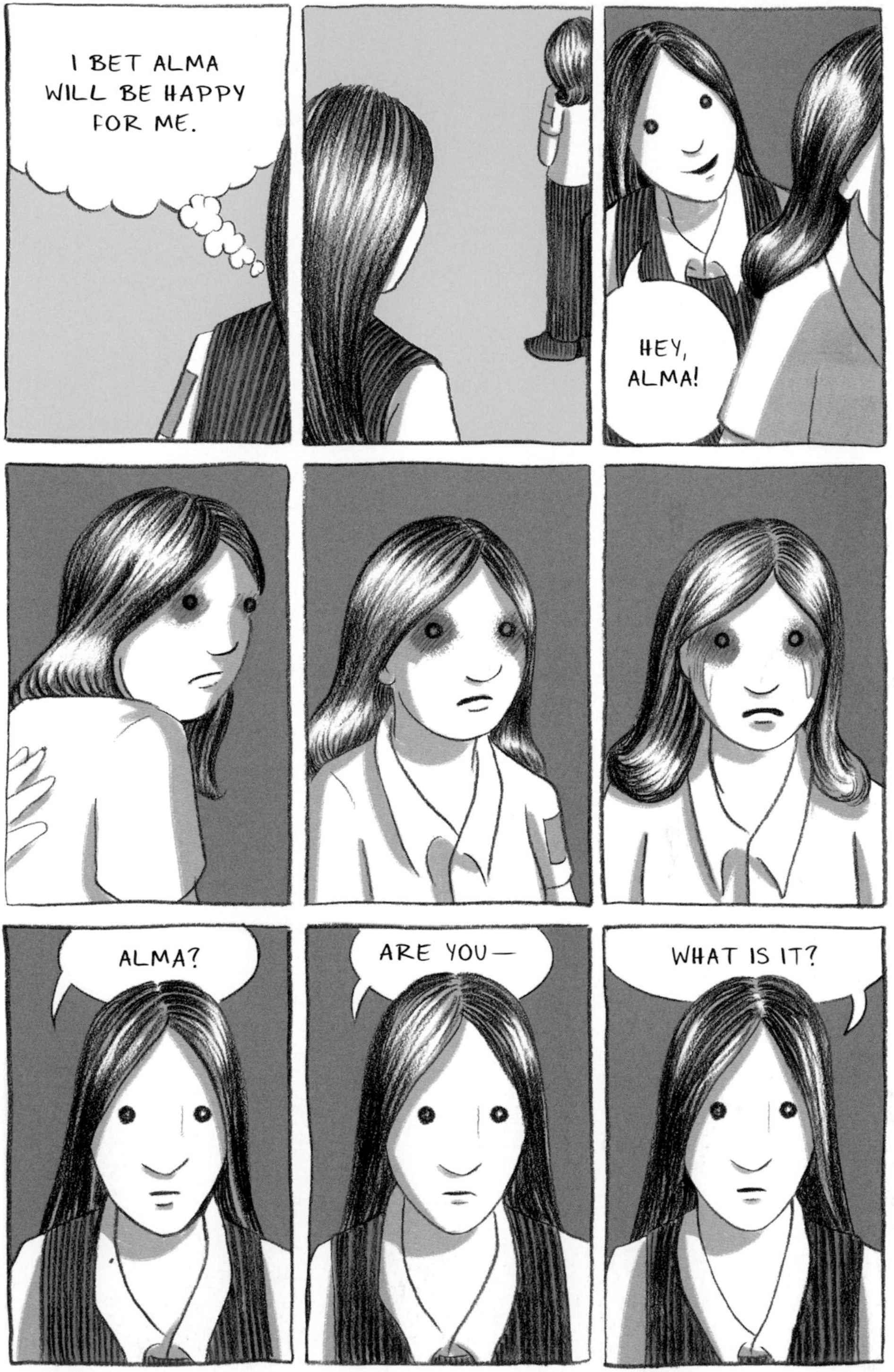
I BET ALMA WILL BE HAPPY FOR ME.
HEY, ALMA!
ALMA?
ARE YOU—
WHAT IS IT?

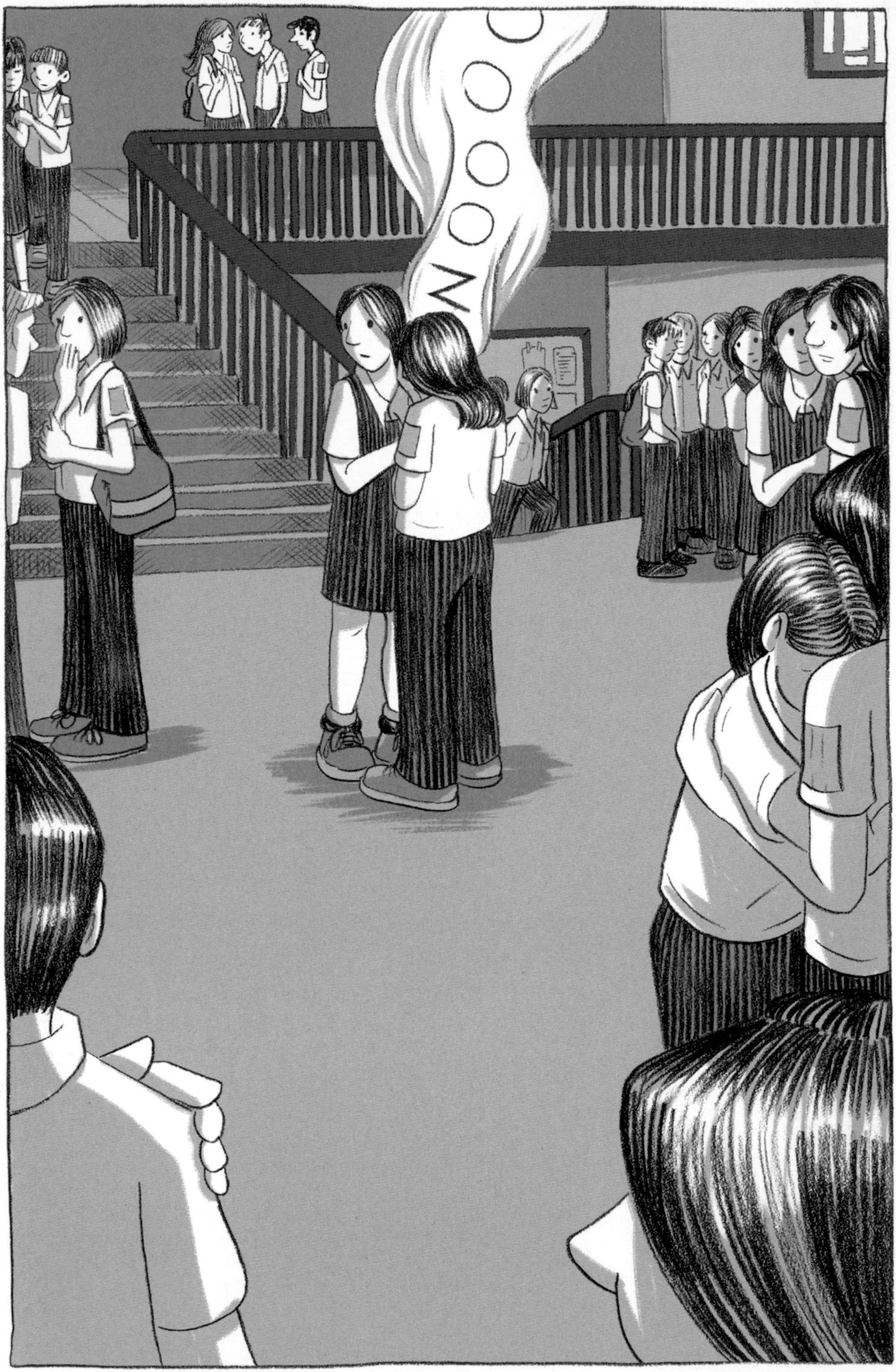
NOOOO

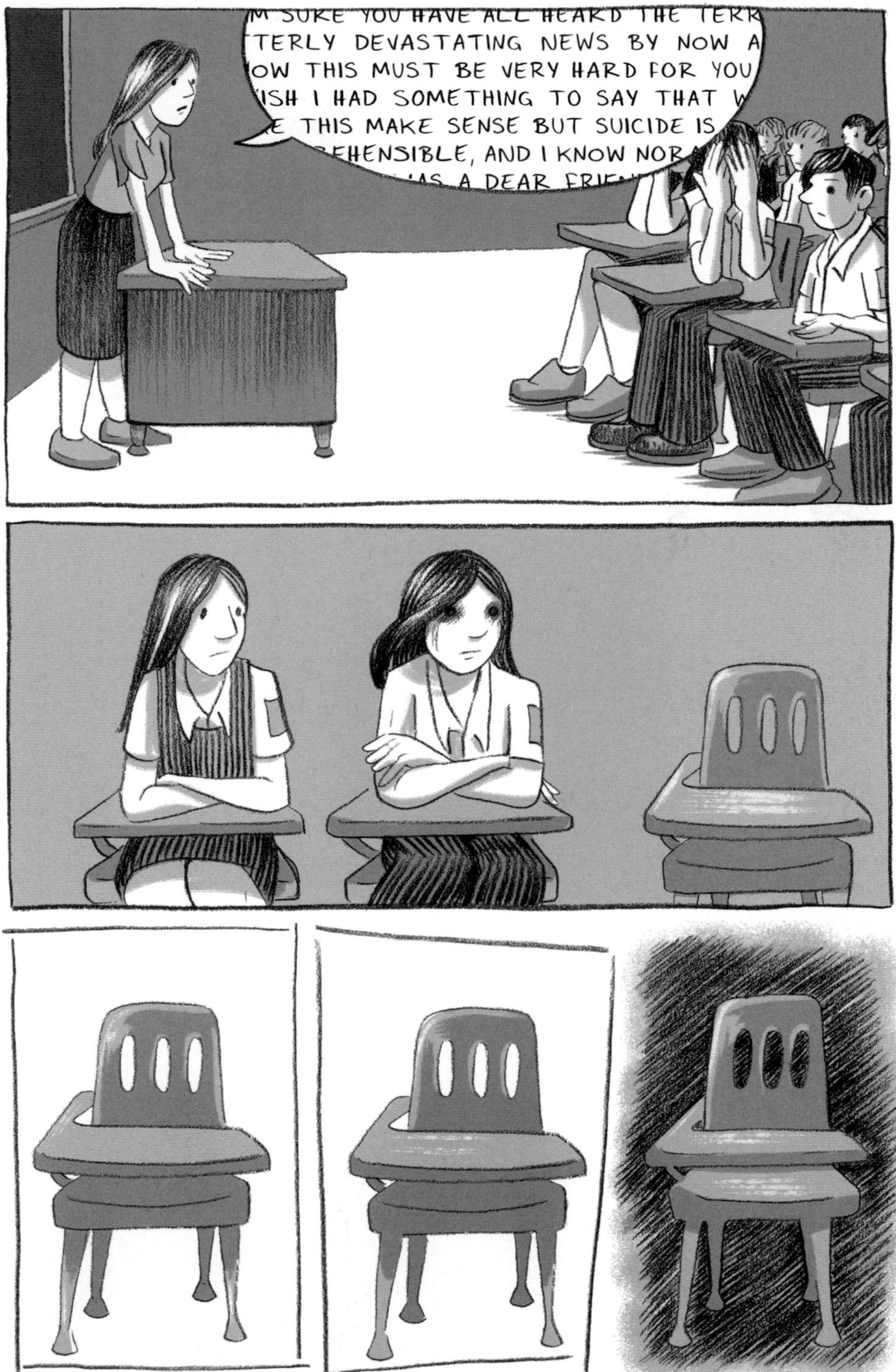
SURE YOU HAVE ALL HEARD THE
DEVASTATING NEWS BY NOW
THIS MUST BE VERY HARD FOR YOU
I HAD SOMETHING TO SAY THAT
THIS MAKE SENSE BUT SUICIDE IS
AND I KNOW
A DEAR

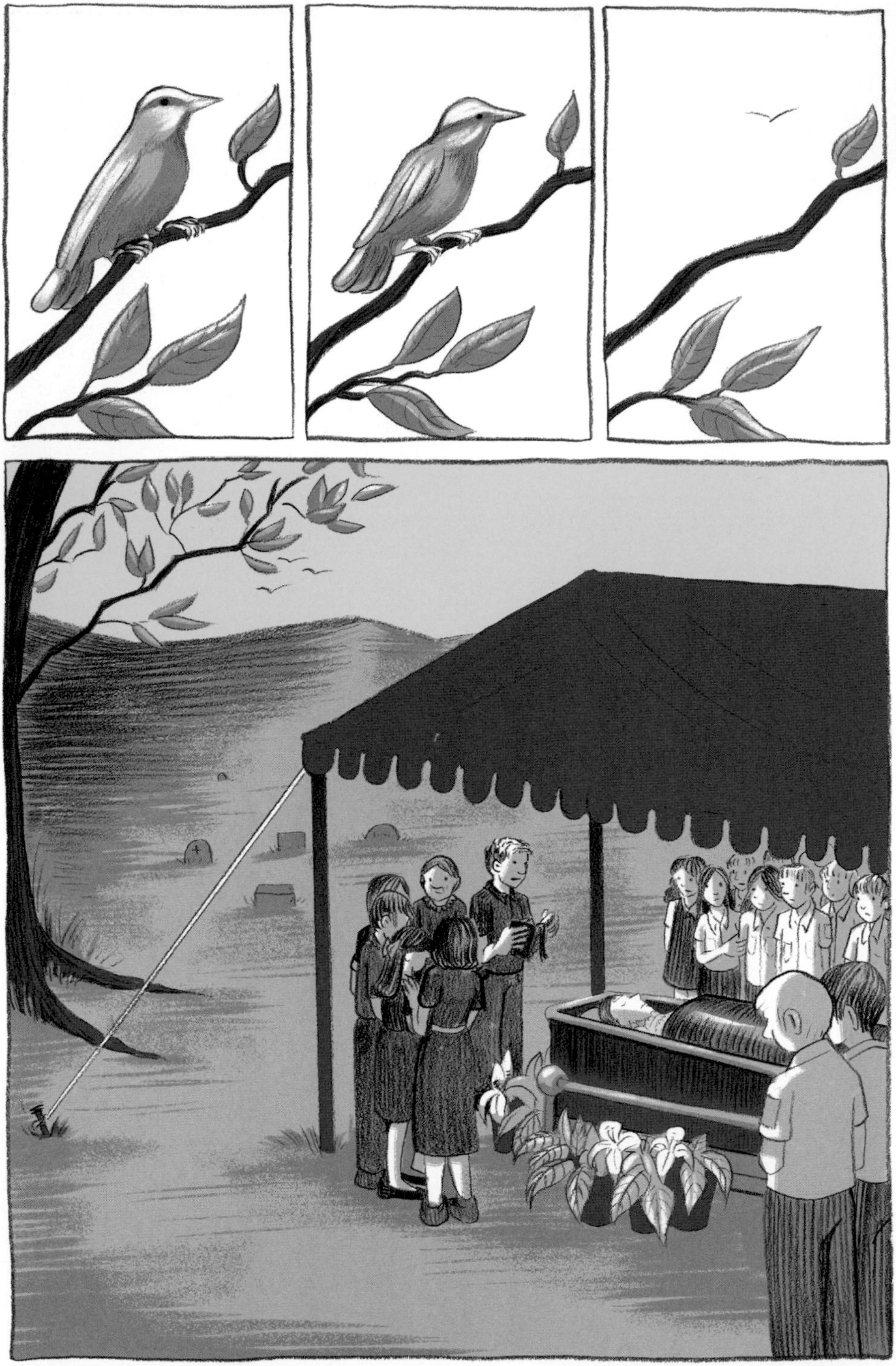

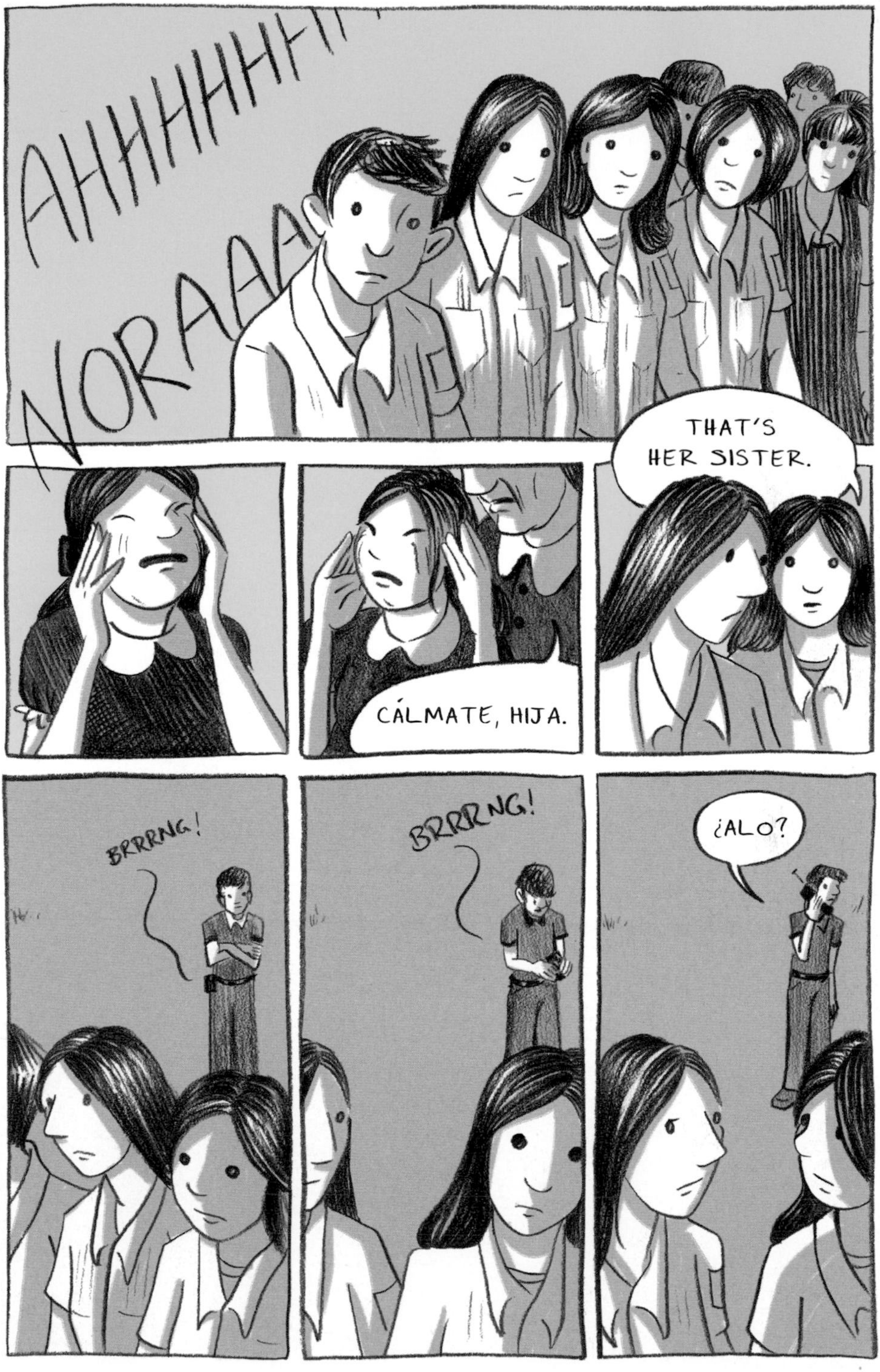
AHHHHHH
NORAAA
THAT'S HER SISTER.
CÁLMATE, HIJA.
BRRRNG!
BRRRNG!
¿ALO?

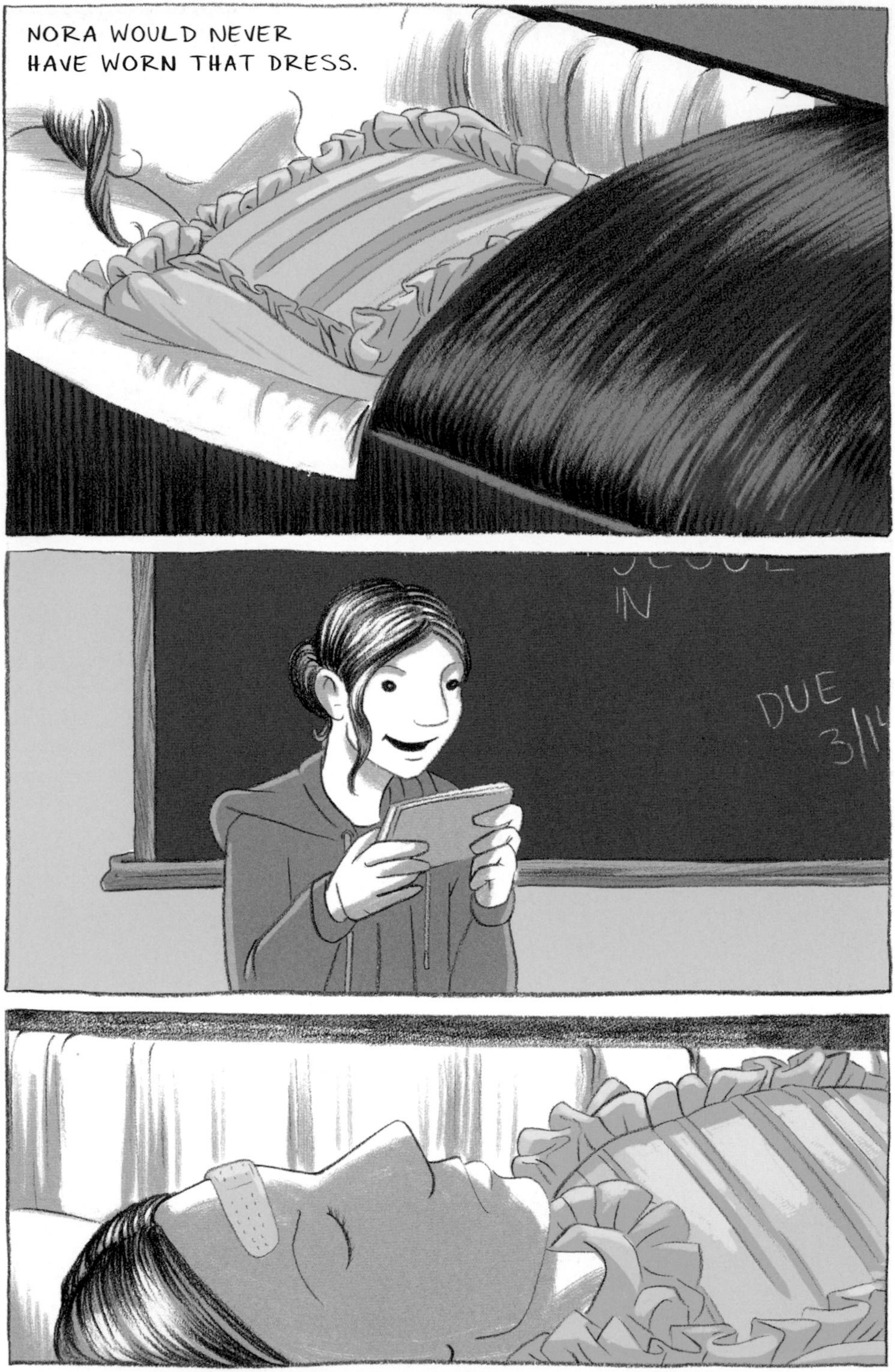
NORA WOULD NEVER HAVE WORN THAT DRESS.
IN
DUE

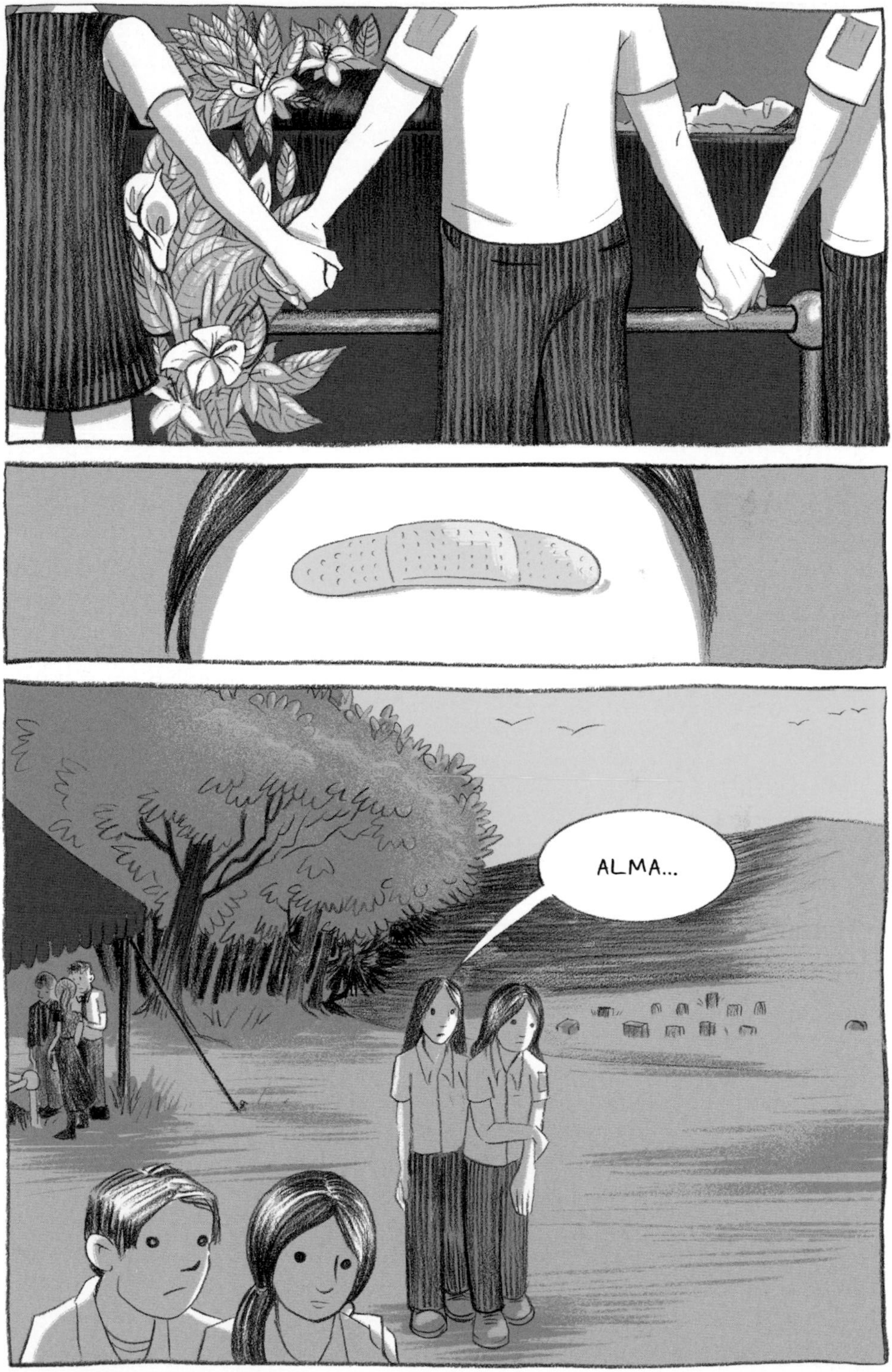
ALMA...

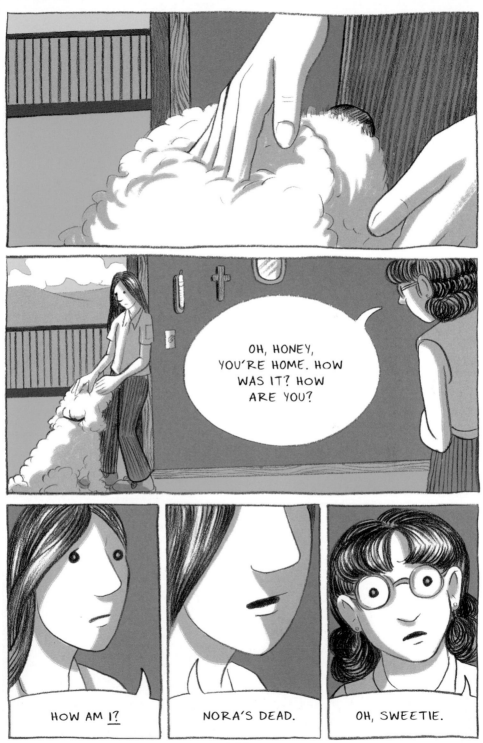

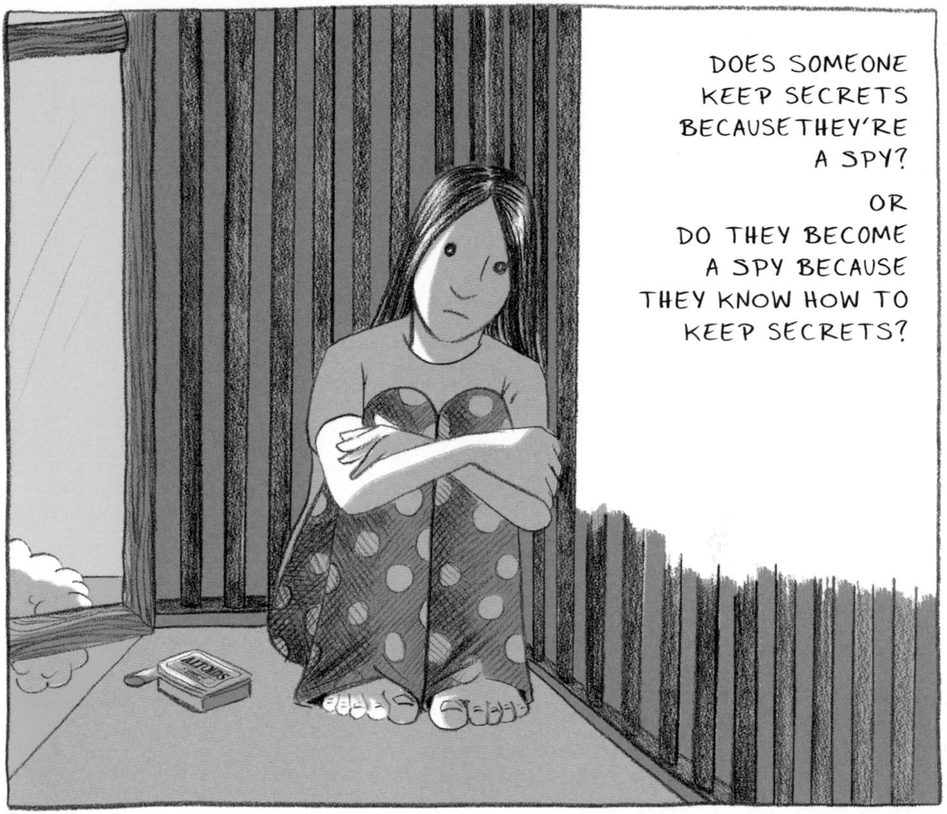
DOES SOMEONE KEEP SECRETS BECAUSE THEY'RE A SPY?
OR DO THEY BECOME A SPY BECAUSE THEY KNOW HOW TO KEEP SECRETS?
ALTOIDS

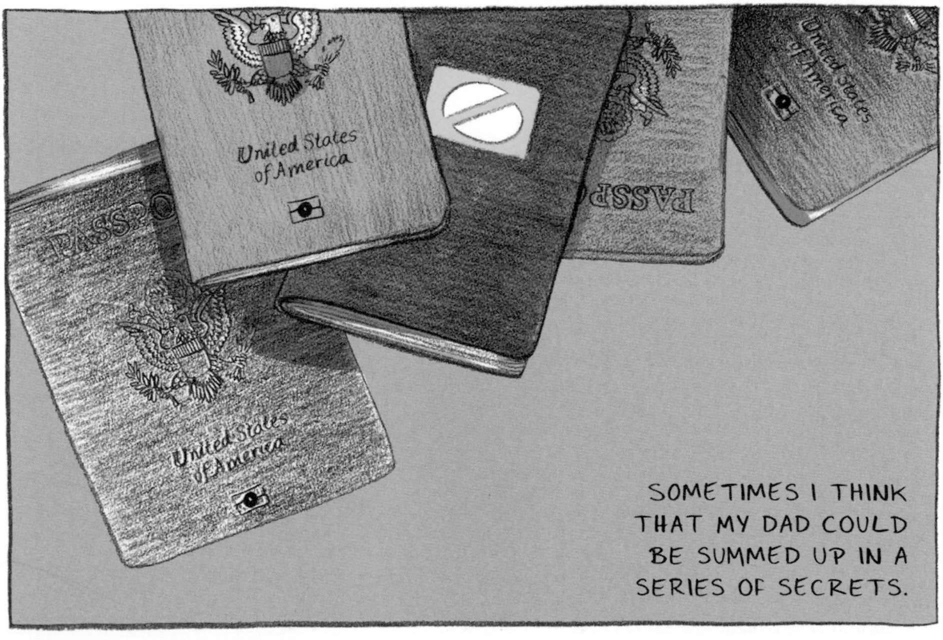
United States of America
PASSPO
United States of America
PASSP
United States of America
SOMETIMES I THINK THAT MY DAD COULD BE SUMMED UP IN A SERIES OF SECRETS.

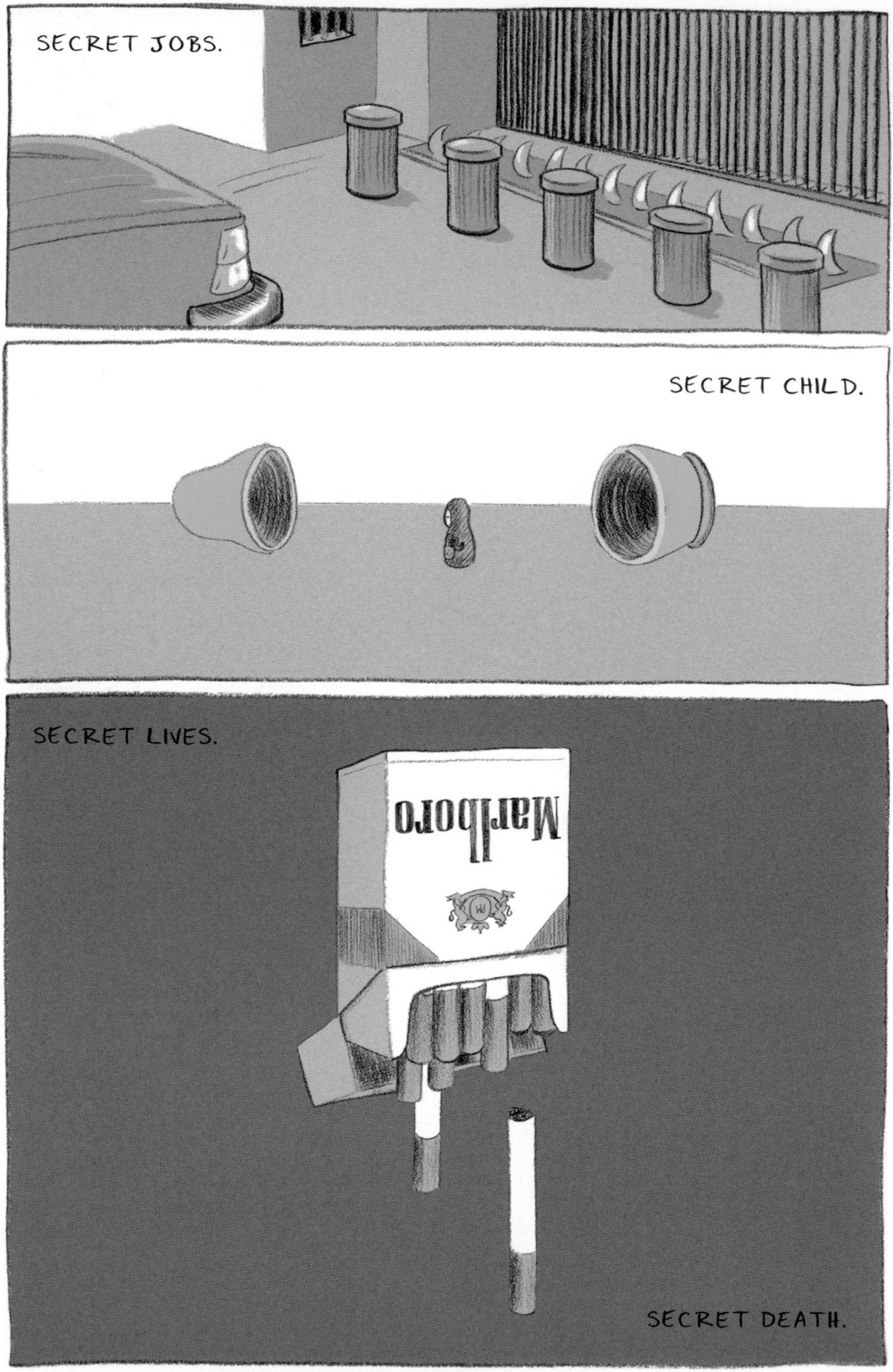
SECRET JOBS.
SECRET CHILD.
SECRET LIVES.
Marlboro
SECRET DEATH.

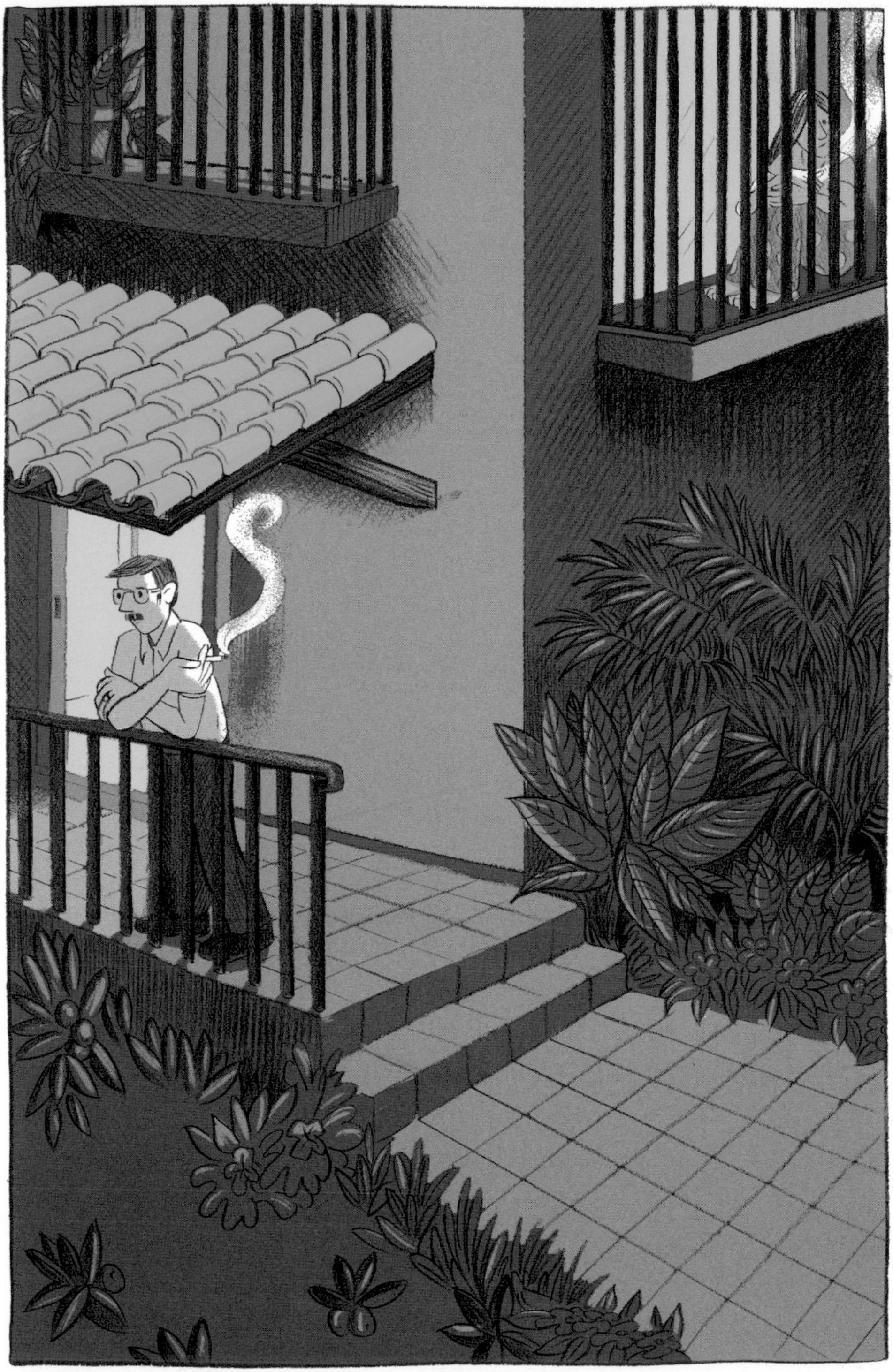

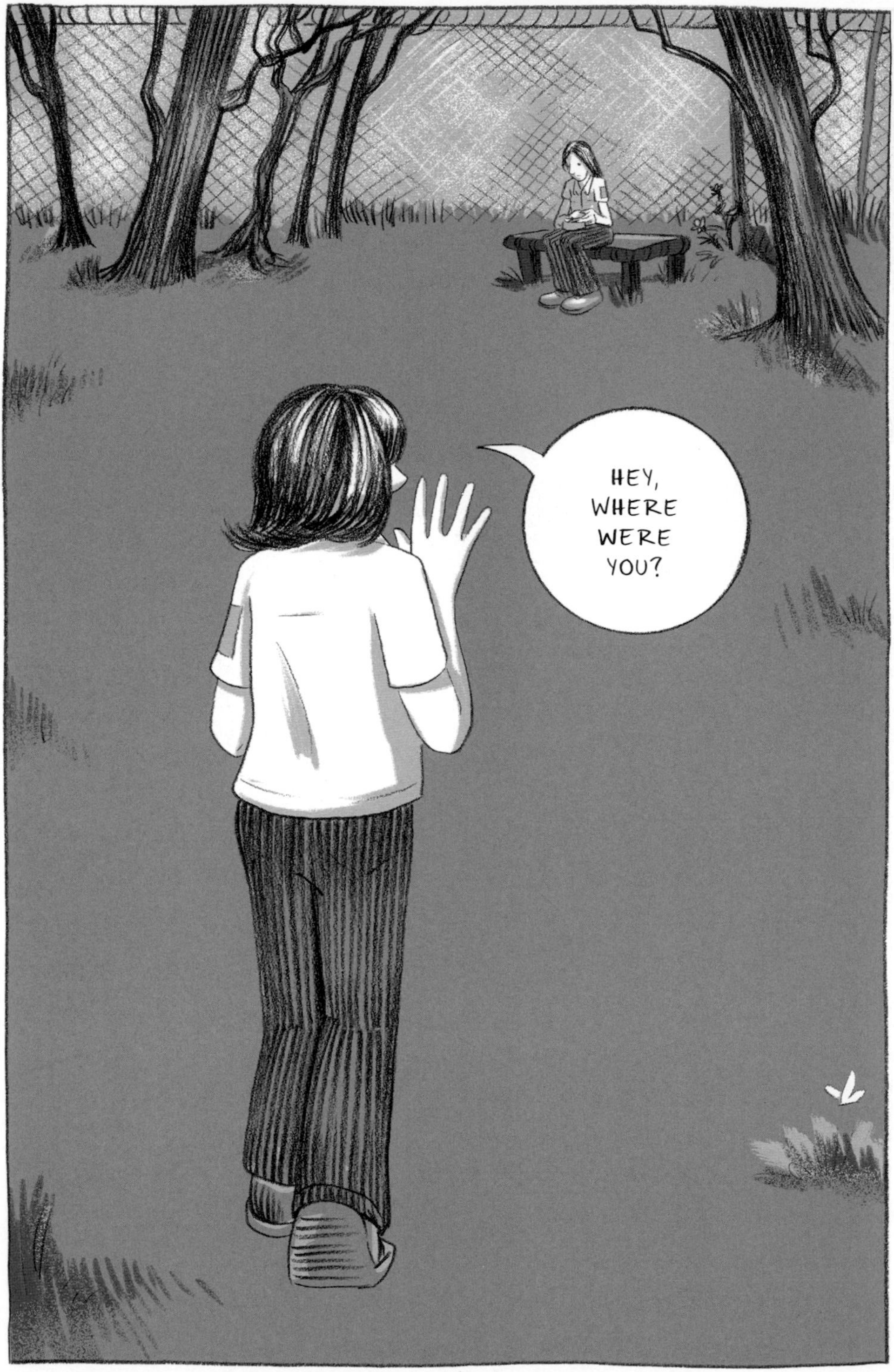
HEY, WHERE WERE YOU?

248

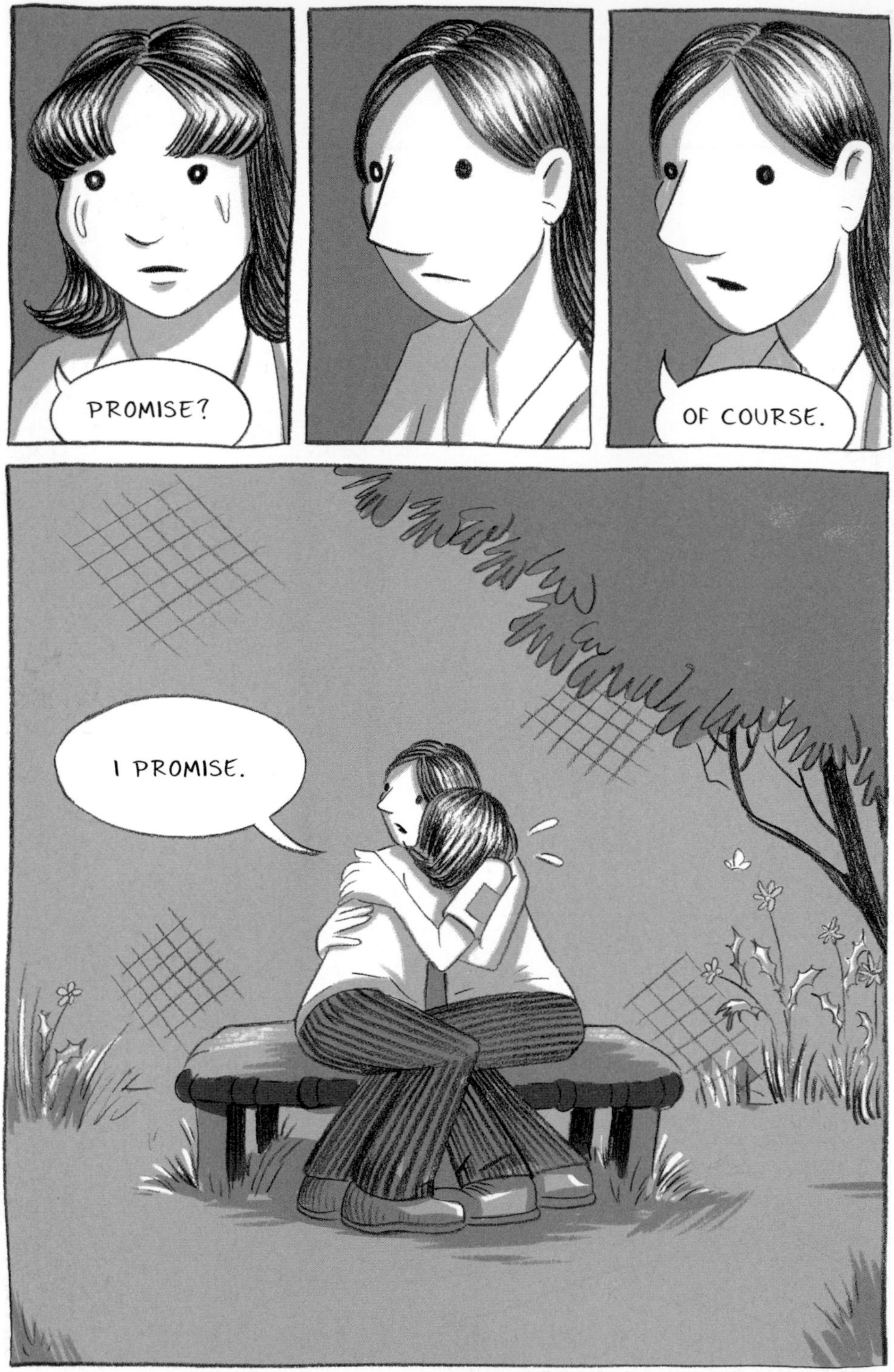
PROMISE?
OF COURSE.
I PROMISE.

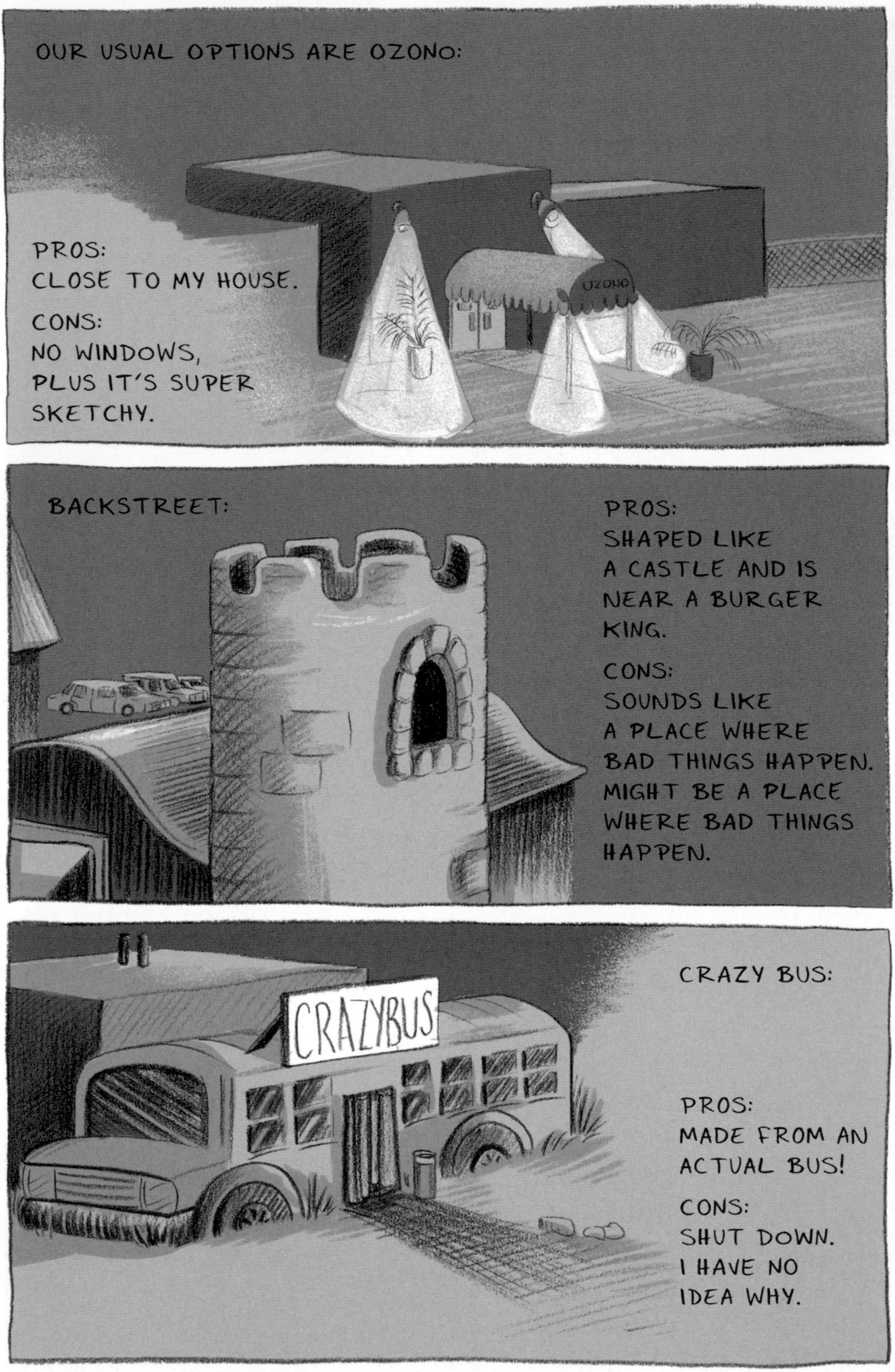
OUR USUAL OPTIONS ARE OZONO:
PROS:
CLOSE TO MY HOUSE.
CONS:
NO WINDOWS, PLUS IT'S SUPER SKETCHY.
BACKSTREET:
PROS:
SHAPED LIKE A CASTLE AND IS NEAR A BURGER KING.
CONS:
SOUNDS LIKE A PLACE WHERE BAD THINGS HAPPEN. MIGHT BE A PLACE WHERE BAD THINGS HAPPEN.
CRAZYBUS
CRAZY BUS:
PROS:
MADE FROM AN ACTUAL BUS!
CONS:
SHUT DOWN. I HAVE NO IDEA WHY.

BUT PRACTICALLY EVERY WEEKEND WE END UP AT ARENAS.
ARENAS
PROS:
THIS IS WHERE EVERYONE GOES.
CONS:
CREEPY OWNER HAS A CRUSH ON BETH.

BETH WOULD CALL THAT A "PRO," SINCE HE USUALLY INSISTS THAT WE HANG OUT IN THE VIP SECTION.

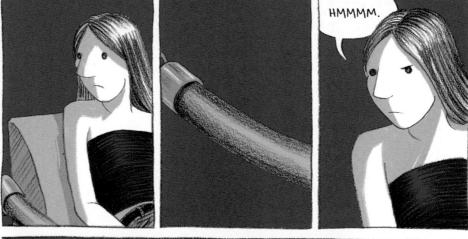

HMMMM.

ISN'T THIS COOL?

IT'S EXACTLY THE SAME. THERE'S JUST THAT STUPID ROPE.

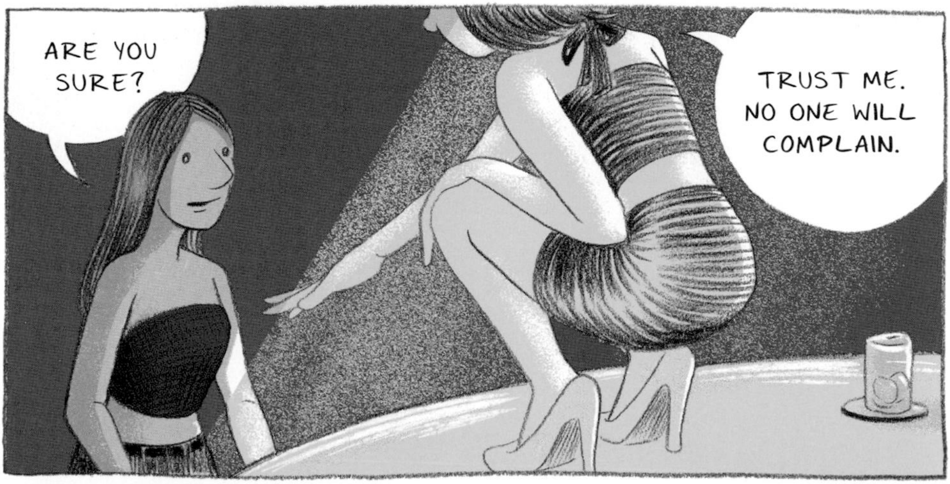
ARE YOU SURE?
TRUST ME. NO ONE WILL COMPLAIN.

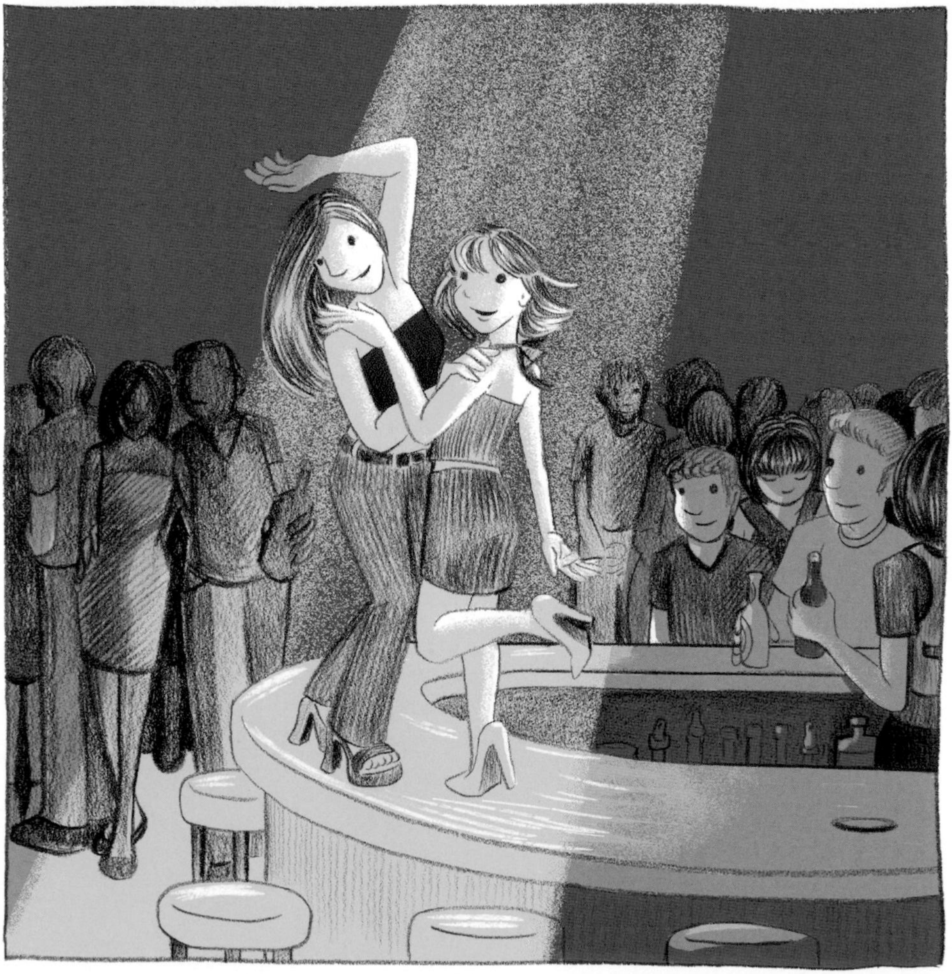

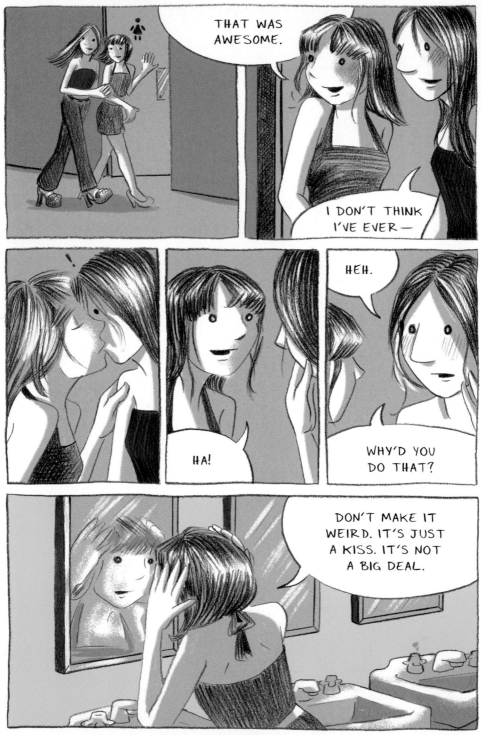

259

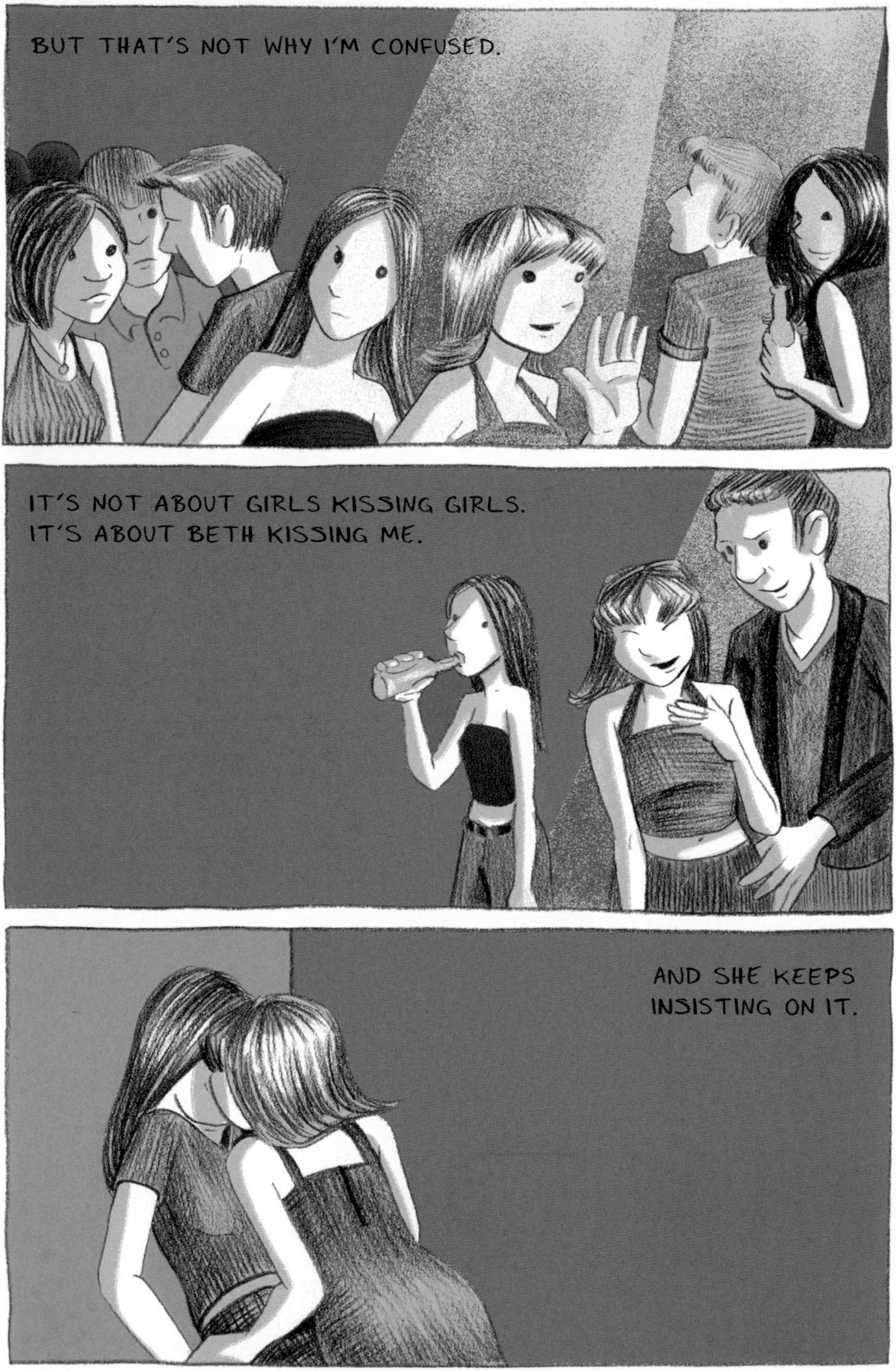
BUT THAT'S NOT WHY I'M CONFUSED.
IT'S NOT ABOUT GIRLS KISSING GIRLS.
IT'S ABOUT BETH KISSING ME.
AND SHE KEEPS
INSISTING ON IT.

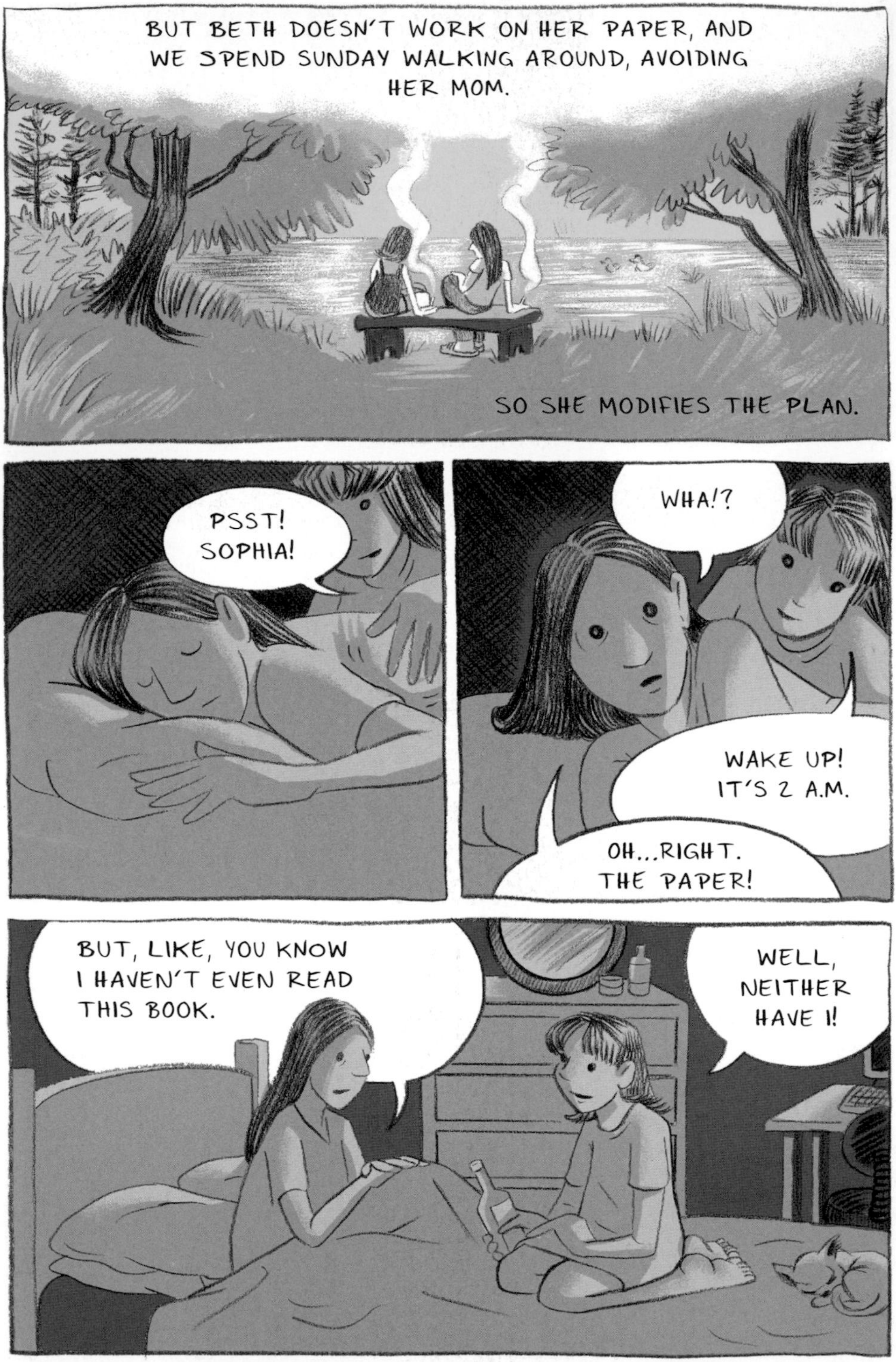
BUT BETH DOESN'T WORK ON HER PAPER, AND WE SPEND SUNDAY WALKING AROUND, AVOIDING HER MOM.
SO SHE MODIFIES THE PLAN.
PSST! SOPHIA!
WHA!?
WAKE UP! IT'S 2 A.M.
OH...RIGHT. THE PAPER!
BUT, LIKE, YOU KNOW I HAVEN'T EVEN READ THIS BOOK.
WELL, NEITHER HAVE I!

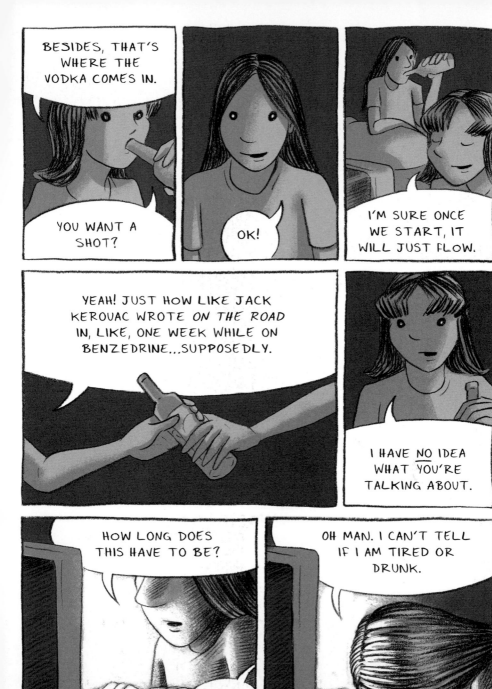

267

268

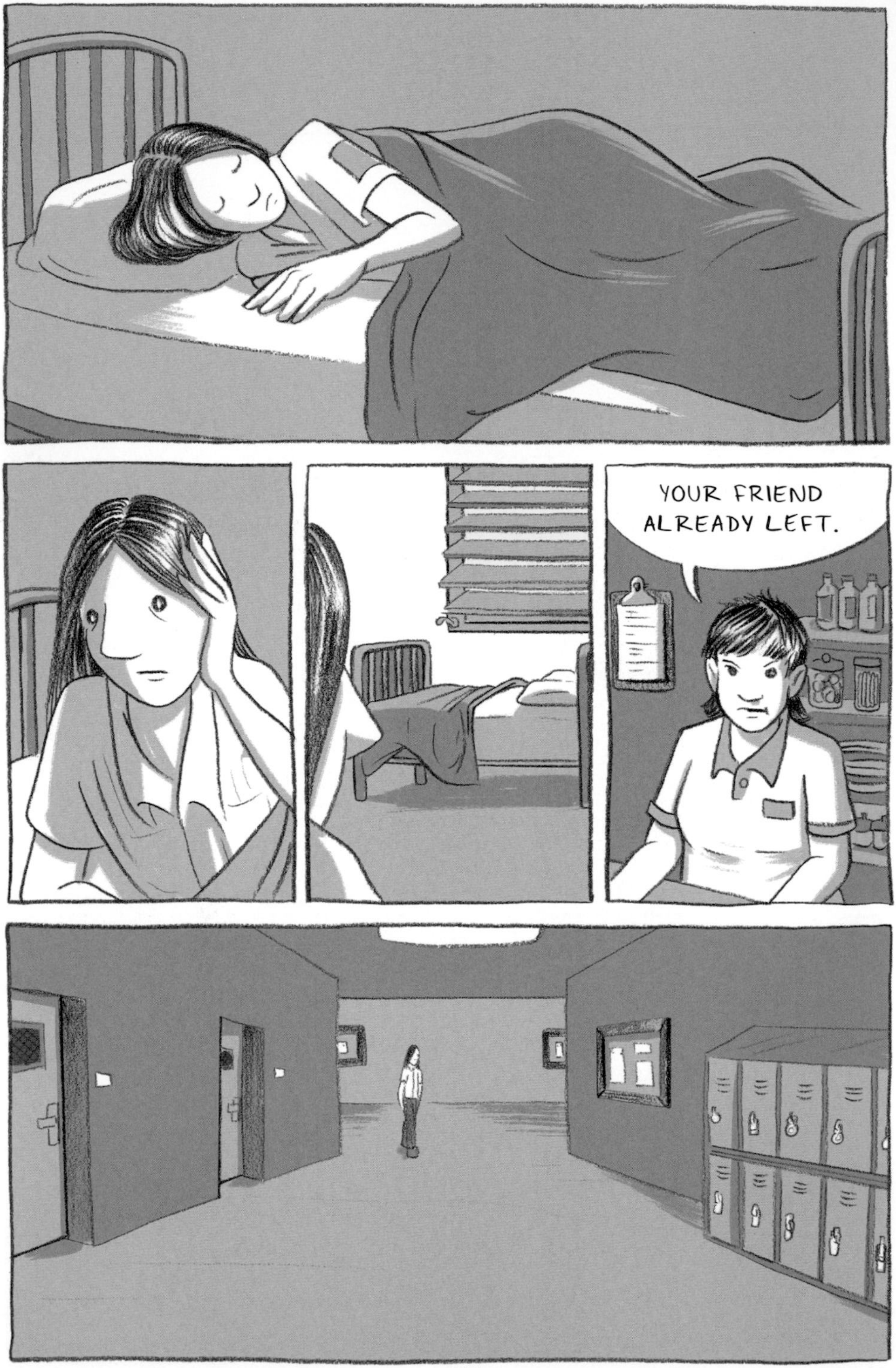
YOUR FRIEND
ALREADY LEFT.

271

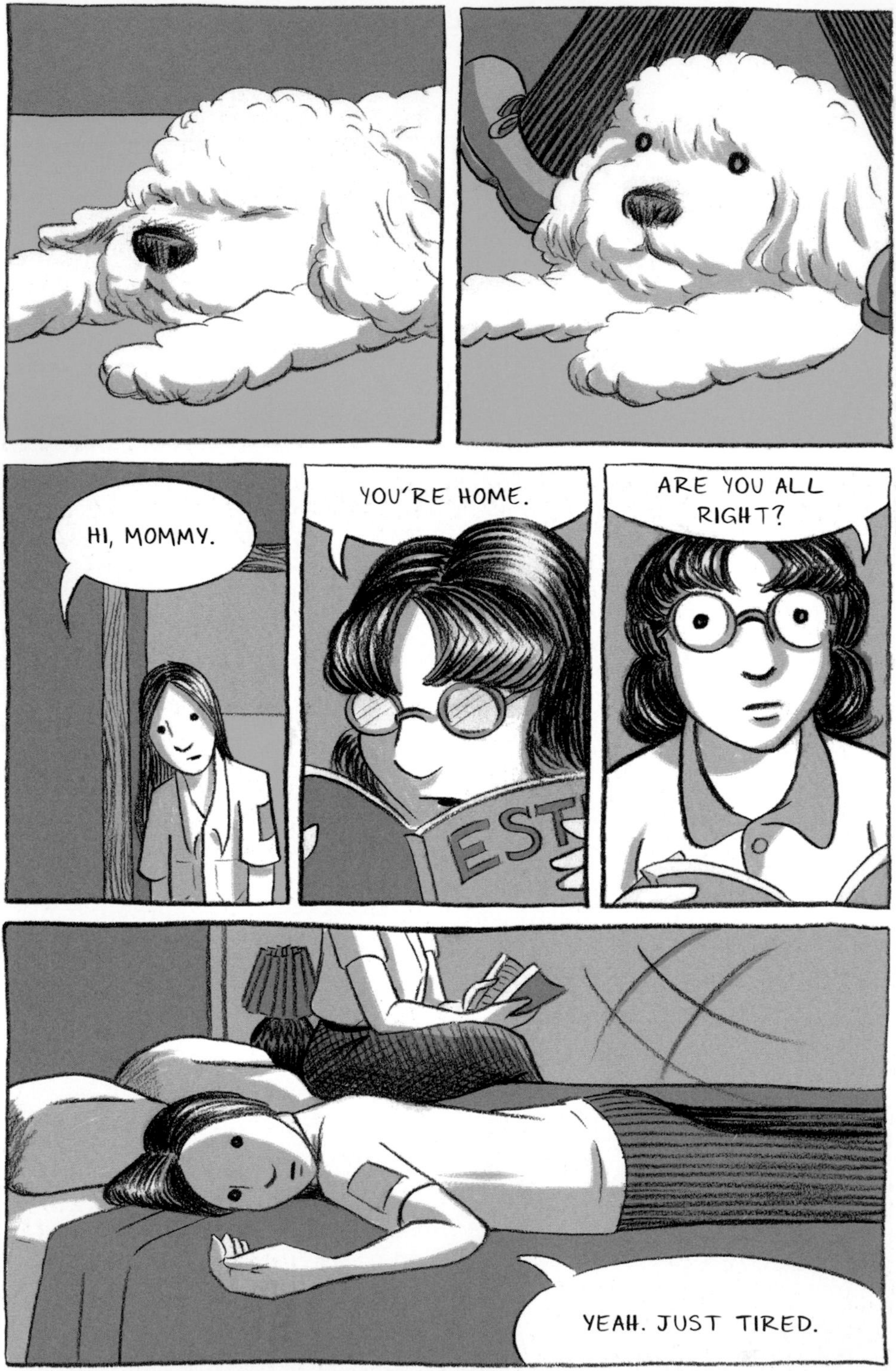
HI, MOMMY.
YOU'RE HOME.
ARE YOU ALL RIGHT?
YEAH. JUST TIRED.

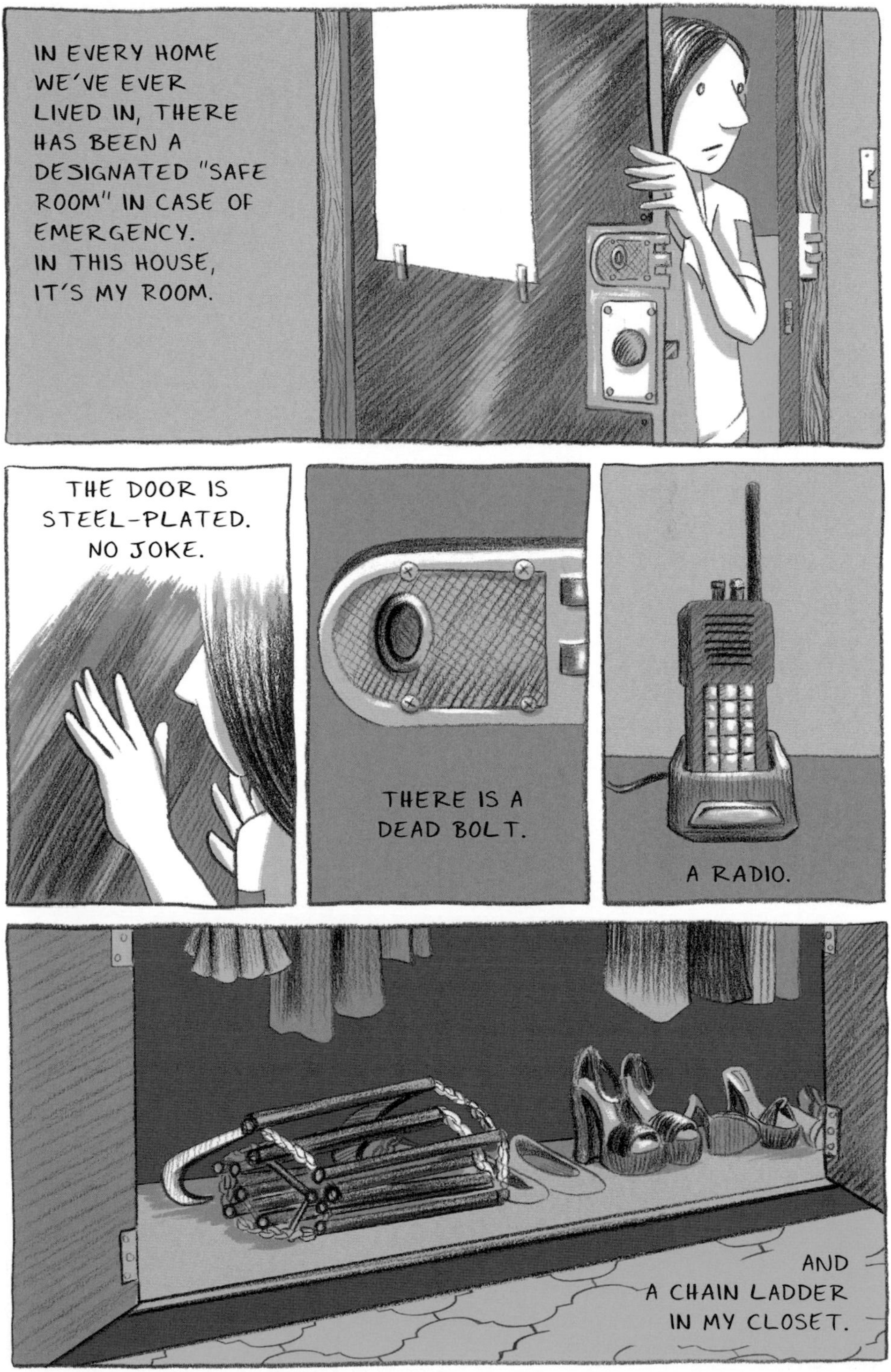
IN EVERY HOME WE'VE EVER LIVED IN, THERE HAS BEEN A DESIGNATED "SAFE ROOM" IN CASE OF EMERGENCY.
IN THIS HOUSE, IT'S MY ROOM.
THE DOOR IS STEEL-PLATED. NO JOKE.
THERE IS A DEAD BOLT.
A RADIO.
AND A CHAIN LADDER IN MY CLOSET.

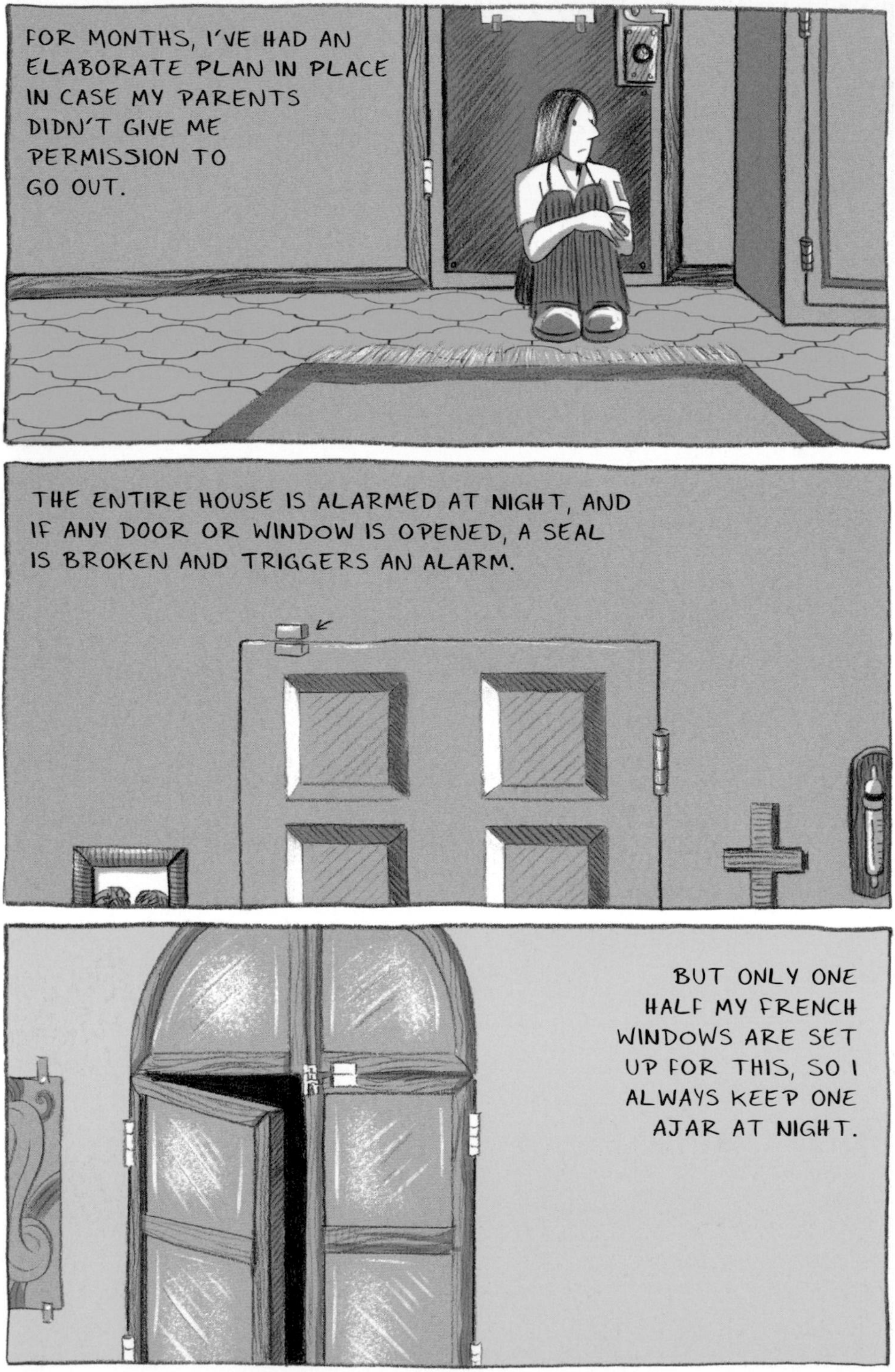
FOR MONTHS, I'VE HAD AN ELABORATE PLAN IN PLACE IN CASE MY PARENTS DIDN'T GIVE ME PERMISSION TO GO OUT.
THE ENTIRE HOUSE IS ALARMED AT NIGHT, AND IF ANY DOOR OR WINDOW IS OPENED, A SEAL IS BROKEN AND TRIGGERS AN ALARM.
BUT ONLY ONE HALF MY FRENCH WINDOWS ARE SET UP FOR THIS, SO I ALWAYS KEEP ONE AJAR AT NIGHT.

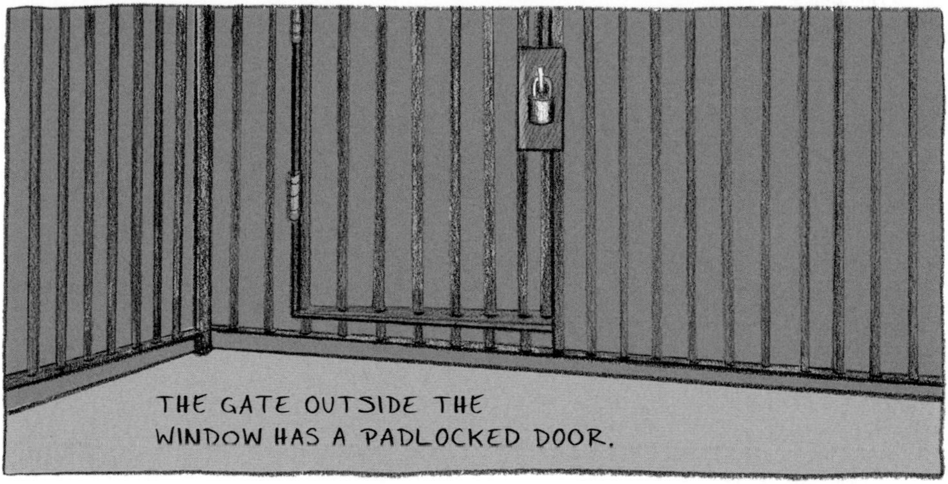
THE GATE OUTSIDE THE
WINDOW HAS A PADLOCKED DOOR.

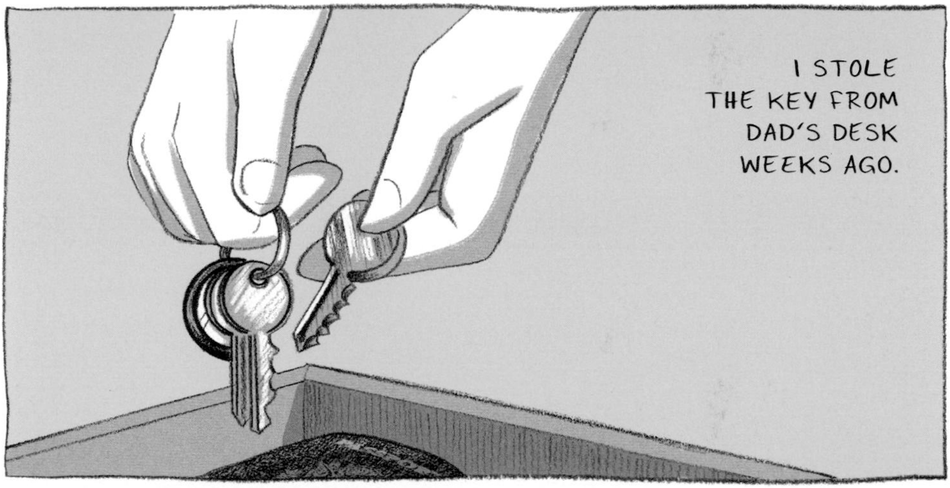
I STOLE
THE KEY FROM
DAD'S DESK
WEEKS AGO.

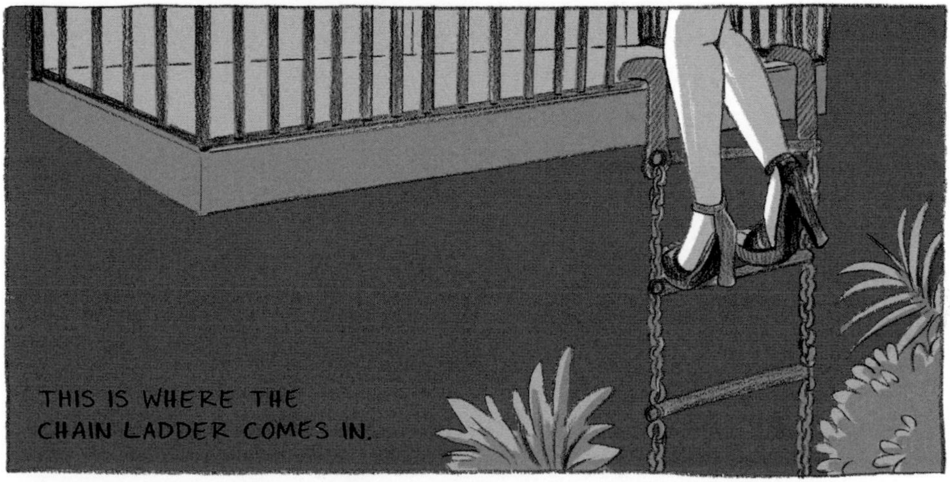
THIS IS WHERE THE
CHAIN LADDER COMES IN.

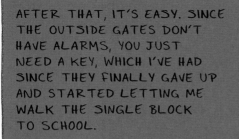

AFTER THAT, IT'S EASY. SINCE THE OUTSIDE GATES DON'T HAVE ALARMS, YOU JUST NEED A KEY, WHICH I'VE HAD SINCE THEY FINALLY GAVE UP AND STARTED LETTING ME WALK THE SINGLE BLOCK TO SCHOOL.

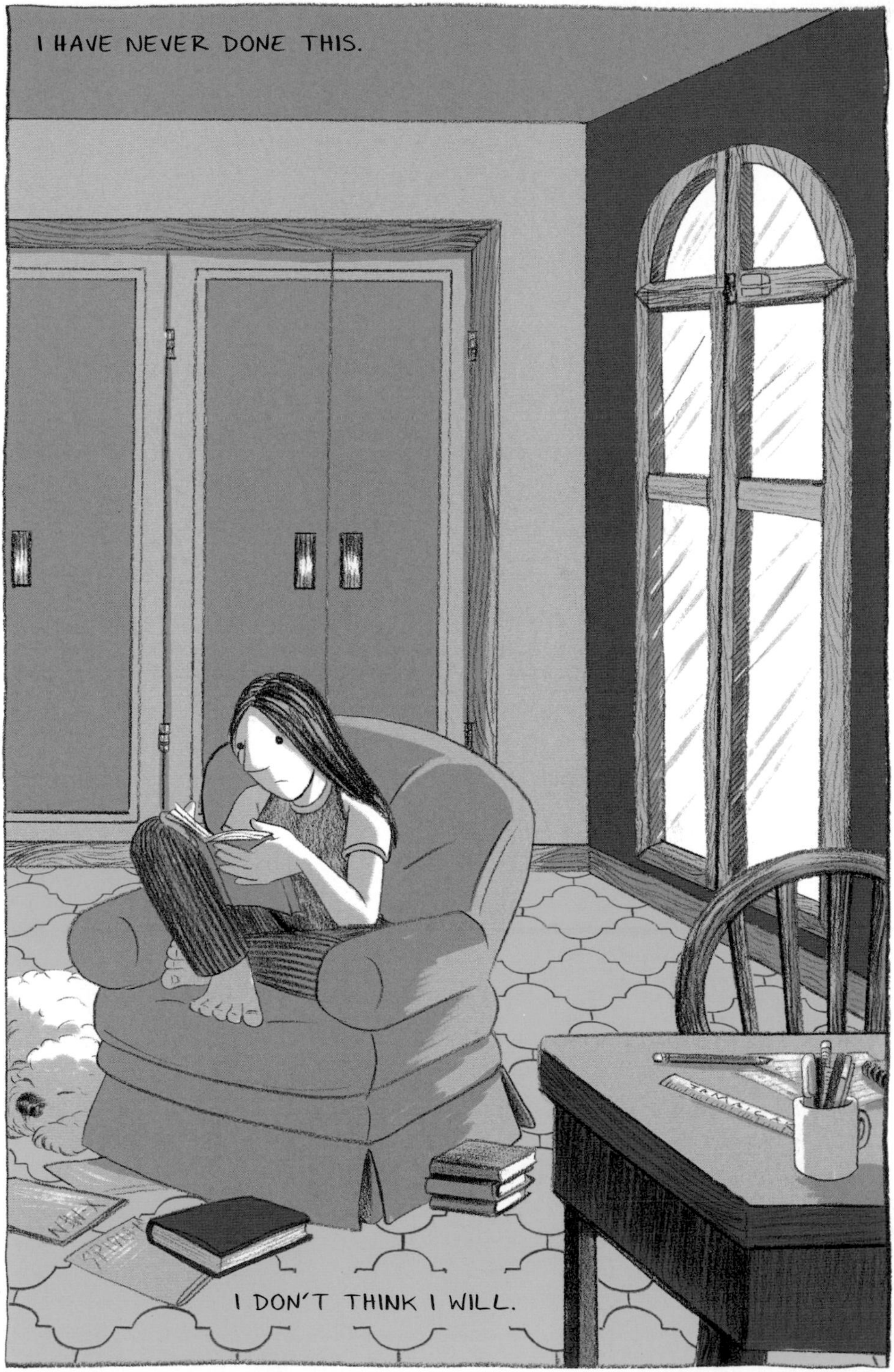
I HAVE NEVER DONE THIS.
I DON'T THINK I WILL.

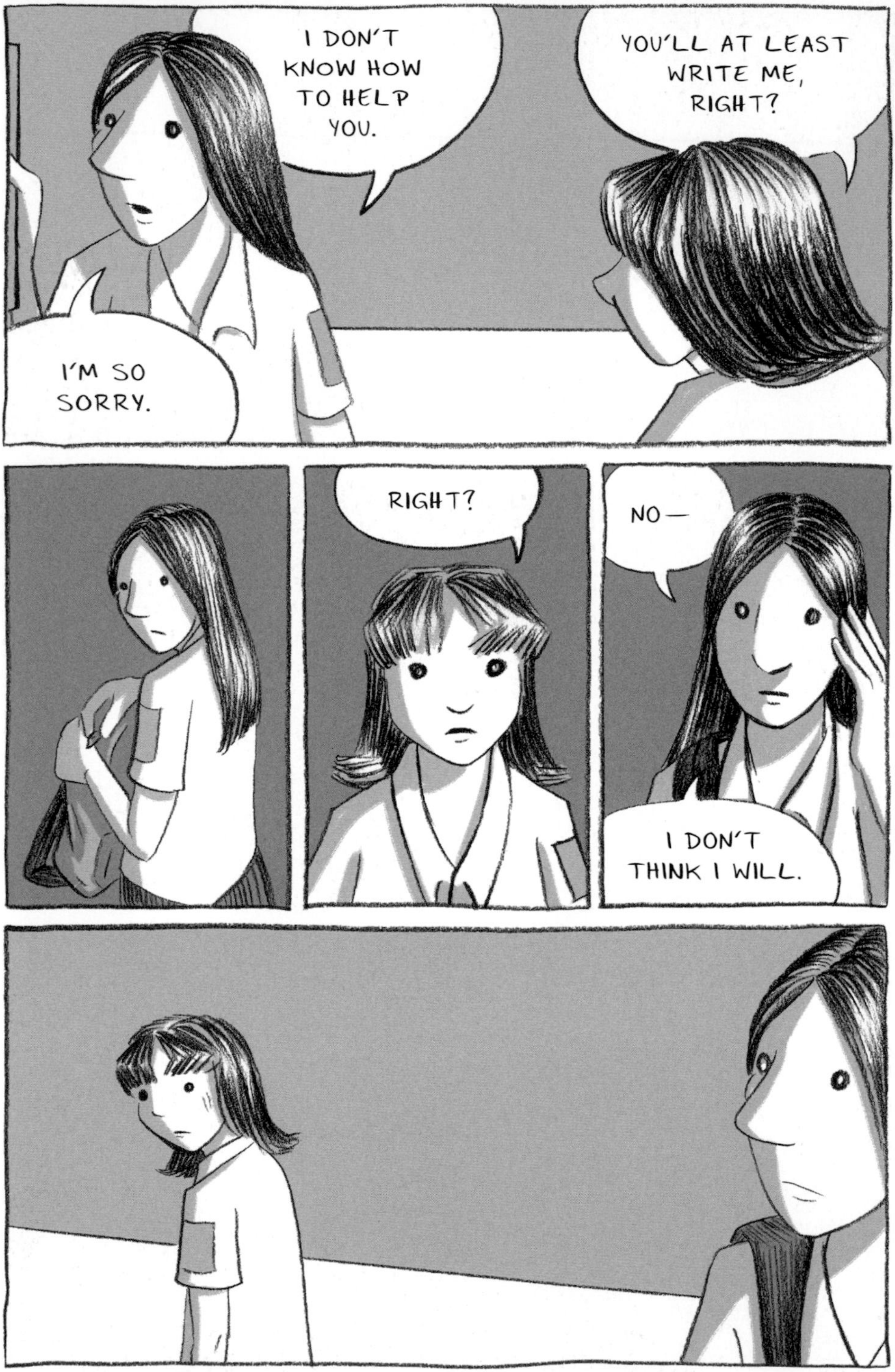
I DON'T KNOW HOW TO HELP YOU.
I'M SO SORRY.
YOU'LL AT LEAST WRITE ME, RIGHT?
RIGHT?
NO—
I DON'T THINK I WILL.

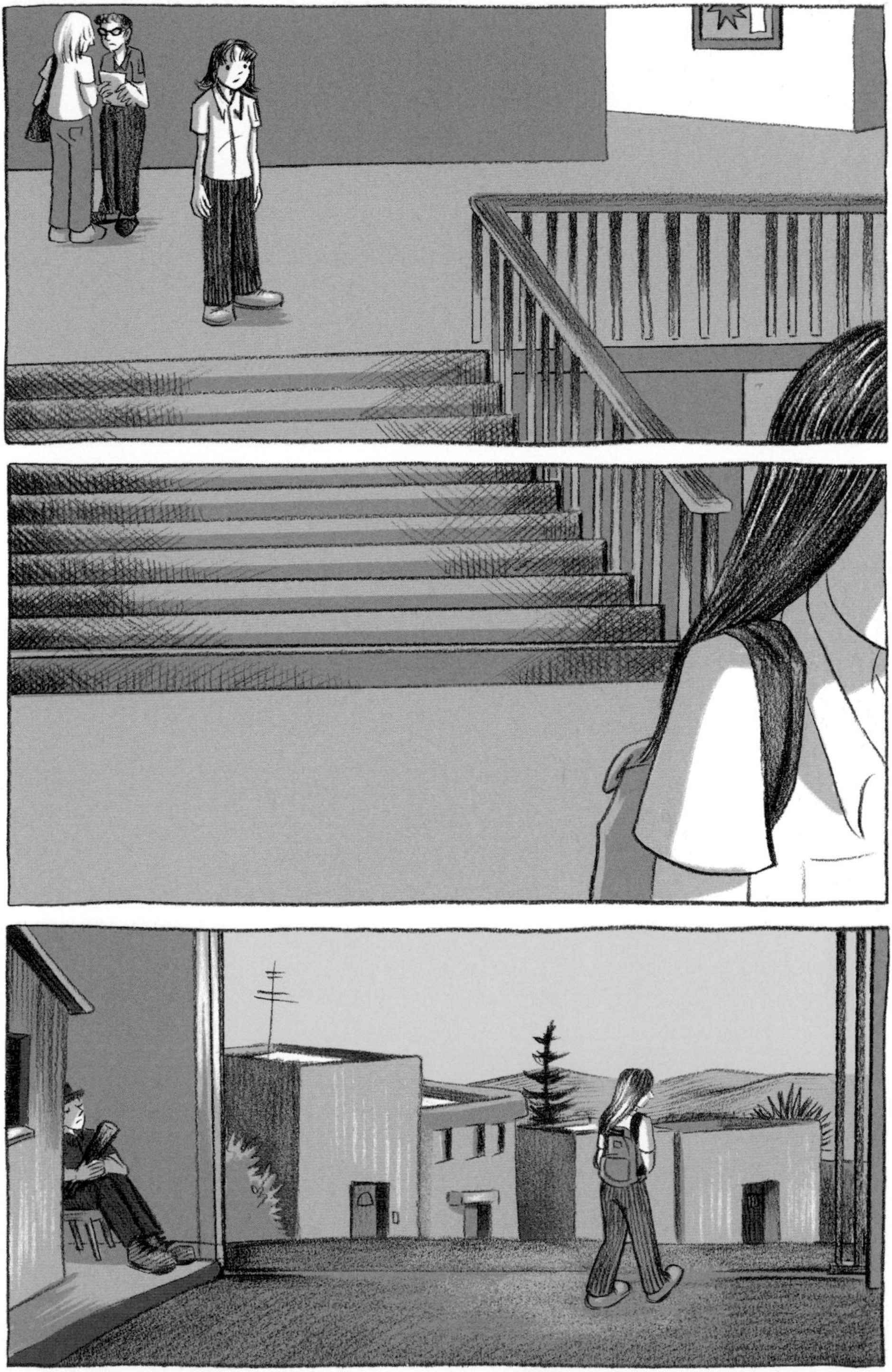

THEY TELL ME.

ON A SUNDAY.

AFTER BREAKFAST.

WE KNOW YOU'RE MATURE ENOUGH TO BE TRUSTED WITH THIS.

BUT SERIOUSLY, YOU CAN'T TELL ANYONE.

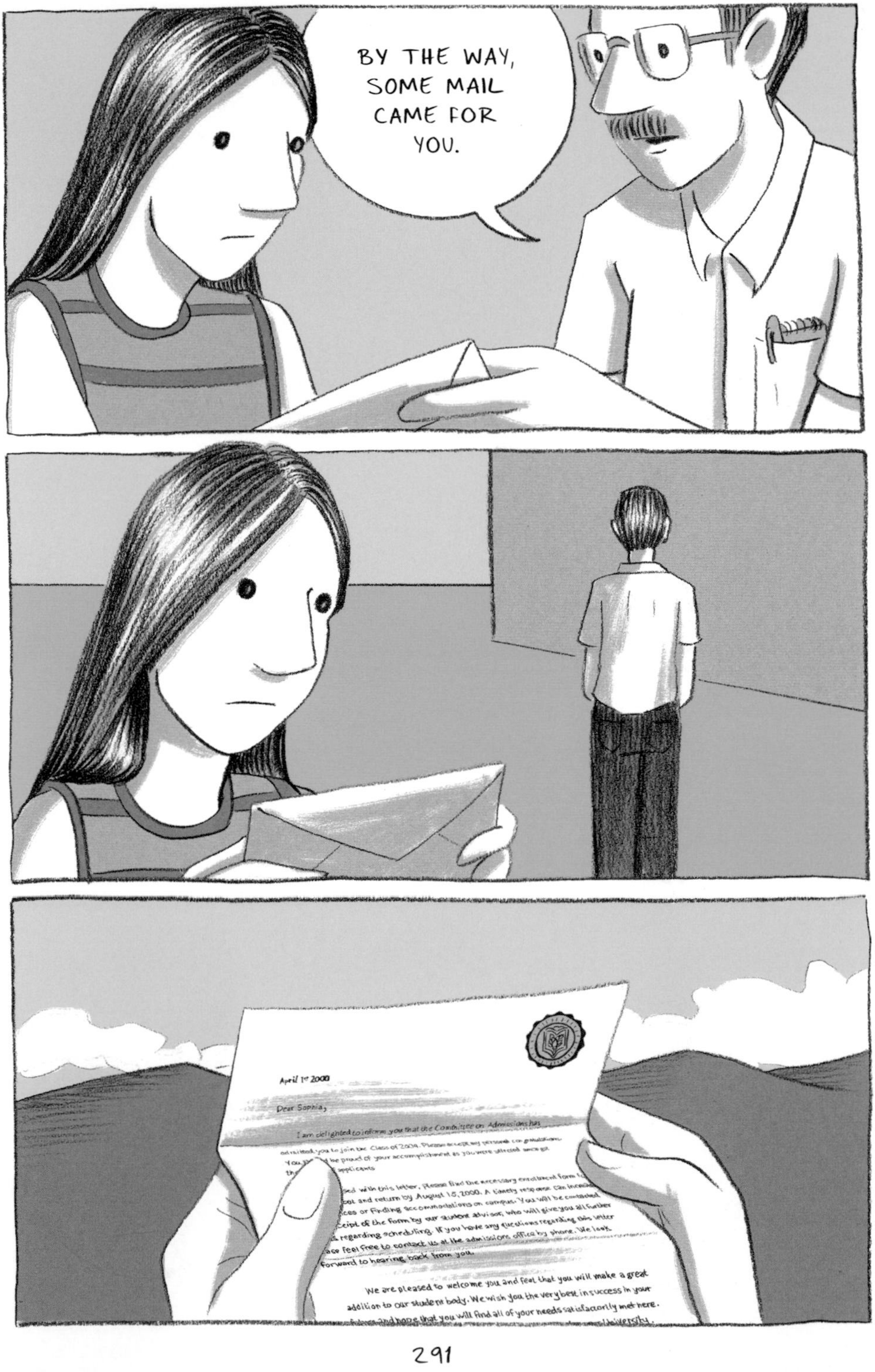
BY THE WAY, SOME MAIL CAME FOR YOU.
April 1st 2000
Dear Sophia,
I am delighted to inform you that the Committee on Admissions has
admitted you to join the Class of 2004.
applicants
sed with this letter, please find the necessary enrollment form
out and return by August 15, 2000. A timely response can
ices or finding accommodations on campus. You will be contacted
ceipt of the form by our student advisor, who will give you all further
regarding scheduling. If you have any questions regarding this letter
ase feel free to contact us at the admissions office by phone. We look
forward to hearing back from you.
We are pleased to welcome you and feel that you will make a great
addition to our student body. We wish you the very best in success in your
and hope that you will find all of your needs satisfactorily met here.

292

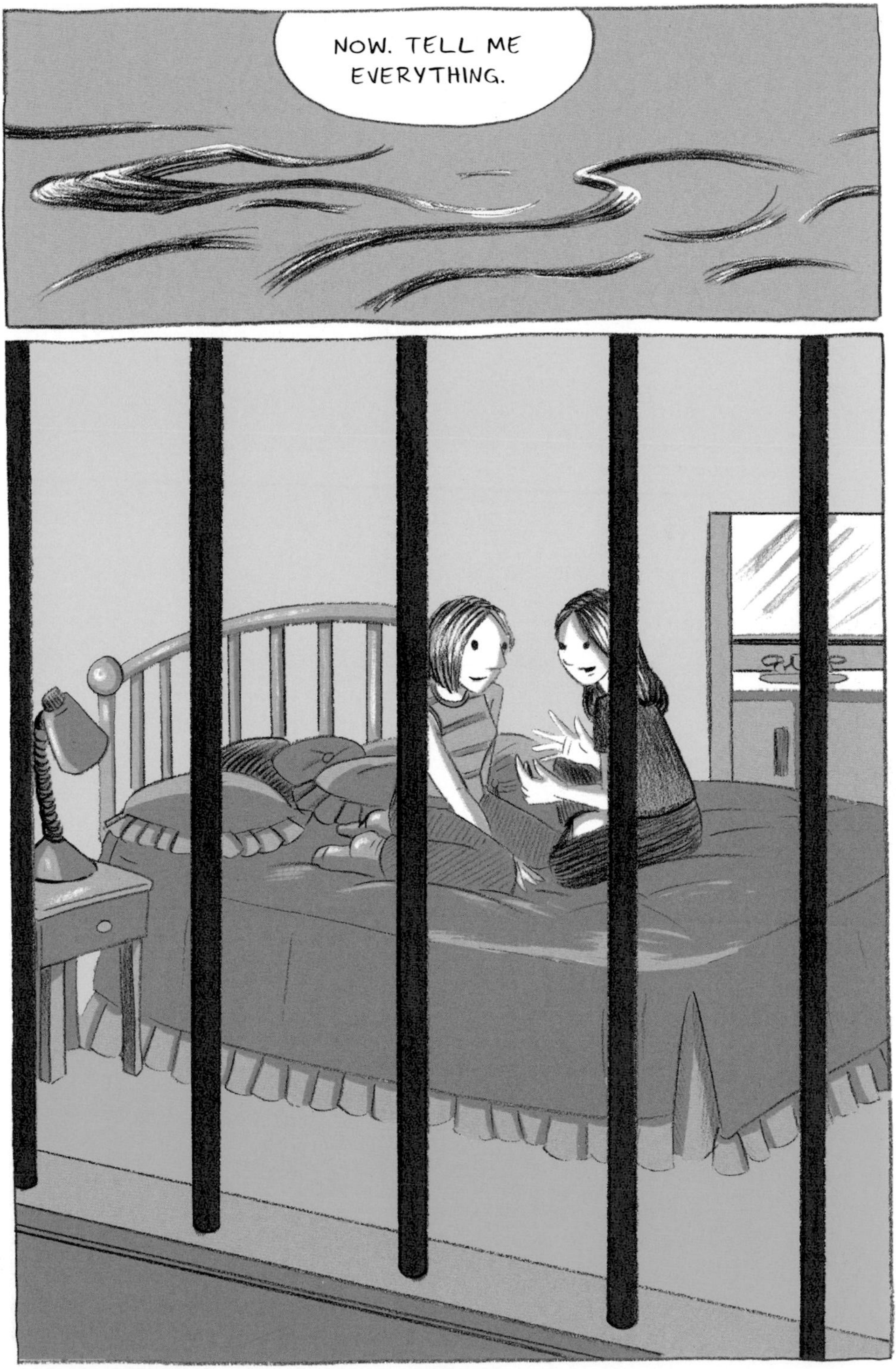
NOW. TELL ME EVERYTHING.

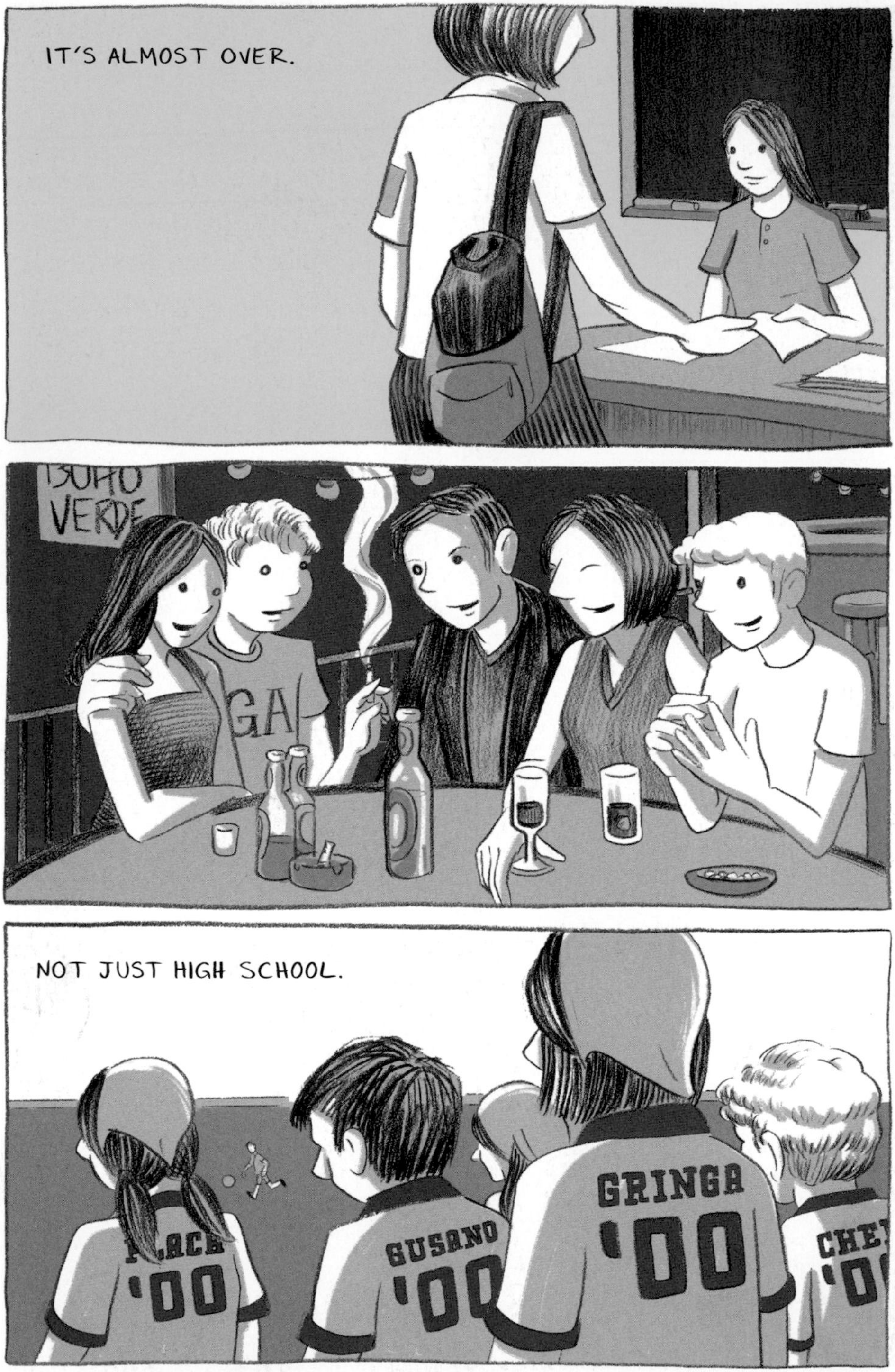
IT'S ALMOST OVER.
VERDE
NOT JUST HIGH SCHOOL.
'00
GUSANO
'00
GRINGA
'00

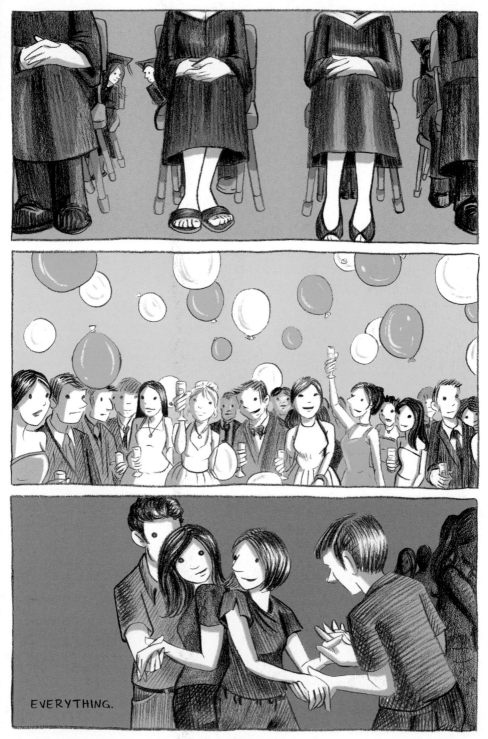

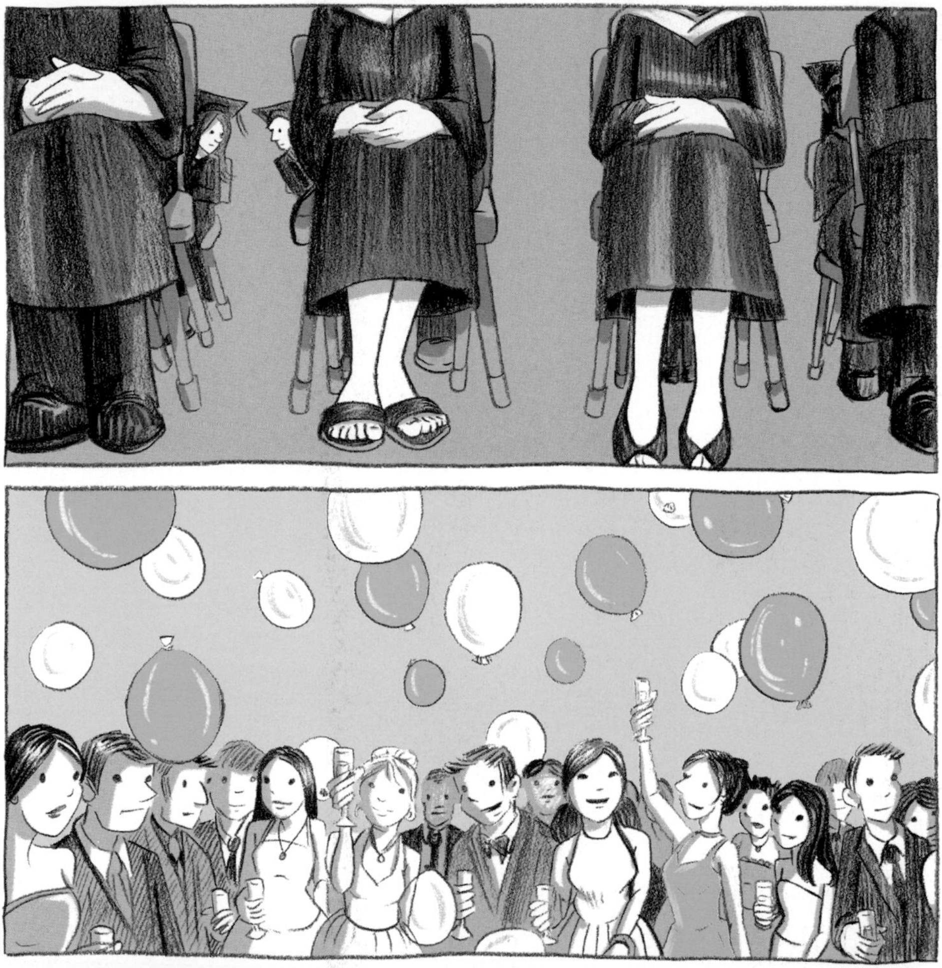
EVERYTHING.

298

BUT IT FEELS
AS IF I AM BEING
PULLED UP BY
THE ROOTS.

299

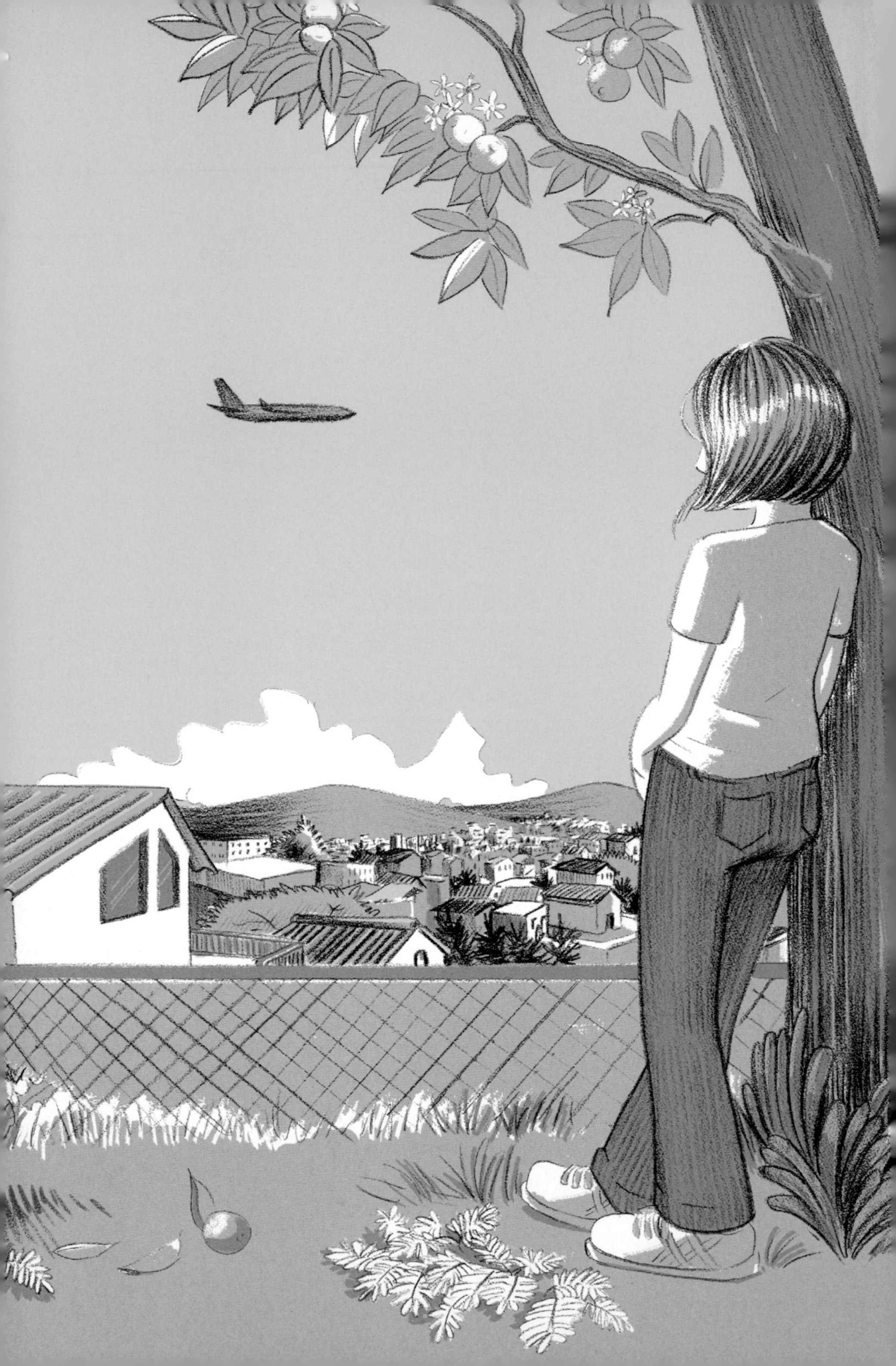

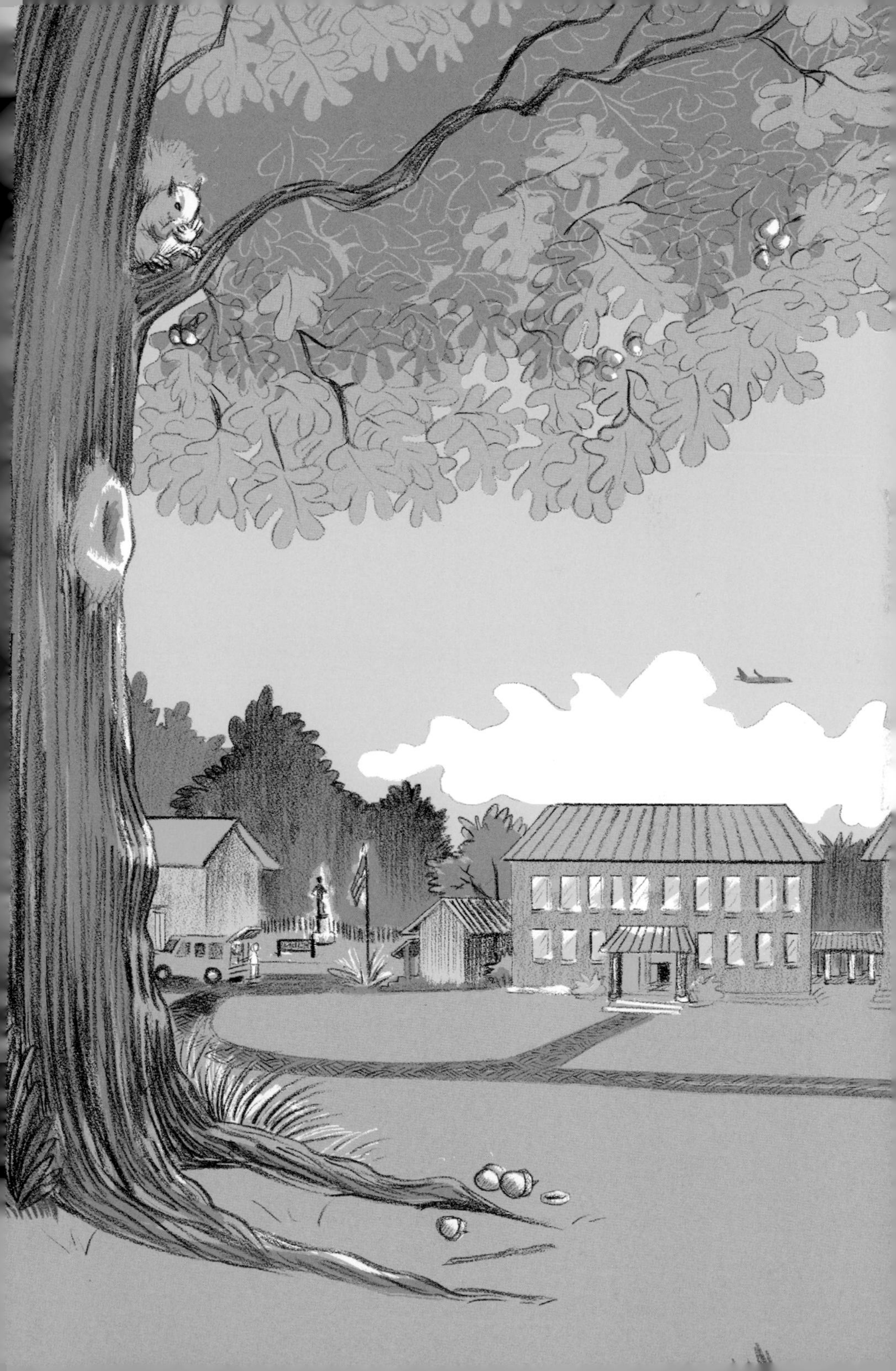

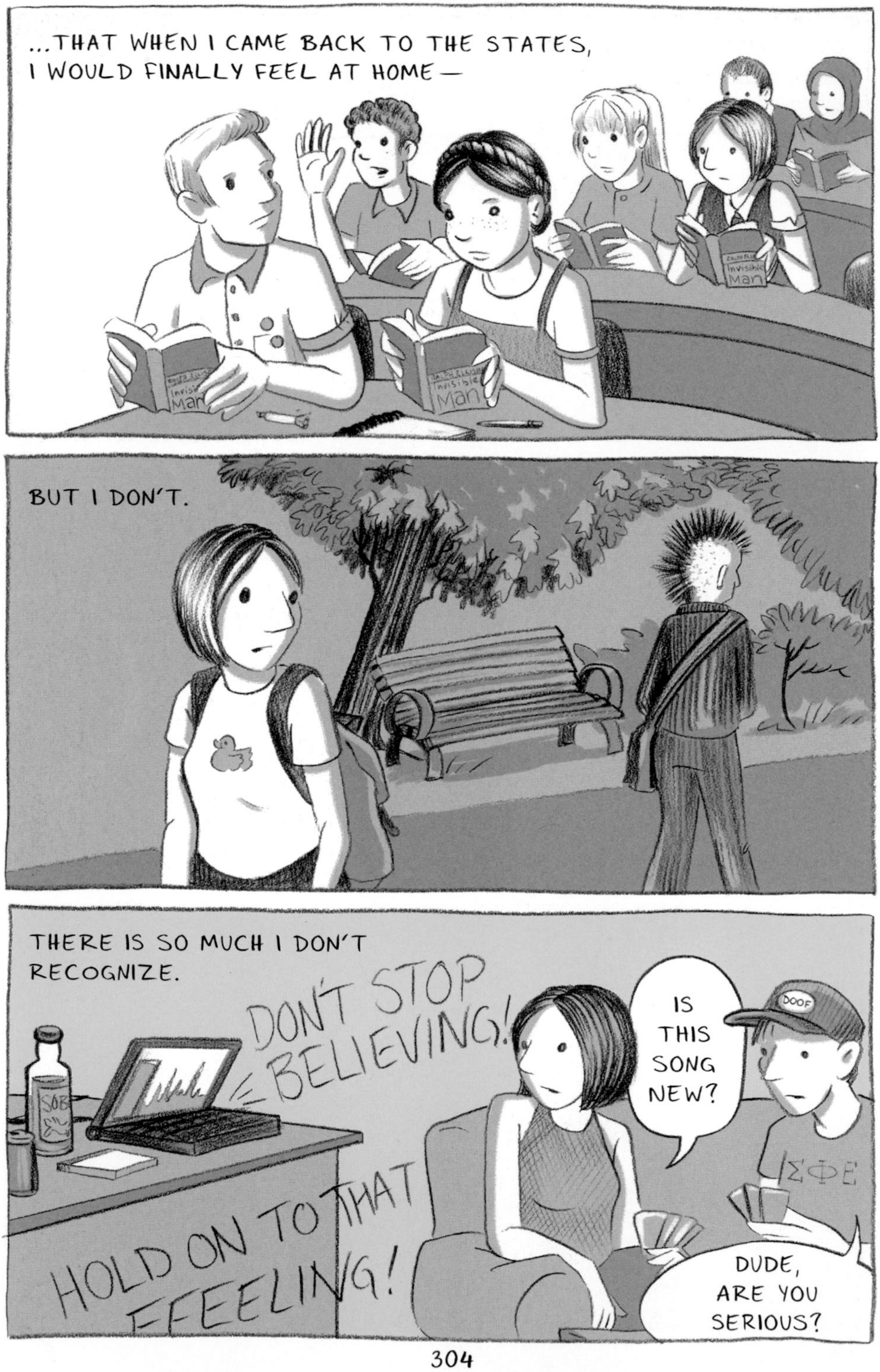
...THAT WHEN I CAME BACK TO THE STATES, I WOULD FINALLY FEEL AT HOME—
Invisible Man
BUT I DON'T.
THERE IS SO MUCH I DON'T RECOGNIZE.
DON'T STOP BELIEVING!
IS THIS SONG NEW?
DOOF
ΣΦΕ
HOLD ON TO THAT FEEELING!
DUDE, ARE YOU SERIOUS?

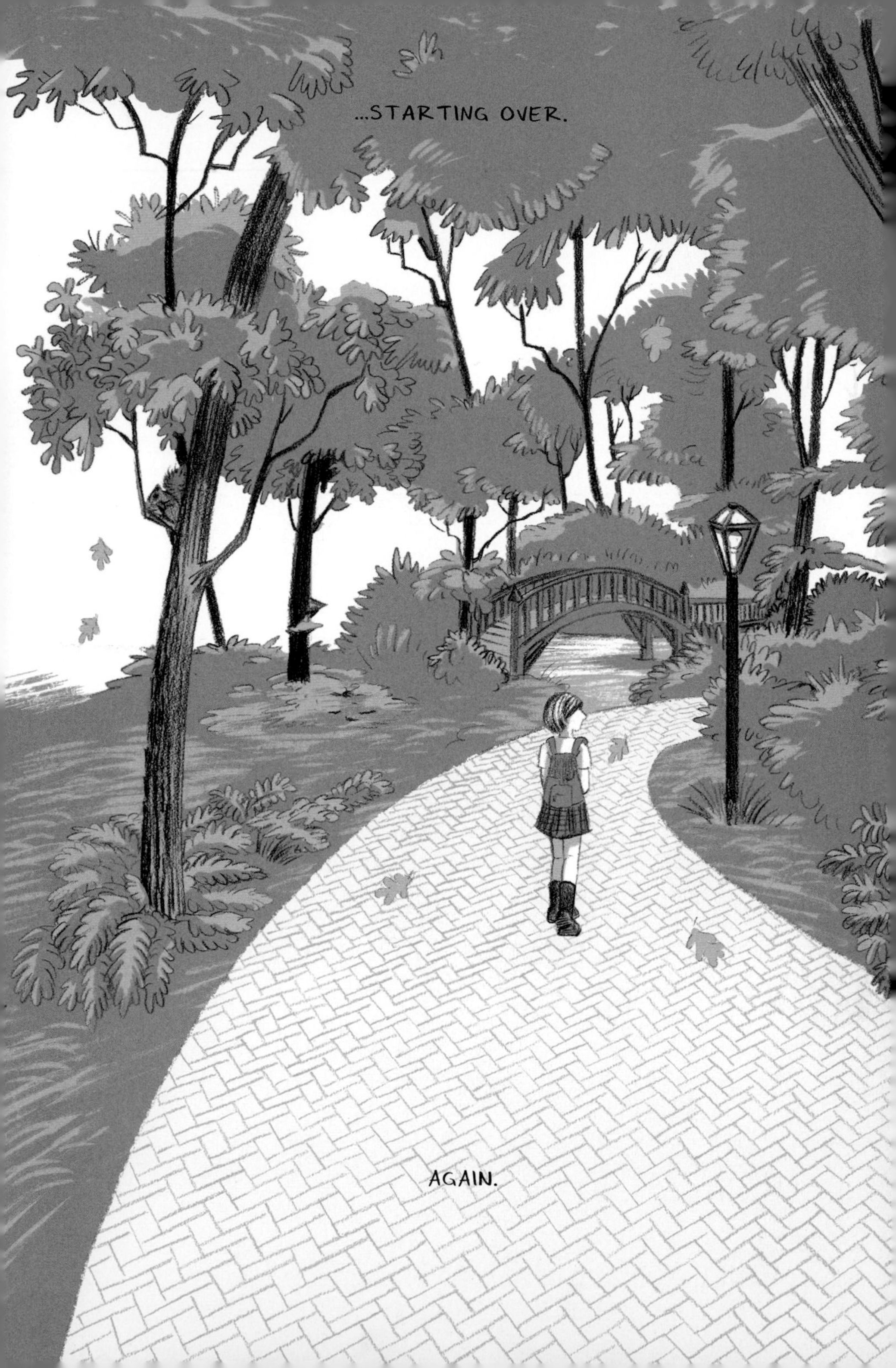
...STARTING OVER.
AGAIN.

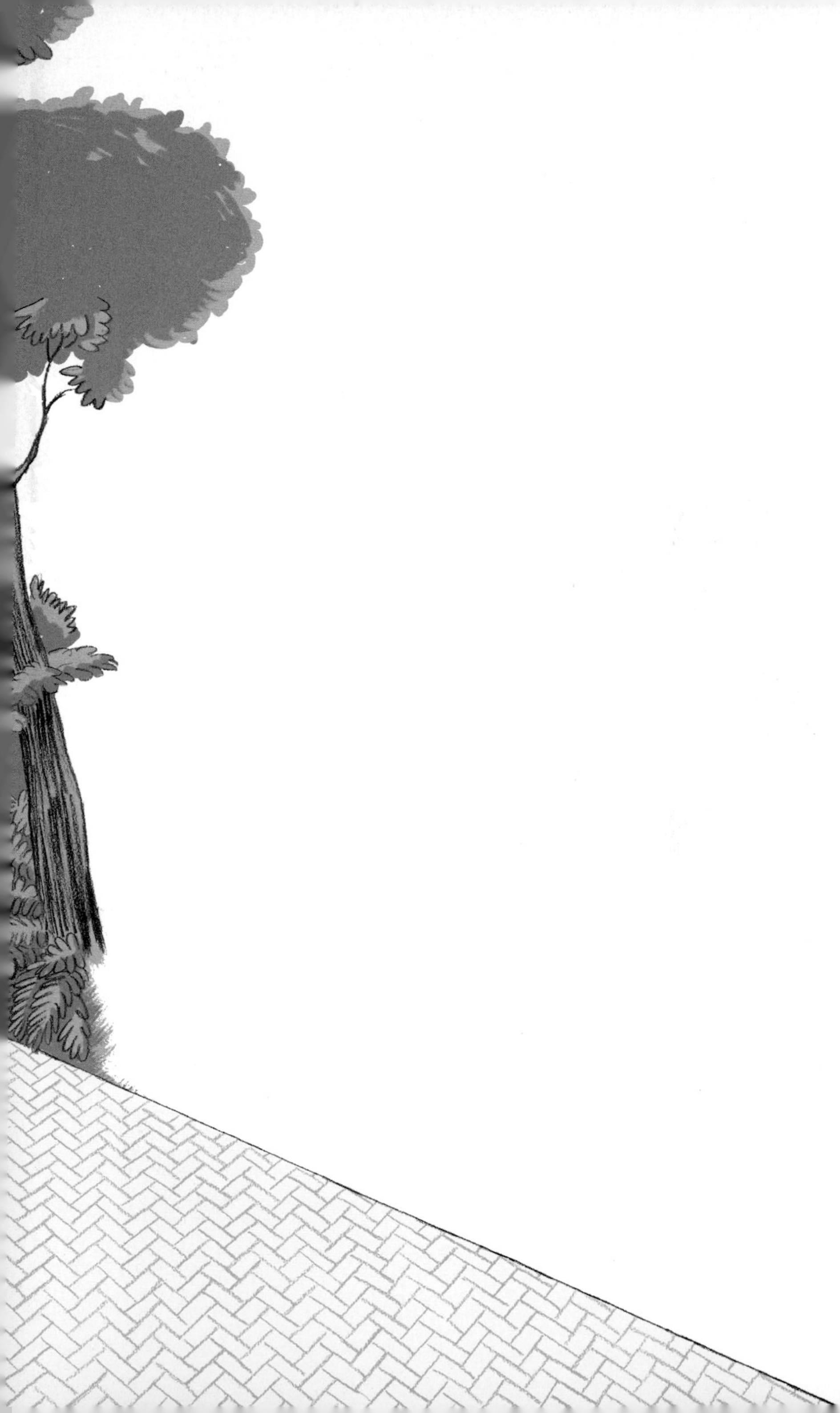

AUTHOR'S NOTE

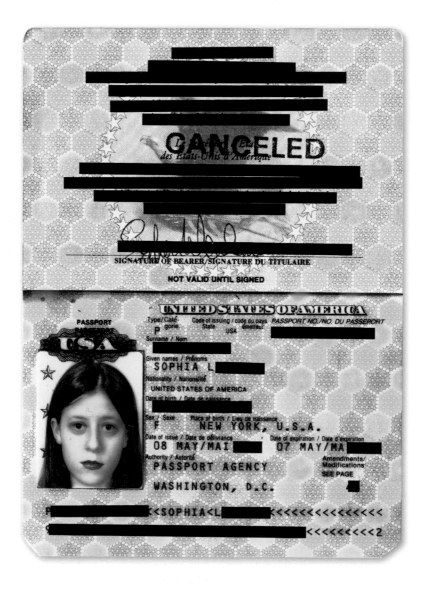

I never thought I would tell this story. For years I deflected and demurred when people asked me questions about where I grew up and what my parents did. Guarding certain secrets was so ingrained in me that I could not imagine a world where I actually discussed them, let alone put them down on paper. But as my comics have become more personal, there has been a small and persistent voice growing within me that has insisted this is my life, my story to tell.

But these stories and secrets also belong to all the other people who share my history, some of whom have devoted their lives to protecting such secrets. At the early stages of this project, I would tie myself up in knots over what to say and how to say it. Would my parents approve? Would I embarrass my family? Would I hurt someone's feelings? But sometimes the trick to writing is giving up the pretense of pleasing anyone at all. So I began to write. When I showed my parents an early draft of my story I was surprised and relieved when they did not hesitate to give me their blessing. Obtaining the permission of the Publication Review Board at the Central Intelligence Agency was a far more daunting and complicated task and is the reason many details have been removed from the book. I stand by my right to tell the truth as I lived it, but in doing so, I have also been extremely careful to protect those who still have secrets to keep and who risk their lives in dedication to their work.

I still flinch around explaining my past. Secrets are sticky. I cling to mine out of habit and in no small part because I sort of love my secrets, having held them close for so long. But here I strove to be as honest as possible. I have a vivid memory, but I am sure I've gotten some of it wrong. There will be people in my family and among my friends who will read this and think, *That's not how it happened*, and I apologize for any discrepancies. I wrote about our experiences from a place of love, and I hope that comes through.

These stories are true as I remember them; however, this is a work of creative non-fiction. I have taken artistic liberties when it was necessary to create a cohesive story. If you ever want to learn how crowded your life is and how deep and myriad the connections you make in this world are, try writing a memoir. The most painful process of this book was not reliving the humiliations of unrequited love but streamlining complicated social relationships into a comprehensible narrative. In short, some events have been rearranged or combined but never invented. Many characters here are composites to protect their privacy as well as maintain narrative clarity. Some conversations are verbatim as I recall them or as I recorded them in my diaries at the time, while others are approximations, meant to illustrate several different events and relationships. As challenging as it felt writing the story, I did find immense pleasure in resurrecting certain parts of my past: the exact pattern of the terra-cotta tiles on my bedroom floor, the unkempt woolly head of my dog, and the friendships that sustained me.

ACKNOWLEDGMENTS

To my classmates who were there at those parties and in the hallways, I may have changed your names, but squint and you will see yourself in these pages. Specifically, I want to thank Carla, Linda, Melissa, and Naa for their assistance in fact-checking my memories and tracking down reference photos. I also want to thank Jorge, Chema, Ana Maria, Ethling, Andrea, Virgilio, Biki, Damien, Carmen, Vivi, Dianne, and Dessiré.

And Cecilia. I wish our story had a different ending, but we had fun, didn't we?

Thank you to Carly, Amie, and Stephanie. I could not imagine a more supportive and inspiring writer's group or group of humans.

Thank you to my ridiculously talented agent, Molly O'Neill, who saw something that I could not yet see. I offer my boundless gratitude to my formidable editor, Susan Rich, who saw what I saw and elevated it. And to the supportive production team at Little, Brown Books for Young Readers, especially Sasha Illingworth and Angelie Yap. And to my adroit and thoughtful colorist, Mike Freiheit.

To my brave and dedicated parents, who gave me the world. Thank you for your unyielding support. To my brother Christopher, who taught me that art is serious business and took mine seriously before anyone else did. Perhaps before even I did. To my sister and second brain, Julia. I could not do this without you. To Byron and Patrick, who remember with me.

And to my first reader and last love, Judge, who encouraged me to tell this story in the first place.

SOPHIA GLOCK

is a cartoonist who lives and draws in Austin, Texas. She attended the College of William & Mary and the School of Visual Arts. Her work has been featured in the *New Yorker*, Buzzfeed, and *Time Out New York*. She talks to her sister every day.